Kieron Gillen story
Omar Francia cover
Omar Francia chapters 1-3
Nahuel Lopez chapters 4-6
Omar Francia interlude
Digikore Studios color
Kurt Hathaway letters

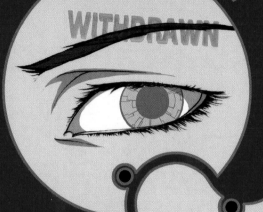

AVATAR

facebook.com/avatarpresscomics
www.avatarpress.com
twitter @avatarpress

William Christensen editor-in-chief
Mark Seifert creative director
Jim Kuhoric managing editor
Ariana Osborne production assistant

Mercury Heat Volume 1

February 2016. Published by Avatar Press, Inc., 515 N. Century Blvd. Rantoul, IL 61866. ©2016 Avatar Press, Inc. Mercury Heat and all related properties TM & ©2016 Avatar Press, Inc. All characters as depicted in this story are over the age of 18. The stories, characters, and institutions mentioned in this magazine are entirely fictional. Printed in Canada.

chapter 1

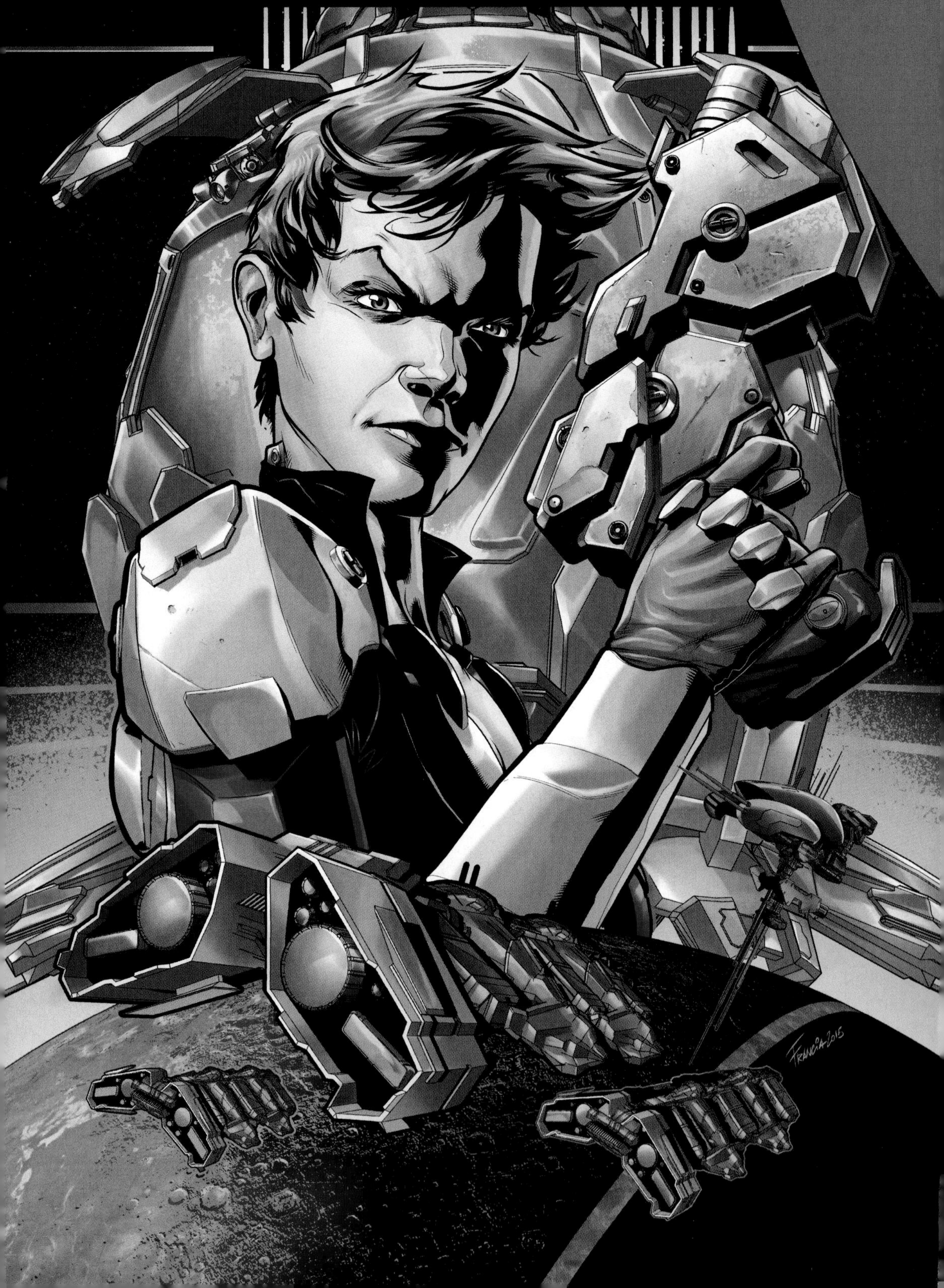
FRANCIA 2015

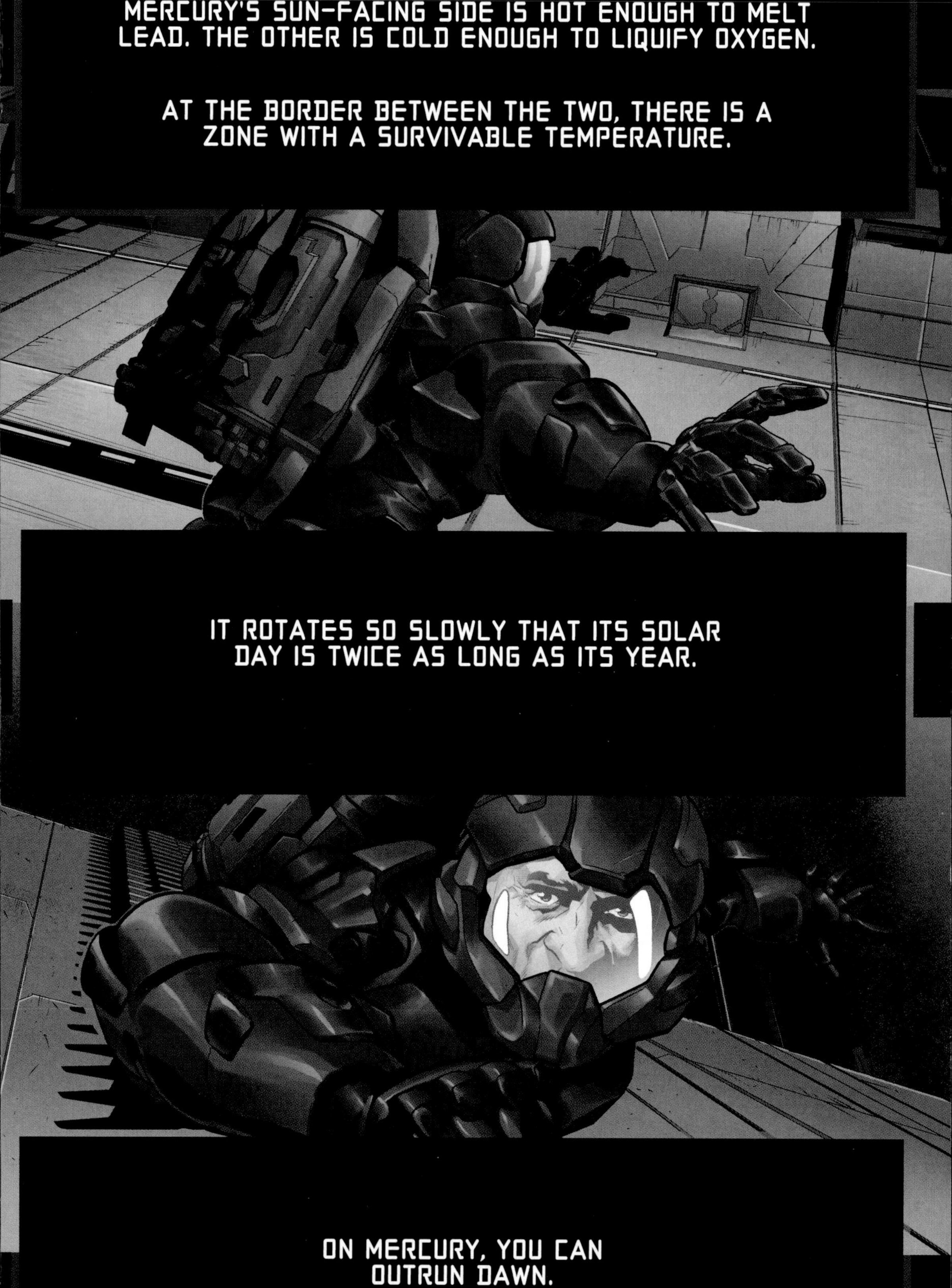
MERCURY'S SUN-FACING SIDE IS HOT ENOUGH TO MELT LEAD. THE OTHER IS COLD ENOUGH TO LIQUIFY OXYGEN.
AT THE BORDER BETWEEN THE TWO, THERE IS A ZONE WITH A SURVIVABLE TEMPERATURE.
IT ROTATES SO SLOWLY THAT ITS SOLAR DAY IS TWICE AS LONG AS ITS YEAR.
ON MERCURY, YOU CAN OUTRUN DAWN.

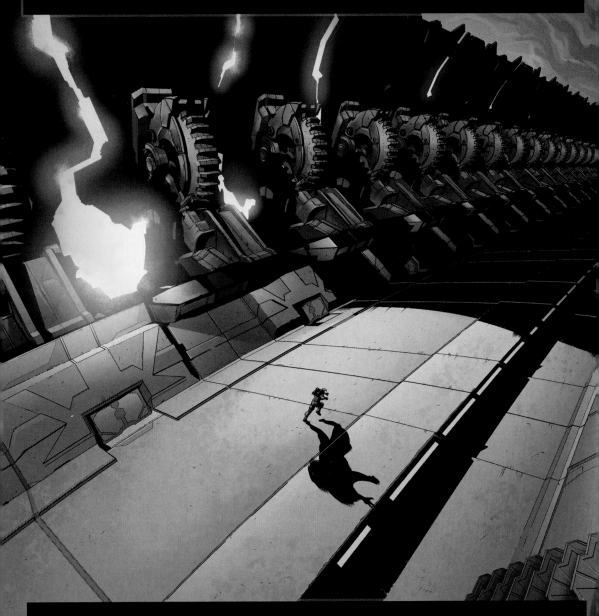

JUST AS LONG AS YOU CAN KEEP MOVING.

MERCURY HEAT:
THE LONG, SLOW DAWN

KIERON GILLEN / OMAR FRANCIA

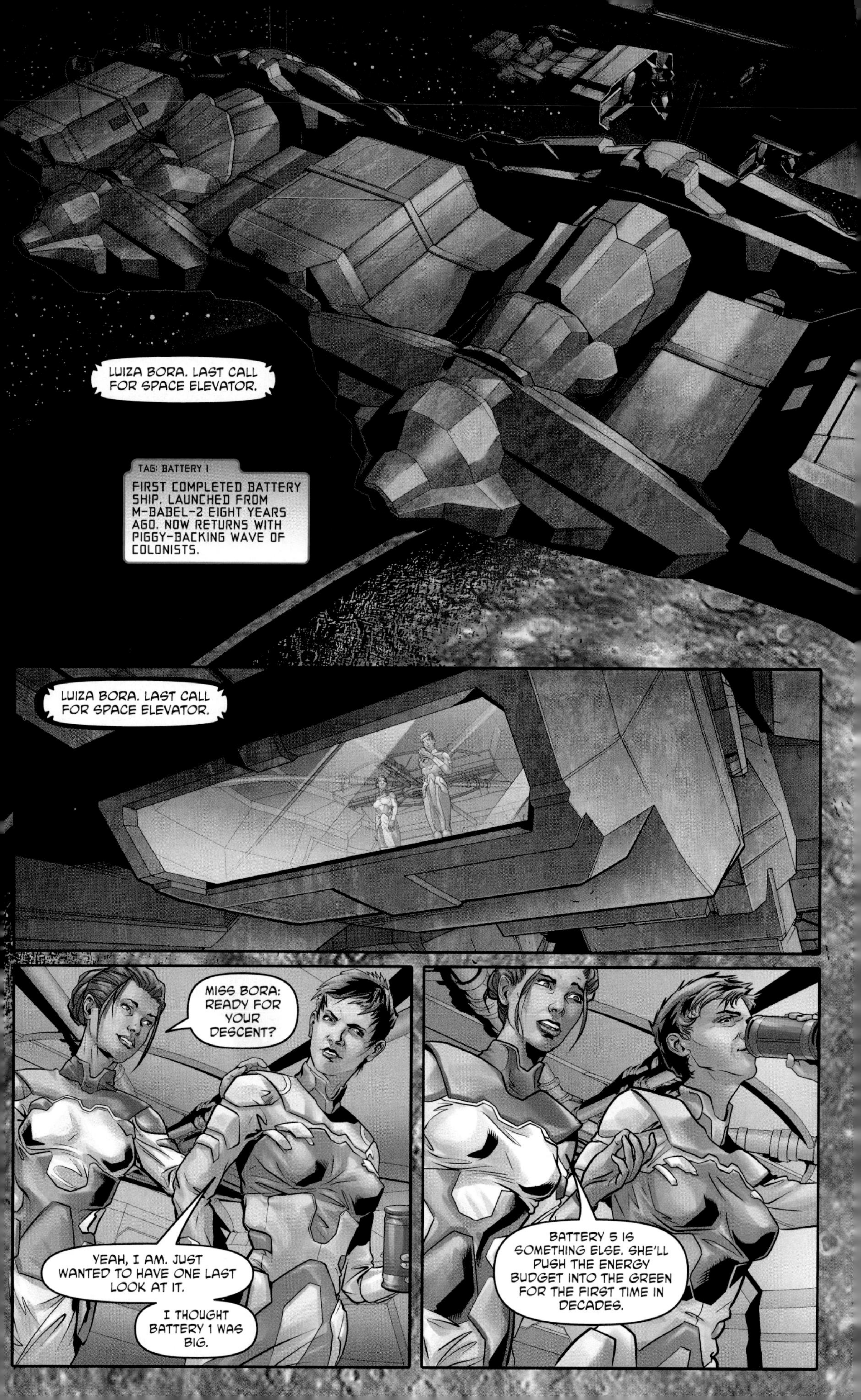
LUIZA BORA. LAST CALL FOR SPACE ELEVATOR.
TAG: BATTERY 1
FIRST COMPLETED BATTERY SHIP. LAUNCHED FROM M-BABEL-2 EIGHT YEARS AGO. NOW RETURNS WITH PIGGY-BACKING WAVE OF COLONISTS.
LUIZA BORA. LAST CALL FOR SPACE ELEVATOR.
MISS BORA: READY FOR YOUR DESCENT?
YEAH, I AM. JUST WANTED TO HAVE ONE LAST LOOK AT IT.
I THOUGHT BATTERY 1 WAS BIG.
BATTERY 5 IS SOMETHING ELSE. SHE'LL PUSH THE ENERGY BUDGET INTO THE GREEN FOR THE FIRST TIME IN DECADES.

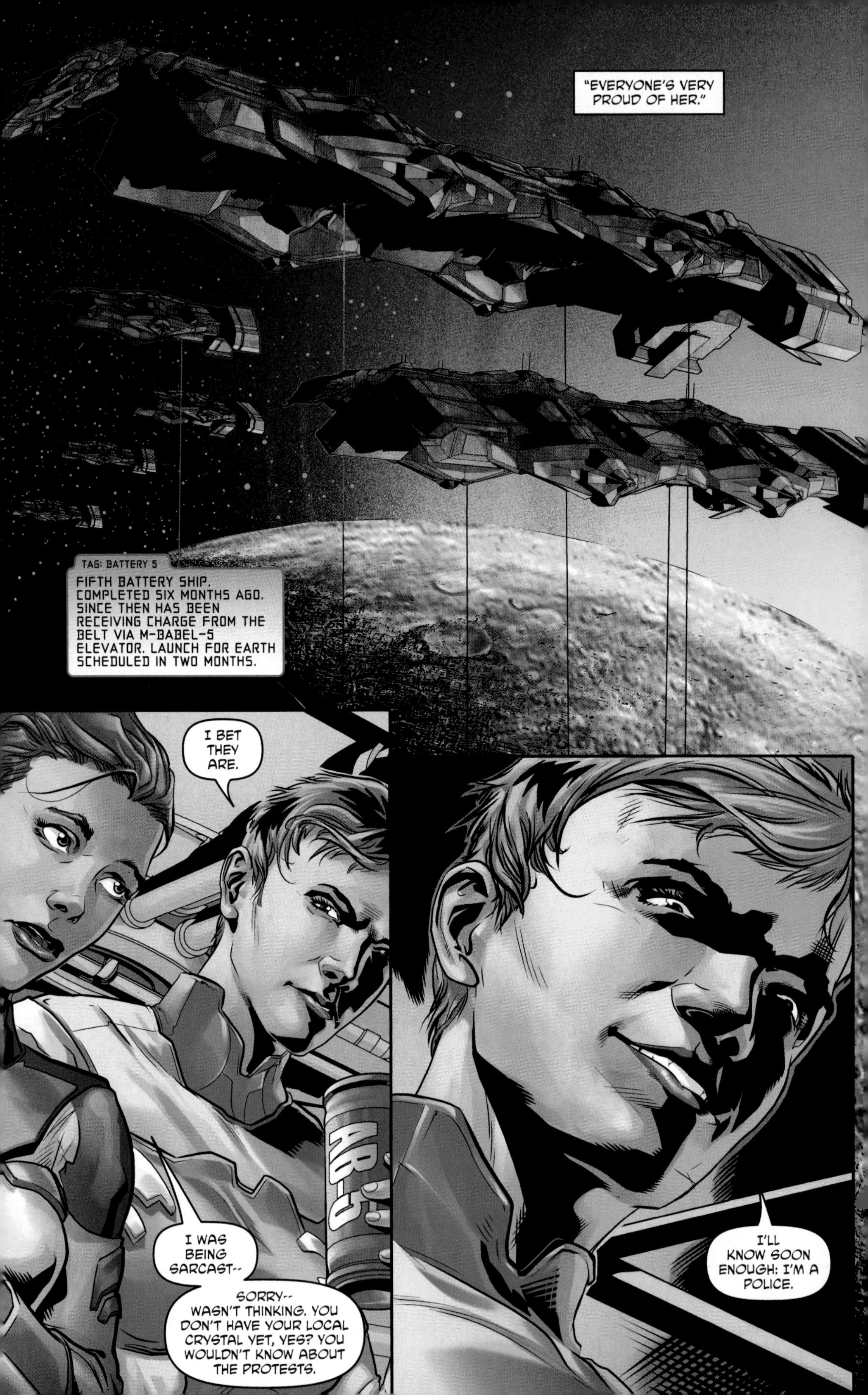
"EVERYONE'S VERY PROUD OF HER."
TAG: BATTERY 5
FIFTH BATTERY SHIP. COMPLETED SIX MONTHS AGO. SINCE THEN HAS BEEN RECEIVING CHARGE FROM THE BELT VIA M-BABEL-5 ELEVATOR. LAUNCH FOR EARTH SCHEDULED IN TWO MONTHS.
I BET THEY ARE.
I WAS BEING SARCAST--
SORRY-- WASN'T THINKING. YOU DON'T HAVE YOUR LOCAL CRYSTAL YET, YES? YOU WOULDN'T KNOW ABOUT THE PROTESTS.
I'LL KNOW SOON ENOUGH: I'M A POLICE.

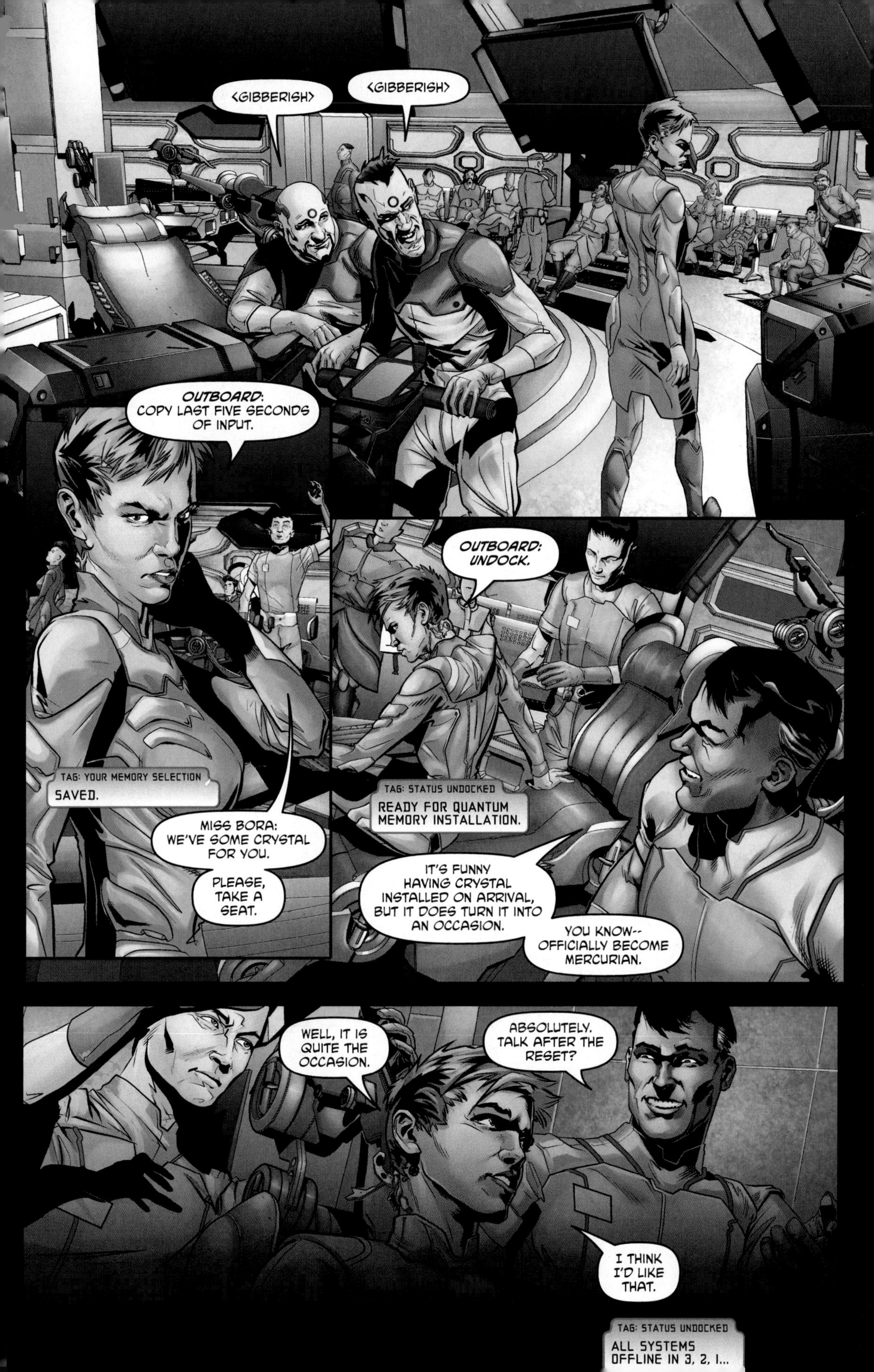
<GIBBERISH>
<GIBBERISH>
OUTBOARD: COPY LAST FIVE SECONDS OF INPUT.
TAG: YOUR MEMORY SELECTION
SAVED.
MISS BORA: WE'VE SOME CRYSTAL FOR YOU.
PLEASE, TAKE A SEAT.
OUTBOARD: UNDOCK.
TAG: STATUS UNDOCKED
READY FOR QUANTUM MEMORY INSTALLATION.
IT'S FUNNY HAVING CRYSTAL INSTALLED ON ARRIVAL, BUT IT DOES TURN IT INTO AN OCCASION.
YOU KNOW-- OFFICIALLY BECOME MERCURIAN.
WELL, IT IS QUITE THE OCCASION.
ABSOLUTELY. TALK AFTER THE RESET?
I THINK I'D LIKE THAT.
TAG: STATUS UNDOCKED
ALL SYSTEMS OFFLINE IN 3, 2, 1...

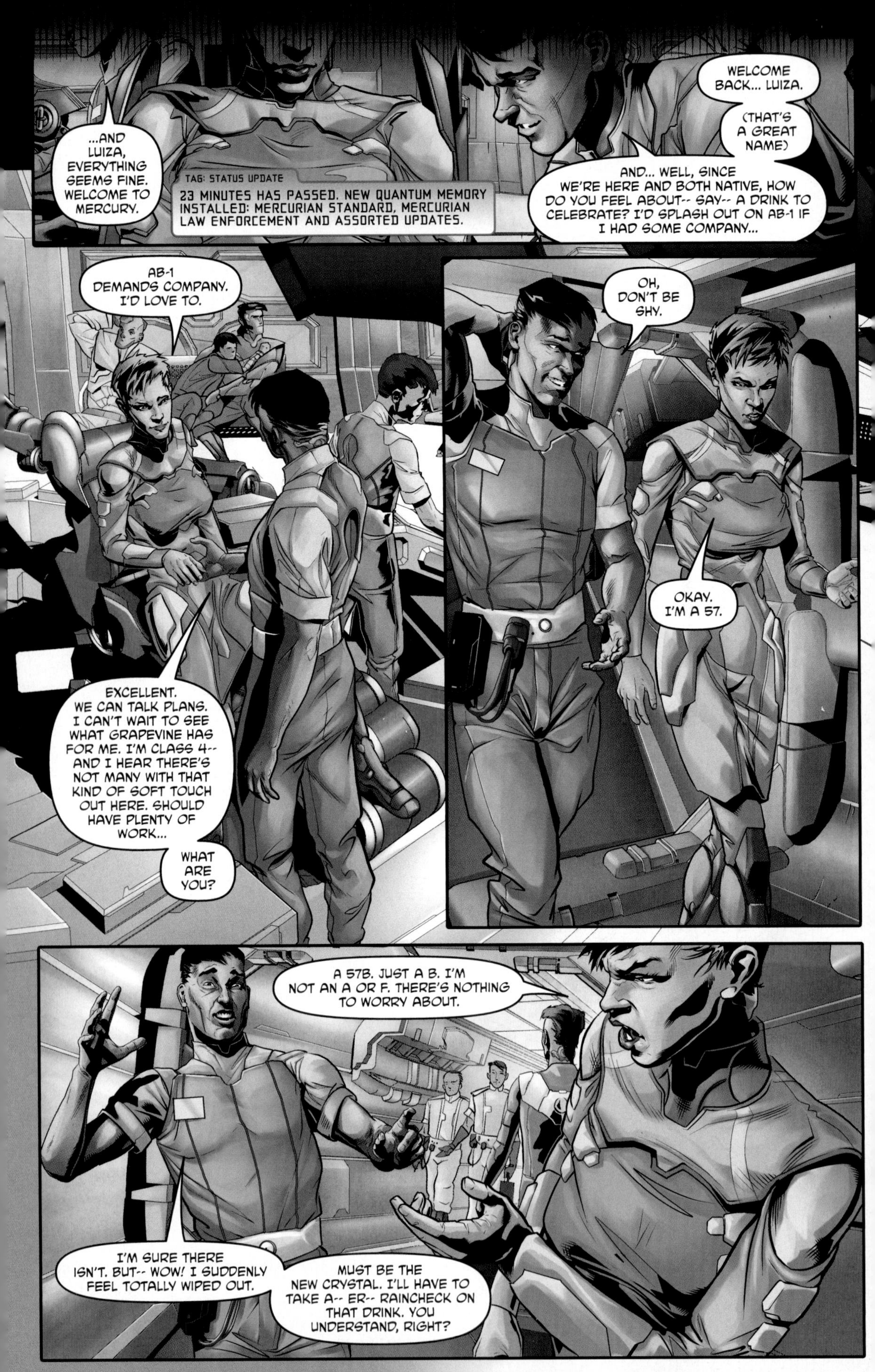

...AND LUIZA, EVERYTHING SEEMS FINE. WELCOME TO MERCURY.
TAG: STATUS UPDATE
23 MINUTES HAS PASSED. NEW QUANTUM MEMORY INSTALLED: MERCURIAN STANDARD, MERCURIAN LAW ENFORCEMENT AND ASSORTED UPDATES.
WELCOME BACK... LUIZA.
(THAT'S A GREAT NAME)
AND... WELL, SINCE WE'RE HERE AND BOTH NATIVE, HOW DO YOU FEEL ABOUT-- SAY-- A DRINK TO CELEBRATE? I'D SPLASH OUT ON AB-1 IF I HAD SOME COMPANY...
AB-1 DEMANDS COMPANY. I'D LOVE TO.
EXCELLENT. WE CAN TALK PLANS. I CAN'T WAIT TO SEE WHAT GRAPEVINE HAS FOR ME. I'M CLASS 4-- AND I HEAR THERE'S NOT MANY WITH THAT KIND OF SOFT TOUCH OUT HERE. SHOULD HAVE PLENTY OF WORK...
WHAT ARE YOU?
OH, DON'T BE SHY.
OKAY. I'M A 57.
A 57B. JUST A B. I'M NOT AN A OR F. THERE'S NOTHING TO WORRY ABOUT.
I'M SURE THERE ISN'T. BUT-- WOW! I SUDDENLY FEEL TOTALLY WIPED OUT.
MUST BE THE NEW CRYSTAL. I'LL HAVE TO TAKE A-- ER-- RAINCHECK ON THAT DRINK. YOU UNDERSTAND, RIGHT?

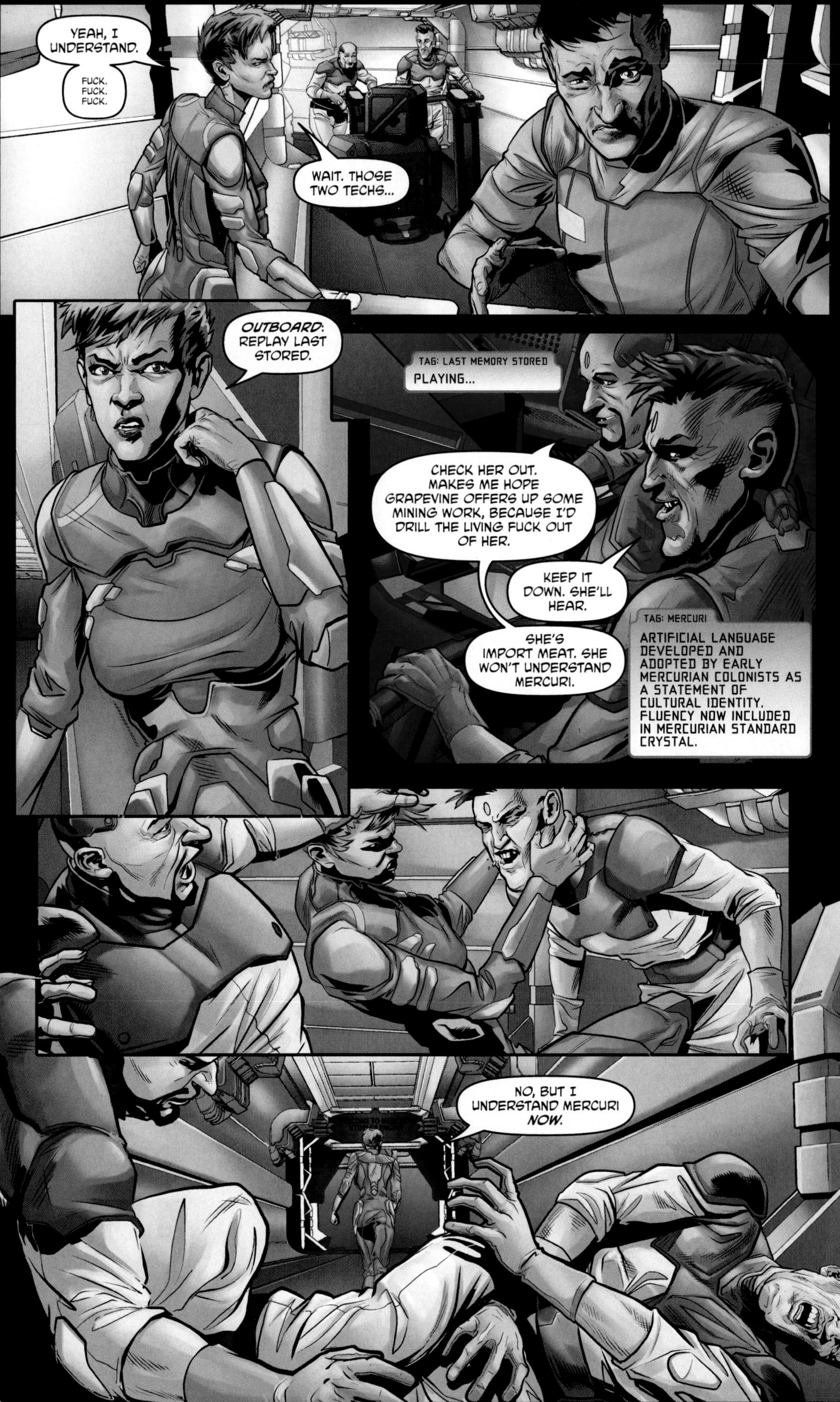
YEAH, I UNDERSTAND.
FUCK. FUCK. FUCK.
WAIT. THOSE TWO TECHS...
OUTBOARD: REPLAY LAST STORED.
TAG: LAST MEMORY STORED
PLAYING...
CHECK HER OUT. MAKES ME HOPE GRAPEVINE OFFERS UP SOME MINING WORK, BECAUSE I'D DRILL THE LIVING FUCK OUT OF HER.
KEEP IT DOWN. SHE'LL HEAR.
SHE'S IMPORT MEAT. SHE WON'T UNDERSTAND MERCURI.
TAG: MERCURI
ARTIFICIAL LANGUAGE DEVELOPED AND ADOPTED BY EARLY MERCURIAN COLONISTS AS A STATEMENT OF CULTURAL IDENTITY. FLUENCY NOW INCLUDED IN MERCURIAN STANDARD CRYSTAL.
NO, BUT I UNDERSTAND MERCURI *NOW*.

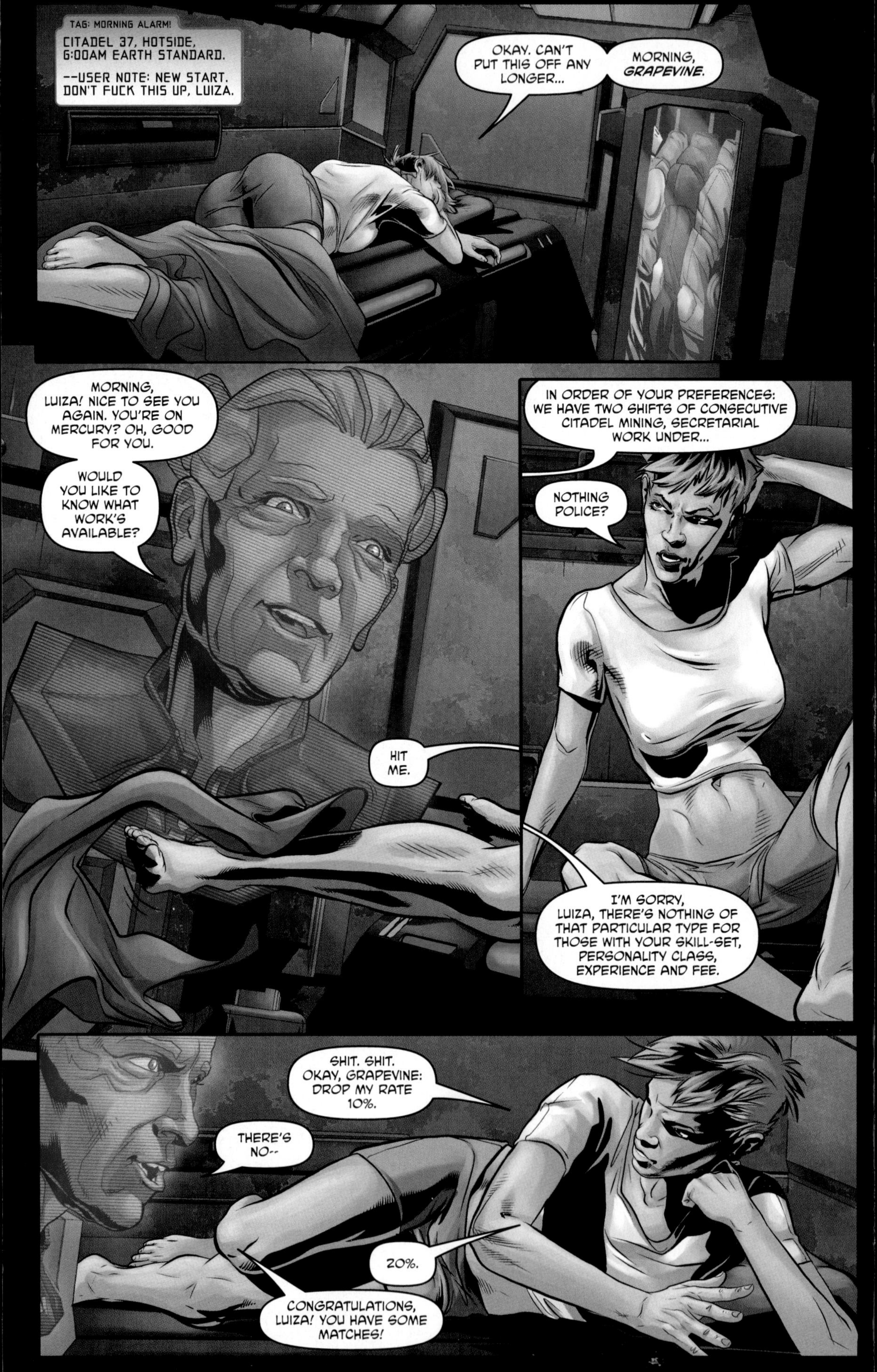
TAG: MORNING ALARM!
CITADEL 37, HOTSIDE, 6:00AM EARTH STANDARD.
--USER NOTE: NEW START. DON'T FUCK THIS UP, LUIZA.
OKAY. CAN'T PUT THIS OFF ANY LONGER...
MORNING, GRAPEVINE.
MORNING, LUIZA! NICE TO SEE YOU AGAIN. YOU'RE ON MERCURY? OH, GOOD FOR YOU.
WOULD YOU LIKE TO KNOW WHAT WORK'S AVAILABLE?
HIT ME.
IN ORDER OF YOUR PREFERENCES: WE HAVE TWO SHIFTS OF CONSECUTIVE CITADEL MINING, SECRETARIAL WORK UNDER...
NOTHING POLICE?
I'M SORRY, LUIZA, THERE'S NOTHING OF THAT PARTICULAR TYPE FOR THOSE WITH YOUR SKILL-SET, PERSONALITY CLASS, EXPERIENCE AND FEE.
SHIT. SHIT. OKAY, GRAPEVINE: DROP MY RATE 10%.
THERE'S NO--
20%.
CONGRATULATIONS, LUIZA! YOU HAVE SOME MATCHES!

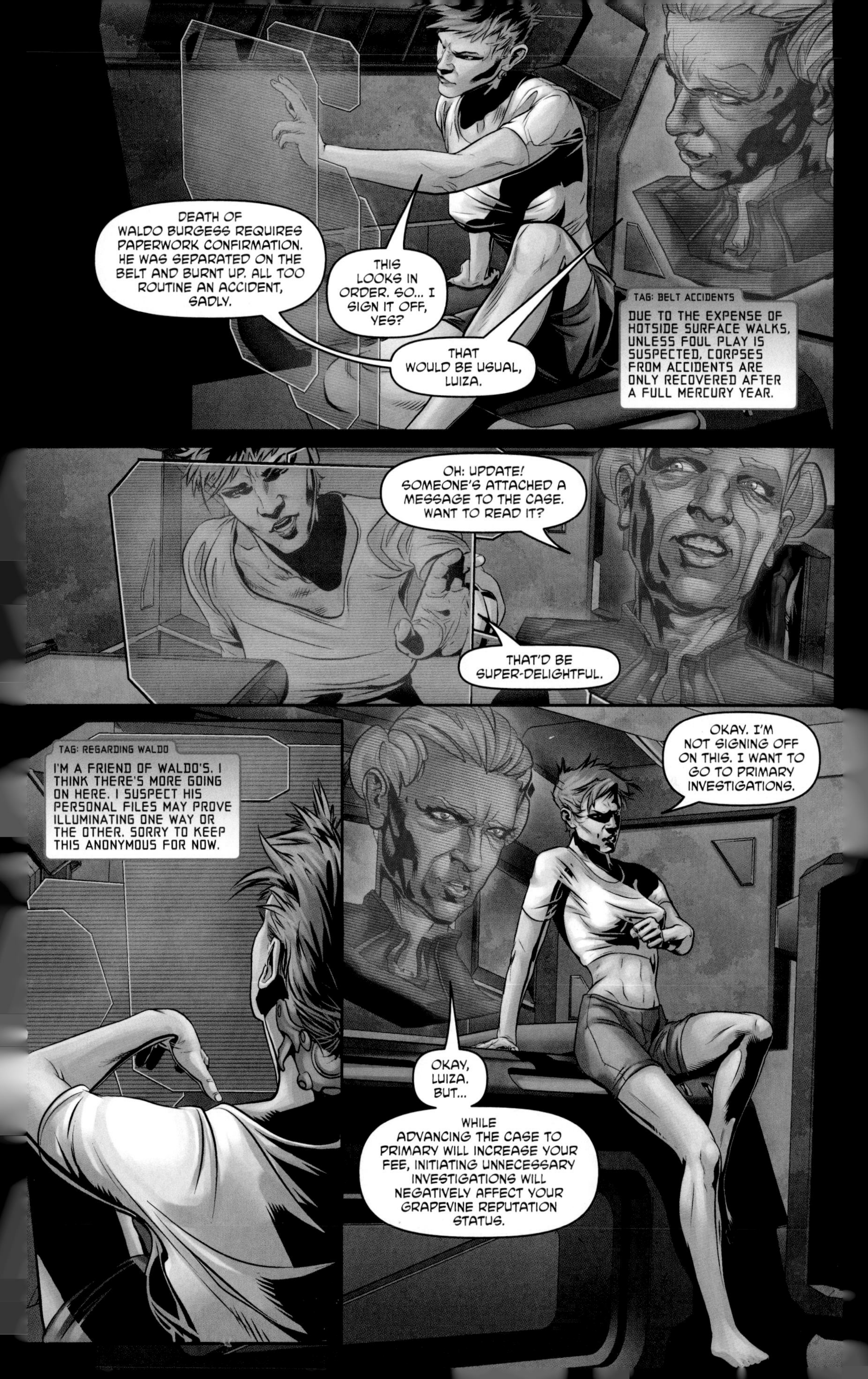
DEATH OF WALDO BURGESS REQUIRES PAPERWORK CONFIRMATION. HE WAS SEPARATED ON THE BELT AND BURNT UP. ALL TOO ROUTINE AN ACCIDENT, SADLY.
THIS LOOKS IN ORDER. SO... I SIGN IT OFF, YES?
THAT WOULD BE USUAL, LUIZA.
TAG: BELT ACCIDENTS
DUE TO THE EXPENSE OF HOTSIDE SURFACE WALKS, UNLESS FOUL PLAY IS SUSPECTED, CORPSES FROM ACCIDENTS ARE ONLY RECOVERED AFTER A FULL MERCURY YEAR.
OH: UPDATE! SOMEONE'S ATTACHED A MESSAGE TO THE CASE. WANT TO READ IT?
THAT'D BE SUPER-DELIGHTFUL.
TAG: REGARDING WALDO
I'M A FRIEND OF WALDO'S. I THINK THERE'S MORE GOING ON HERE. I SUSPECT HIS PERSONAL FILES MAY PROVE ILLUMINATING ONE WAY OR THE OTHER. SORRY TO KEEP THIS ANONYMOUS FOR NOW.
OKAY. I'M NOT SIGNING OFF ON THIS. I WANT TO GO TO PRIMARY INVESTIGATIONS.
OKAY, LUIZA. BUT...
WHILE ADVANCING THE CASE TO PRIMARY WILL INCREASE YOUR FEE, INITIATING UNNECESSARY INVESTIGATIONS WILL NEGATIVELY AFFECT YOUR GRAPEVINE REPUTATION STATUS.

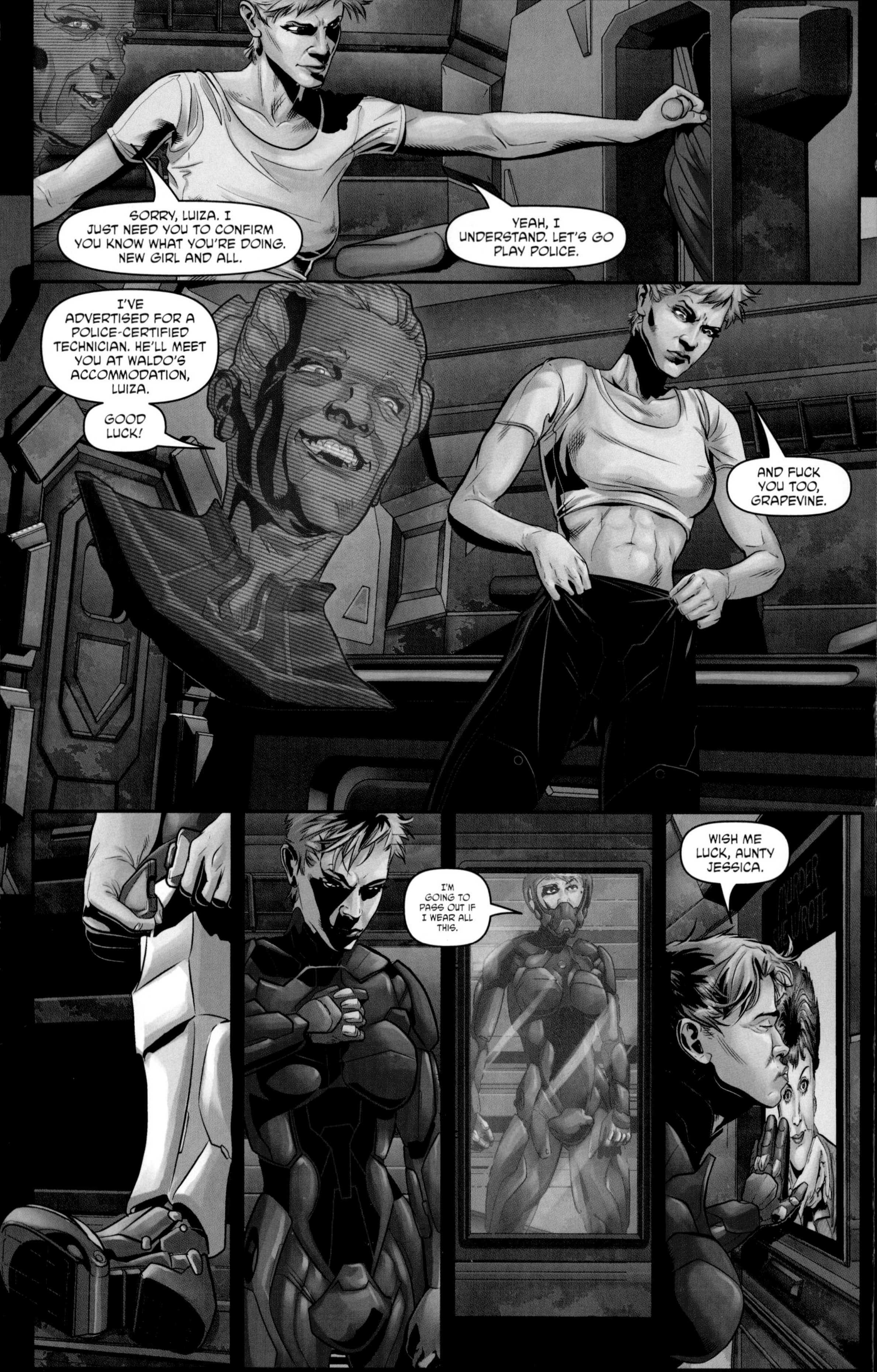
SORRY, LUIZA. I JUST NEED YOU TO CONFIRM YOU KNOW WHAT YOU'RE DOING. NEW GIRL AND ALL.
YEAH, I UNDERSTAND. LET'S GO PLAY POLICE.
I'VE ADVERTISED FOR A POLICE-CERTIFIED TECHNICIAN. HE'LL MEET YOU AT WALDO'S ACCOMMODATION, LUIZA.
GOOD LUCK!
AND FUCK YOU TOO, GRAPEVINE.
I'M GOING TO PASS OUT IF I WEAR ALL THIS.
WISH ME LUCK, AUNTY JESSICA.

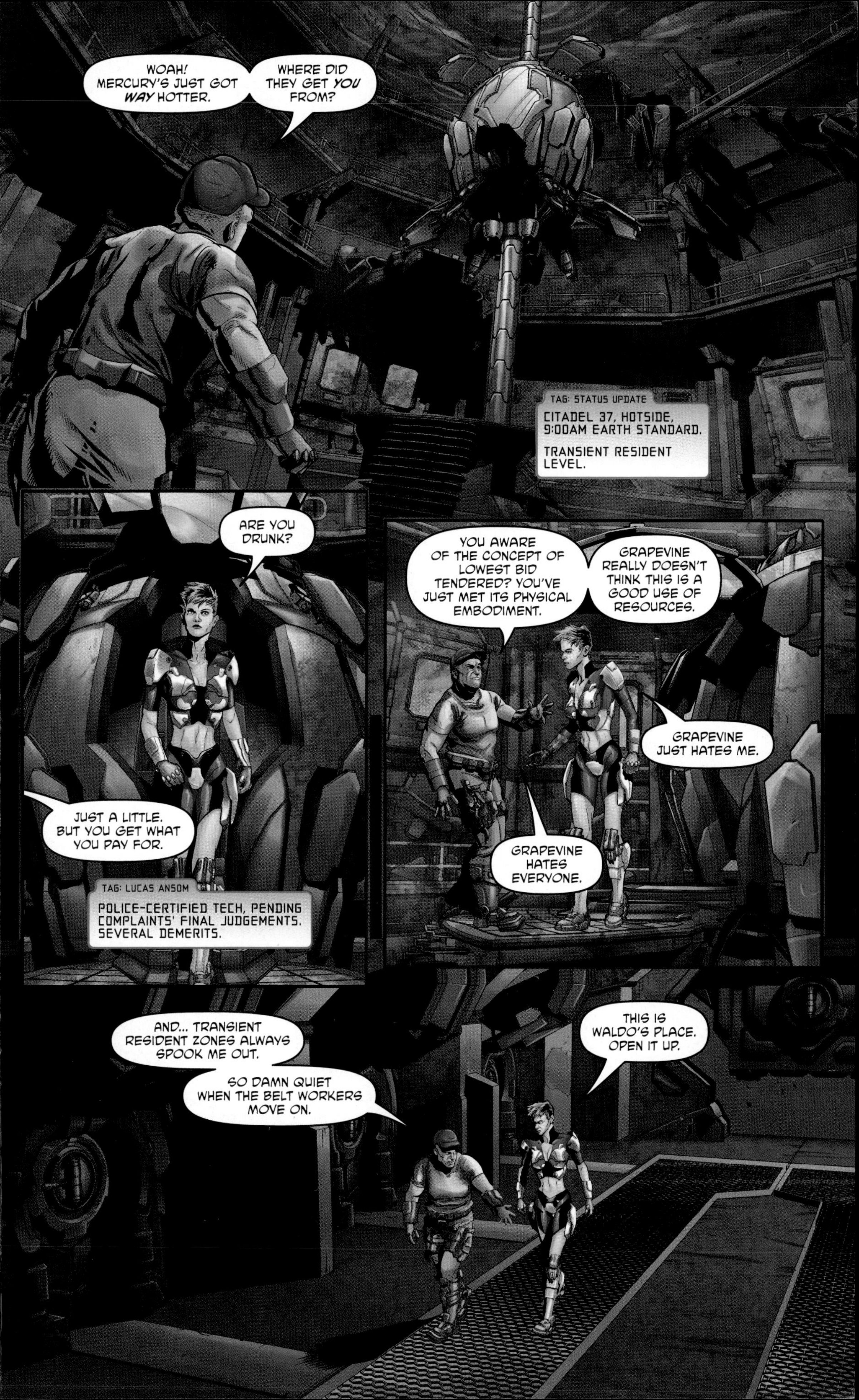
WOAH! MERCURY'S JUST GOT *WAY* HOTTER.
WHERE DID THEY GET *YOU* FROM?
TAG: STATUS UPDATE
CITADEL 37, HOTSIDE, 9:00AM EARTH STANDARD.
TRANSIENT RESIDENT LEVEL.
ARE YOU DRUNK?
JUST A LITTLE. BUT YOU GET WHAT YOU PAY FOR.
TAG: LUCAS ANSOM
POLICE-CERTIFIED TECH, PENDING COMPLAINTS' FINAL JUDGEMENTS. SEVERAL DEMERITS.
YOU AWARE OF THE CONCEPT OF LOWEST BID TENDERED? YOU'VE JUST MET ITS PHYSICAL EMBODIMENT.
GRAPEVINE REALLY DOESN'T THINK THIS IS A GOOD USE OF RESOURCES.
GRAPEVINE JUST HATES ME.
GRAPEVINE HATES EVERYONE.
AND... TRANSIENT RESIDENT ZONES ALWAYS SPOOK ME OUT.
SO DAMN QUIET WHEN THE BELT WORKERS MOVE ON.
THIS IS WALDO'S PLACE. OPEN IT UP.

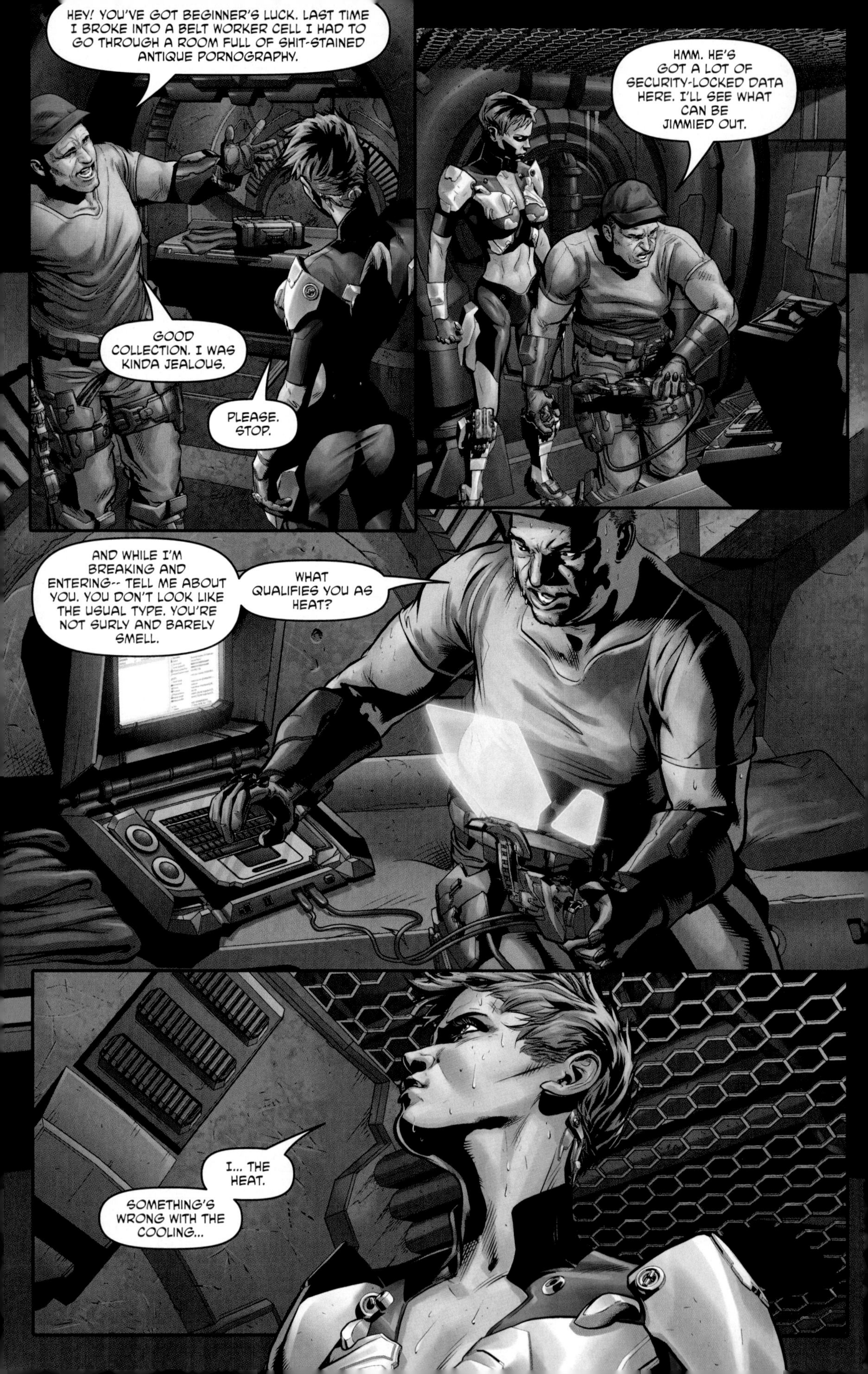
HEY! YOU'VE GOT BEGINNER'S LUCK. LAST TIME I BROKE INTO A BELT WORKER CELL I HAD TO GO THROUGH A ROOM FULL OF SHIT-STAINED ANTIQUE PORNOGRAPHY.
GOOD COLLECTION. I WAS KINDA JEALOUS.
PLEASE. STOP.
HMM. HE'S GOT A LOT OF SECURITY-LOCKED DATA HERE. I'LL SEE WHAT CAN BE JIMMIED OUT.
AND WHILE I'M BREAKING AND ENTERING-- TELL ME ABOUT YOU. YOU DON'T LOOK LIKE THE USUAL TYPE. YOU'RE NOT SURLY AND BARELY SMELL.
WHAT QUALIFIES YOU AS HEAT?
I... THE HEAT.
SOMETHING'S WRONG WITH THE COOLING...

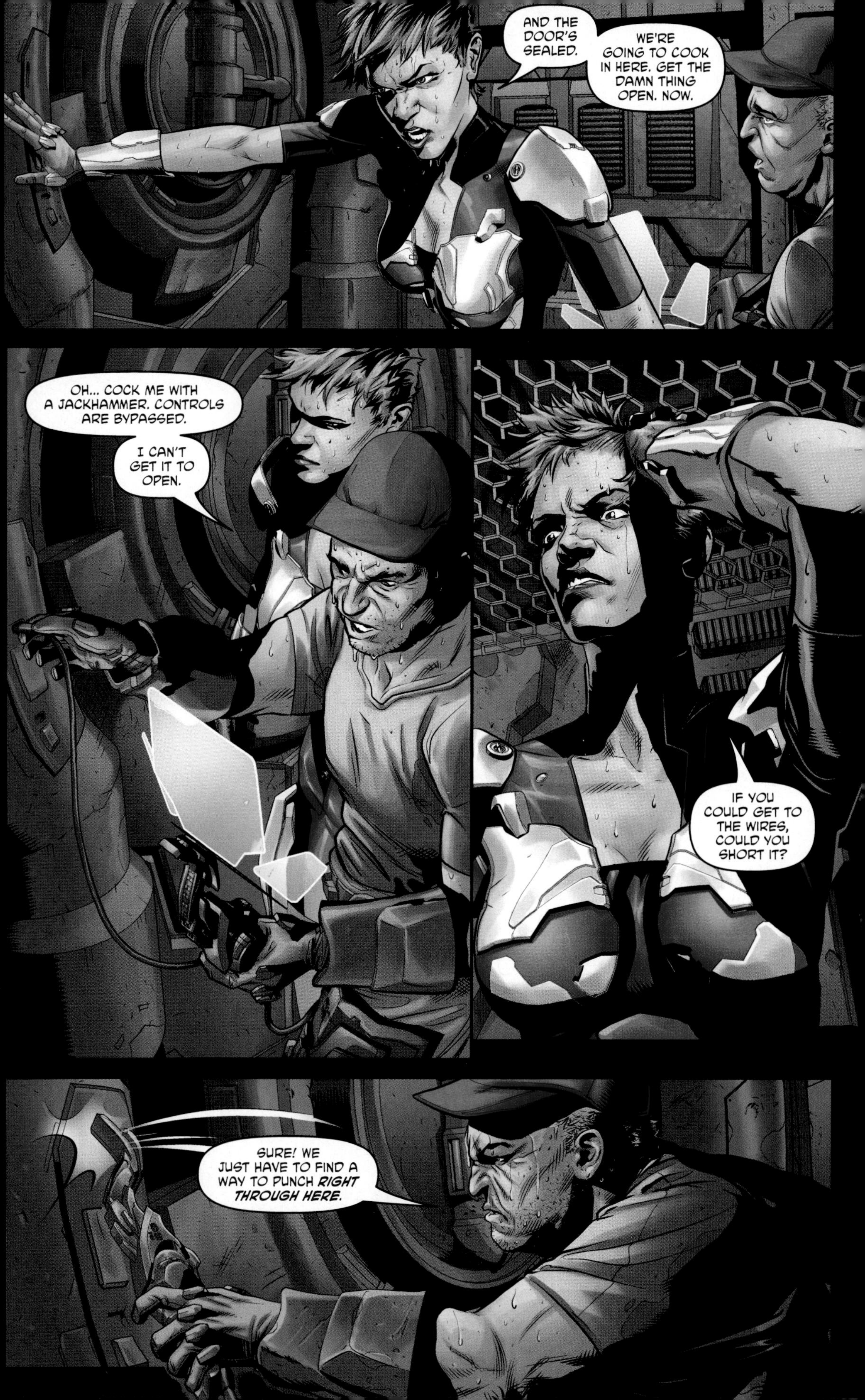
AND THE DOOR'S SEALED.
WE'RE GOING TO COOK IN HERE. GET THE DAMN THING OPEN. NOW.
OH... COCK ME WITH A JACKHAMMER. CONTROLS ARE BYPASSED.
I CAN'T GET IT TO OPEN.
IF YOU COULD GET TO THE WIRES, COULD YOU SHORT IT?
SURE! WE JUST HAVE TO FIND A WAY TO PUNCH *RIGHT THROUGH HERE*.

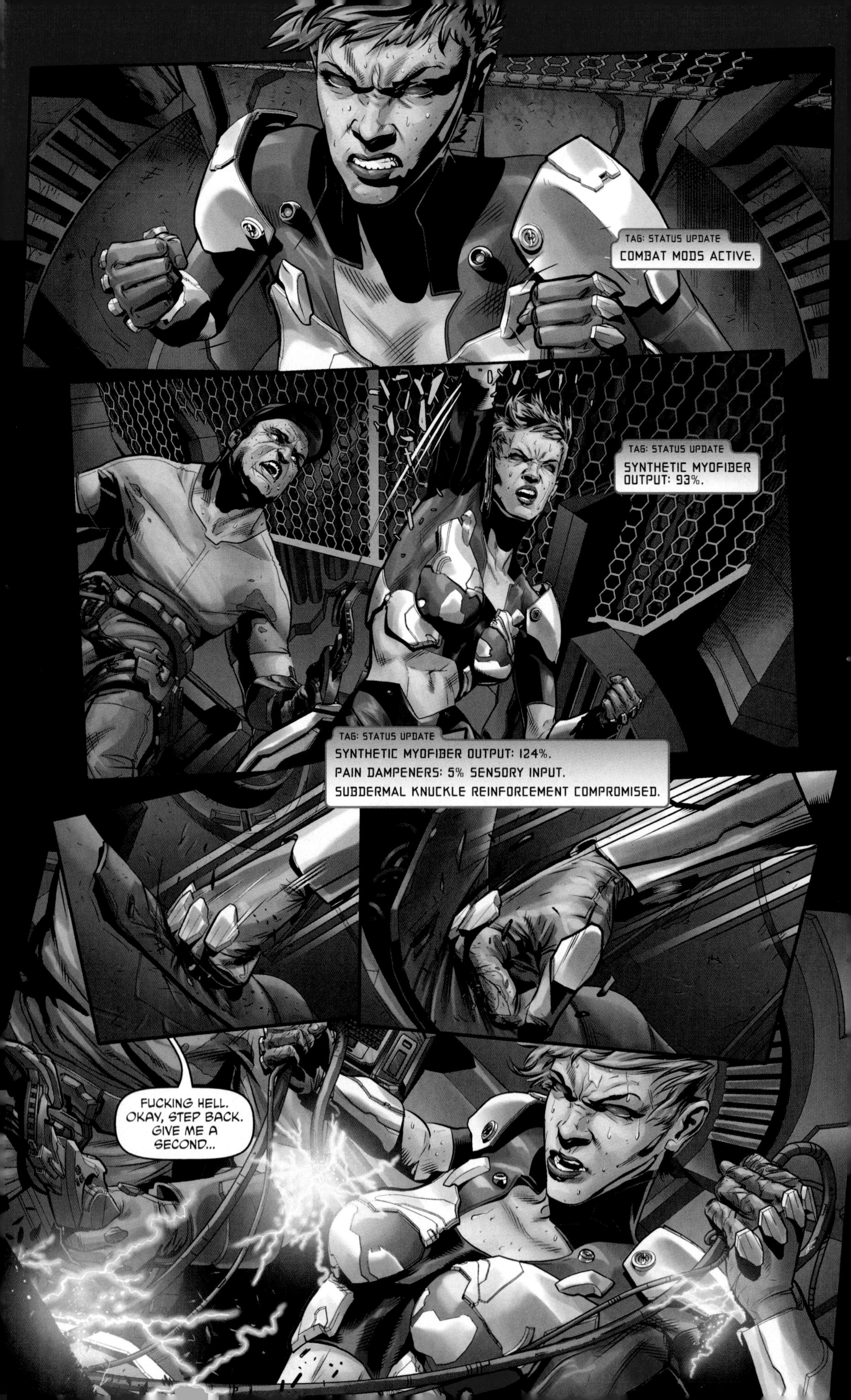
TAG: STATUS UPDATE
COMBAT MODS ACTIVE.
TAG: STATUS UPDATE
SYNTHETIC MYOFIBER OUTPUT: 93%.
TAG: STATUS UPDATE
SYNTHETIC MYOFIBER OUTPUT: 124%.
PAIN DAMPENERS: 5% SENSORY INPUT.
SUBDERMAL KNUCKLE REINFORCEMENT COMPROMISED.
FUCKING HELL. OKAY, STEP BACK. GIVE ME A SECOND...

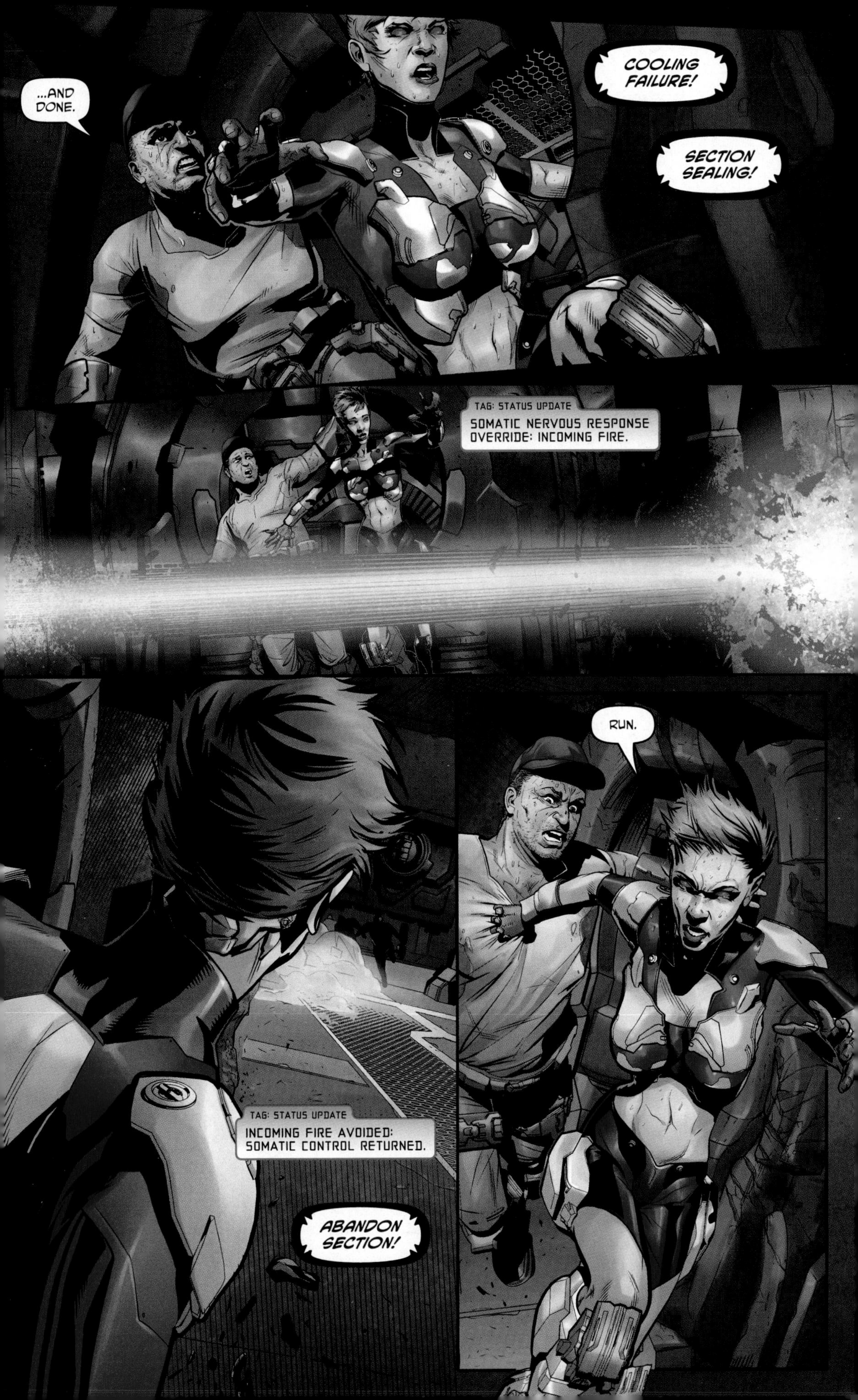
...AND DONE.
COOLING FAILURE!
SECTION SEALING!
TAG: STATUS UPDATE
SOMATIC NERVOUS RESPONSE OVERRIDE: INCOMING FIRE.
TAG: STATUS UPDATE
INCOMING FIRE AVOIDED: SOMATIC CONTROL RETURNED.
ABANDON SECTION!
RUN.

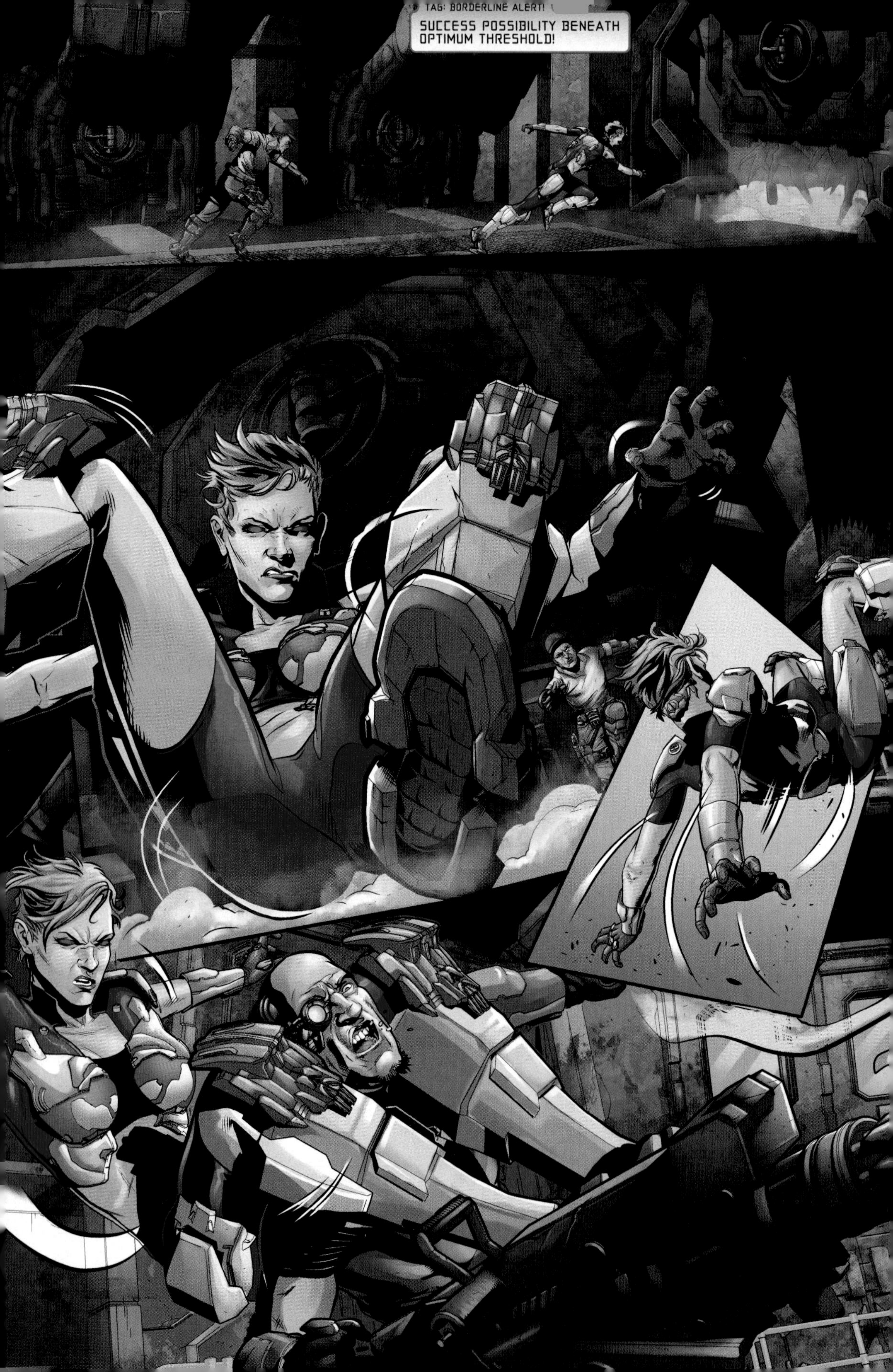
TAG: BORDERLINE ALERT!
SUCCESS POSSIBILITY BENEATH OPTIMUM THRESHOLD!

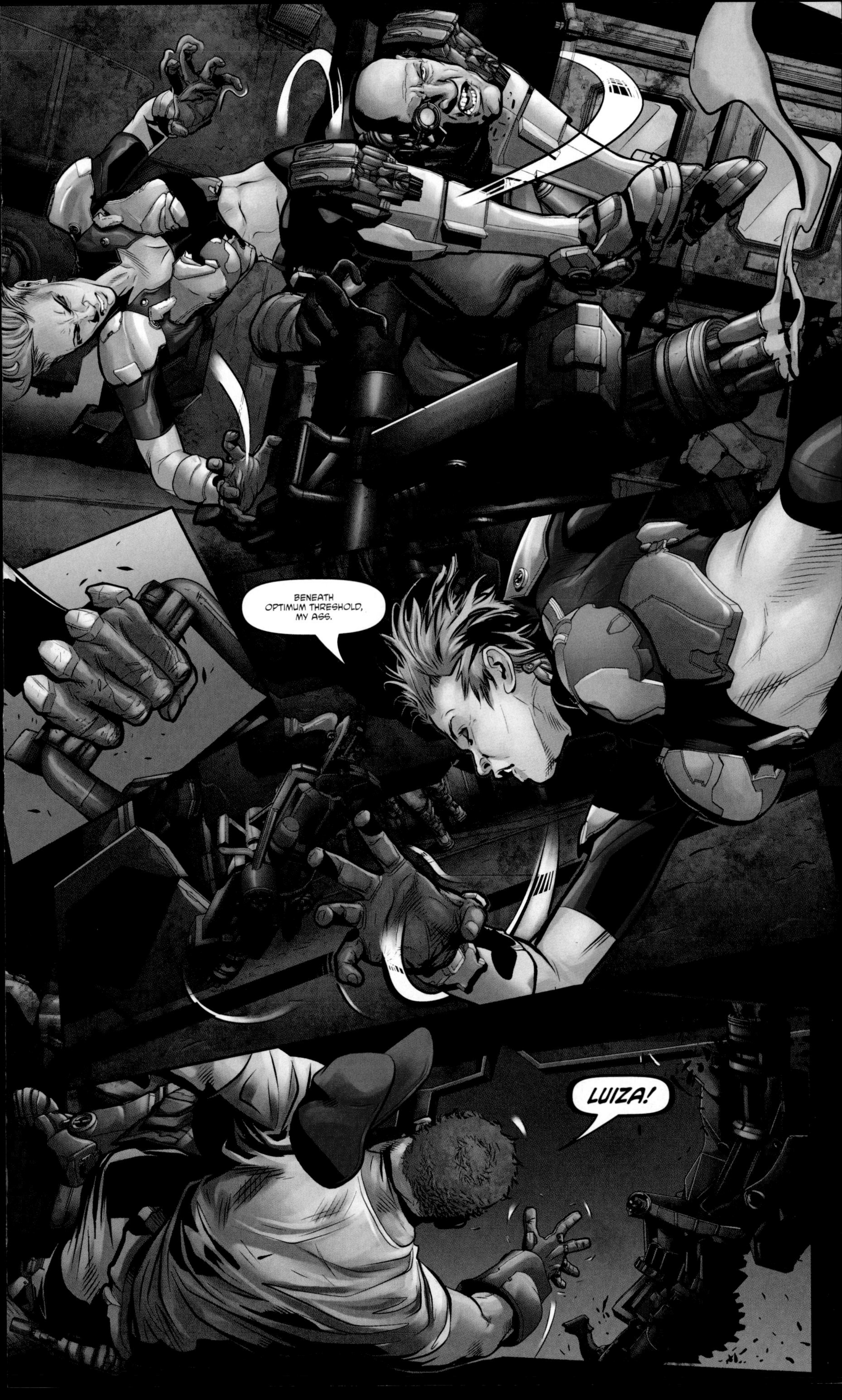
BENEATH OPTIMUM THRESHOLD, MY ASS.
LUIZA!

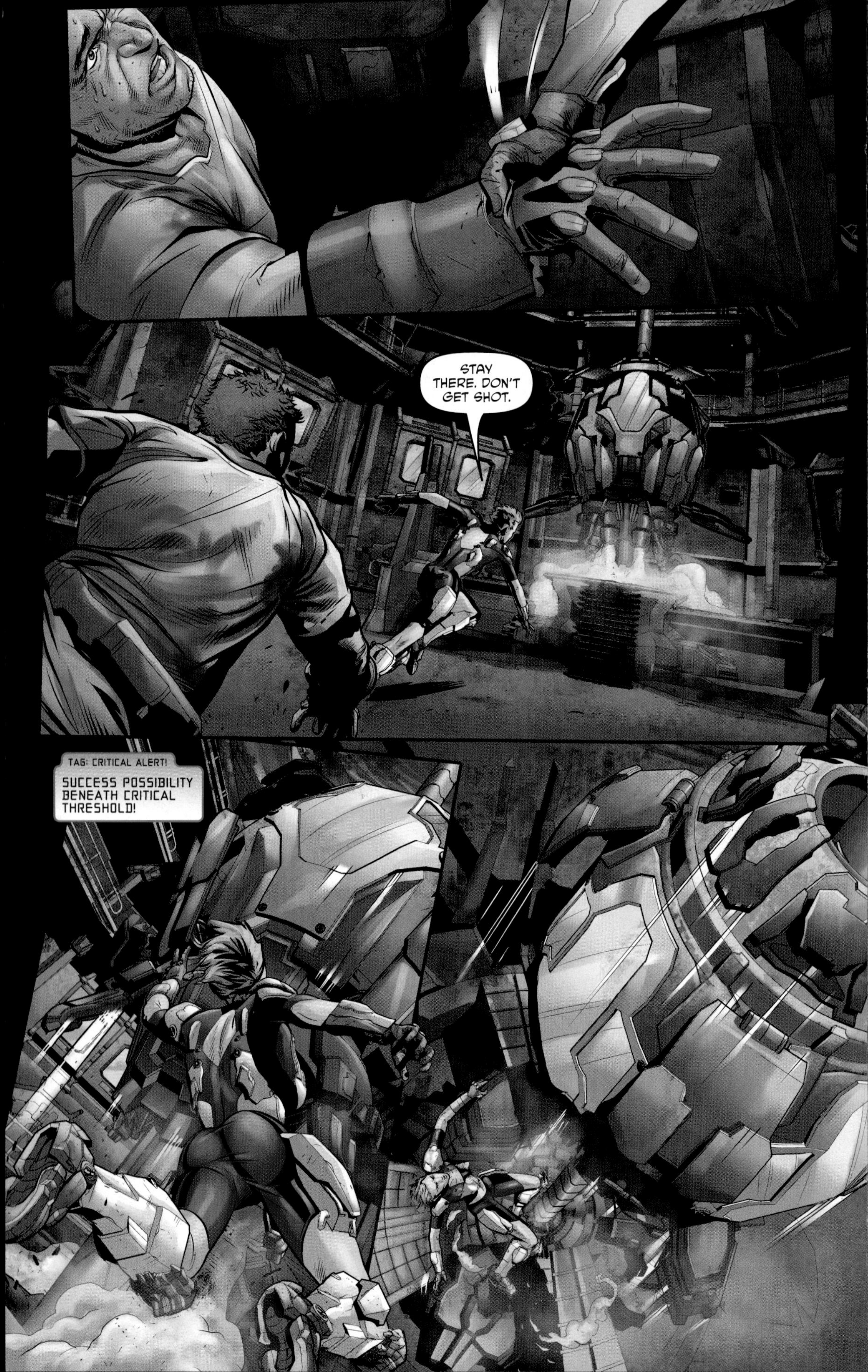
STAY THERE. DON'T GET SHOT.
TAG: CRITICAL ALERT!
SUCCESS POSSIBILITY BENEATH CRITICAL THRESHOLD!

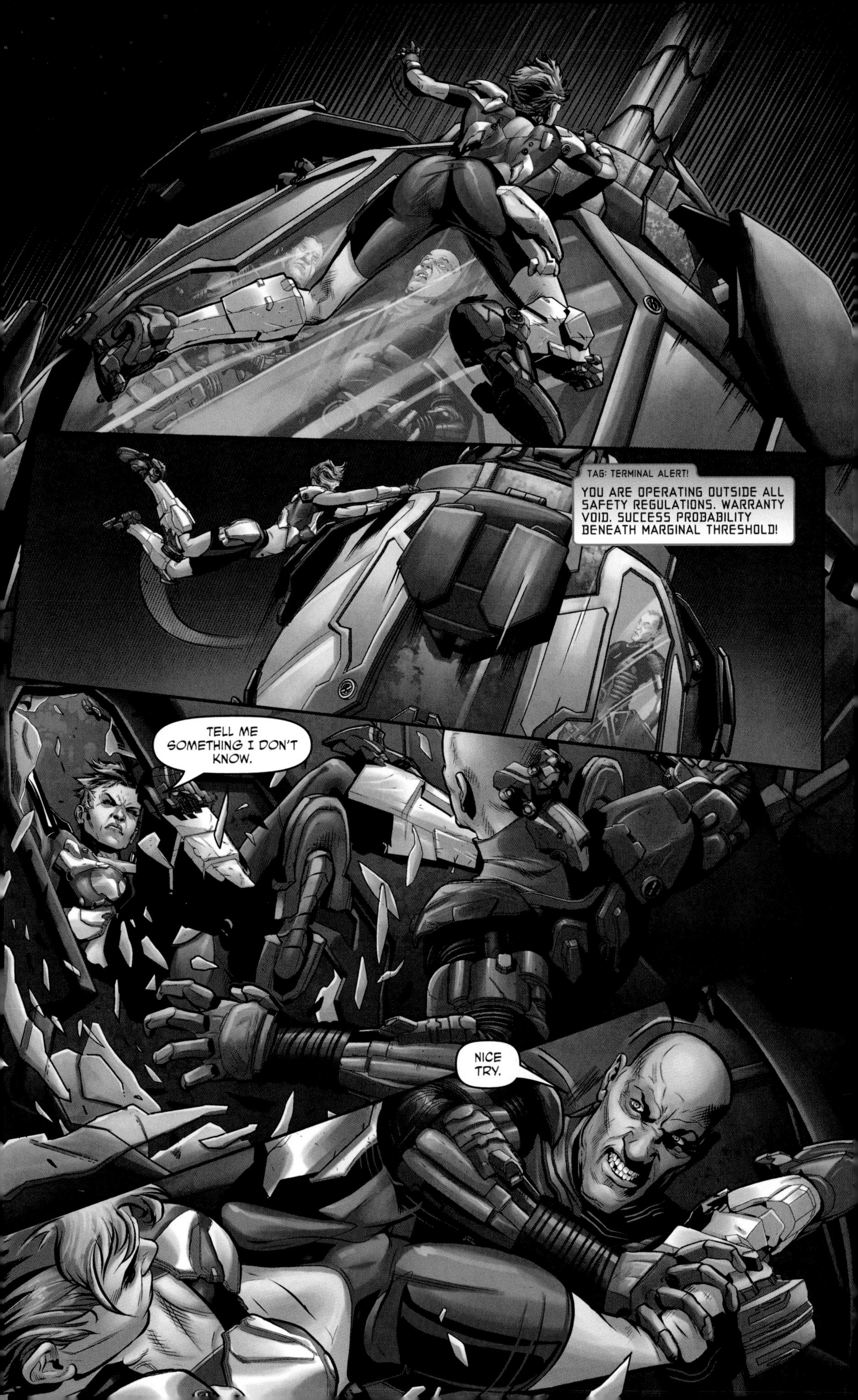
TAG: TERMINAL ALERT!
YOU ARE OPERATING OUTSIDE ALL SAFETY REGULATIONS. WARRANTY VOID. SUCCESS PROBABILITY BENEATH MARGINAL THRESHOLD!
TELL ME SOMETHING I DON'T KNOW.
NICE TRY.

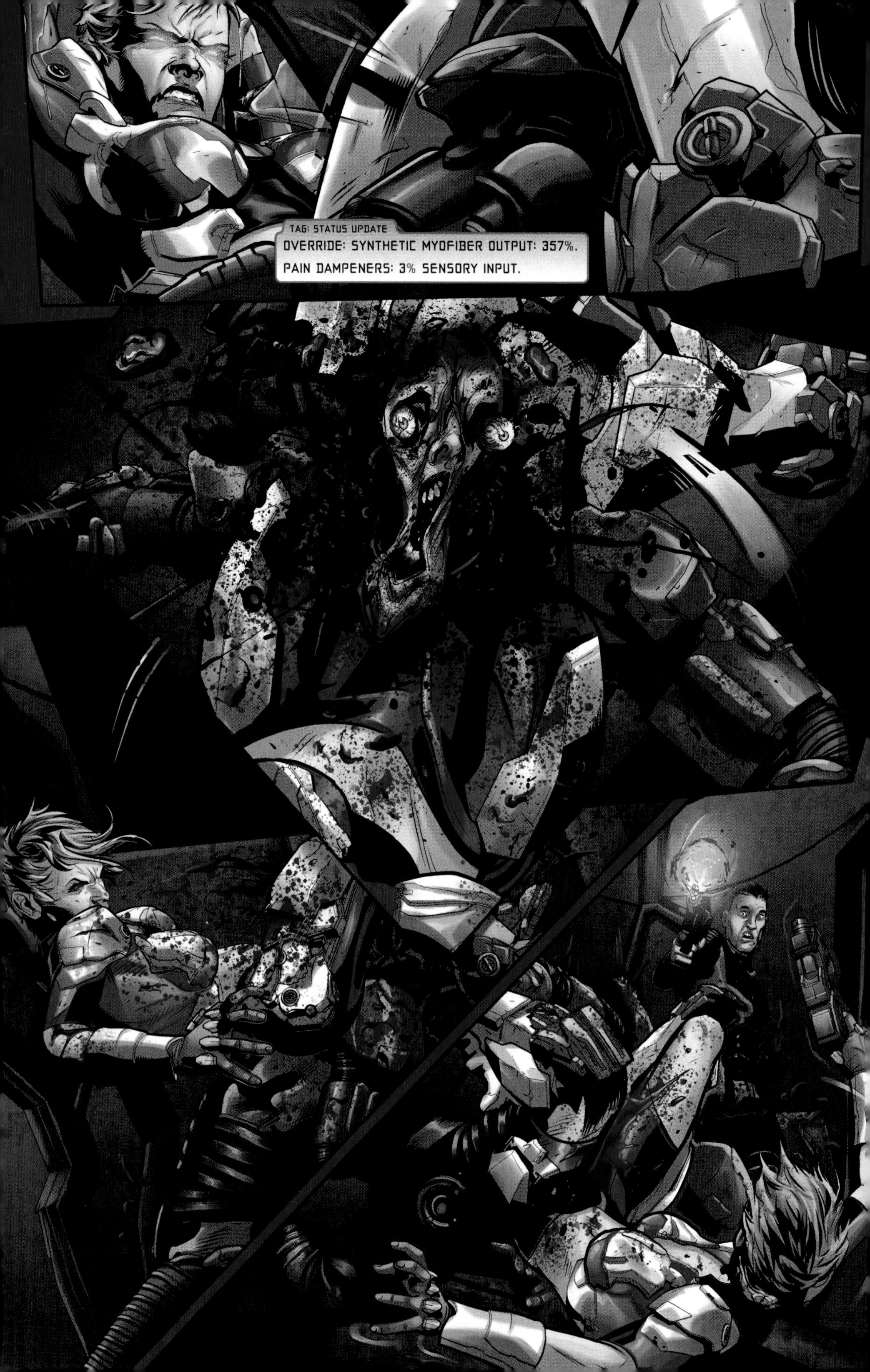
TAG: STATUS UPDATE
OVERRIDE: SYNTHETIC MYOFIBER OUTPUT: 357%.
PAIN DAMPENERS: 3% SENSORY INPUT.

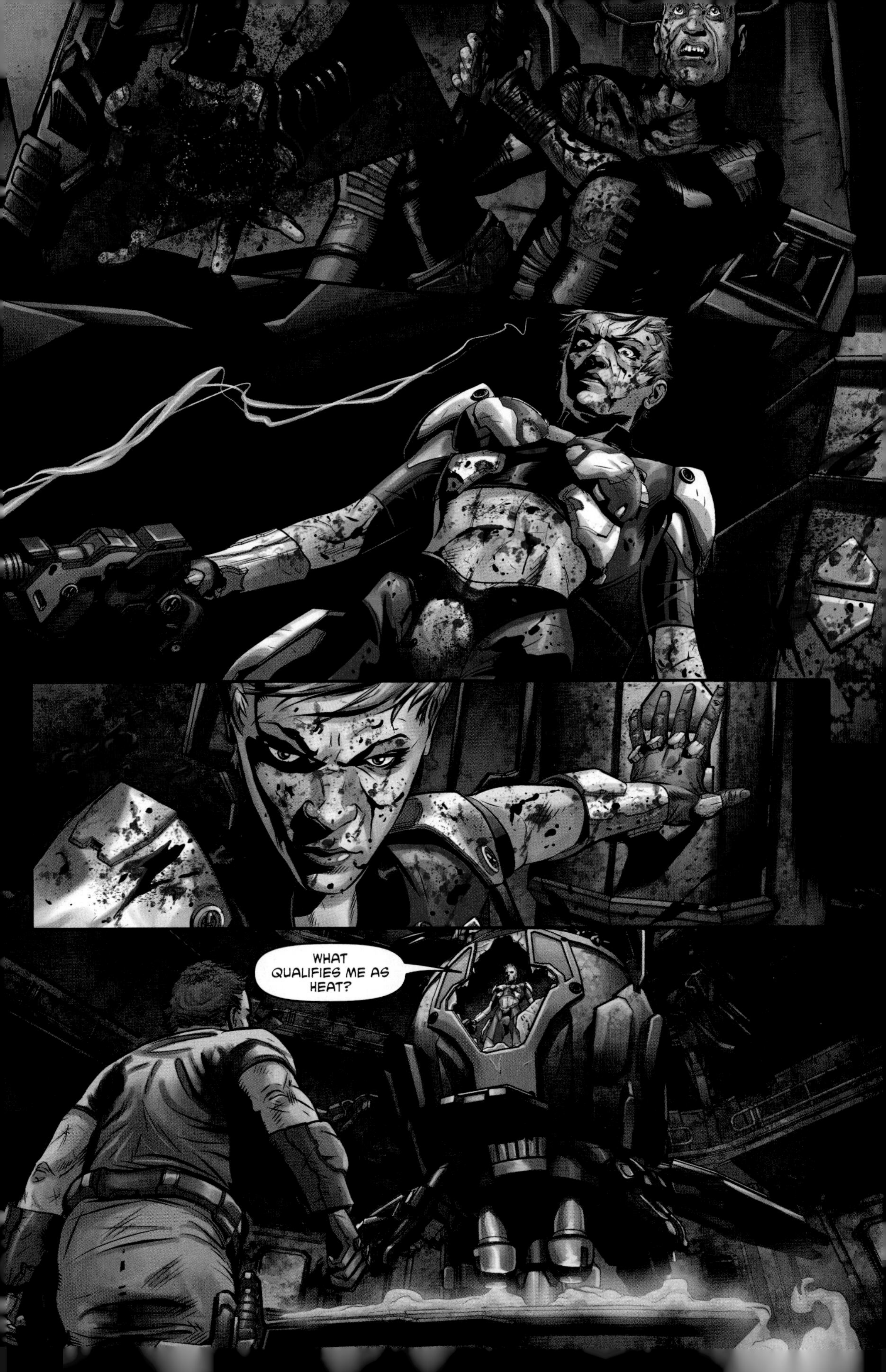
WHAT QUALIFIES ME AS HEAT?

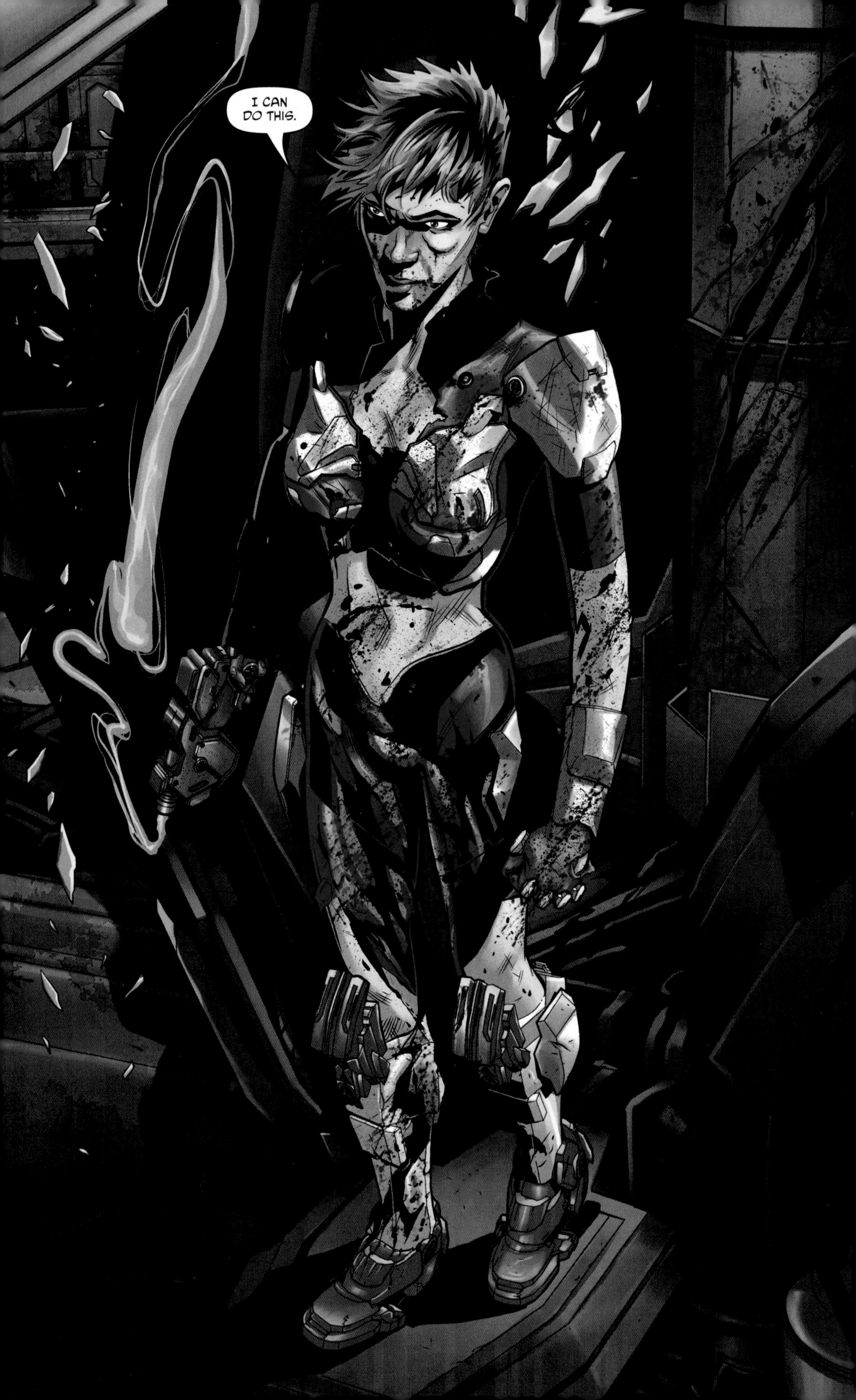
I CAN DO THIS.

chapter 2

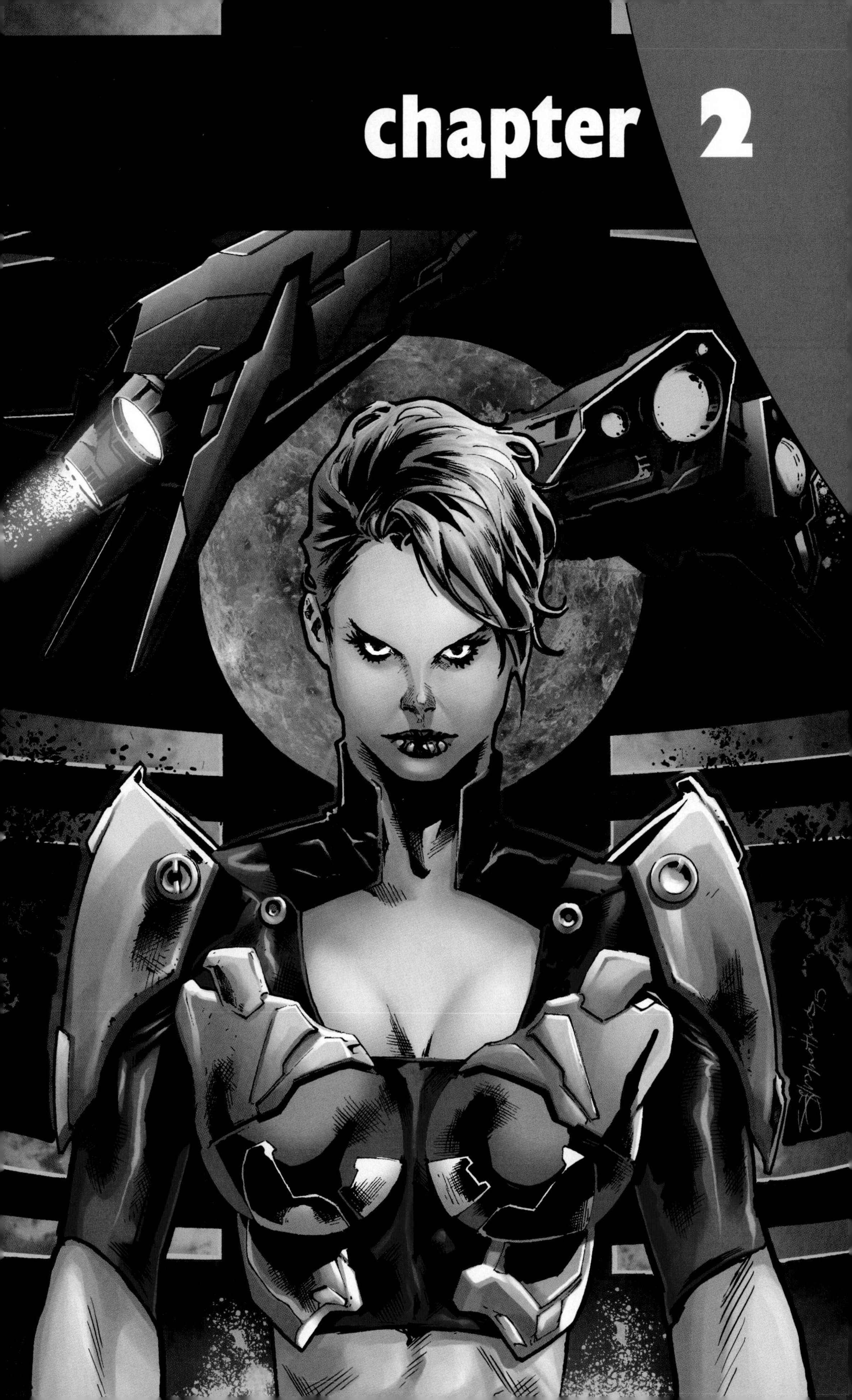

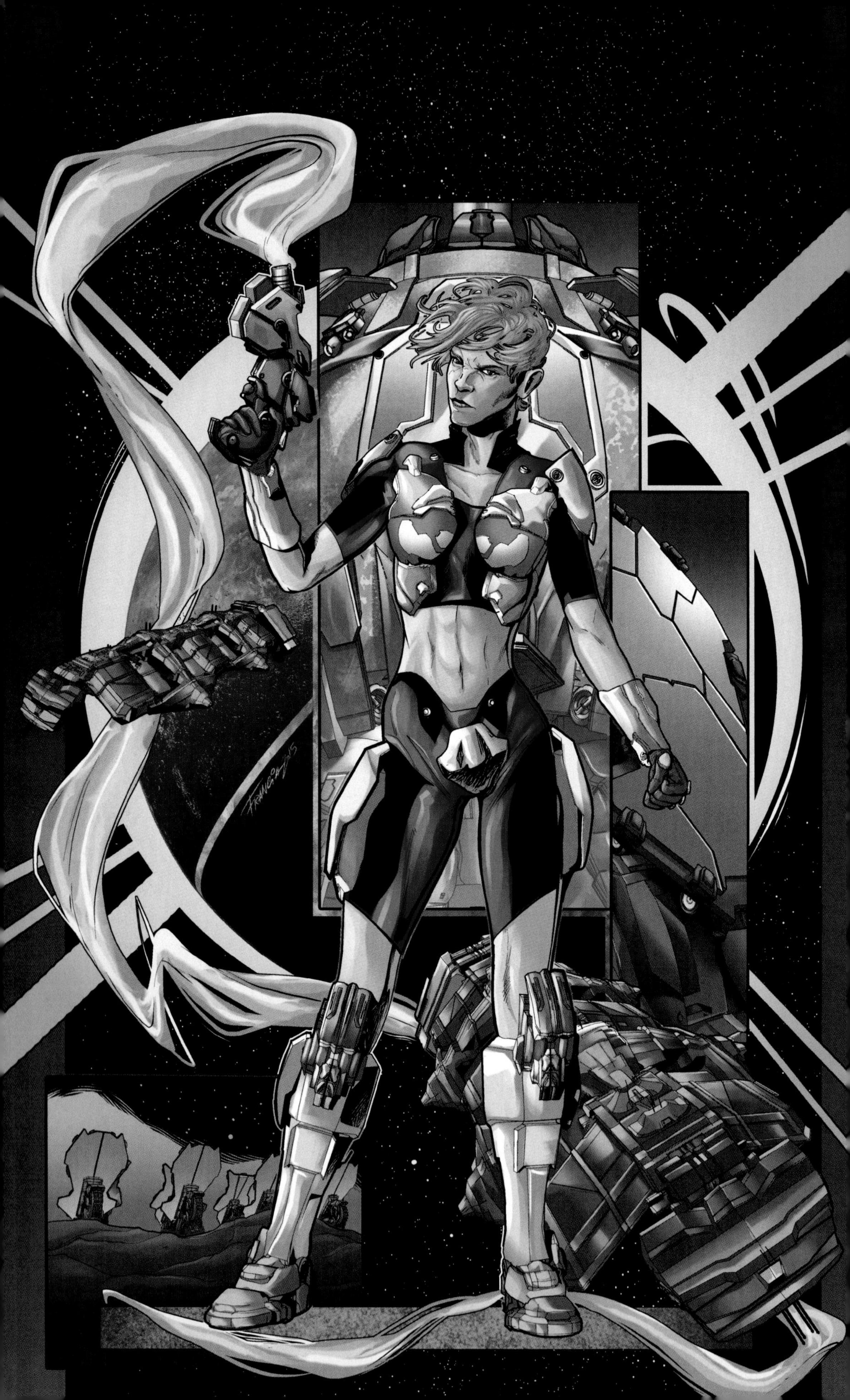

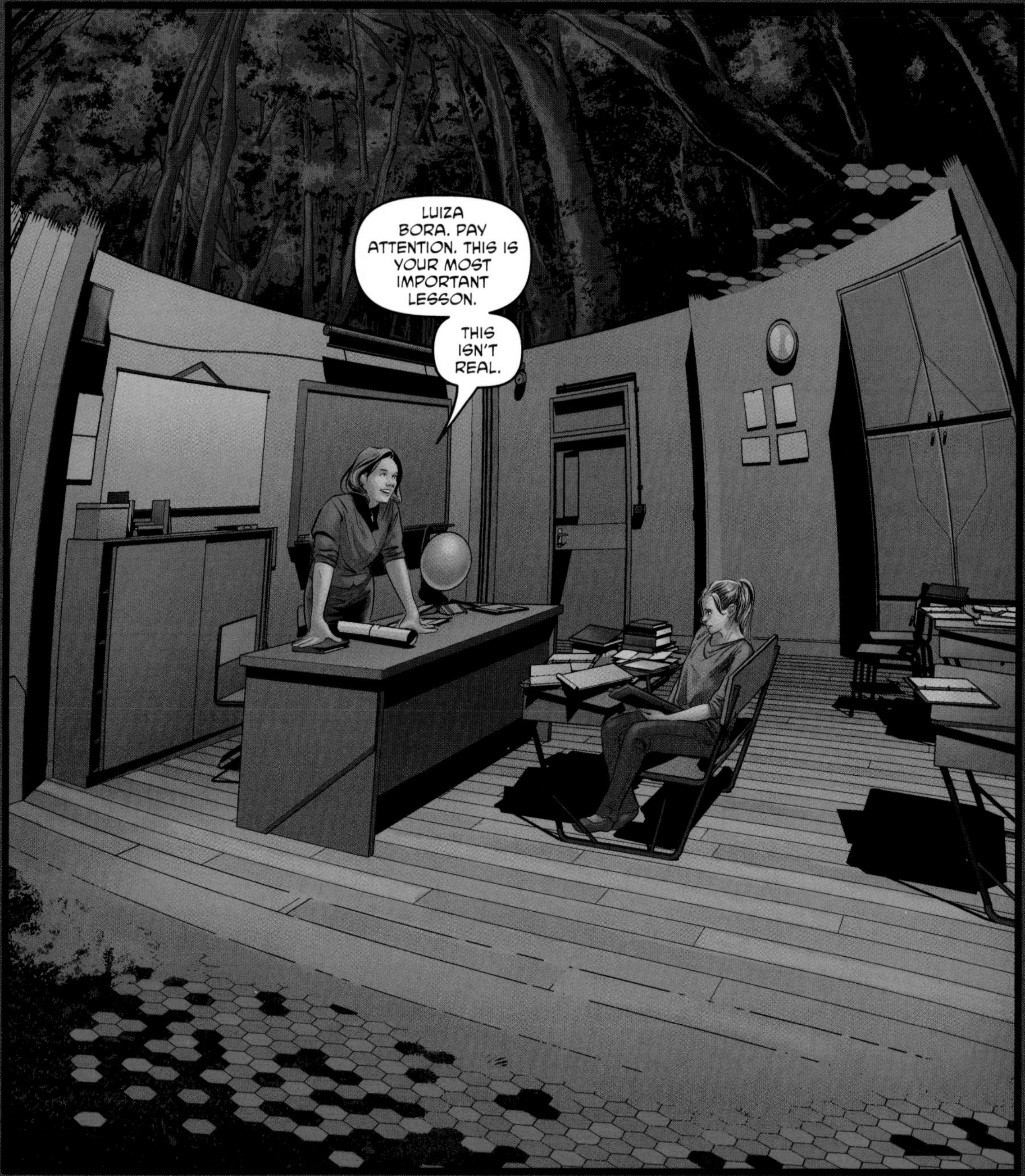
LUIZA BORA. PAY ATTENTION. THIS IS YOUR MOST IMPORTANT LESSON.
THIS ISN'T REAL.

MERCURY HEAT: THE LONG, SLOW DAWN

KIERON GILLEN / OMAR FRANCIA

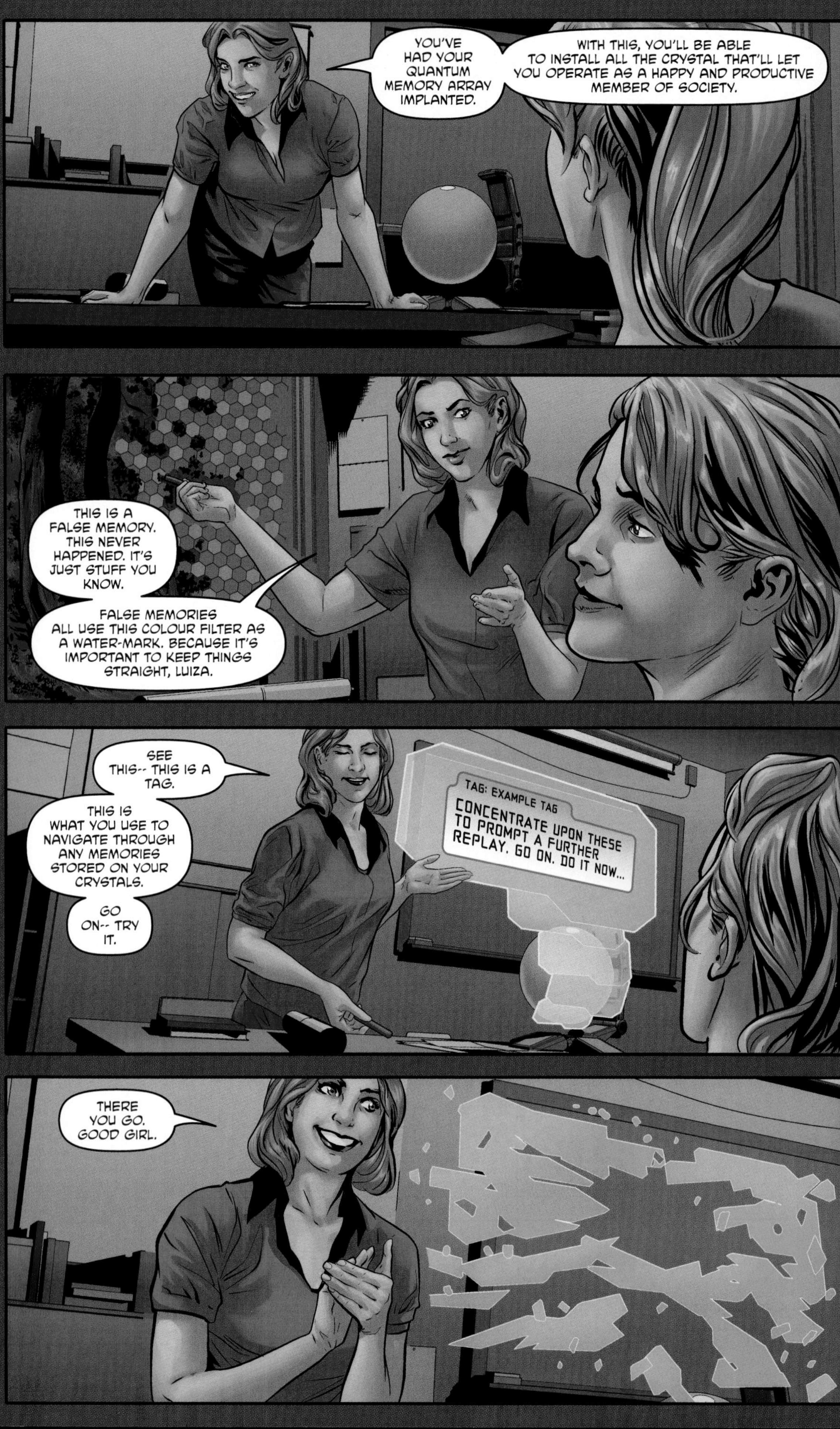
YOU'VE HAD YOUR QUANTUM MEMORY ARRAY IMPLANTED.
WITH THIS, YOU'LL BE ABLE TO INSTALL ALL THE CRYSTAL THAT'LL LET YOU OPERATE AS A HAPPY AND PRODUCTIVE MEMBER OF SOCIETY.
THIS IS A FALSE MEMORY. THIS NEVER HAPPENED. IT'S JUST STUFF YOU KNOW.
FALSE MEMORIES ALL USE THIS COLOUR FILTER AS A WATER-MARK. BECAUSE IT'S IMPORTANT TO KEEP THINGS STRAIGHT, LUIZA.
SEE THIS-- THIS IS A TAG.
THIS IS WHAT YOU USE TO NAVIGATE THROUGH ANY MEMORIES STORED ON YOUR CRYSTALS.
GO ON-- TRY IT.
TAG: EXAMPLE TAG
CONCENTRATE UPON THESE TO PROMPT A FURTHER REPLAY. GO ON. DO IT NOW...
THERE YOU GO. GOOD GIRL.

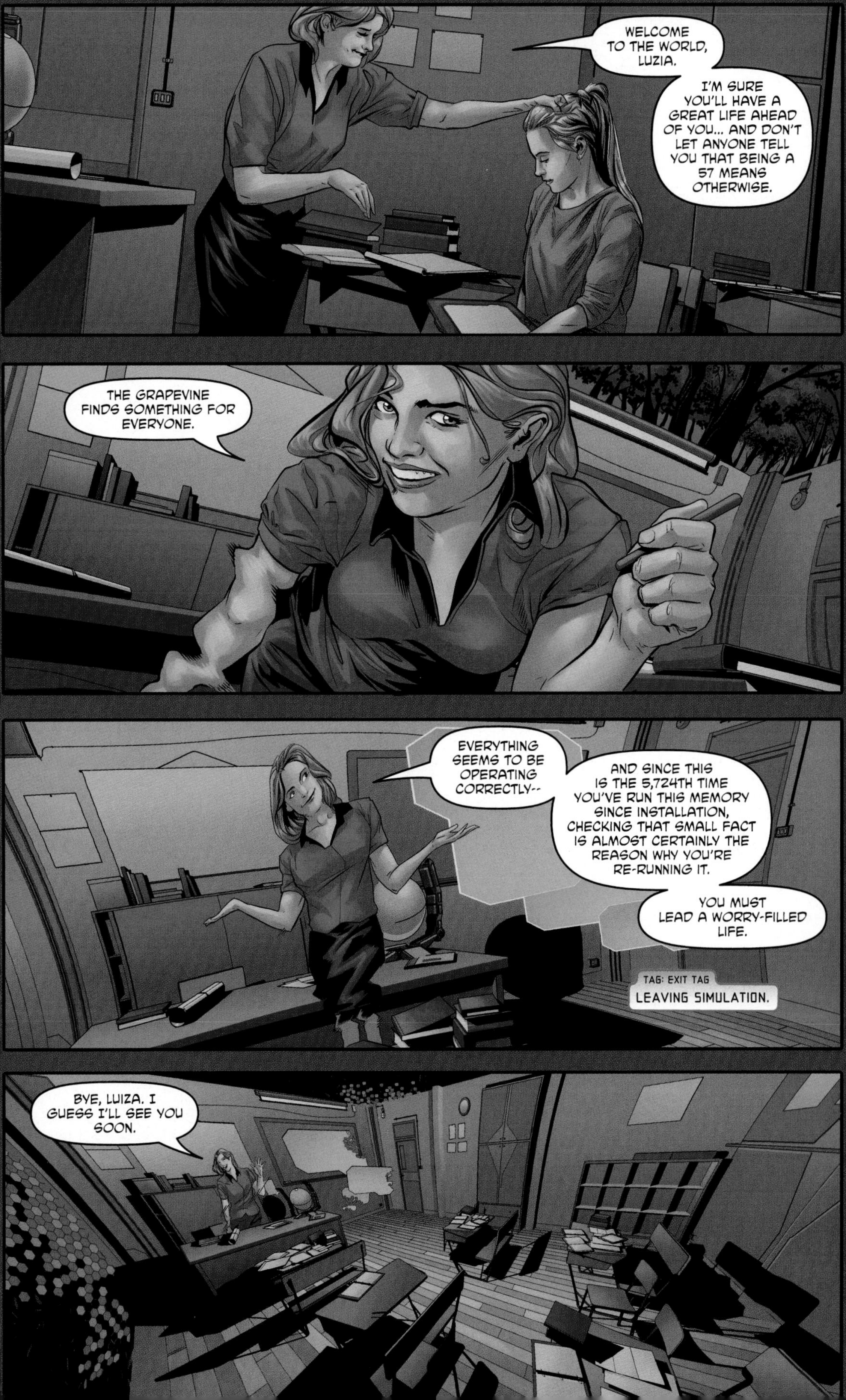

WELCOME TO THE WORLD, LUZIA.
I'M SURE YOU'LL HAVE A GREAT LIFE AHEAD OF YOU... AND DON'T LET ANYONE TELL YOU THAT BEING A 57 MEANS OTHERWISE.
THE GRAPEVINE FINDS SOMETHING FOR EVERYONE.
EVERYTHING SEEMS TO BE OPERATING CORRECTLY--
AND SINCE THIS IS THE 5,724TH TIME YOU'VE RUN THIS MEMORY SINCE INSTALLATION, CHECKING THAT SMALL FACT IS ALMOST CERTAINLY THE REASON WHY YOU'RE RE-RUNNING IT.
YOU MUST LEAD A WORRY-FILLED LIFE.
TAG: EXIT TAG
LEAVING SIMULATION.
BYE, LUIZA. I GUESS I'LL SEE YOU SOON.

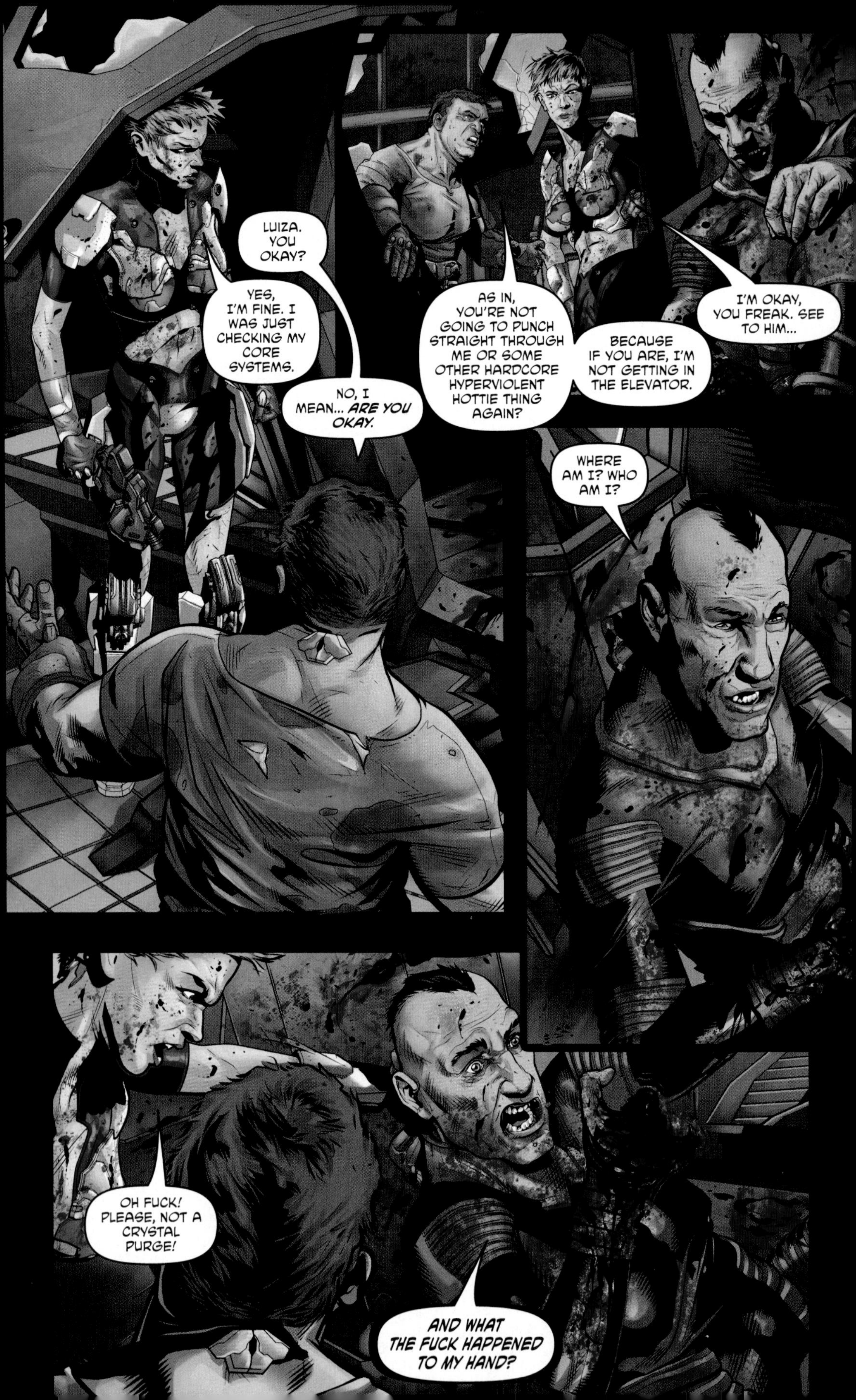
LUIZA. YOU OKAY?
YES, I'M FINE. I WAS JUST CHECKING MY CORE SYSTEMS.
NO, I MEAN... ARE YOU OKAY.
AS IN, YOU'RE NOT GOING TO PUNCH STRAIGHT THROUGH ME OR SOME OTHER HARDCORE HYPERVIOLENT HOTTIE THING AGAIN?
BECAUSE IF YOU ARE, I'M NOT GETTING IN THE ELEVATOR.
I'M OKAY, YOU FREAK. SEE TO HIM...
WHERE AM I? WHO AM I?
OH FUCK! PLEASE, NOT A CRYSTAL PURGE!
AND WHAT THE FUCK HAPPENED TO MY HAND?

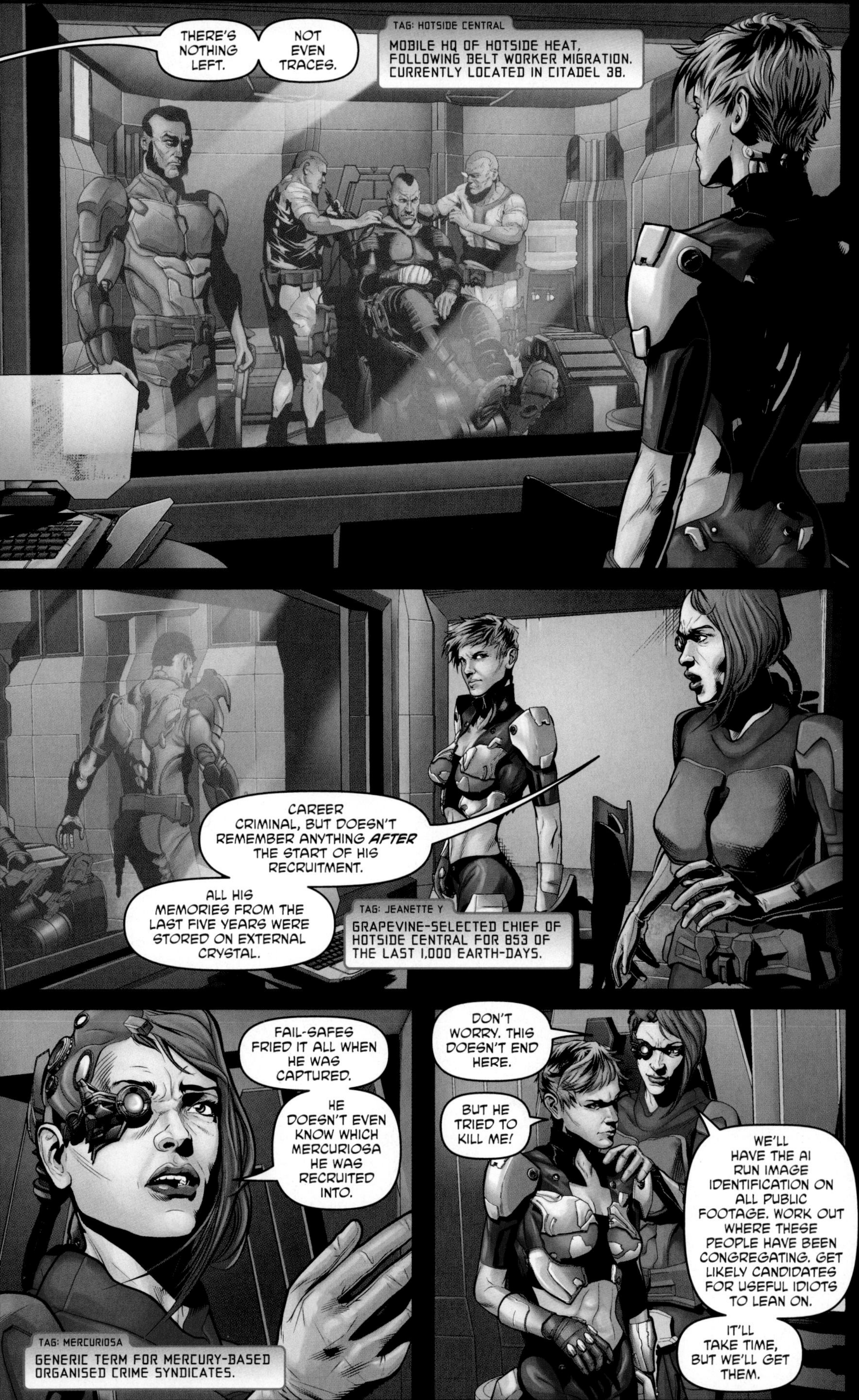
THERE'S NOTHING LEFT.
NOT EVEN TRACES.
TAG: HOTSIDE CENTRAL
MOBILE HQ OF HOTSIDE HEAT, FOLLOWING BELT WORKER MIGRATION. CURRENTLY LOCATED IN CITADEL 38.
CAREER CRIMINAL, BUT DOESN'T REMEMBER ANYTHING *AFTER* THE START OF HIS RECRUITMENT.
ALL HIS MEMORIES FROM THE LAST FIVE YEARS WERE STORED ON EXTERNAL CRYSTAL.
TAG: JEANETTE Y
GRAPEVINE-SELECTED CHIEF OF HOTSIDE CENTRAL FOR 853 OF THE LAST 1,000 EARTH-DAYS.
FAIL-SAFES FRIED IT ALL WHEN HE WAS CAPTURED.
HE DOESN'T EVEN KNOW WHICH MERCURIOSA HE WAS RECRUITED INTO.
TAG: MERCURIOSA
GENERIC TERM FOR MERCURY-BASED ORGANISED CRIME SYNDICATES.
DON'T WORRY. THIS DOESN'T END HERE.
BUT HE TRIED TO KILL ME!
WE'LL HAVE THE AI RUN IMAGE IDENTIFICATION ON ALL PUBLIC FOOTAGE. WORK OUT WHERE THESE PEOPLE HAVE BEEN CONGREGATING. GET LIKELY CANDIDATES FOR USEFUL IDIOTS TO LEAN ON.
IT'LL TAKE TIME, BUT WE'LL GET THEM.

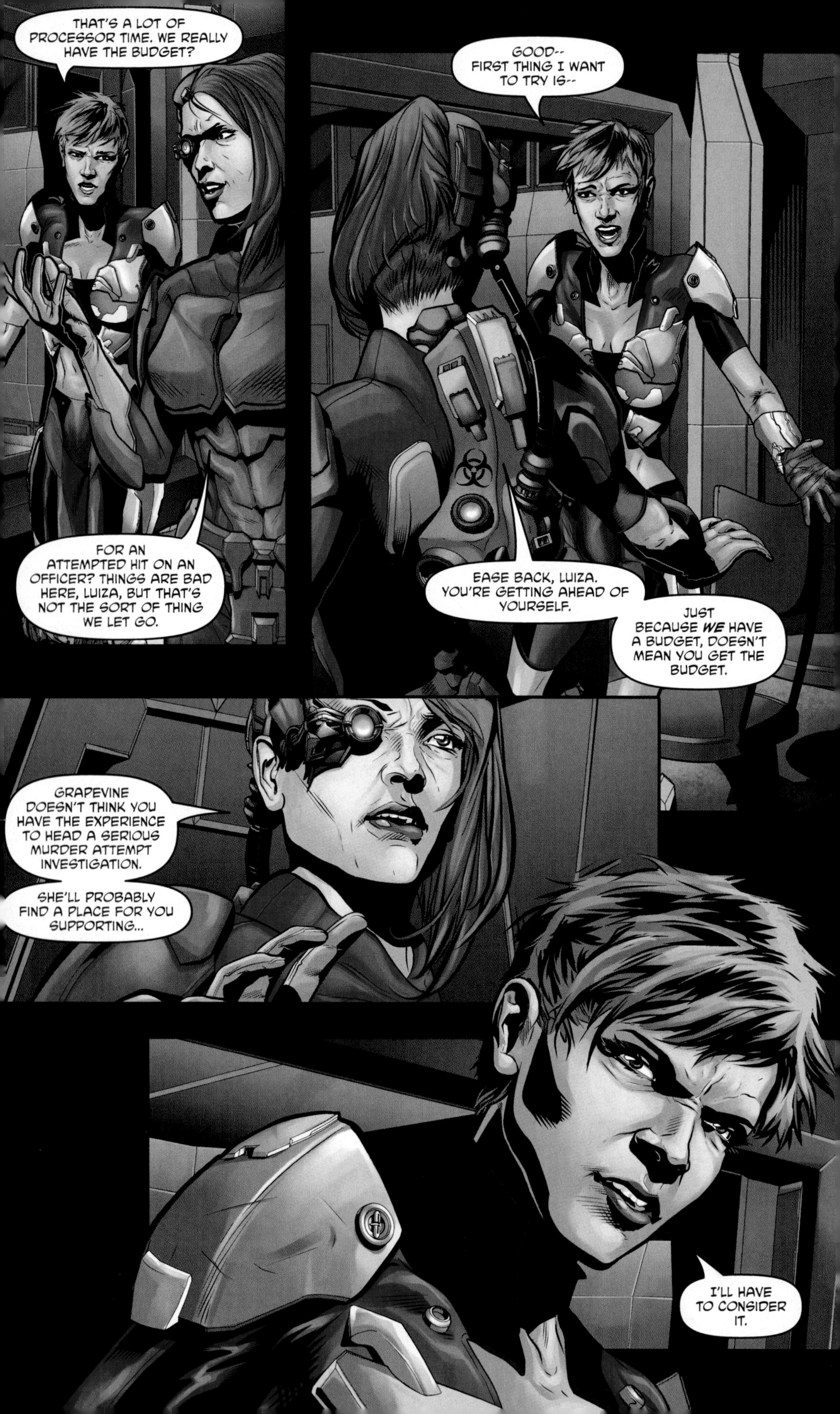
THAT'S A LOT OF PROCESSOR TIME. WE REALLY HAVE THE BUDGET?
FOR AN ATTEMPTED HIT ON AN OFFICER? THINGS ARE BAD HERE, LUIZA, BUT THAT'S NOT THE SORT OF THING WE LET GO.
GOOD-- FIRST THING I WANT TO TRY IS--
EASE BACK, LUIZA. YOU'RE GETTING AHEAD OF YOURSELF.
JUST BECAUSE *WE* HAVE A BUDGET, DOESN'T MEAN YOU GET THE BUDGET.
GRAPEVINE DOESN'T THINK YOU HAVE THE EXPERIENCE TO HEAD A SERIOUS MURDER ATTEMPT INVESTIGATION.
SHE'LL PROBABLY FIND A PLACE FOR YOU SUPPORTING...
I'LL HAVE TO CONSIDER IT.

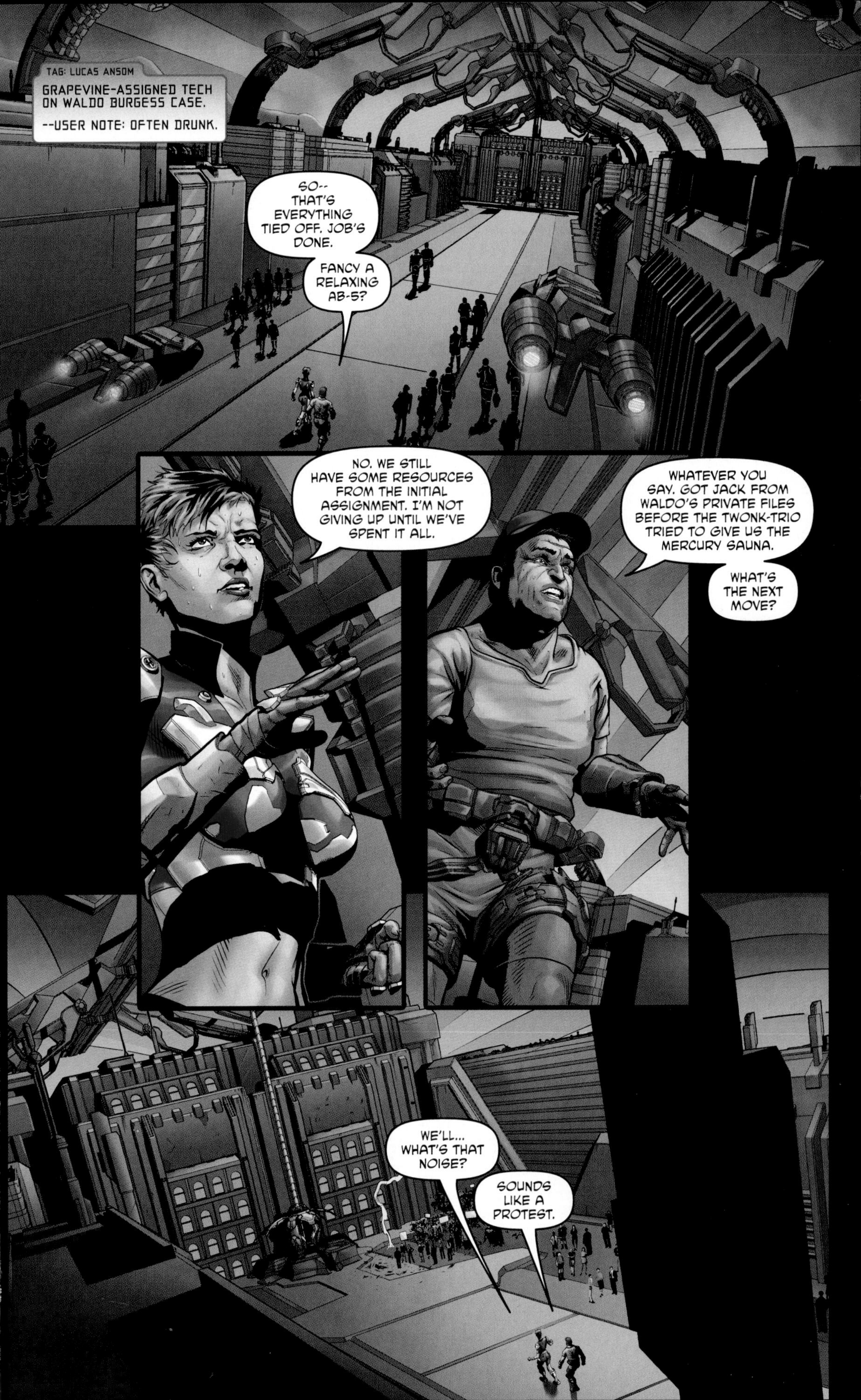
TAG: LUCAS ANSOM
GRAPEVINE-ASSIGNED TECH ON WALDO BURGESS CASE.
--USER NOTE: OFTEN DRUNK.
SO-- THAT'S EVERYTHING TIED OFF. JOB'S DONE.
FANCY A RELAXING AB-5?
NO. WE STILL HAVE SOME RESOURCES FROM THE INITIAL ASSIGNMENT. I'M NOT GIVING UP UNTIL WE'VE SPENT IT ALL.
WHATEVER YOU SAY. GOT JACK FROM WALDO'S PRIVATE FILES BEFORE THE TWONK-TRIO TRIED TO GIVE US THE MERCURY SAUNA.
WHAT'S THE NEXT MOVE?
WE'LL... WHAT'S THAT NOISE?
SOUNDS LIKE A PROTEST.

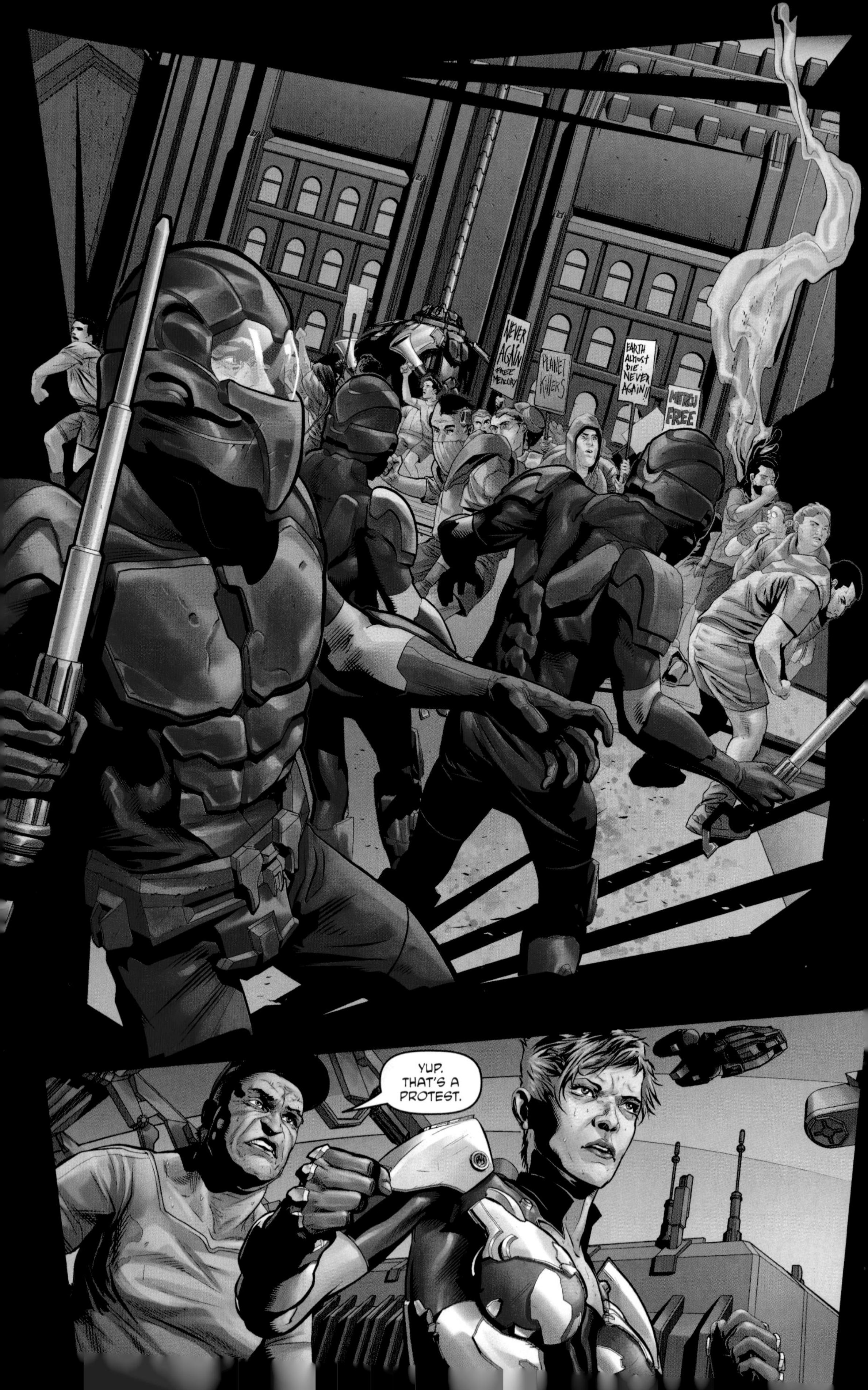
NEVER AGAIN FREE MERCURY
PLANET KILLERS
EARTH ALMOST DIE: NEVER AGAIN!!
MERCU FREE
YUP. THAT'S A PROTEST.

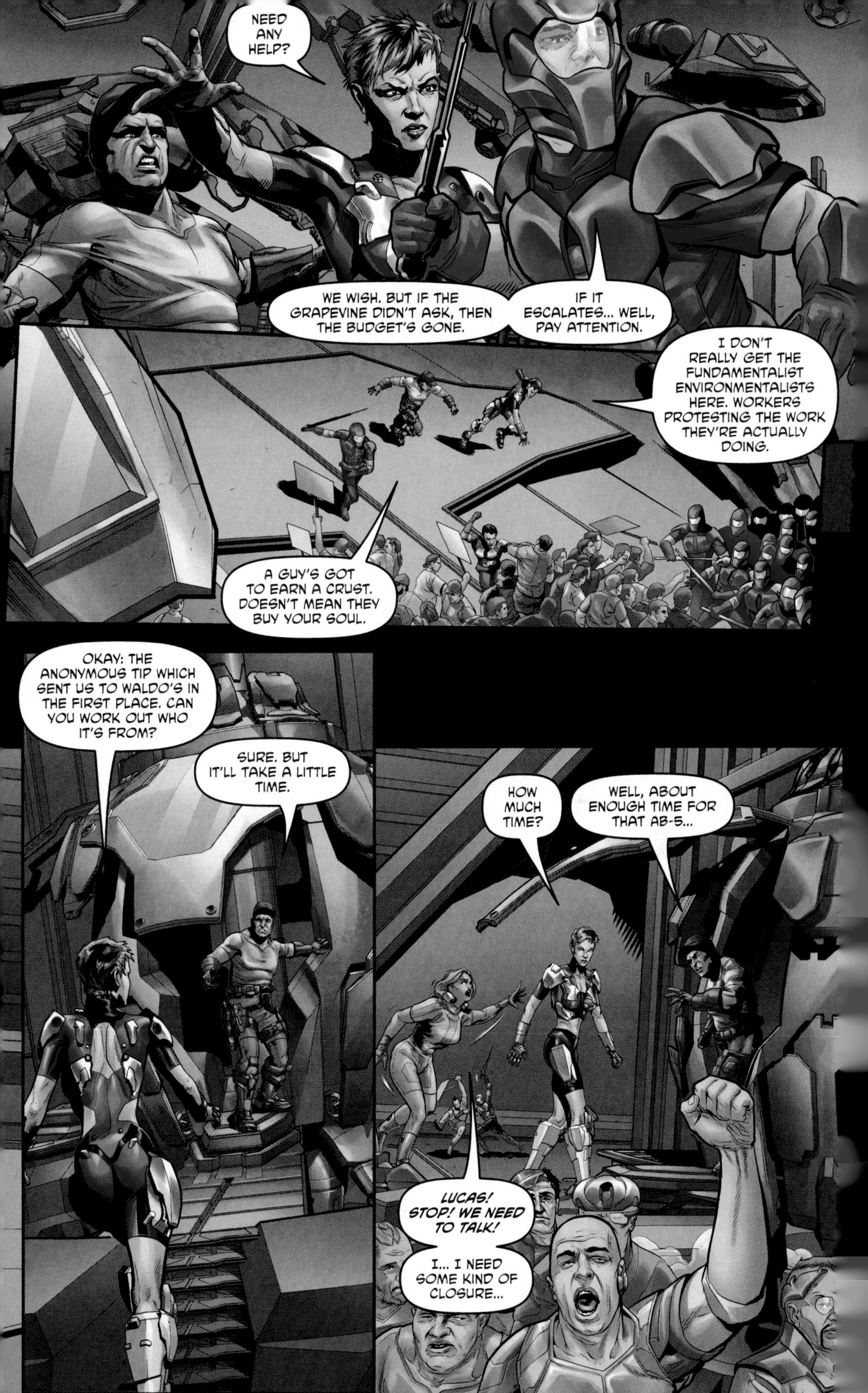
NEED ANY HELP?
WE WISH. BUT IF THE GRAPEVINE DIDN'T ASK, THEN THE BUDGET'S GONE.
IF IT ESCALATES... WELL, PAY ATTENTION.
I DON'T REALLY GET THE FUNDAMENTALIST ENVIRONMENTALISTS HERE. WORKERS PROTESTING THE WORK THEY'RE ACTUALLY DOING.
A GUY'S GOT TO EARN A CRUST. DOESN'T MEAN THEY BUY YOUR SOUL.
OKAY: THE ANONYMOUS TIP WHICH SENT US TO WALDO'S IN THE FIRST PLACE. CAN YOU WORK OUT WHO IT'S FROM?
SURE. BUT IT'LL TAKE A LITTLE TIME.
HOW MUCH TIME?
WELL, ABOUT ENOUGH TIME FOR THAT AB-5...
LUCAS! STOP! WE NEED TO TALK!
I... I NEED SOME KIND OF CLOSURE...

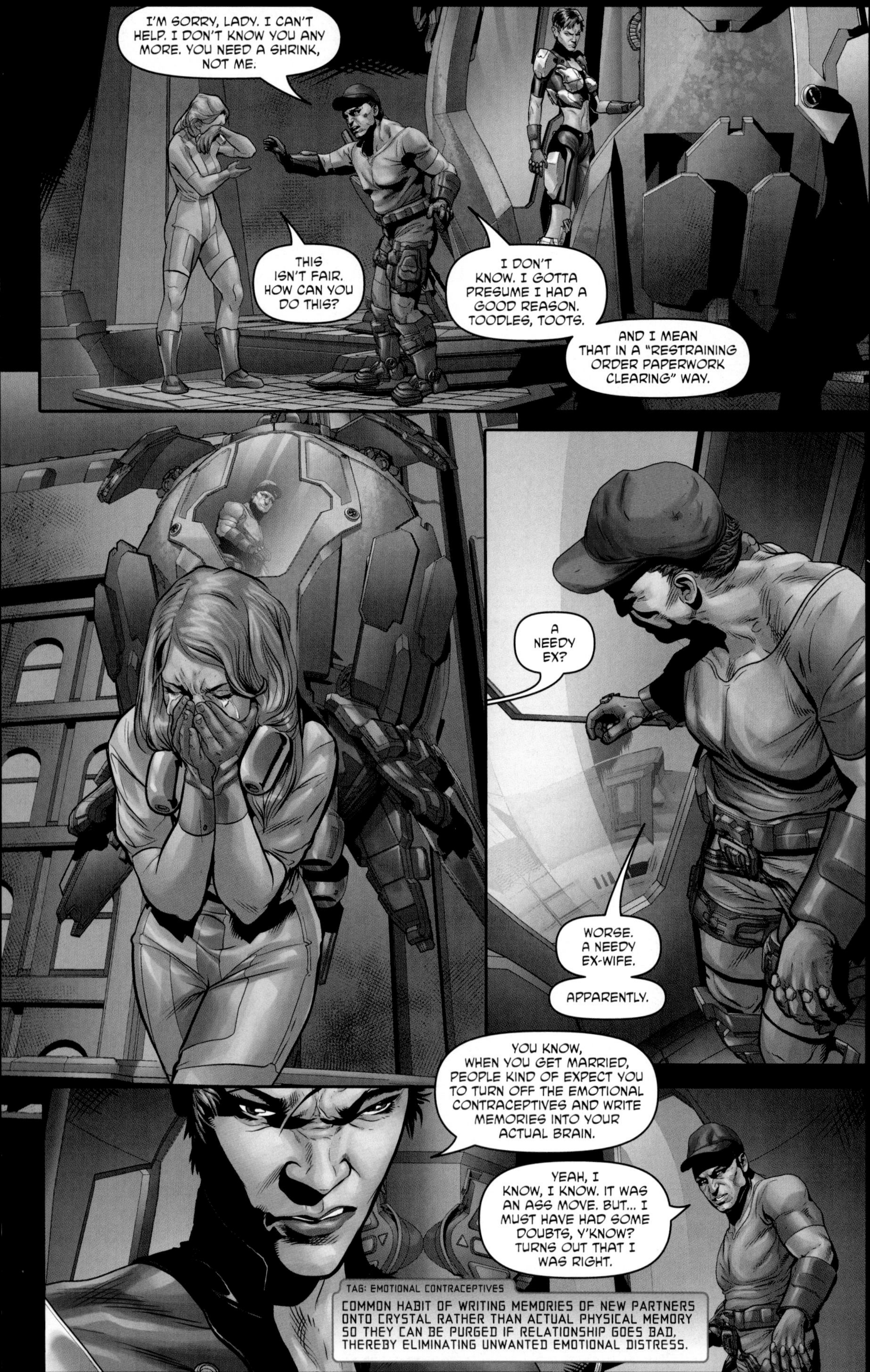
I'M SORRY, LADY. I CAN'T HELP. I DON'T KNOW YOU ANY MORE. YOU NEED A SHRINK, NOT ME.
THIS ISN'T FAIR. HOW CAN YOU DO THIS?
I DON'T KNOW. I GOTTA PRESUME I HAD A GOOD REASON. TOODLES, TOOTS.
AND I MEAN THAT IN A "RESTRAINING ORDER PAPERWORK CLEARING" WAY.
A NEEDY EX?
WORSE. A NEEDY EX-WIFE.
APPARENTLY.
YOU KNOW, WHEN YOU GET MARRIED, PEOPLE KIND OF EXPECT YOU TO TURN OFF THE EMOTIONAL CONTRACEPTIVES AND WRITE MEMORIES INTO YOUR ACTUAL BRAIN.
YEAH, I KNOW, I KNOW. IT WAS AN ASS MOVE. BUT... I MUST HAVE HAD SOME DOUBTS, Y'KNOW? TURNS OUT THAT I WAS RIGHT.
TAG: EMOTIONAL CONTRACEPTIVES
COMMON HABIT OF WRITING MEMORIES OF NEW PARTNERS ONTO CRYSTAL RATHER THAN ACTUAL PHYSICAL MEMORY SO THEY CAN BE PURGED IF RELATIONSHIP GOES BAD, THEREBY ELIMINATING UNWANTED EMOTIONAL DISTRESS.

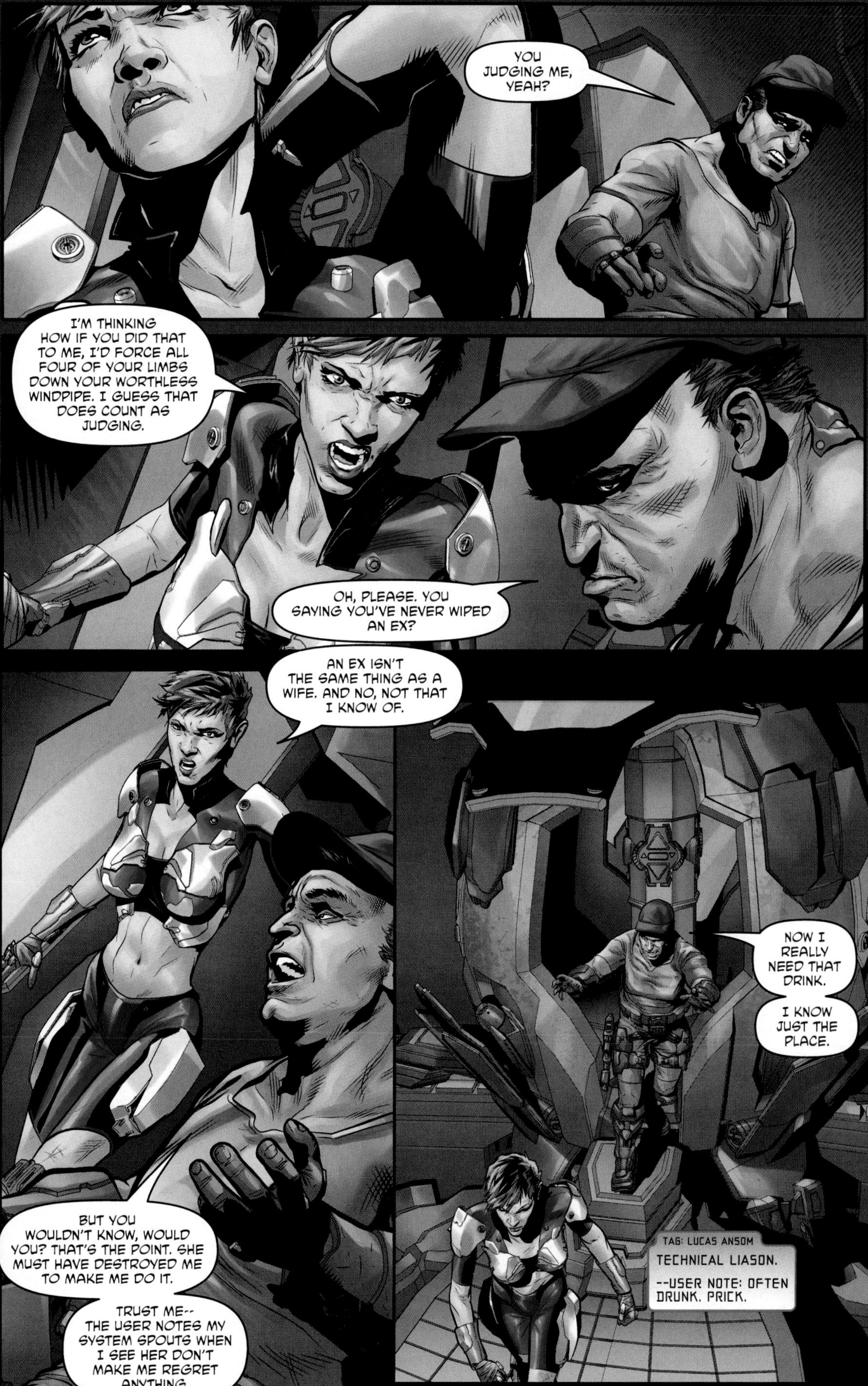
YOU JUDGING ME, YEAH?
I'M THINKING HOW IF YOU DID THAT TO ME, I'D FORCE ALL FOUR OF YOUR LIMBS DOWN YOUR WORTHLESS WINDPIPE. I GUESS THAT DOES COUNT AS JUDGING.
OH, PLEASE. YOU SAYING YOU'VE NEVER WIPED AN EX?
AN EX ISN'T THE SAME THING AS A WIFE. AND NO, NOT THAT I KNOW OF.
BUT YOU WOULDN'T KNOW, WOULD YOU? THAT'S THE POINT. SHE MUST HAVE DESTROYED ME TO MAKE ME DO IT.
TRUST ME-- THE USER NOTES MY SYSTEM SPOUTS WHEN I SEE HER DON'T MAKE ME REGRET ANYTHING.
NOW I REALLY NEED THAT DRINK.
I KNOW JUST THE PLACE.
TAG: LUCAS ANSOM
TECHNICAL LIASON.
--USER NOTE: OFTEN DRUNK. PRICK.

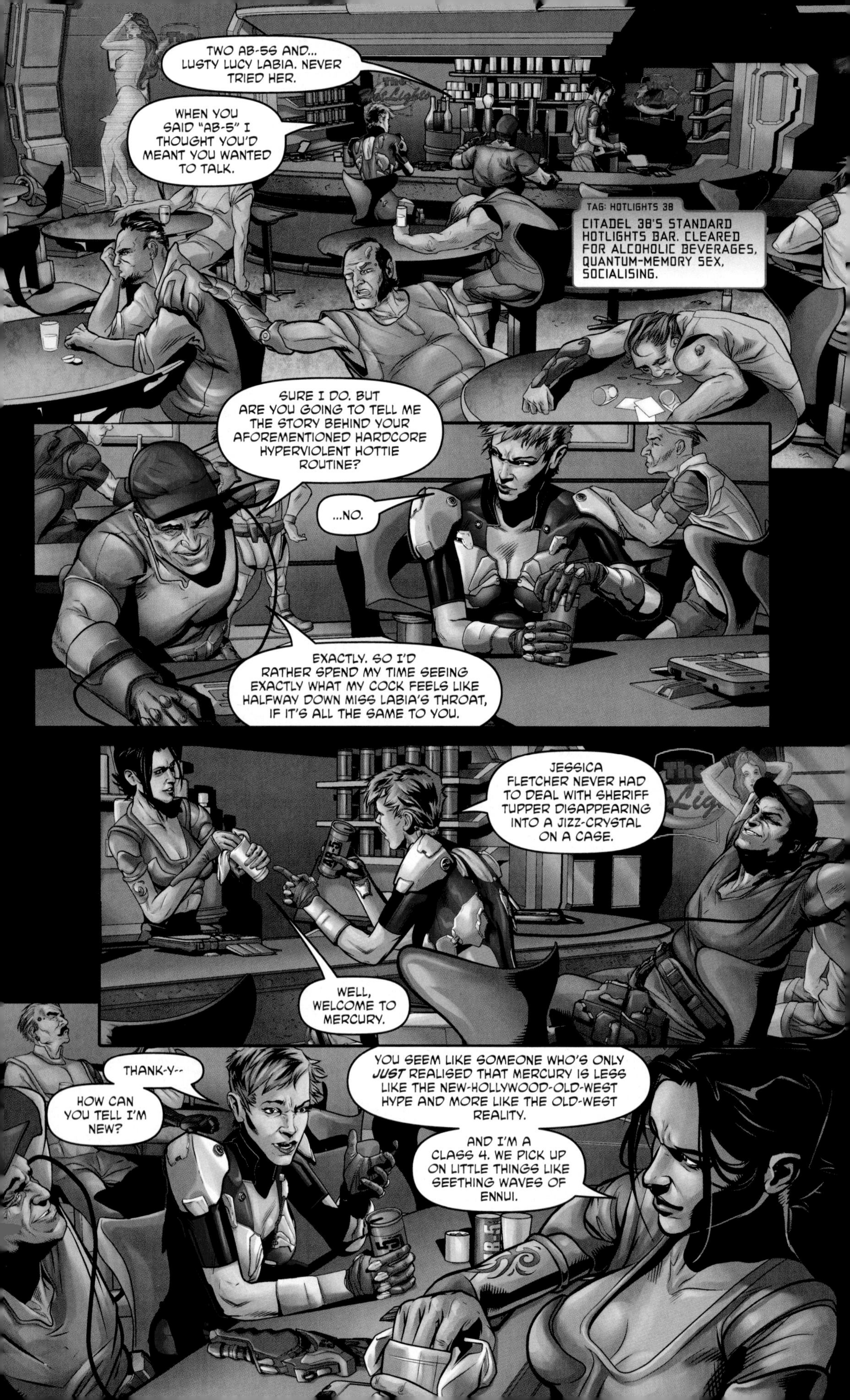
TWO AB-5S AND... LUSTY LUCY LABIA. NEVER TRIED HER.
WHEN YOU SAID "AB-5" I THOUGHT YOU'D MEANT YOU WANTED TO TALK.
TAG: HOTLIGHTS 38
CITADEL 38'S STANDARD HOTLIGHTS BAR. CLEARED FOR ALCOHOLIC BEVERAGES, QUANTUM-MEMORY SEX, SOCIALISING.
SURE I DO. BUT ARE YOU GOING TO TELL ME THE STORY BEHIND YOUR AFOREMENTIONED HARDCORE HYPERVIOLENT HOTTIE ROUTINE?
...NO.
EXACTLY. SO I'D RATHER SPEND MY TIME SEEING EXACTLY WHAT MY COCK FEELS LIKE HALFWAY DOWN MISS LABIA'S THROAT, IF IT'S ALL THE SAME TO YOU.
JESSICA FLETCHER NEVER HAD TO DEAL WITH SHERIFF TUPPER DISAPPEARING INTO A JIZZ-CRYSTAL ON A CASE.
WELL, WELCOME TO MERCURY.
THANK-Y--
HOW CAN YOU TELL I'M NEW?
YOU SEEM LIKE SOMEONE WHO'S ONLY *JUST* REALISED THAT MERCURY IS LESS LIKE THE NEW-HOLLYWOOD-OLD-WEST HYPE AND MORE LIKE THE OLD-WEST REALITY.
AND I'M A CLASS 4. WE PICK UP ON LITTLE THINGS LIKE SEETHING WAVES OF ENNUI.

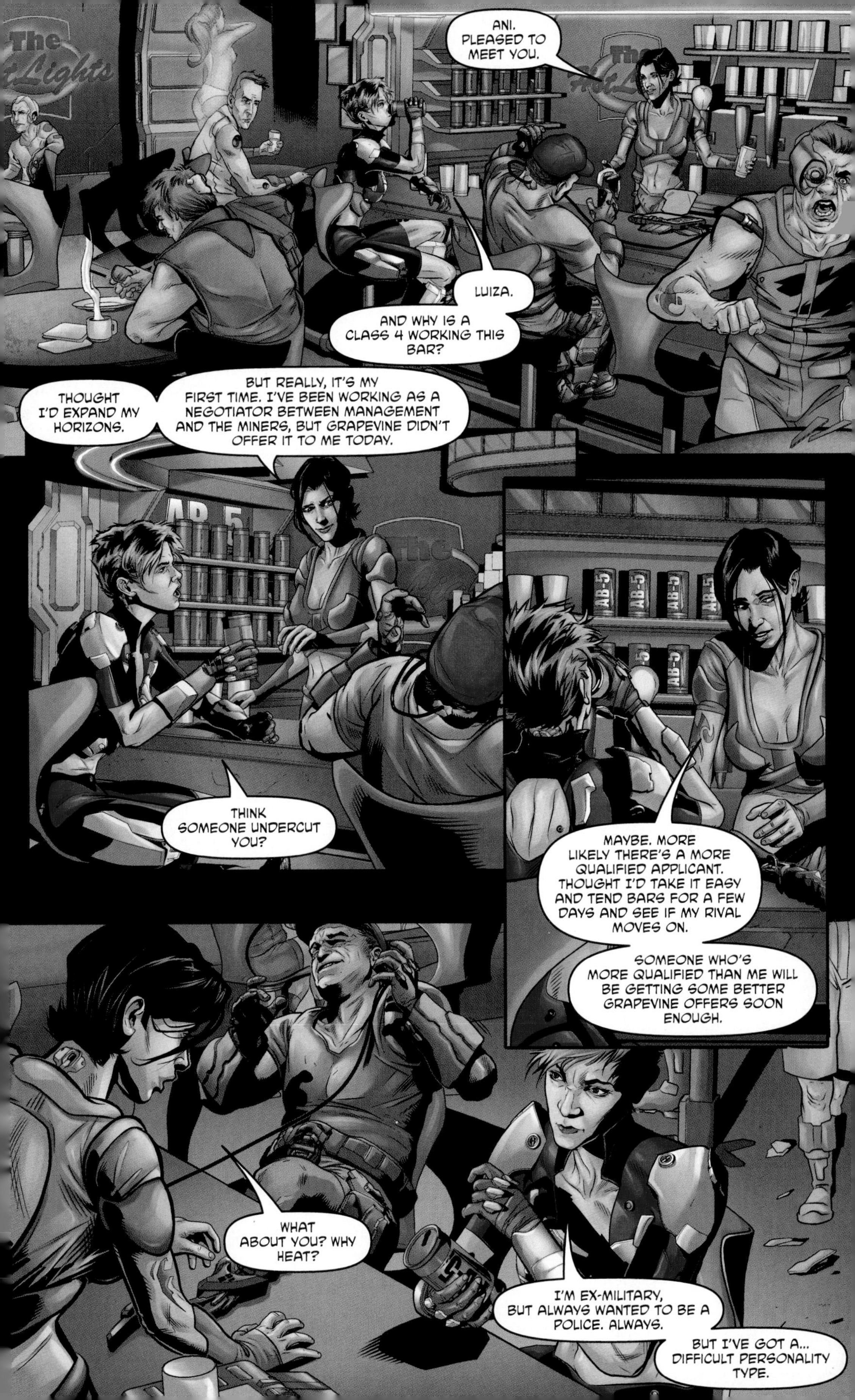
ANI. PLEASED TO MEET YOU.
LUIZA.
AND WHY IS A CLASS 4 WORKING THIS BAR?
THOUGHT I'D EXPAND MY HORIZONS.
BUT REALLY, IT'S MY FIRST TIME. I'VE BEEN WORKING AS A NEGOTIATOR BETWEEN MANAGEMENT AND THE MINERS, BUT GRAPEVINE DIDN'T OFFER IT TO ME TODAY.
THINK SOMEONE UNDERCUT YOU?
MAYBE. MORE LIKELY THERE'S A MORE QUALIFIED APPLICANT. THOUGHT I'D TAKE IT EASY AND TEND BARS FOR A FEW DAYS AND SEE IF MY RIVAL MOVES ON.
SOMEONE WHO'S MORE QUALIFIED THAN ME WILL BE GETTING SOME BETTER GRAPEVINE OFFERS SOON ENOUGH.
WHAT ABOUT YOU? WHY HEAT?
I'M EX-MILITARY, BUT ALWAYS WANTED TO BE A POLICE. ALWAYS.
BUT I'VE GOT A... DIFFICULT PERSONALITY TYPE.

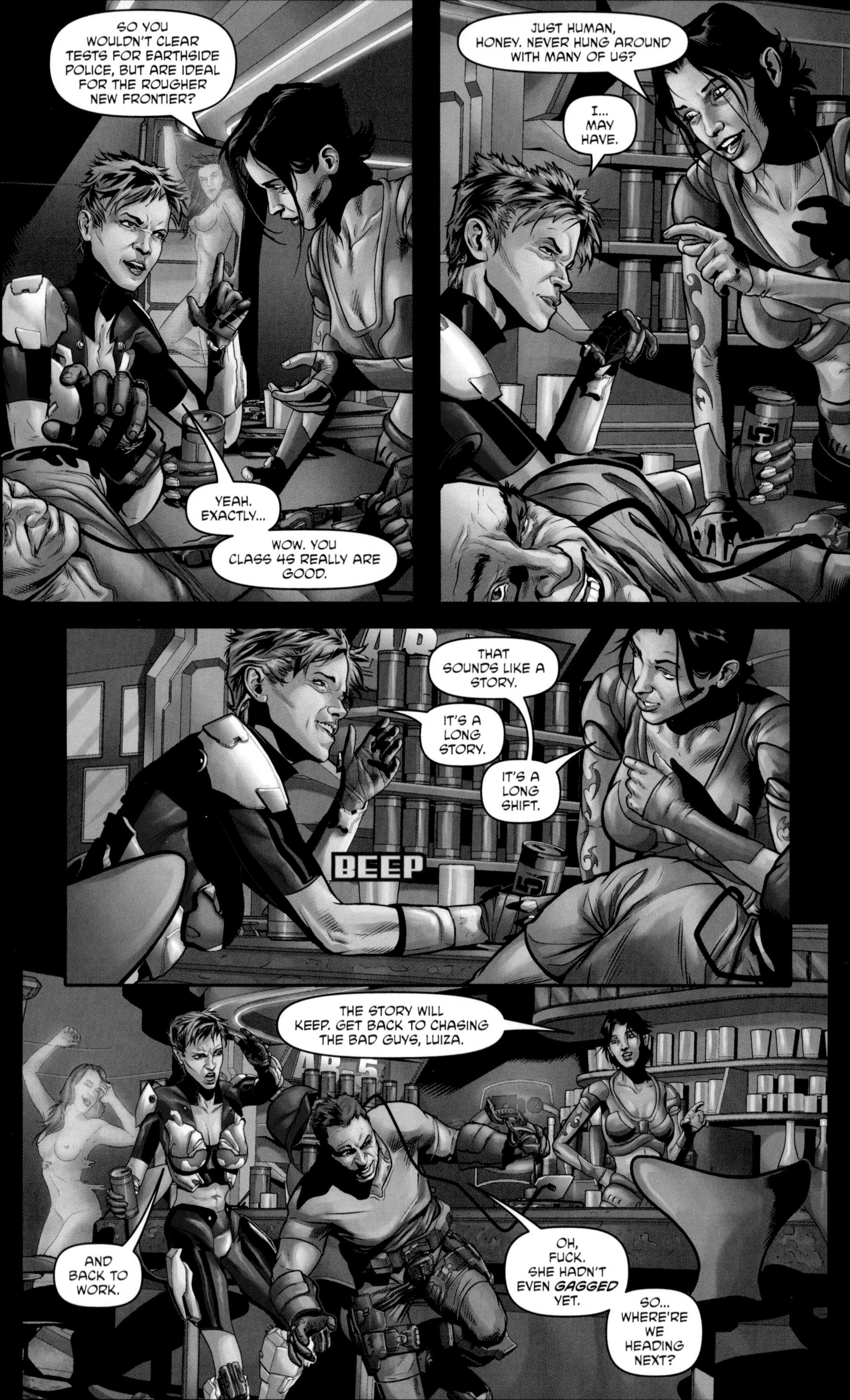
SO YOU WOULDN'T CLEAR TESTS FOR EARTHSIDE POLICE, BUT ARE IDEAL FOR THE ROUGHER NEW FRONTIER?
YEAH. EXACTLY...
WOW. YOU CLASS 4S REALLY ARE GOOD.
JUST HUMAN, HONEY. NEVER HUNG AROUND WITH MANY OF US?
I... MAY HAVE.
THAT SOUNDS LIKE A STORY.
IT'S A LONG STORY.
IT'S A LONG SHIFT.
BEEP
THE STORY WILL KEEP. GET BACK TO CHASING THE BAD GUYS, LUIZA.
AND BACK TO WORK.
OH, FUCK. SHE HADN'T EVEN GAGGED YET.
SO... WHERE'RE WE HEADING NEXT?

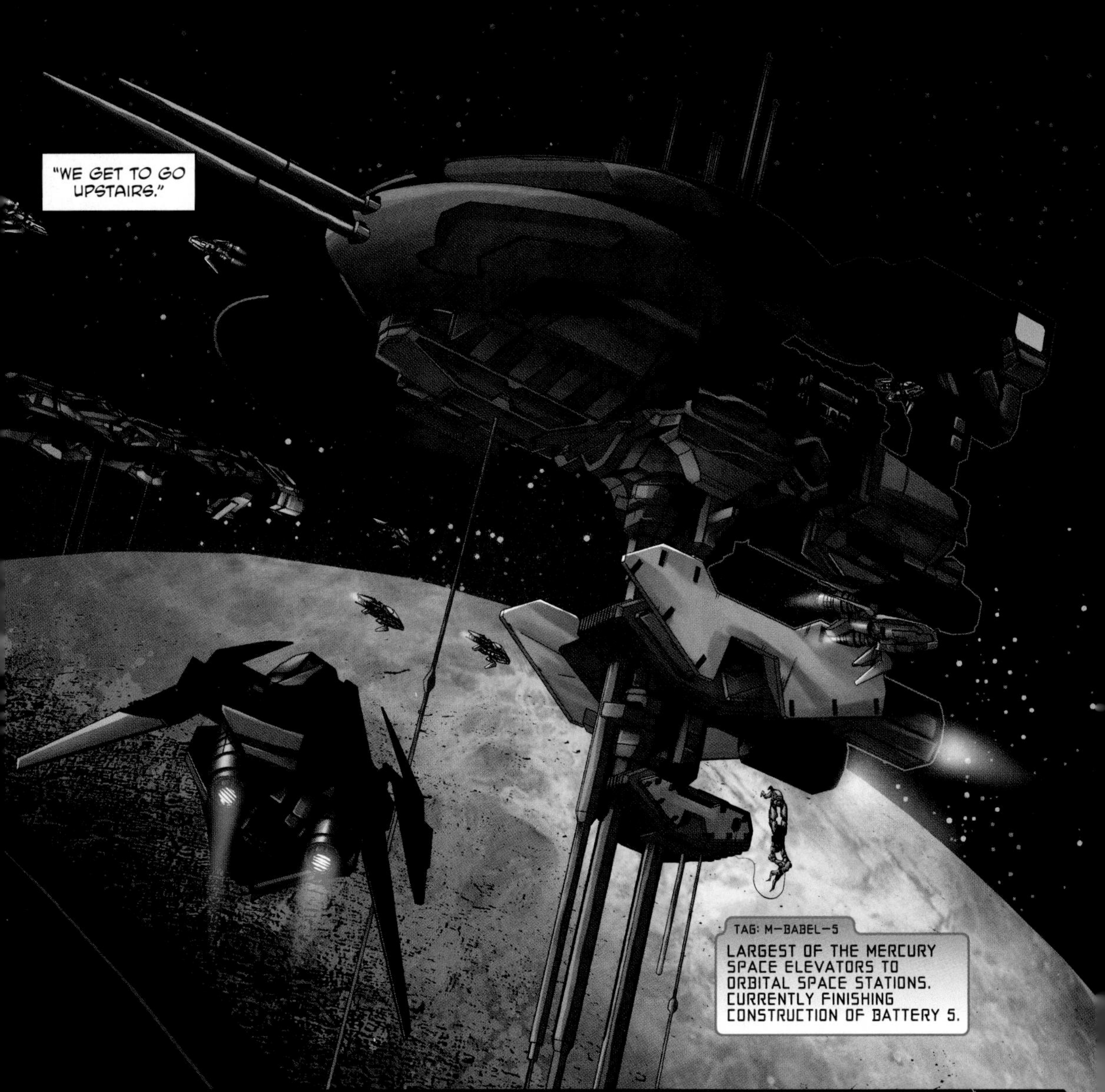
"WE GET TO GO UPSTAIRS."
TAG: M-BABEL-5
LARGEST OF THE MERCURY SPACE ELEVATORS TO ORBITAL SPACE STATIONS. CURRENTLY FINISHING CONSTRUCTION OF BATTERY 5.

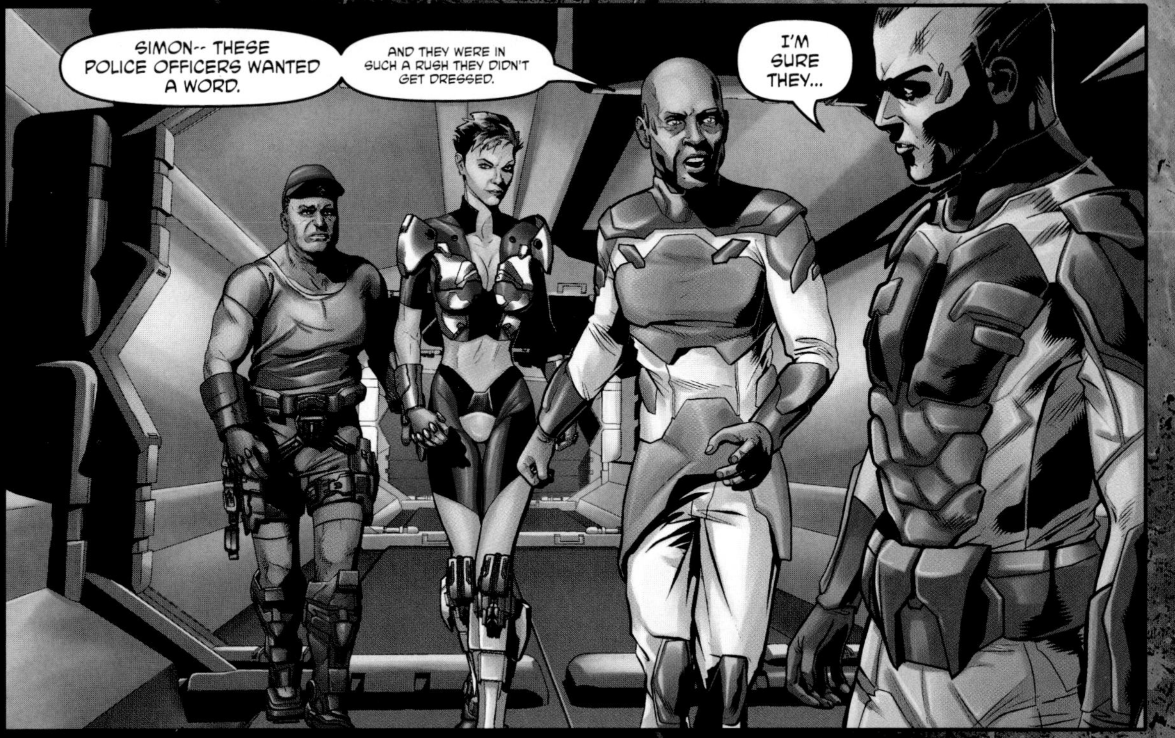
SIMON-- THESE POLICE OFFICERS WANTED A WORD.
AND THEY WERE IN SUCH A RUSH THEY DIDN'T GET DRESSED.
I'M SURE THEY...

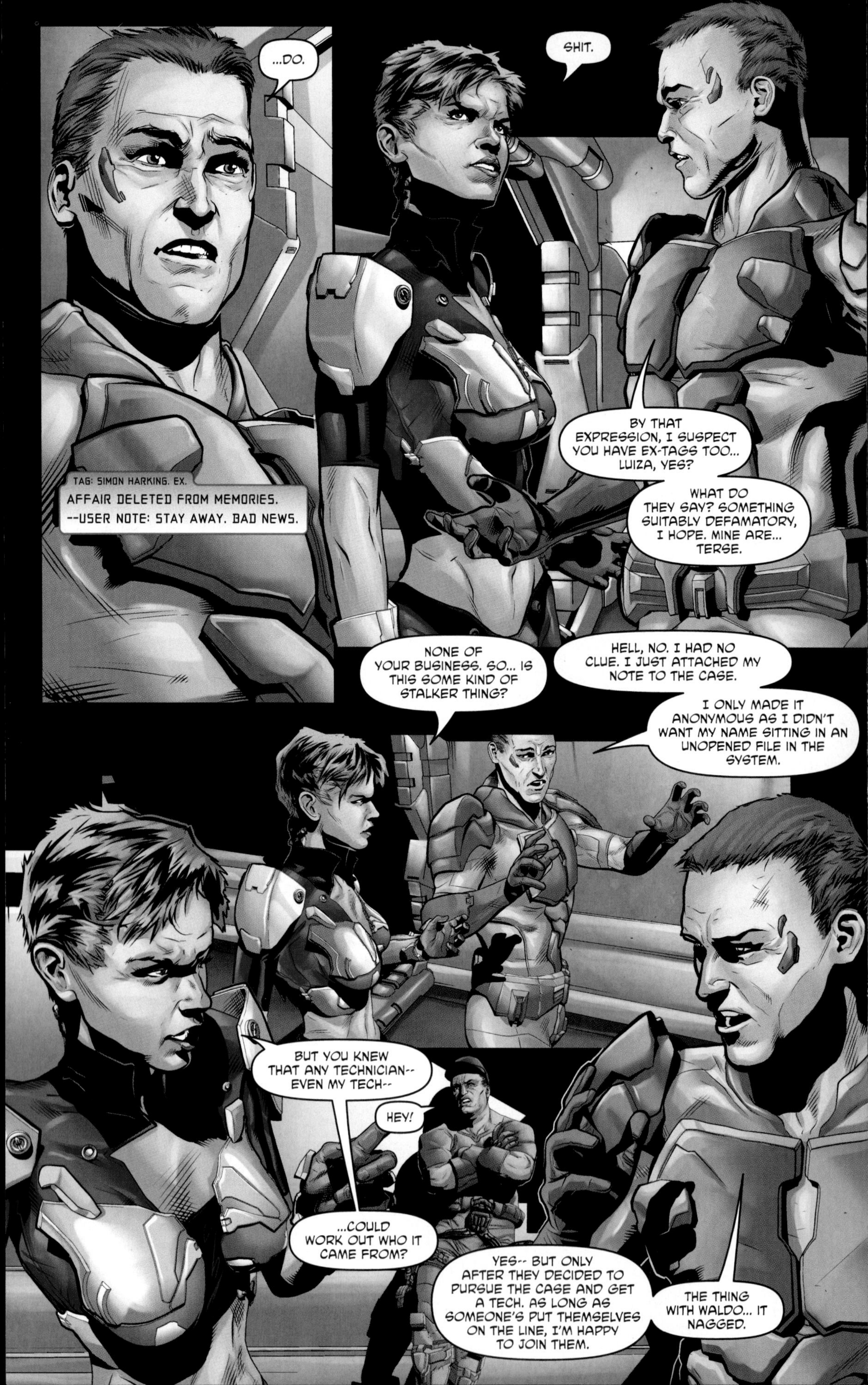
...DO.
TAG: SIMON HARKING. EX.
AFFAIR DELETED FROM MEMORIES.
--USER NOTE: STAY AWAY. BAD NEWS.
SHIT.
BY THAT EXPRESSION, I SUSPECT YOU HAVE EX-TAGS TOO... LUIZA, YES?
WHAT DO THEY SAY? SOMETHING SUITABLY DEFAMATORY, I HOPE. MINE ARE... TERSE.
NONE OF YOUR BUSINESS. SO... IS THIS SOME KIND OF STALKER THING?
HELL, NO. I HAD NO CLUE. I JUST ATTACHED MY NOTE TO THE CASE.
I ONLY MADE IT ANONYMOUS AS I DIDN'T WANT MY NAME SITTING IN AN UNOPENED FILE IN THE SYSTEM.
BUT YOU KNEW THAT ANY TECHNICIAN-- EVEN MY TECH--
HEY!
...COULD WORK OUT WHO IT CAME FROM?
YES-- BUT ONLY AFTER THEY DECIDED TO PURSUE THE CASE AND GET A TECH. AS LONG AS SOMEONE'S PUT THEMSELVES ON THE LINE, I'M HAPPY TO JOIN THEM.
THE THING WITH WALDO... IT NAGGED.

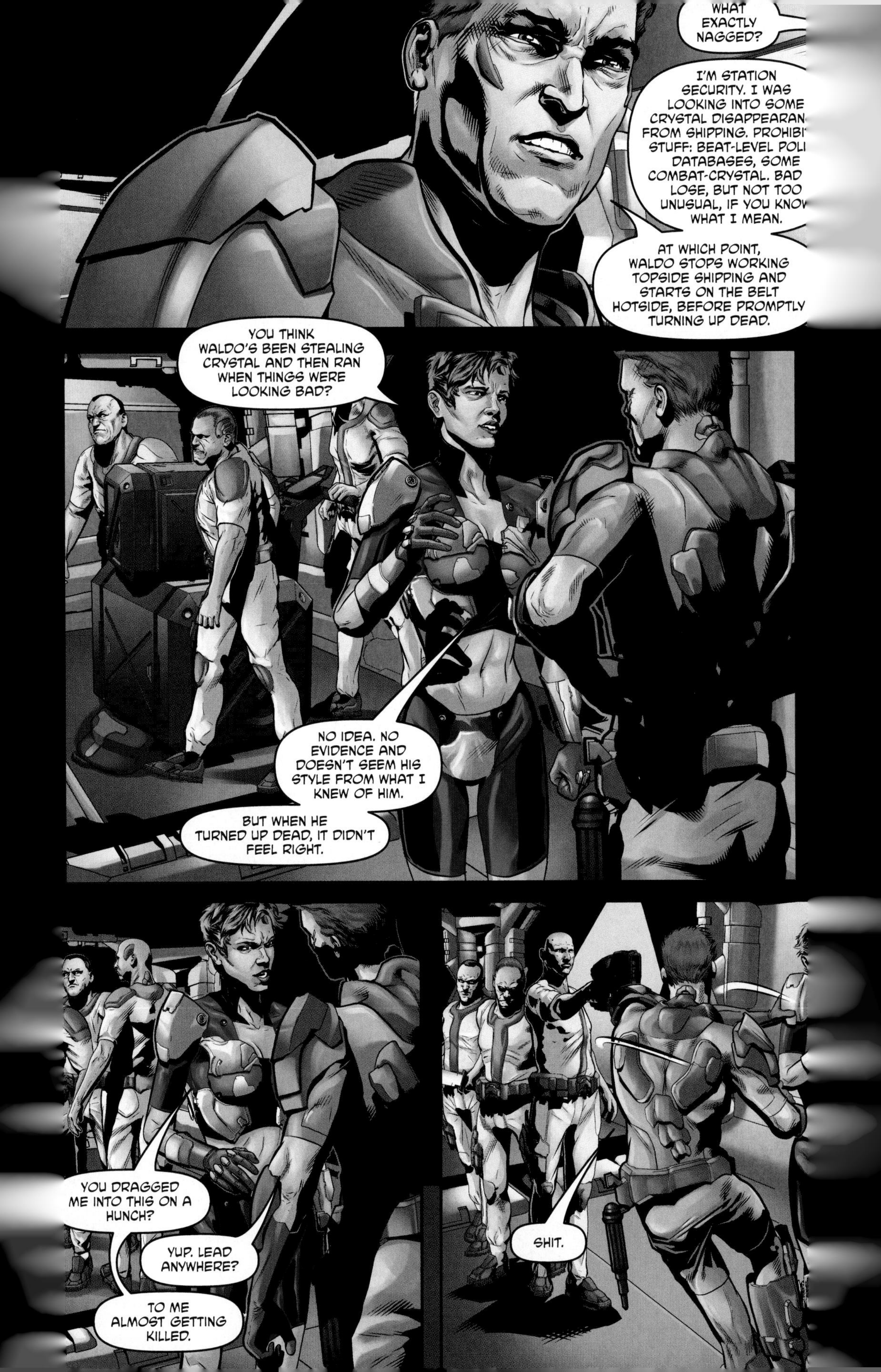
WHAT EXACTLY NAGGED?
I'M STATION SECURITY. I WAS LOOKING INTO SOME CRYSTAL DISAPPEARAN FROM SHIPPING. PROHIBI STUFF: BEAT-LEVEL POLI DATABASES, SOME COMBAT-CRYSTAL. BAD LOSE, BUT NOT TOO UNUSUAL, IF YOU KNOV WHAT I MEAN.
AT WHICH POINT, WALDO STOPS WORKING TOPSIDE SHIPPING AND STARTS ON THE BELT HOTSIDE, BEFORE PROMPTLY TURNING UP DEAD.
YOU THINK WALDO'S BEEN STEALING CRYSTAL AND THEN RAN WHEN THINGS WERE LOOKING BAD?
NO IDEA. NO EVIDENCE AND DOESN'T SEEM HIS STYLE FROM WHAT I KNEW OF HIM.
BUT WHEN HE TURNED UP DEAD, IT DIDN'T FEEL RIGHT.
YOU DRAGGED ME INTO THIS ON A HUNCH?
YUP. LEAD ANYWHERE?
TO ME ALMOST GETTING KILLED.
SHIT.

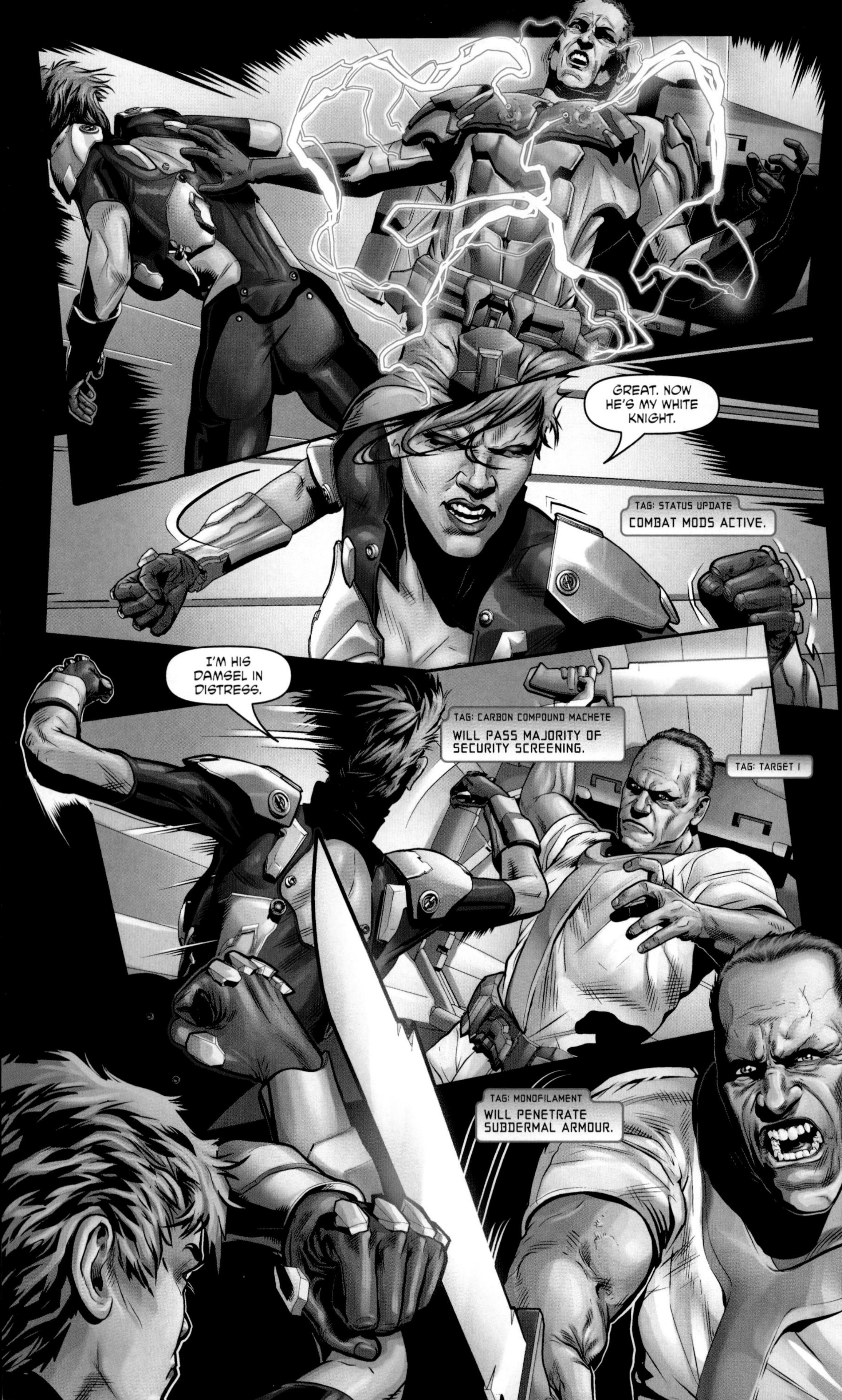

GREAT. NOW HE'S MY WHITE KNIGHT.
TAG: STATUS UPDATE
COMBAT MODS ACTIVE.
I'M HIS DAMSEL IN DISTRESS.
TAG: CARBON COMPOUND MACHETE
WILL PASS MAJORITY OF SECURITY SCREENING.
TAG: TARGET 1
TAG: MONOFILAMENT
WILL PENETRATE SUBDERMAL ARMOUR.

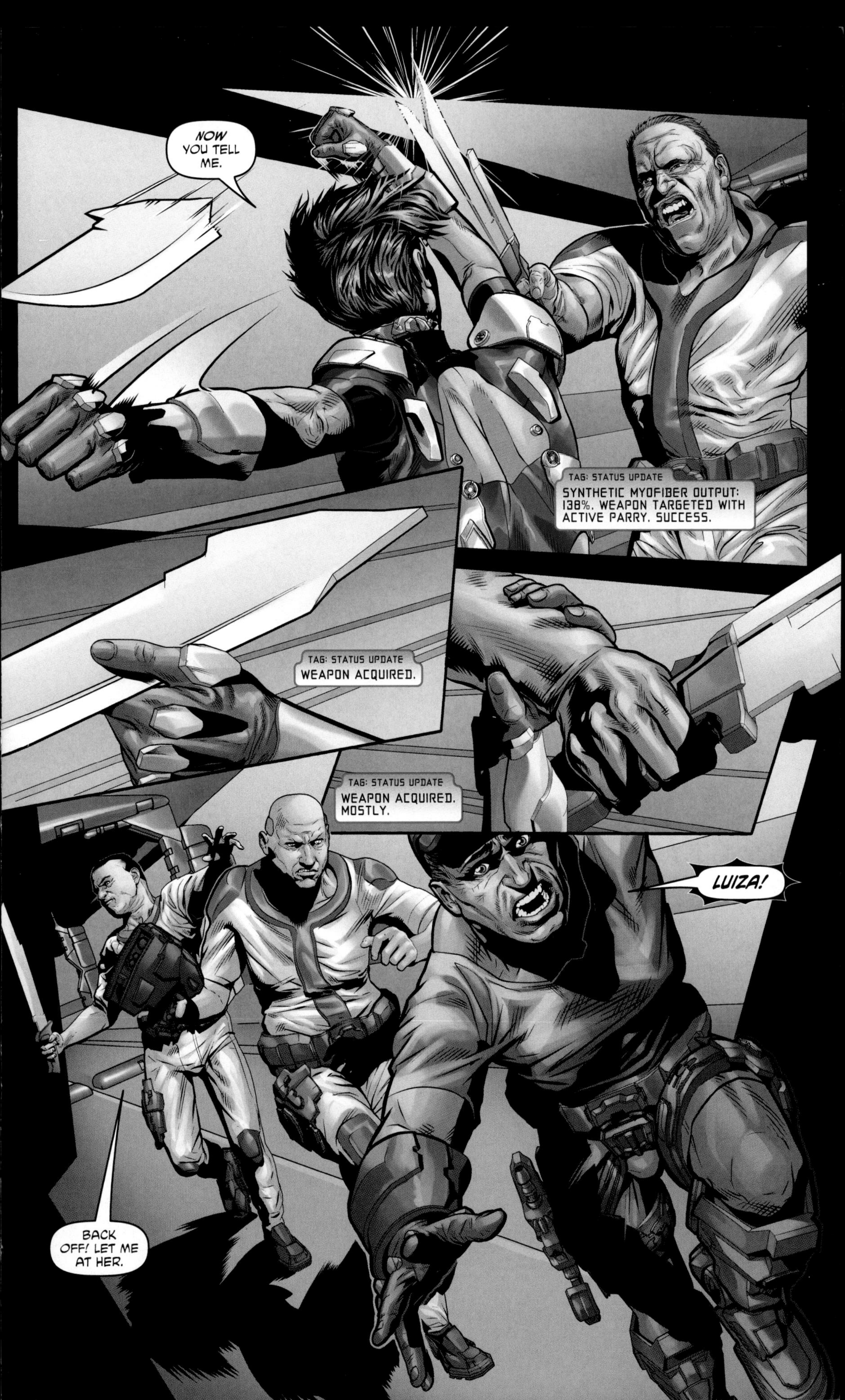
NOW YOU TELL ME.
TAG: STATUS UPDATE
SYNTHETIC MYOFIBER OUTPUT: 138%. WEAPON TARGETED WITH ACTIVE PARRY. SUCCESS.
TAG: STATUS UPDATE
WEAPON ACQUIRED.
TAG: STATUS UPDATE
WEAPON ACQUIRED. MOSTLY.
LUIZA!
BACK OFF! LET ME AT HER.

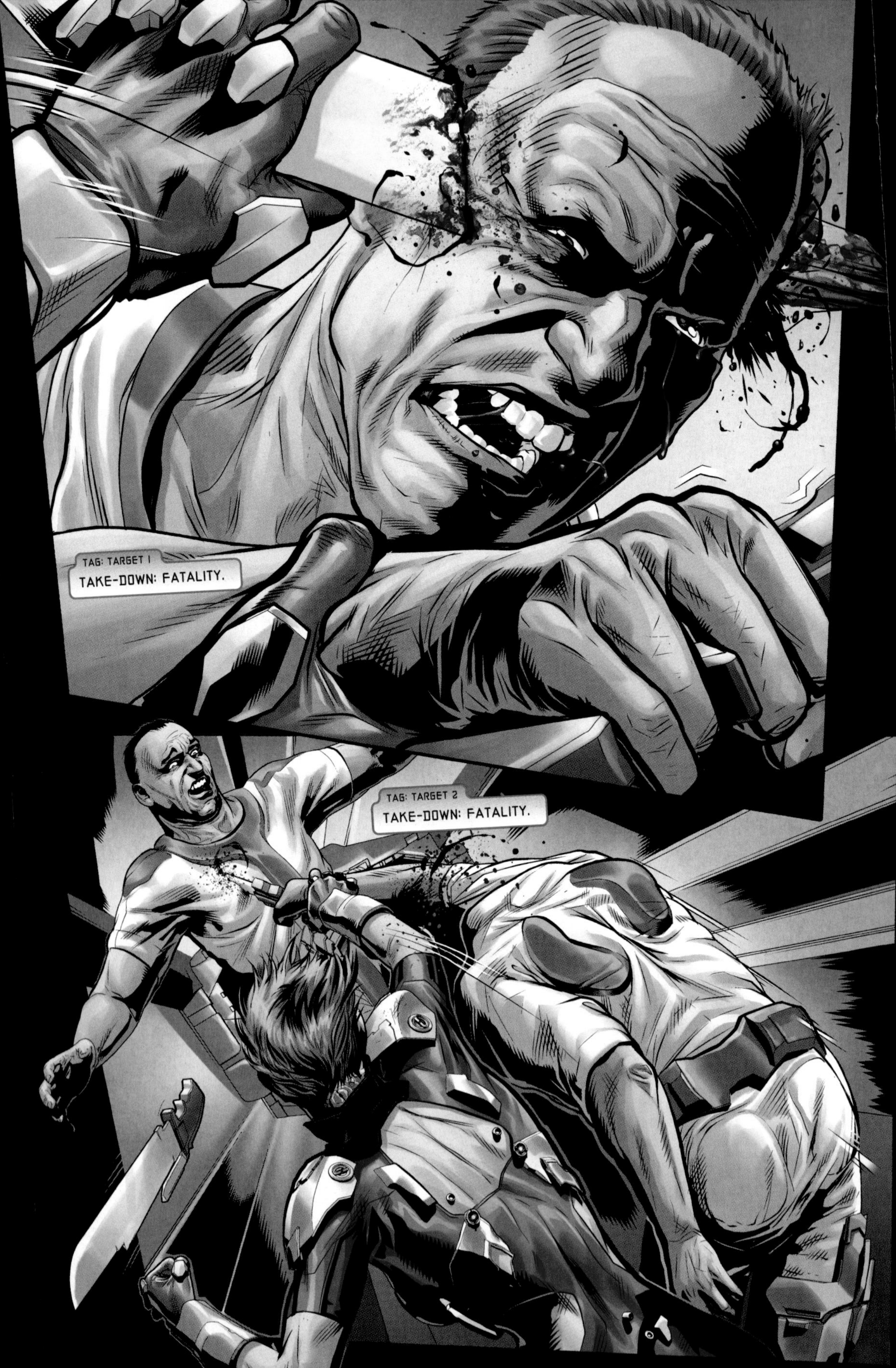
TAG: TARGET 1
TAKE-DOWN: FATALITY.
TAG: TARGET 2
TAKE-DOWN: FATALITY.

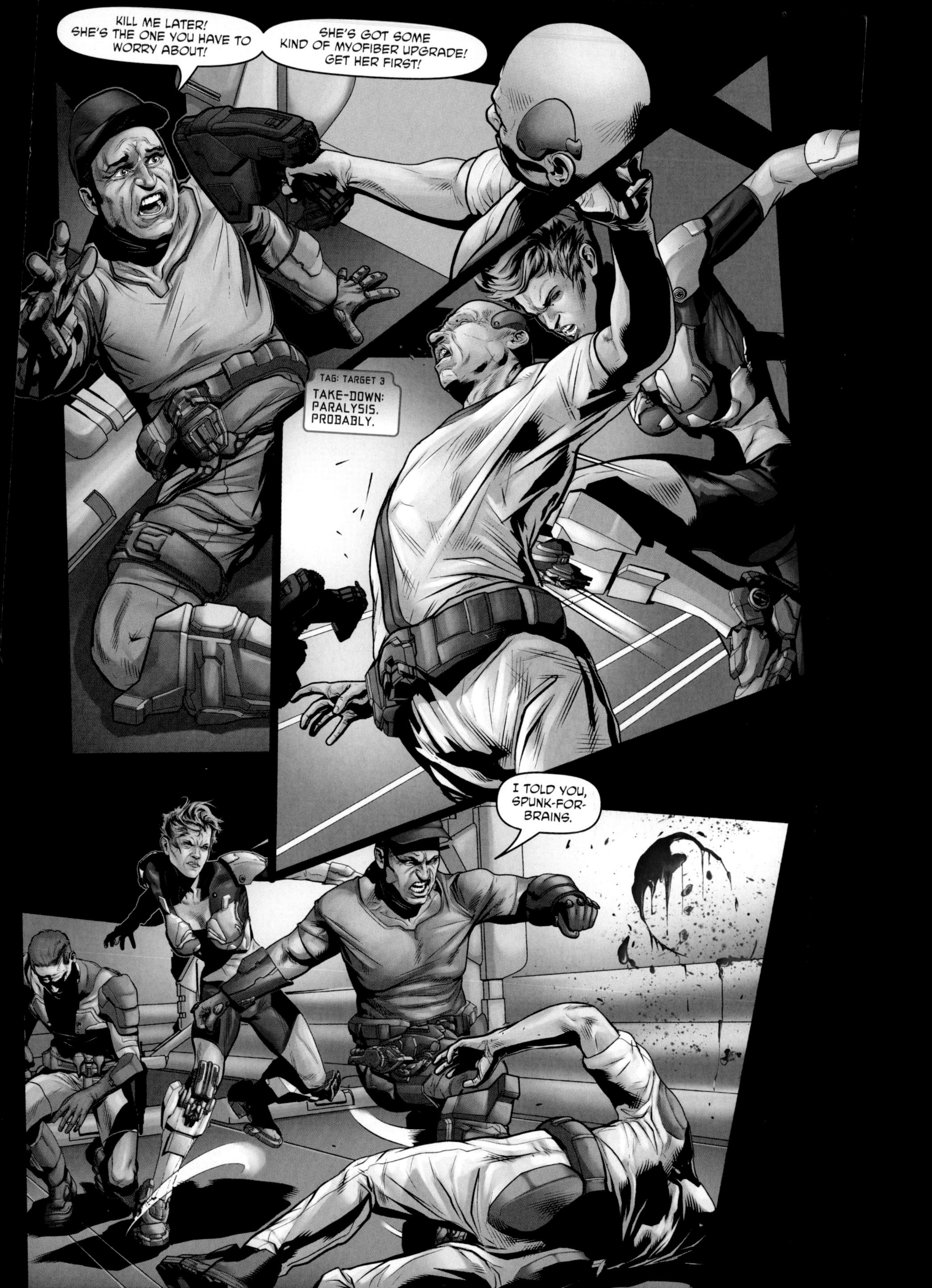
KILL ME LATER! SHE'S THE ONE YOU HAVE TO WORRY ABOUT!
SHE'S GOT SOME KIND OF MYOFIBER UPGRADE! GET HER FIRST!
TAG: TARGET 3
TAKE-DOWN: PARALYSIS. PROBABLY.
I TOLD YOU, SPUNK-FOR-BRAINS.

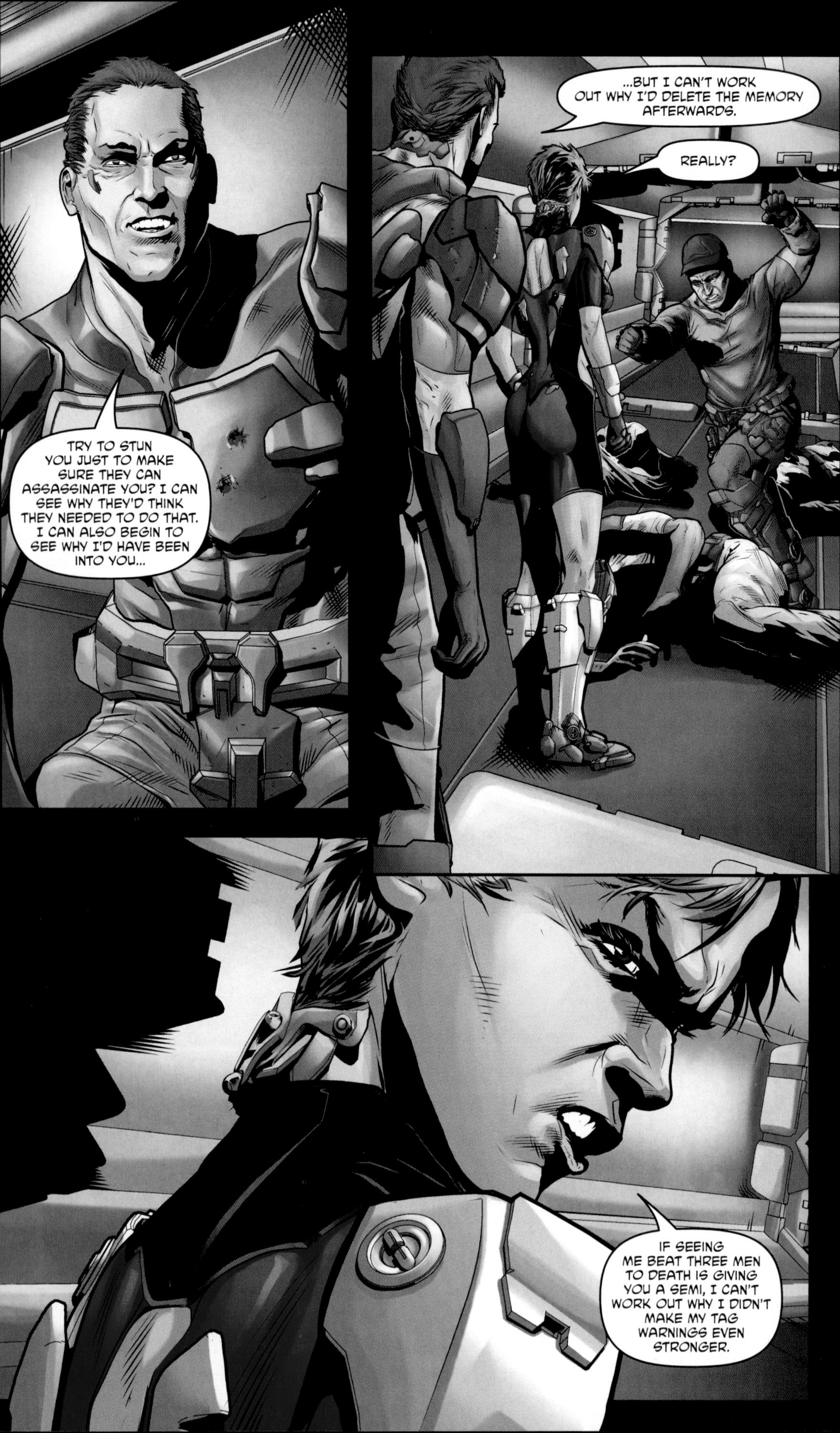
TRY TO STUN YOU JUST TO MAKE SURE THEY CAN ASSASSINATE YOU? I CAN SEE WHY THEY'D THINK THEY NEEDED TO DO THAT. I CAN ALSO BEGIN TO SEE WHY I'D HAVE BEEN INTO YOU...
...BUT I CAN'T WORK OUT WHY I'D DELETE THE MEMORY AFTERWARDS.
REALLY?
IF SEEING ME BEAT THREE MEN TO DEATH IS GIVING YOU A SEMI, I CAN'T WORK OUT WHY I DIDN'T MAKE MY TAG WARNINGS EVEN STRONGER.

chapter 3

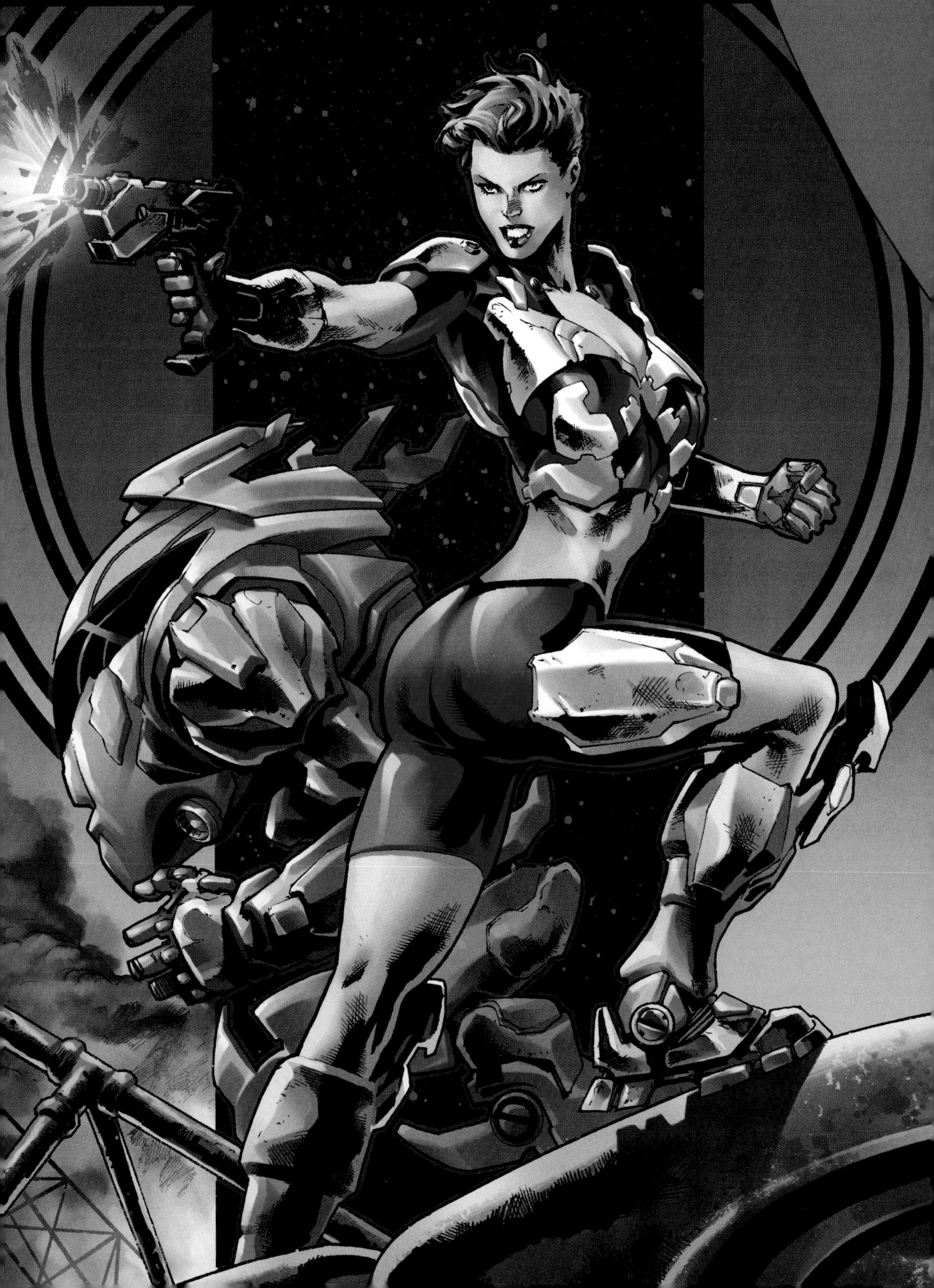

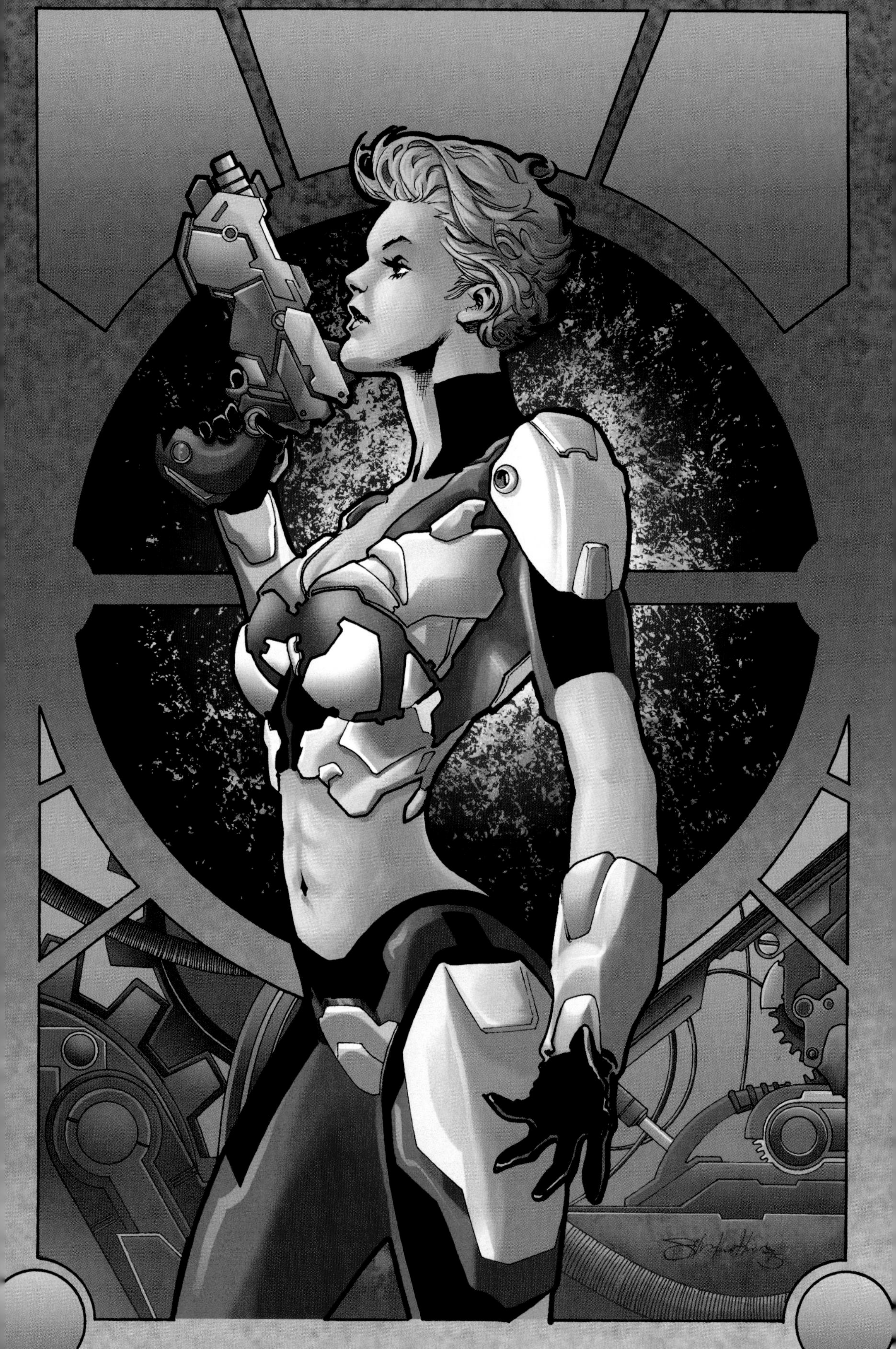

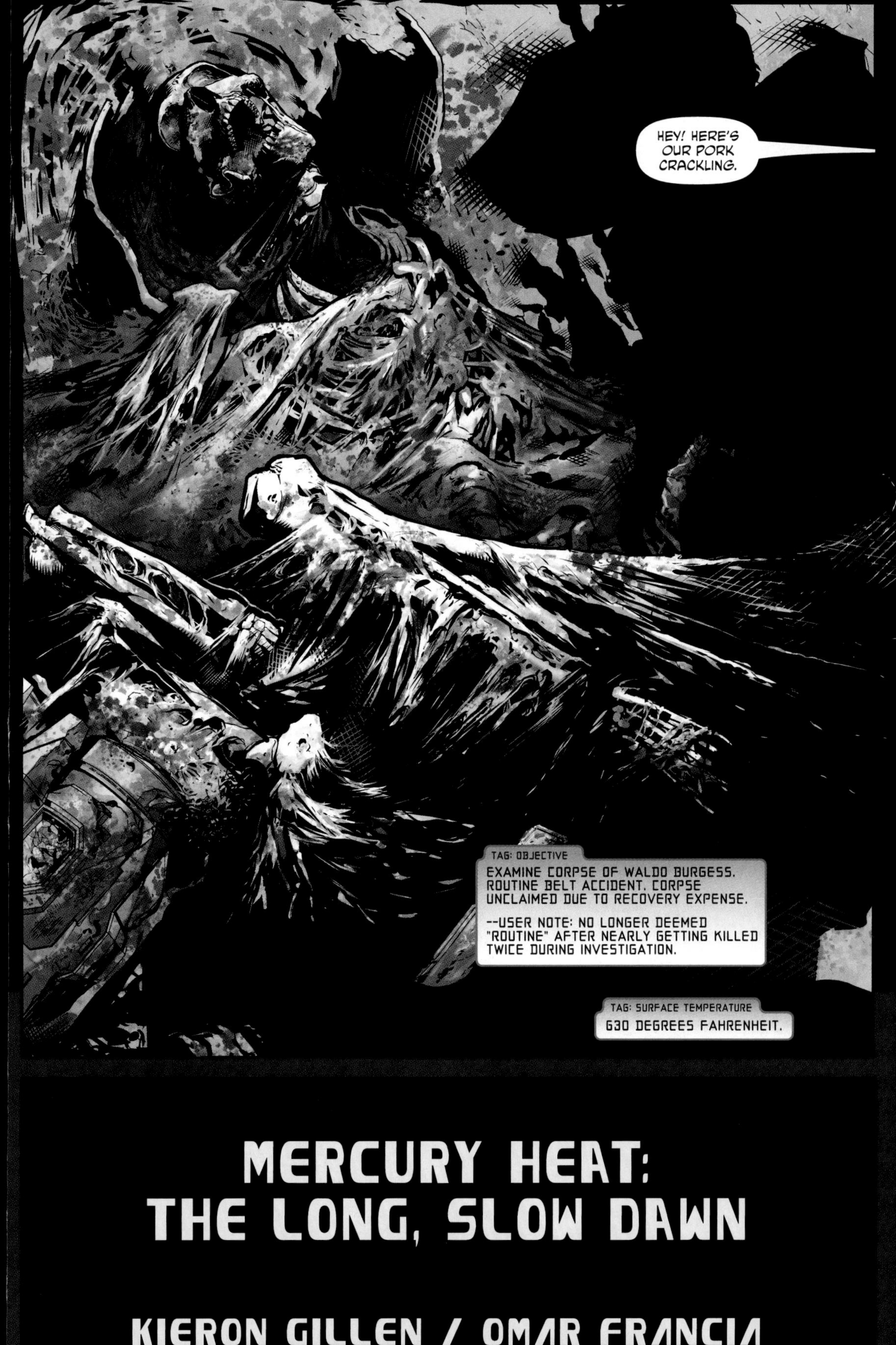
HEY! HERE'S OUR PORK CRACKLING.
TAG: OBJECTIVE
EXAMINE CORPSE OF WALDO BURGESS. ROUTINE BELT ACCIDENT. CORPSE UNCLAIMED DUE TO RECOVERY EXPENSE.
--USER NOTE: NO LONGER DEEMED "ROUTINE" AFTER NEARLY GETTING KILLED TWICE DURING INVESTIGATION.
TAG: SURFACE TEMPERATURE
630 DEGREES FAHRENHEIT.

MERCURY HEAT: THE LONG, SLOW DAWN

KIERON GILLEN / OMAR FRANCIA

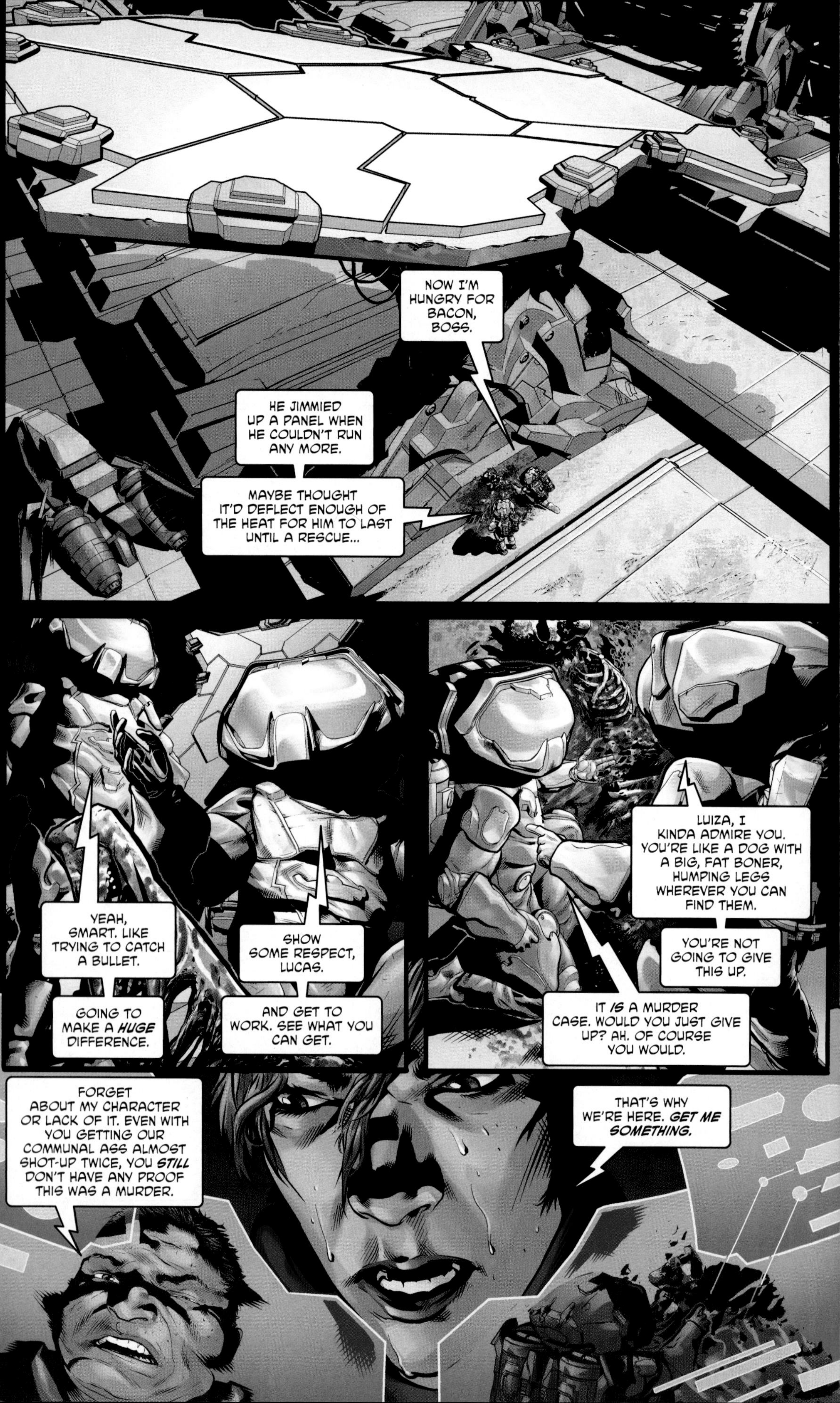
NOW I'M HUNGRY FOR BACON, BOSS.
HE JIMMIED UP A PANEL WHEN HE COULDN'T RUN ANY MORE.
MAYBE THOUGHT IT'D DEFLECT ENOUGH OF THE HEAT FOR HIM TO LAST UNTIL A RESCUE...
YEAH, SMART. LIKE TRYING TO CATCH A BULLET.
GOING TO MAKE A *HUGE* DIFFERENCE.
SHOW SOME RESPECT, LUCAS.
AND GET TO WORK. SEE WHAT YOU CAN GET.
LUIZA, I KINDA ADMIRE YOU. YOU'RE LIKE A DOG WITH A BIG, FAT BONER, HUMPING LEGS WHEREVER YOU CAN FIND THEM.
YOU'RE NOT GOING TO GIVE THIS UP.
IT *IS* A MURDER CASE. WOULD YOU JUST GIVE UP? AH. OF COURSE YOU WOULD.
FORGET ABOUT MY CHARACTER OR LACK OF IT. EVEN WITH YOU GETTING OUR COMMUNAL ASS ALMOST SHOT-UP TWICE, YOU *STILL* DON'T HAVE ANY PROOF THIS WAS A MURDER.
THAT'S WHY WE'RE HERE. *GET ME SOMETHING.*

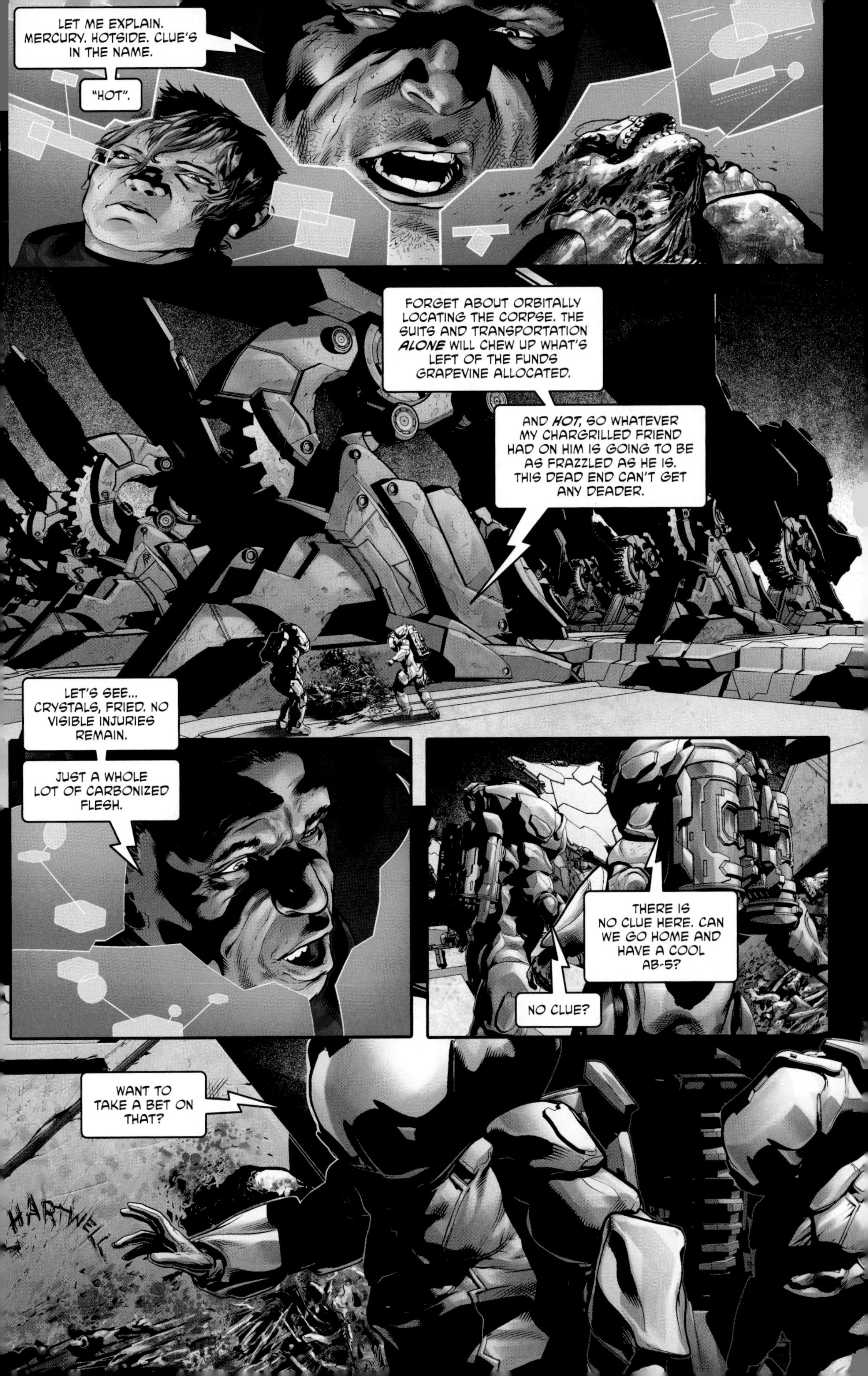
LET ME EXPLAIN. MERCURY. HOTSIDE. CLUE'S IN THE NAME.
"HOT".
FORGET ABOUT ORBITALLY LOCATING THE CORPSE. THE SUITS AND TRANSPORTATION ALONE WILL CHEW UP WHAT'S LEFT OF THE FUNDS GRAPEVINE ALLOCATED.
AND HOT, SO WHATEVER MY CHARGRILLED FRIEND HAD ON HIM IS GOING TO BE AS FRAZZLED AS HE IS. THIS DEAD END CAN'T GET ANY DEADER.
LET'S SEE... CRYSTALS, FRIED. NO VISIBLE INJURIES REMAIN.
JUST A WHOLE LOT OF CARBONIZED FLESH.
THERE IS NO CLUE HERE. CAN WE GO HOME AND HAVE A COOL AB-5?
NO CLUE?
WANT TO TAKE A BET ON THAT?
HARTWELL

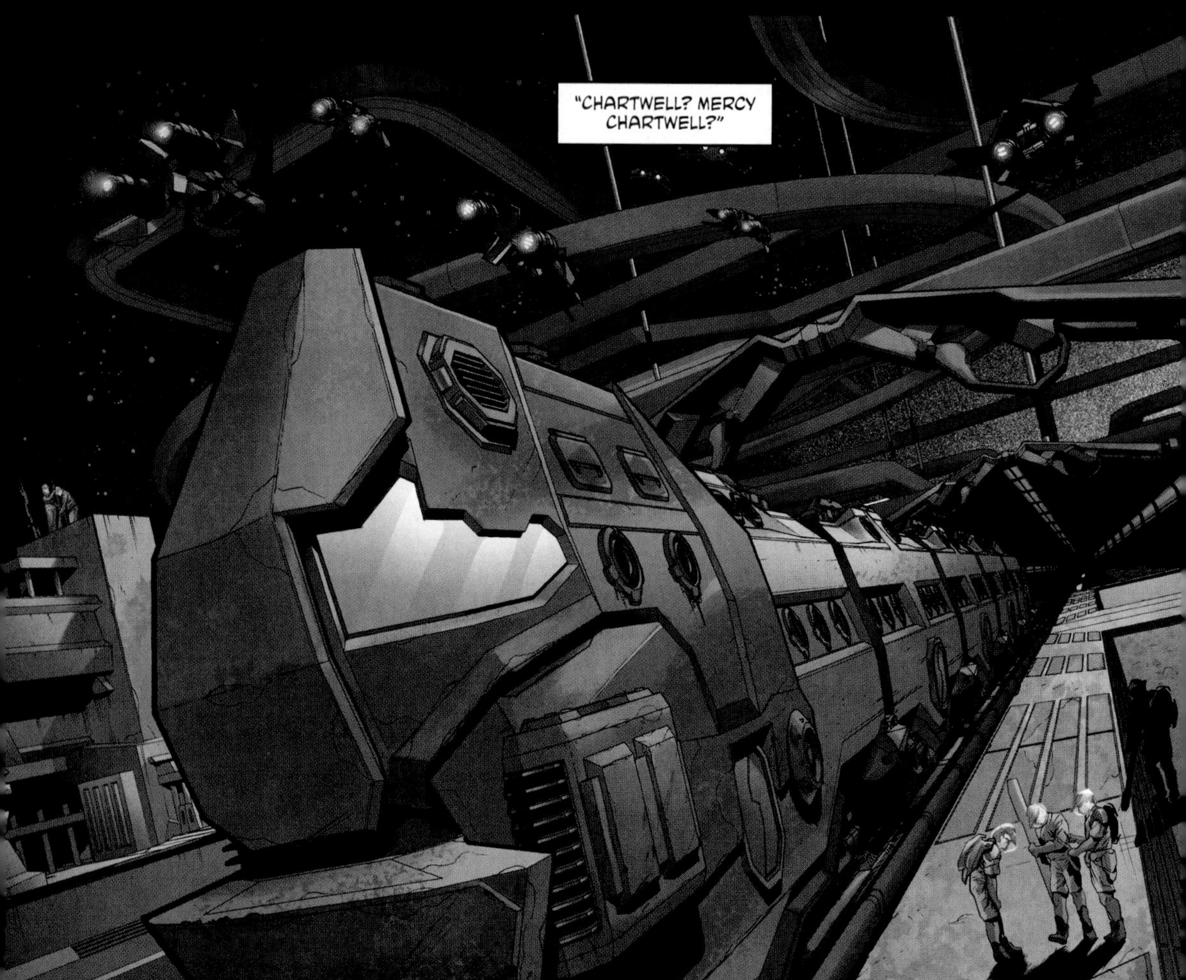
"CHARTWELL? MERCY CHARTWELL?"
TAG: BELT WORKER CAMP 4
LOCALIZED HEADQUARTERS OF BELT WORKERS IN PRESENT TEMPERATE ZONE. ALSO, TRANSPORT CENTER FOR OFF-SHIFT WORKERS TRAVELING TO LOCALIZED CITADEL FOR RECREATIONAL ACTIVITIES.

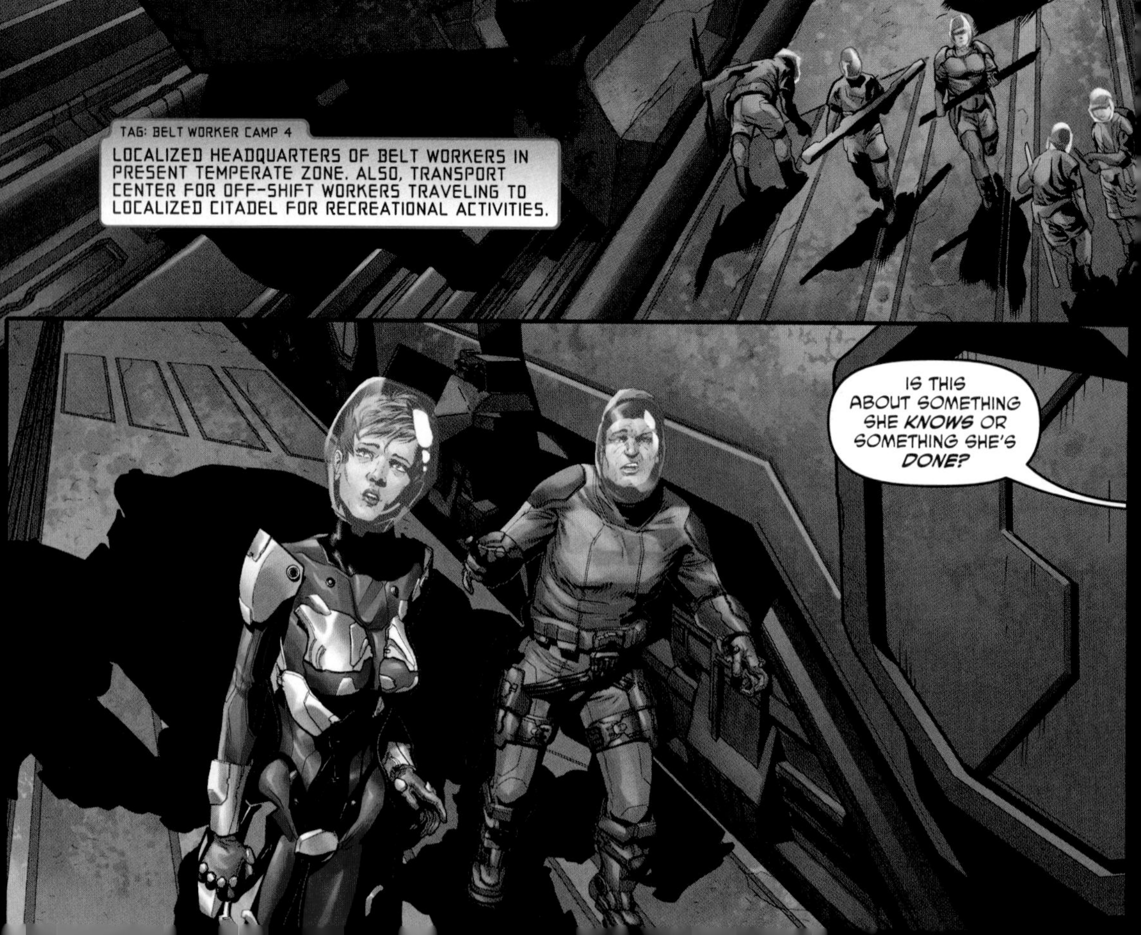
IS THIS ABOUT SOMETHING SHE *KNOWS* OR SOMETHING SHE'S *DONE?*

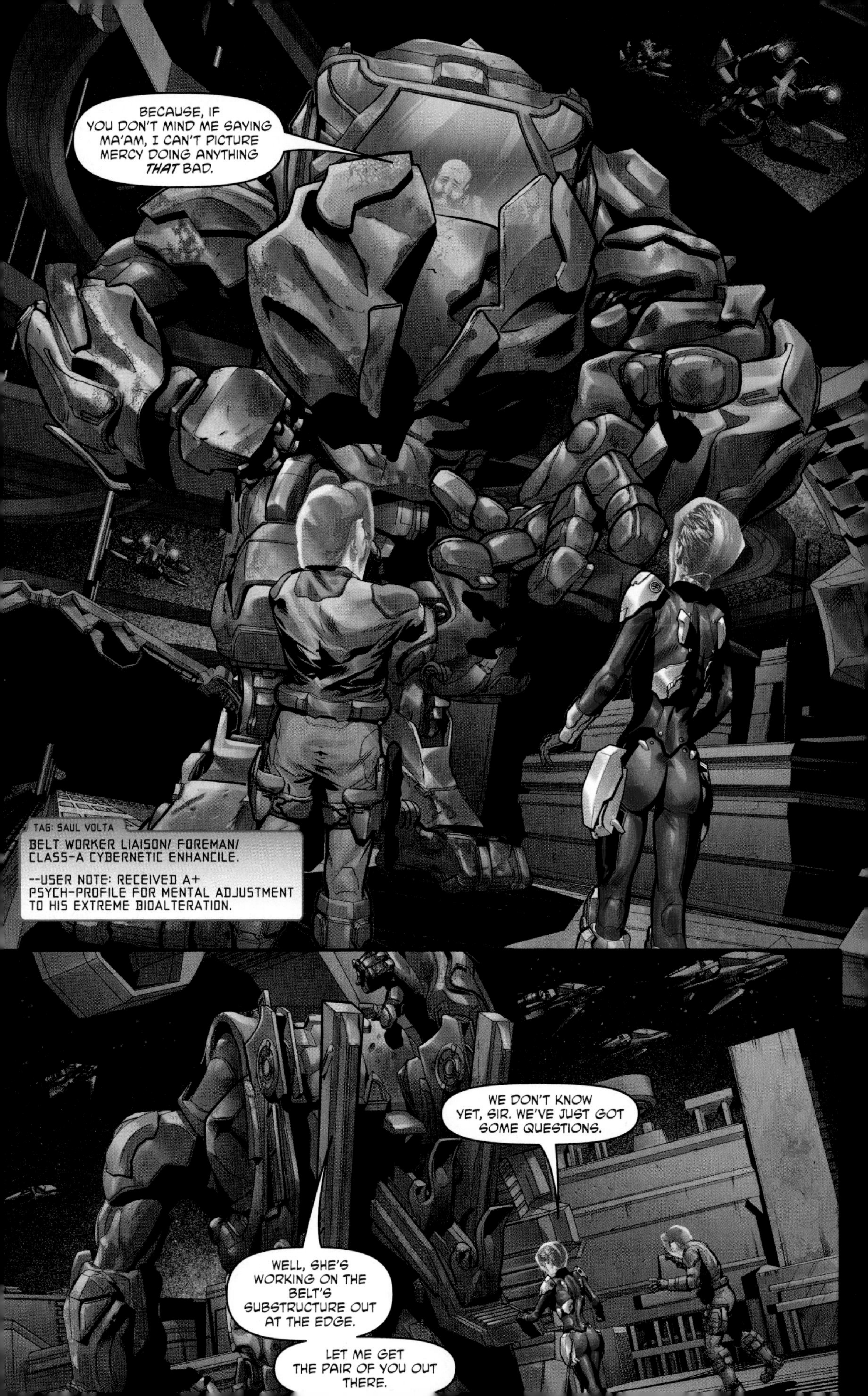
BECAUSE, IF YOU DON'T MIND ME SAYING MA'AM, I CAN'T PICTURE MERCY DOING ANYTHING *THAT* BAD.
TAG: SAUL VOLTA
BELT WORKER LIAISON/ FOREMAN/ CLASS-A CYBERNETIC ENHANCILE.
--USER NOTE: RECEIVED A+ PSYCH-PROFILE FOR MENTAL ADJUSTMENT TO HIS EXTREME BIOALTERATION.
WE DON'T KNOW YET, SIR. WE'VE JUST GOT SOME QUESTIONS.
WELL, SHE'S WORKING ON THE BELT'S SUBSTRUCTURE OUT AT THE EDGE.
LET ME GET THE PAIR OF YOU OUT THERE.

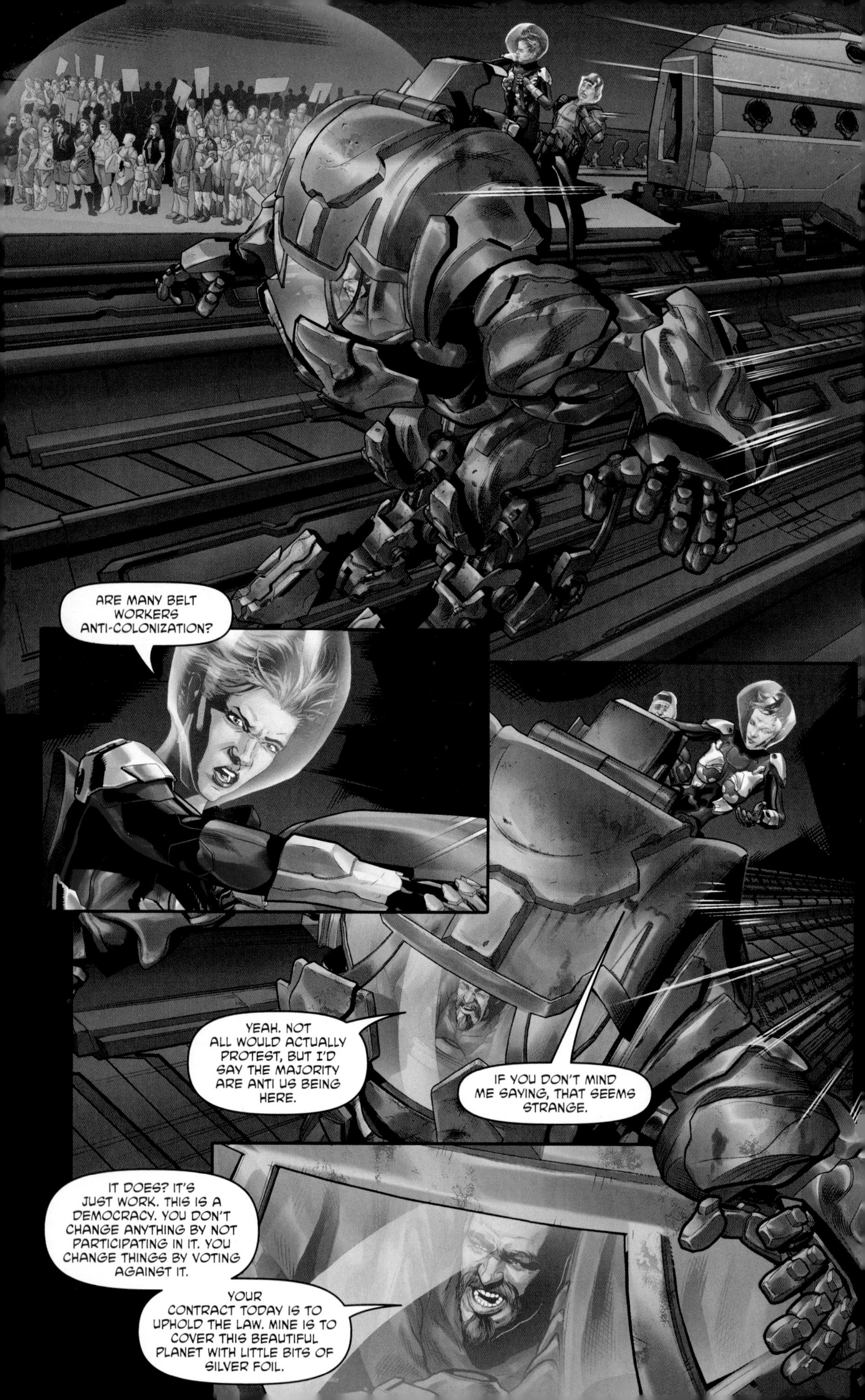
ARE MANY BELT WORKERS ANTI-COLONIZATION?
YEAH. NOT ALL WOULD ACTUALLY PROTEST, BUT I'D SAY THE MAJORITY ARE ANTI US BEING HERE.
IF YOU DON'T MIND ME SAYING, THAT SEEMS STRANGE.
IT DOES? IT'S JUST WORK. THIS IS A DEMOCRACY. YOU DON'T CHANGE ANYTHING BY NOT PARTICIPATING IN IT. YOU CHANGE THINGS BY VOTING AGAINST IT.
YOUR CONTRACT TODAY IS TO UPHOLD THE LAW. MINE IS TO COVER THIS BEAUTIFUL PLANET WITH LITTLE BITS OF SILVER FOIL.

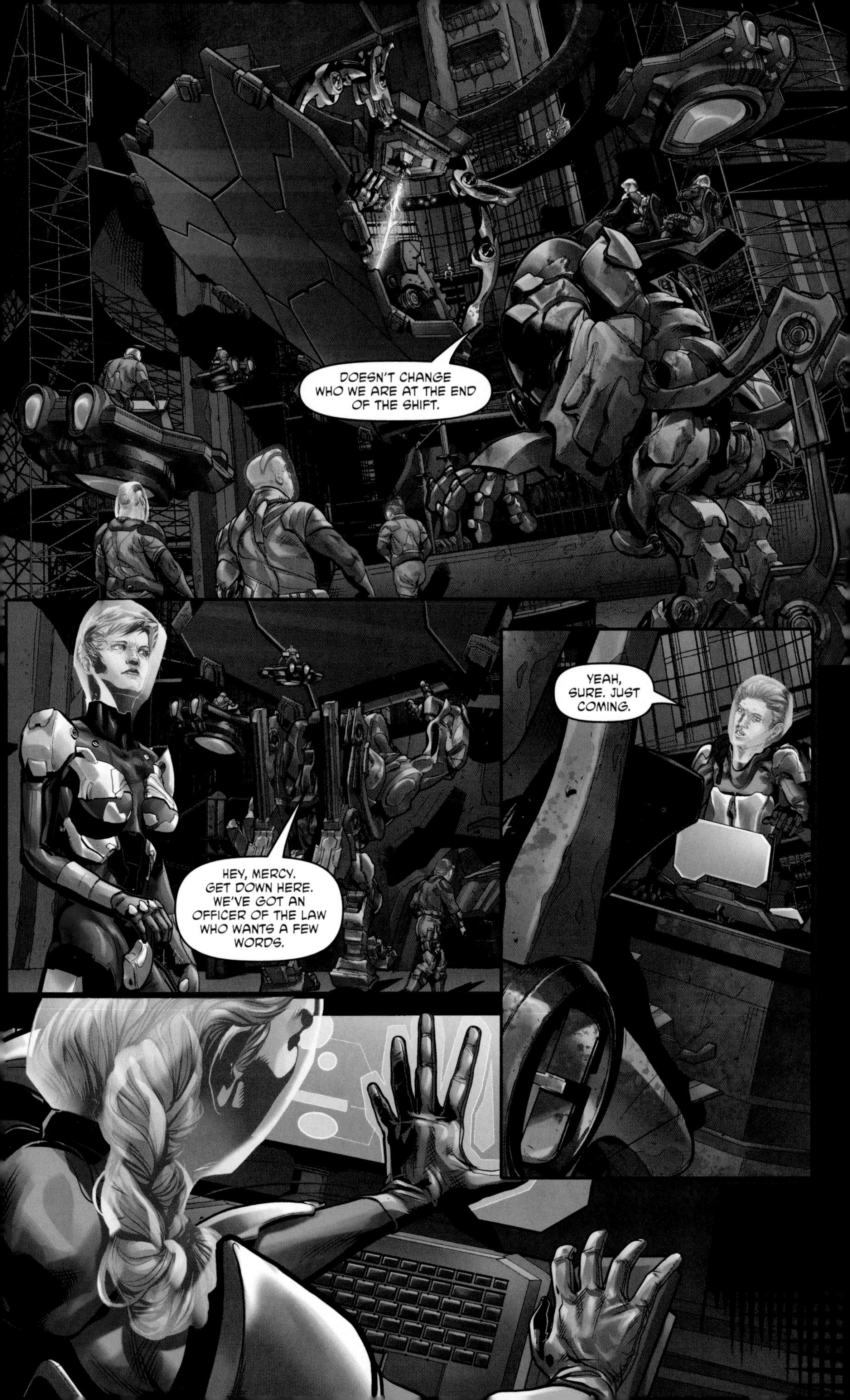
DOESN'T CHANGE WHO WE ARE AT THE END OF THE SHIFT.
HEY, MERCY. GET DOWN HERE. WE'VE GOT AN OFFICER OF THE LAW WHO WANTS A FEW WORDS.
YEAH, SURE. JUST COMING.

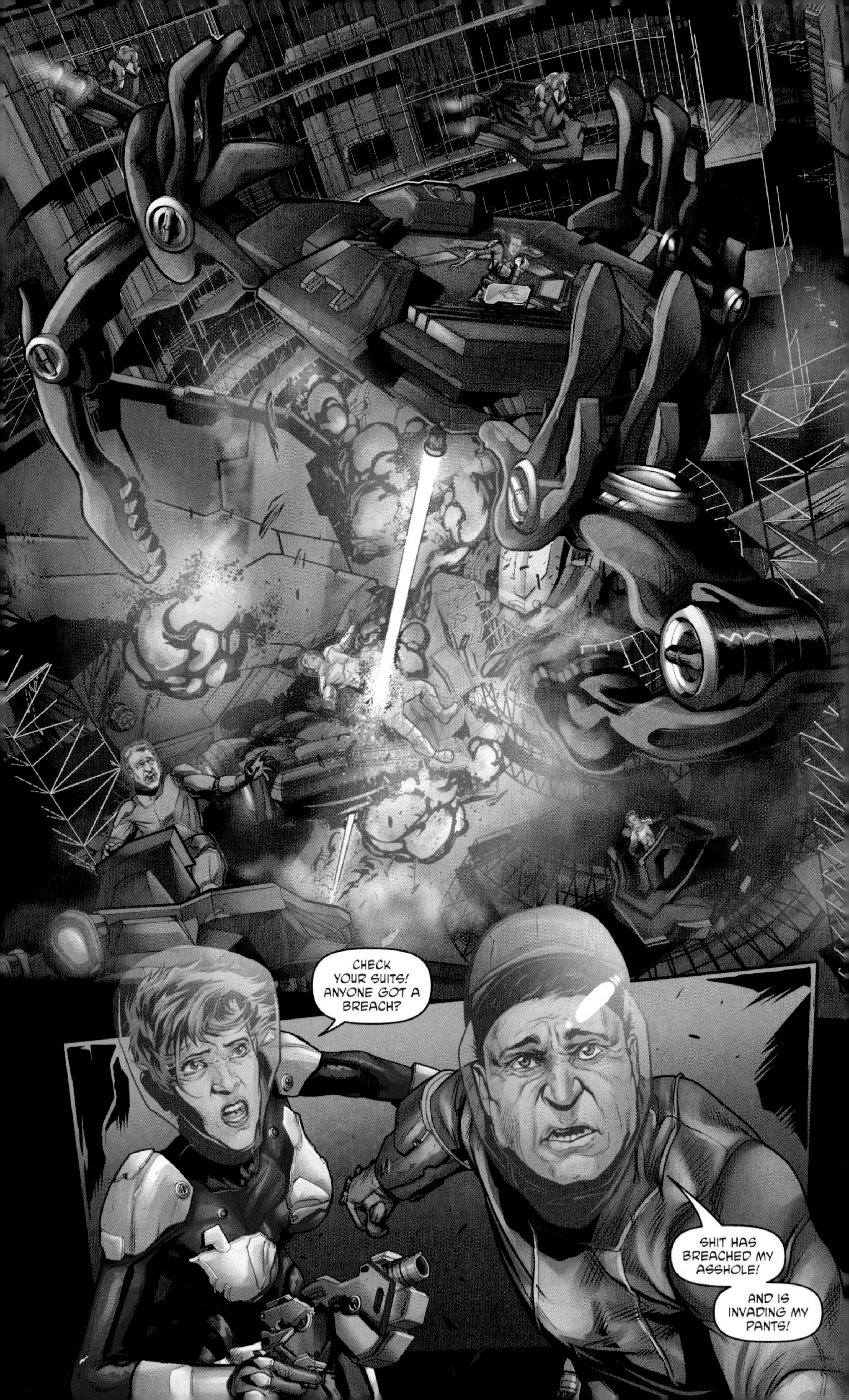
CHECK YOUR SUITS! ANYONE GOT A BREACH?
SHIT HAS BREACHED MY ASSHOLE!
AND IS INVADING MY PANTS!

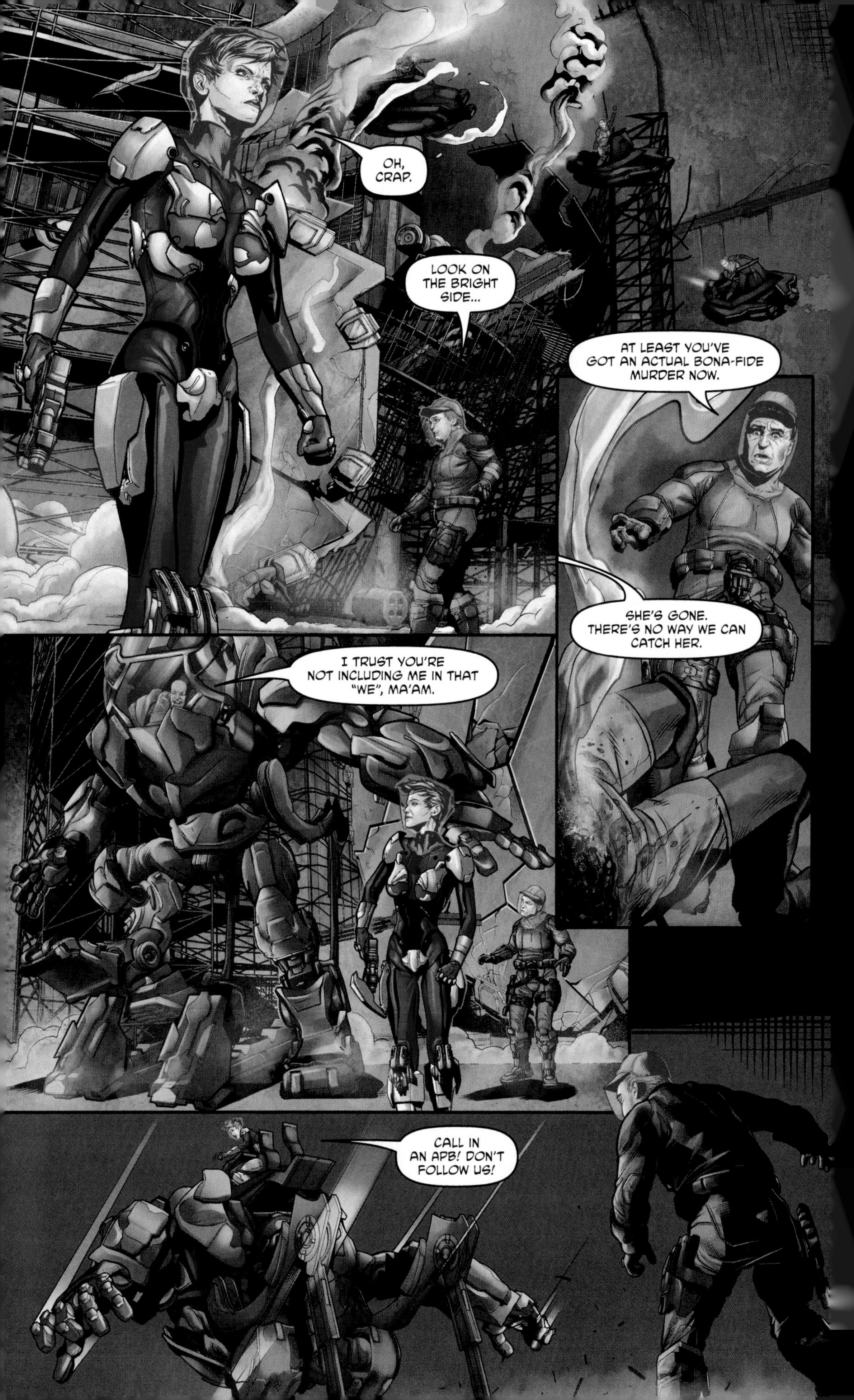
OH, CRAP.
LOOK ON THE BRIGHT SIDE...
AT LEAST YOU'VE GOT AN ACTUAL BONA-FIDE MURDER NOW.
SHE'S GONE. THERE'S NO WAY WE CAN CATCH HER.
I TRUST YOU'RE NOT INCLUDING ME IN THAT "WE", MA'AM.
CALL IN AN APB! DON'T FOLLOW US!

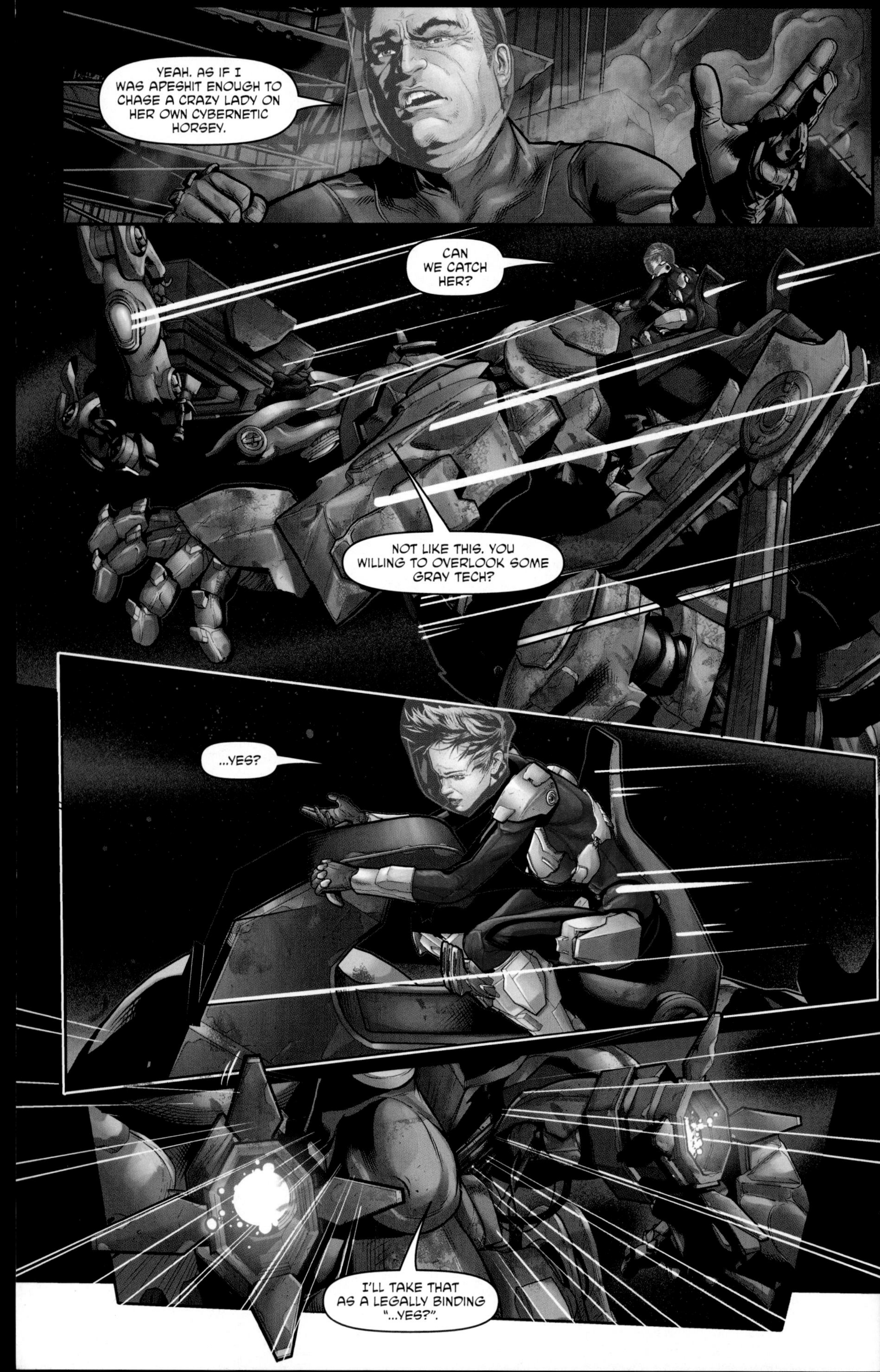
YEAH. AS IF I WAS APESHIT ENOUGH TO CHASE A CRAZY LADY ON HER OWN CYBERNETIC HORSEY.
CAN WE CATCH HER?
NOT LIKE THIS. YOU WILLING TO OVERLOOK SOME GRAY TECH?
...YES?
I'LL TAKE THAT AS A LEGALLY BINDING "...YES?".

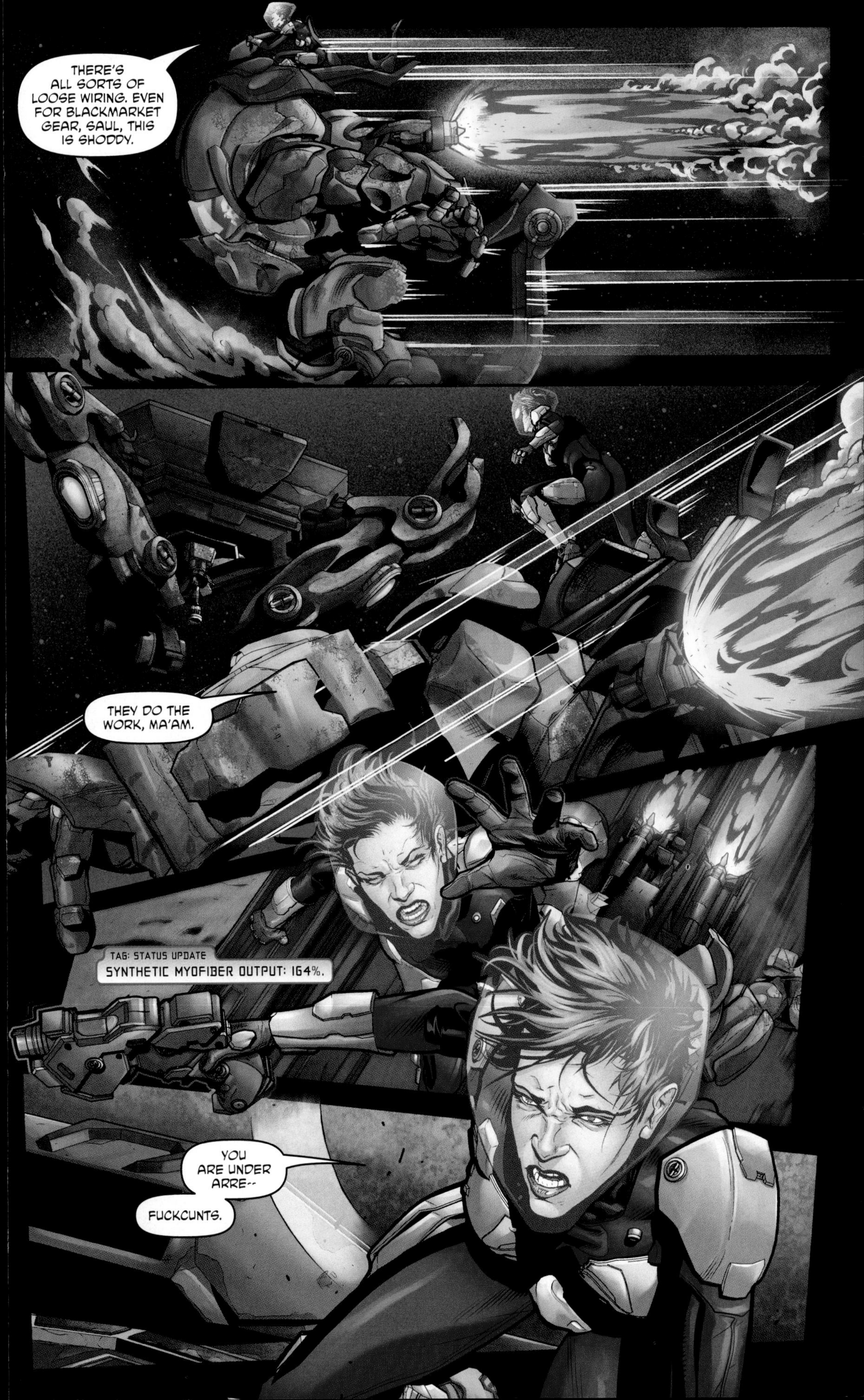
THERE'S ALL SORTS OF LOOSE WIRING. EVEN FOR BLACKMARKET GEAR, SAUL, THIS IS SHODDY.
THEY DO THE WORK, MA'AM.
TAG: STATUS UPDATE
SYNTHETIC MYOFIBER OUTPUT: 164%.
YOU ARE UNDER ARRE--
FUCKCUNTS.

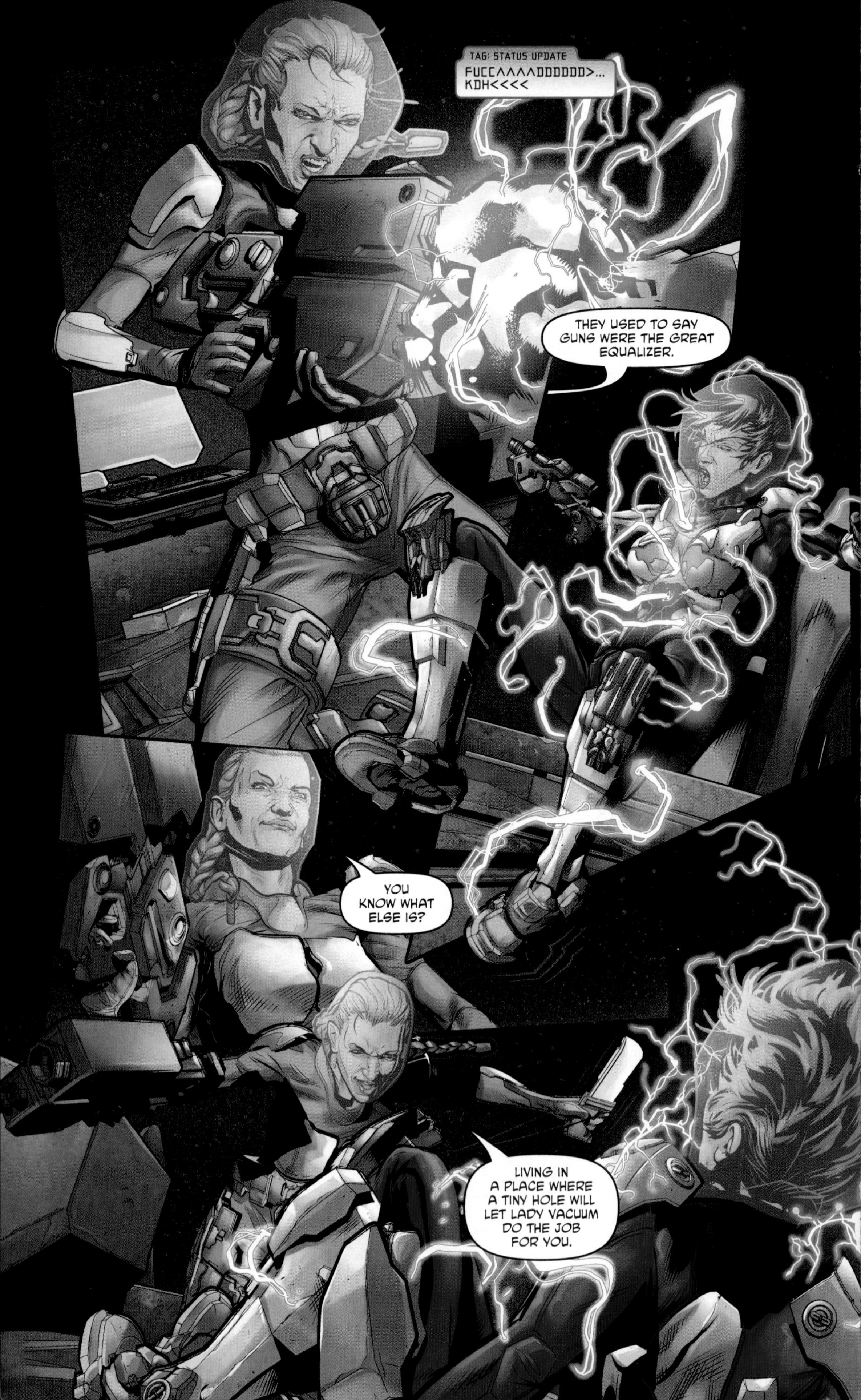
TAG: STATUS UPDATE
FUCCAAAADDDDDD>...
KDH<<<<
THEY USED TO SAY GUNS WERE THE GREAT EQUALIZER.
YOU KNOW WHAT ELSE IS?
LIVING IN A PLACE WHERE A TINY HOLE WILL LET LADY VACUUM DO THE JOB FOR YOU.

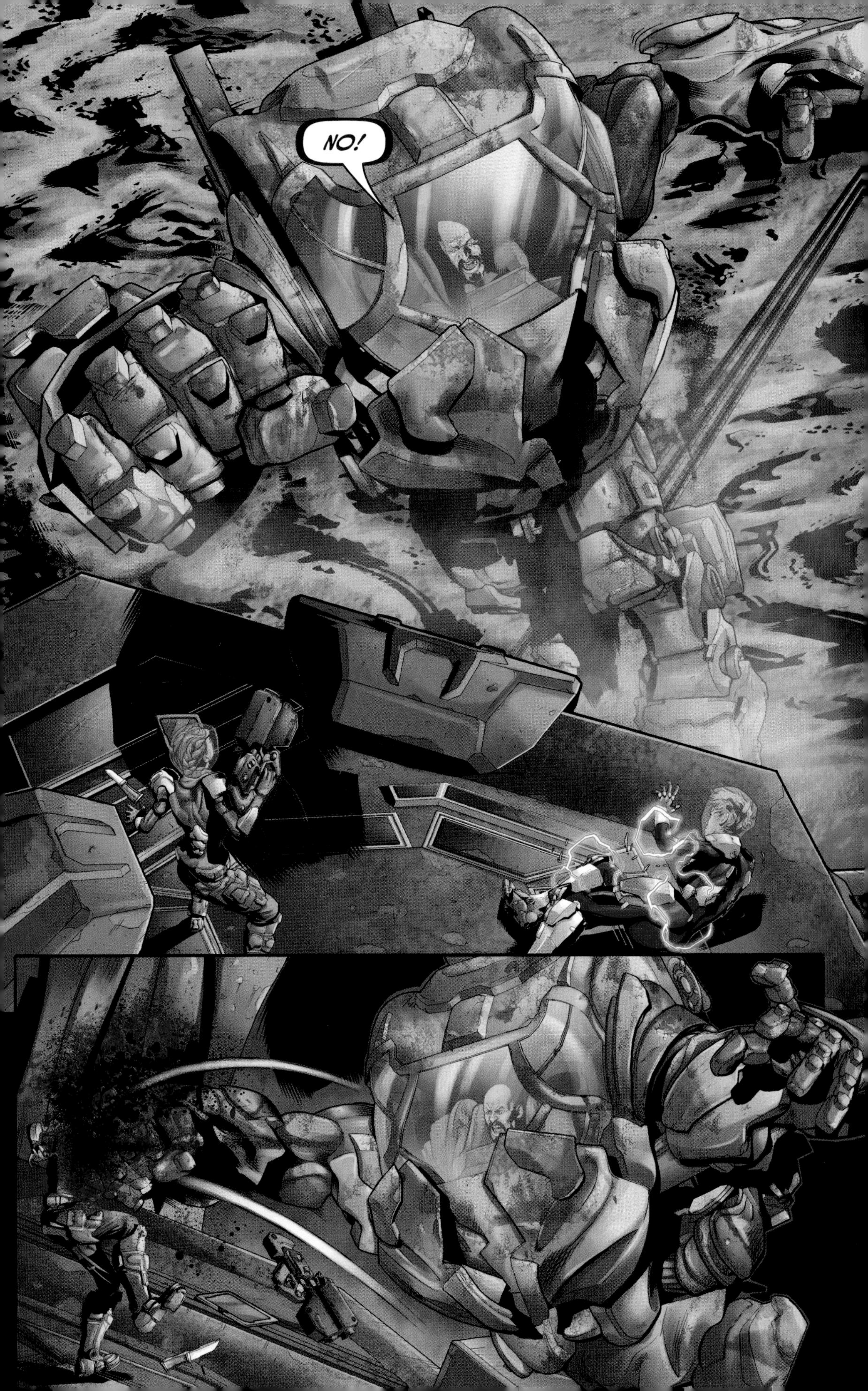
NO!

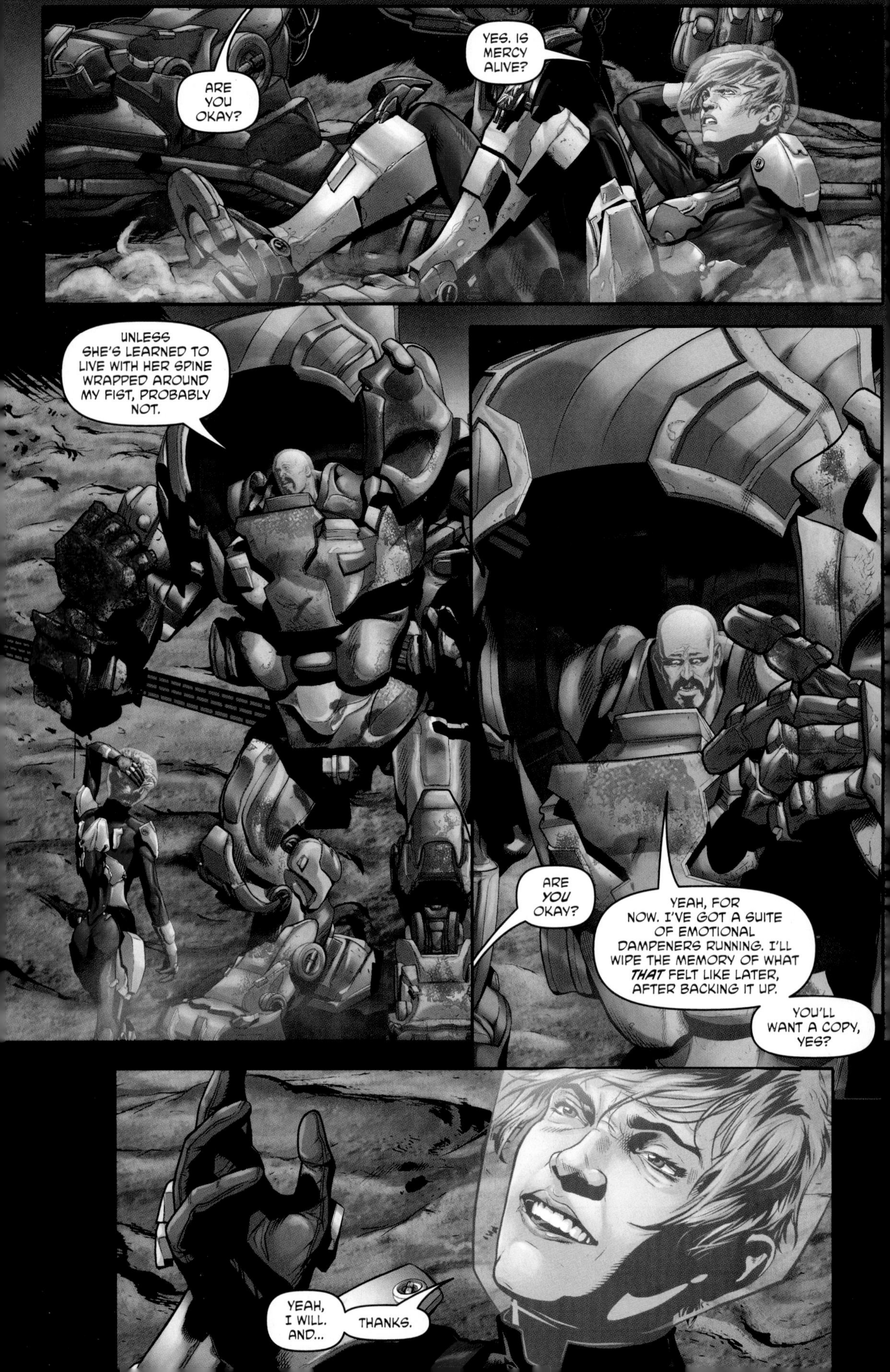
ARE YOU OKAY?
YES. IS MERCY ALIVE?
UNLESS SHE'S LEARNED TO LIVE WITH HER SPINE WRAPPED AROUND MY FIST, PROBABLY NOT.
ARE *YOU* OKAY?
YEAH, FOR NOW. I'VE GOT A SUITE OF EMOTIONAL DAMPENERS RUNNING. I'LL WIPE THE MEMORY OF WHAT *THAT* FELT LIKE LATER, AFTER BACKING IT UP.
YOU'LL WANT A COPY, YES?
YEAH, I WILL. AND...
THANKS.

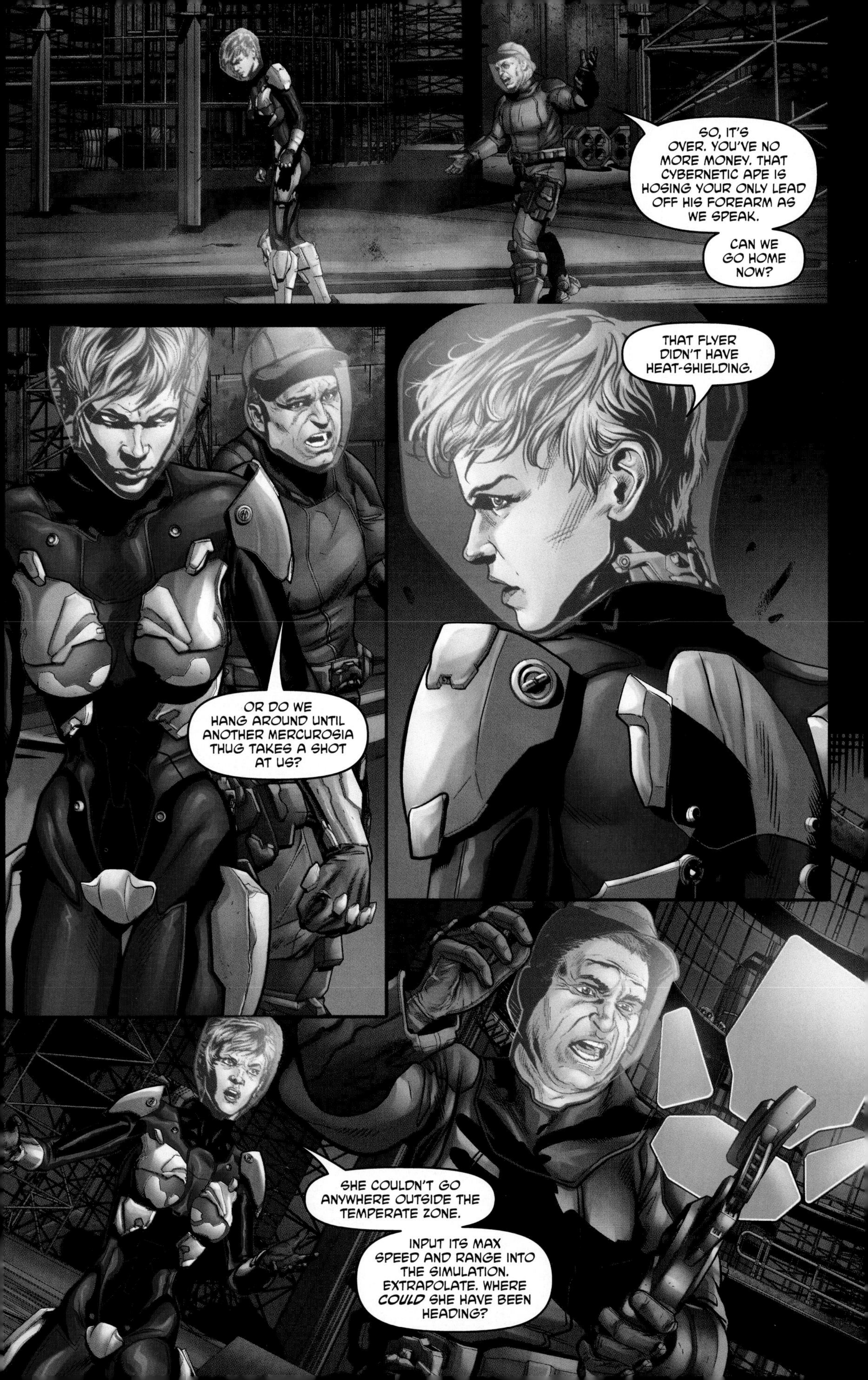
SO, IT'S OVER. YOU'VE NO MORE MONEY. THAT CYBERNETIC APE IS HOSING YOUR ONLY LEAD OFF HIS FOREARM AS WE SPEAK.
CAN WE GO HOME NOW?
OR DO WE HANG AROUND UNTIL ANOTHER MERCUROSIA THUG TAKES A SHOT AT US?
THAT FLYER DIDN'T HAVE HEAT-SHIELDING.
SHE COULDN'T GO ANYWHERE OUTSIDE THE TEMPERATE ZONE.
INPUT ITS MAX SPEED AND RANGE INTO THE SIMULATION. EXTRAPOLATE. WHERE *COULD* SHE HAVE BEEN HEADING?

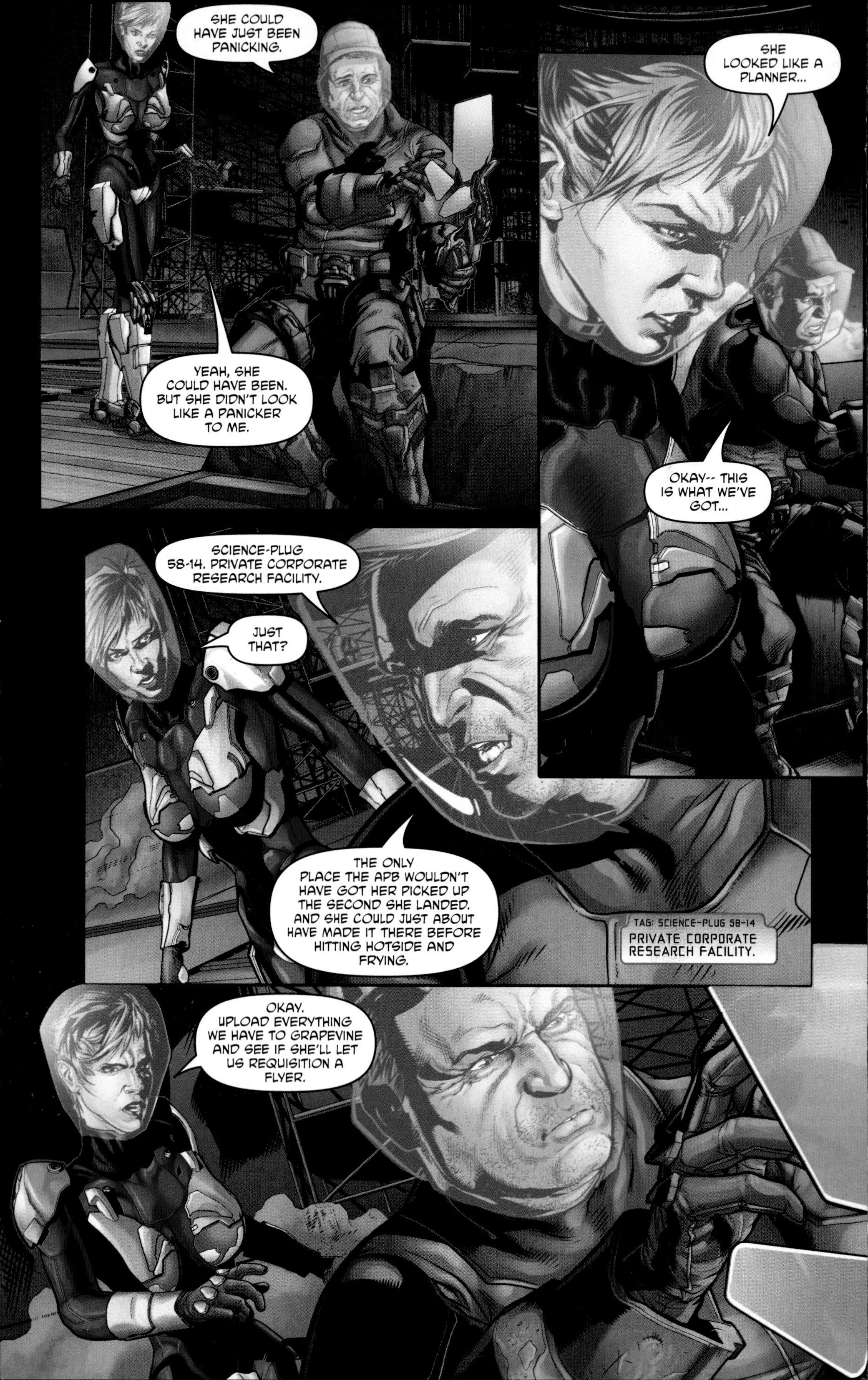
SHE COULD HAVE JUST BEEN PANICKING.
YEAH, SHE COULD HAVE BEEN. BUT SHE DIDN'T LOOK LIKE A PANICKER TO ME.
SHE LOOKED LIKE A PLANNER...
OKAY-- THIS IS WHAT WE'VE GOT...
SCIENCE-PLUG 58-14. PRIVATE CORPORATE RESEARCH FACILITY.
JUST THAT?
THE ONLY PLACE THE APB WOULDN'T HAVE GOT HER PICKED UP THE SECOND SHE LANDED. AND SHE COULD JUST ABOUT HAVE MADE IT THERE BEFORE HITTING HOTSIDE AND FRYING.
TAG: SCIENCE-PLUG 58-14
PRIVATE CORPORATE RESEARCH FACILITY.
OKAY. UPLOAD EVERYTHING WE HAVE TO GRAPEVINE AND SEE IF SHE'LL LET US REQUISITION A FLYER.

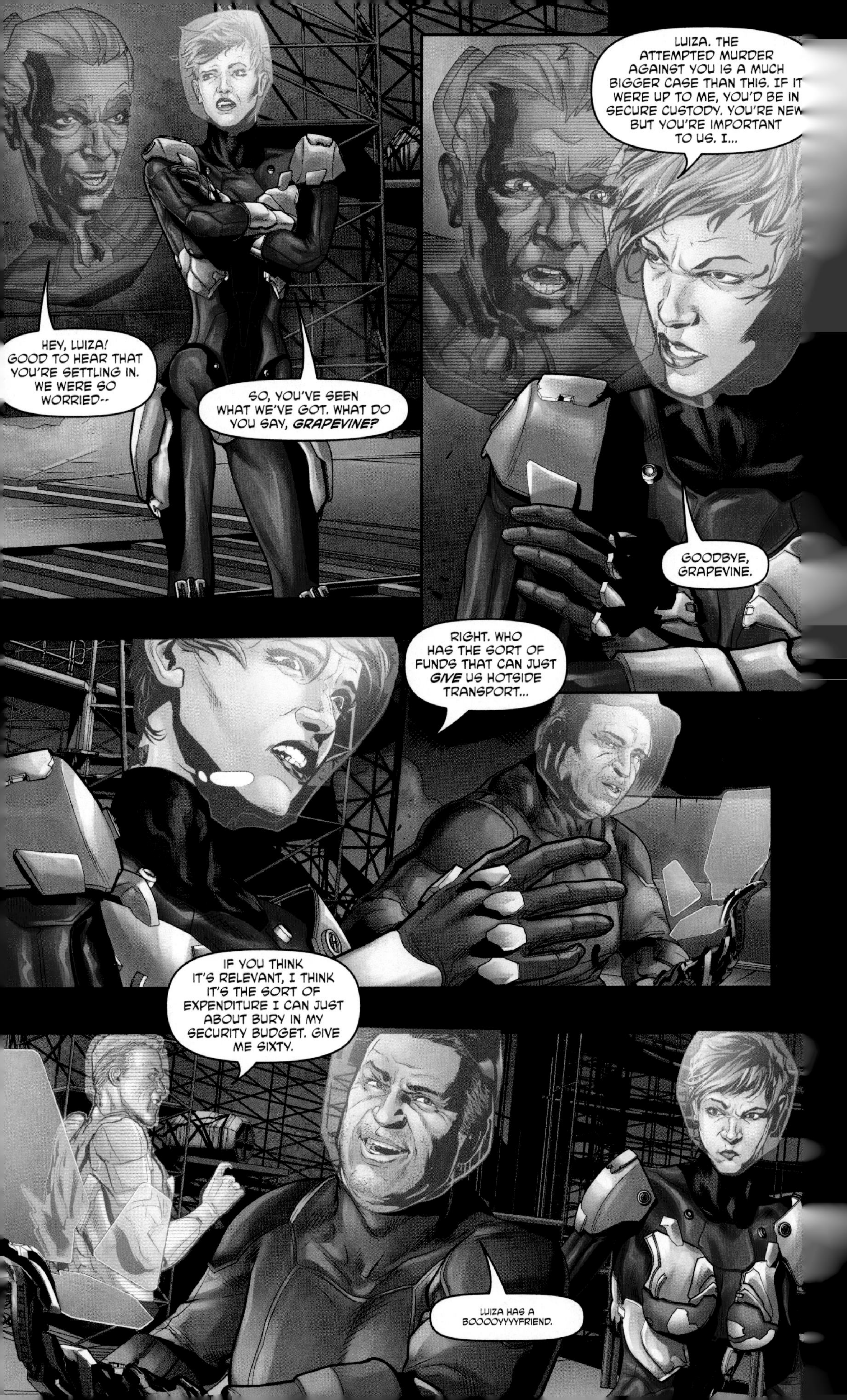
HEY, LUIZA! GOOD TO HEAR THAT YOU'RE SETTLING IN. WE WERE SO WORRIED--
SO, YOU'VE SEEN WHAT WE'VE GOT. WHAT DO YOU SAY, *GRAPEVINE?*
LUIZA. THE ATTEMPTED MURDER AGAINST YOU IS A MUCH BIGGER CASE THAN THIS. IF IT WERE UP TO ME, YOU'D BE IN SECURE CUSTODY. YOU'RE NEW BUT YOU'RE IMPORTANT TO US. I...
GOODBYE, GRAPEVINE.
RIGHT. WHO HAS THE SORT OF FUNDS THAT CAN JUST *GIVE* US HOTSIDE TRANSPORT...
IF YOU THINK IT'S RELEVANT, I THINK IT'S THE SORT OF EXPENDITURE I CAN JUST ABOUT BURY IN MY SECURITY BUDGET. GIVE ME SIXTY.
LUIZA HAS A BOOOOYYYYFRIEND.

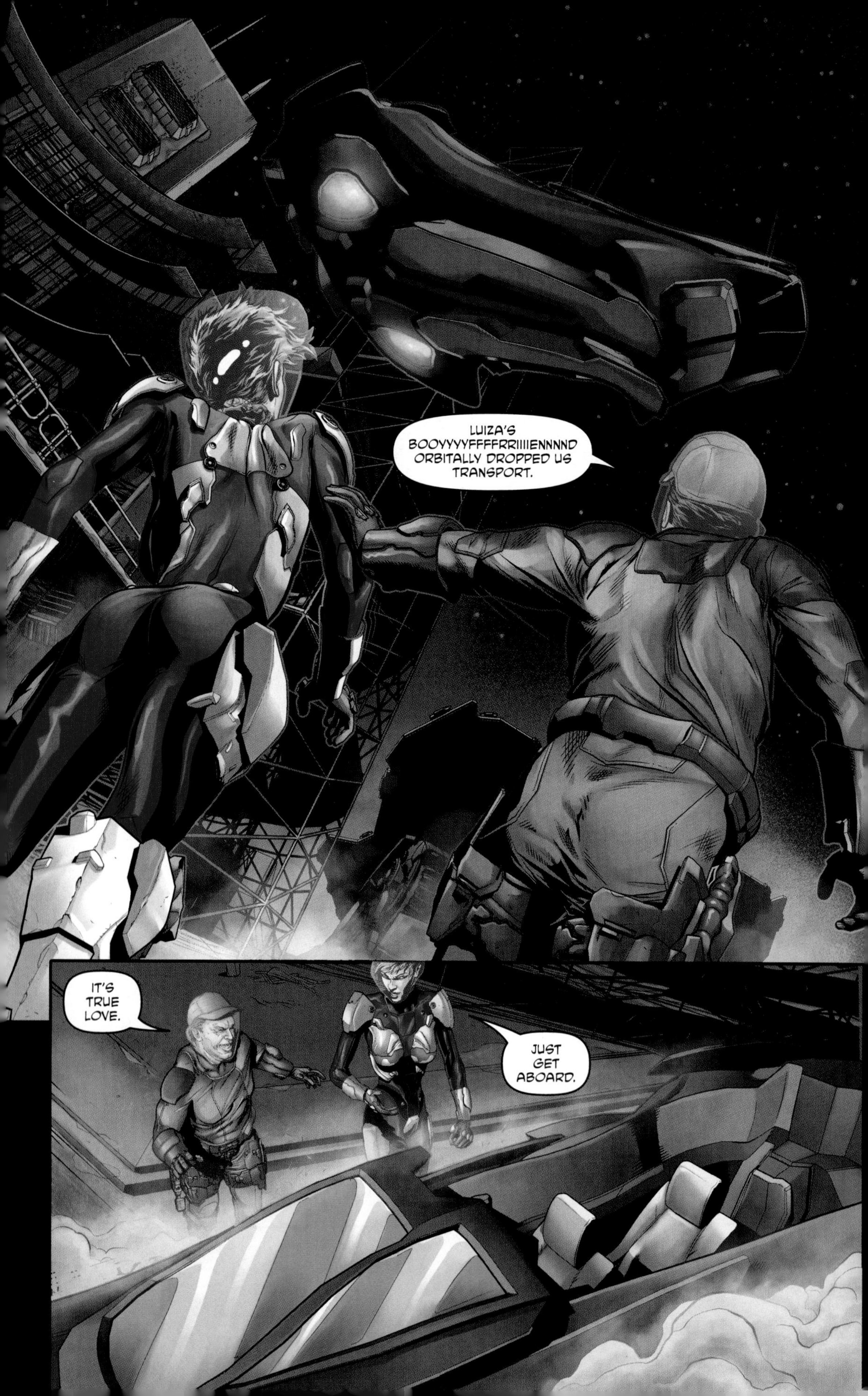
LUIZA'S BOOYYYYFFFFRRIIIIENNNND ORBITALLY DROPPED US TRANSPORT.
IT'S TRUE LOVE.
JUST GET ABOARD.

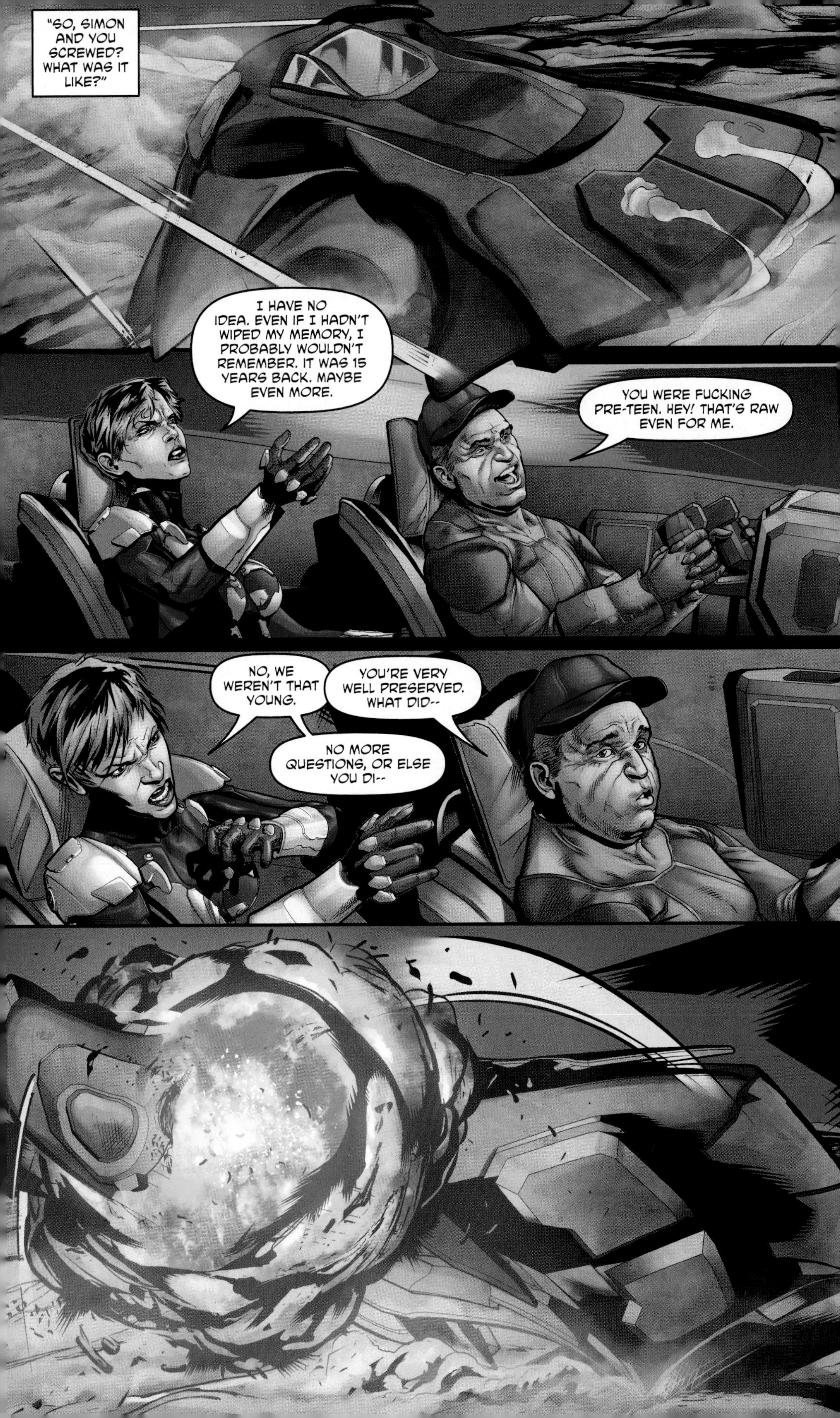
"SO, SIMON AND YOU SCREWED? WHAT WAS IT LIKE?"
I HAVE NO IDEA. EVEN IF I HADN'T WIPED MY MEMORY, I PROBABLY WOULDN'T REMEMBER. IT WAS 15 YEARS BACK. MAYBE EVEN MORE.
YOU WERE FUCKING PRE-TEEN. HEY! THAT'S RAW EVEN FOR ME.
NO, WE WEREN'T THAT YOUNG.
YOU'RE VERY WELL PRESERVED. WHAT DID--
NO MORE QUESTIONS, OR ELSE YOU DI--

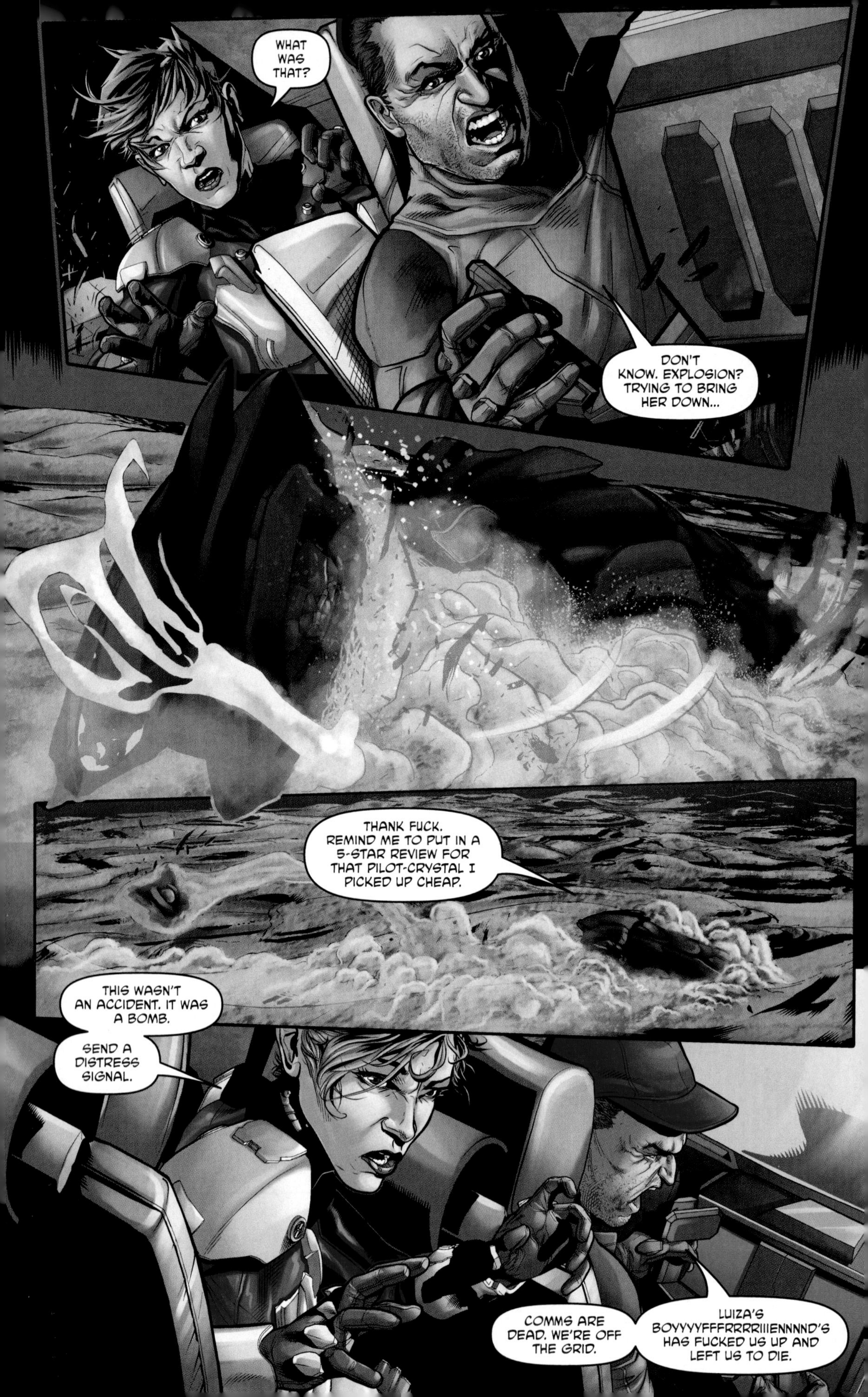

WHAT WAS THAT?
DON'T KNOW. EXPLOSION? TRYING TO BRING HER DOWN...
THANK FUCK. REMIND ME TO PUT IN A 5-STAR REVIEW FOR THAT PILOT-CRYSTAL I PICKED UP CHEAP.
THIS WASN'T AN ACCIDENT. IT WAS A BOMB.
SEND A DISTRESS SIGNAL.
COMMS ARE DEAD. WE'RE OFF THE GRID.
LUIZA'S BOYYYYFFFRRRRIIIENNNND'S HAS FUCKED US UP AND LEFT US TO DIE.

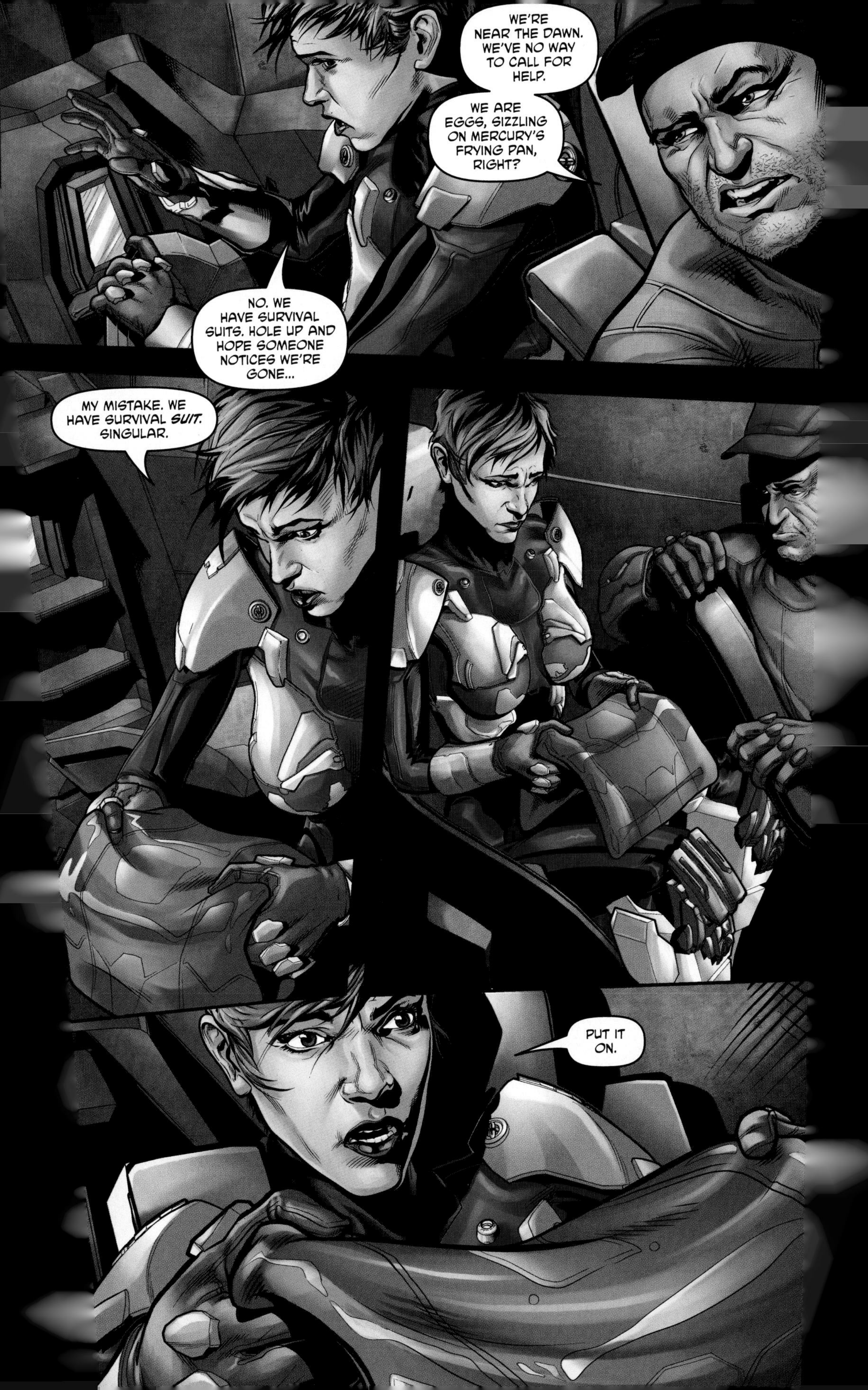
WE'RE NEAR THE DAWN. WE'VE NO WAY TO CALL FOR HELP.
WE ARE EGGS, SIZZLING ON MERCURY'S FRYING PAN, RIGHT?
NO. WE HAVE SURVIVAL SUITS. HOLE UP AND HOPE SOMEONE NOTICES WE'RE GONE...
MY MISTAKE. WE HAVE SURVIVAL *SUIT*. SINGULAR.
PUT IT ON.

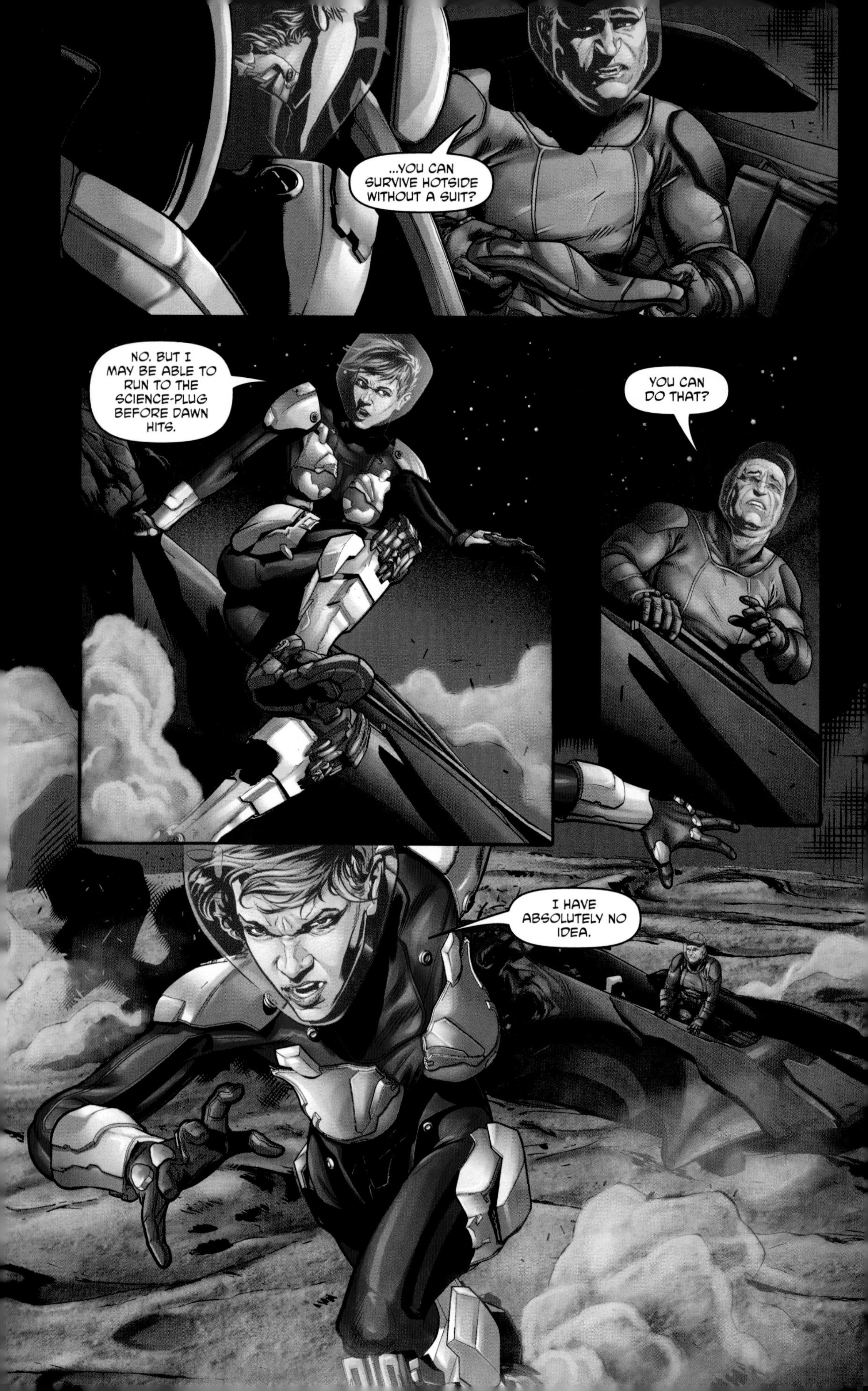
...YOU CAN SURVIVE HOTSIDE WITHOUT A SUIT?
NO. BUT I MAY BE ABLE TO RUN TO THE SCIENCE-PLUG BEFORE DAWN HITS.
YOU CAN DO THAT?
I HAVE ABSOLUTELY NO IDEA.

chapter 4

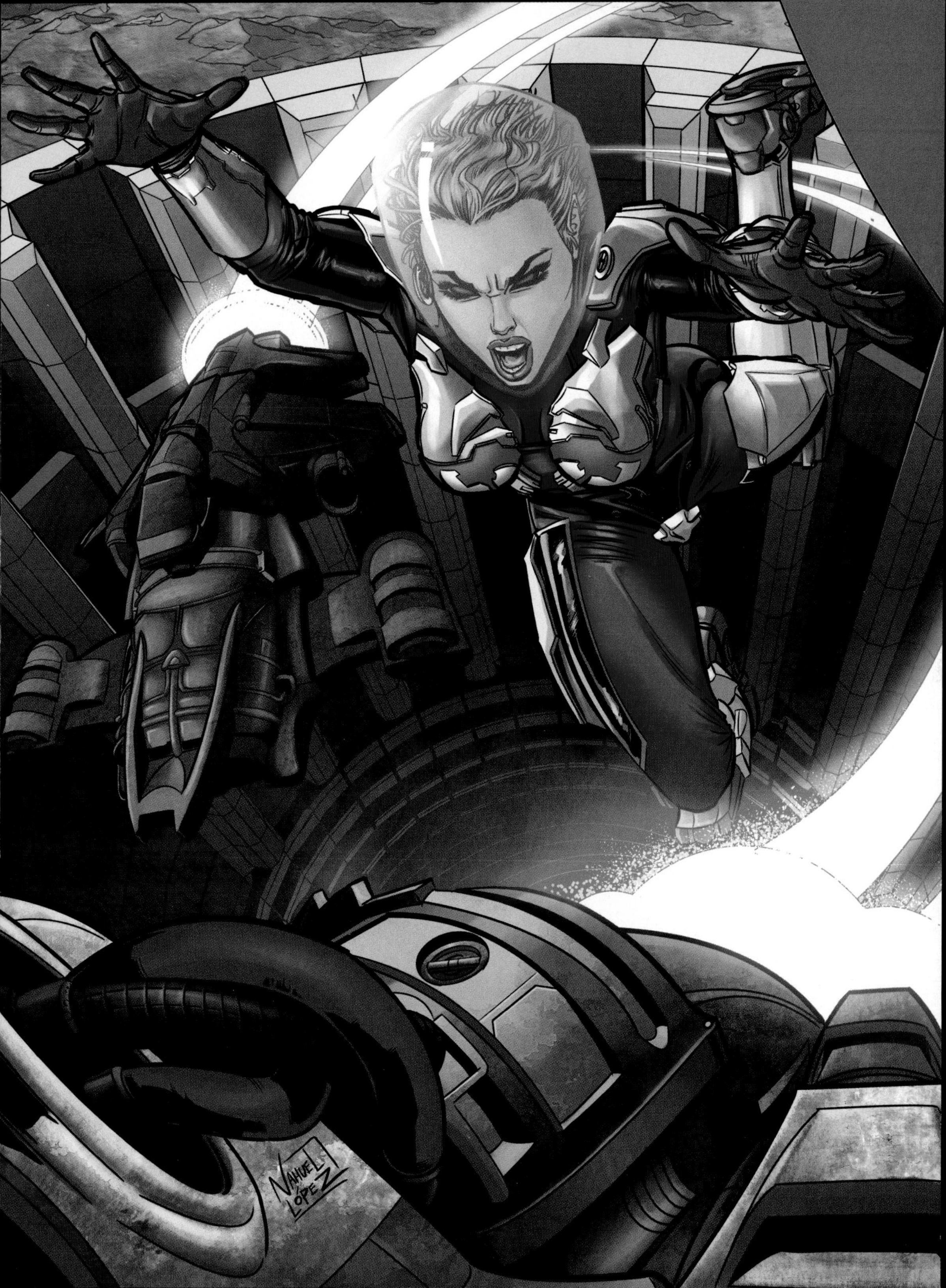
NAHUEL LÓPEZ

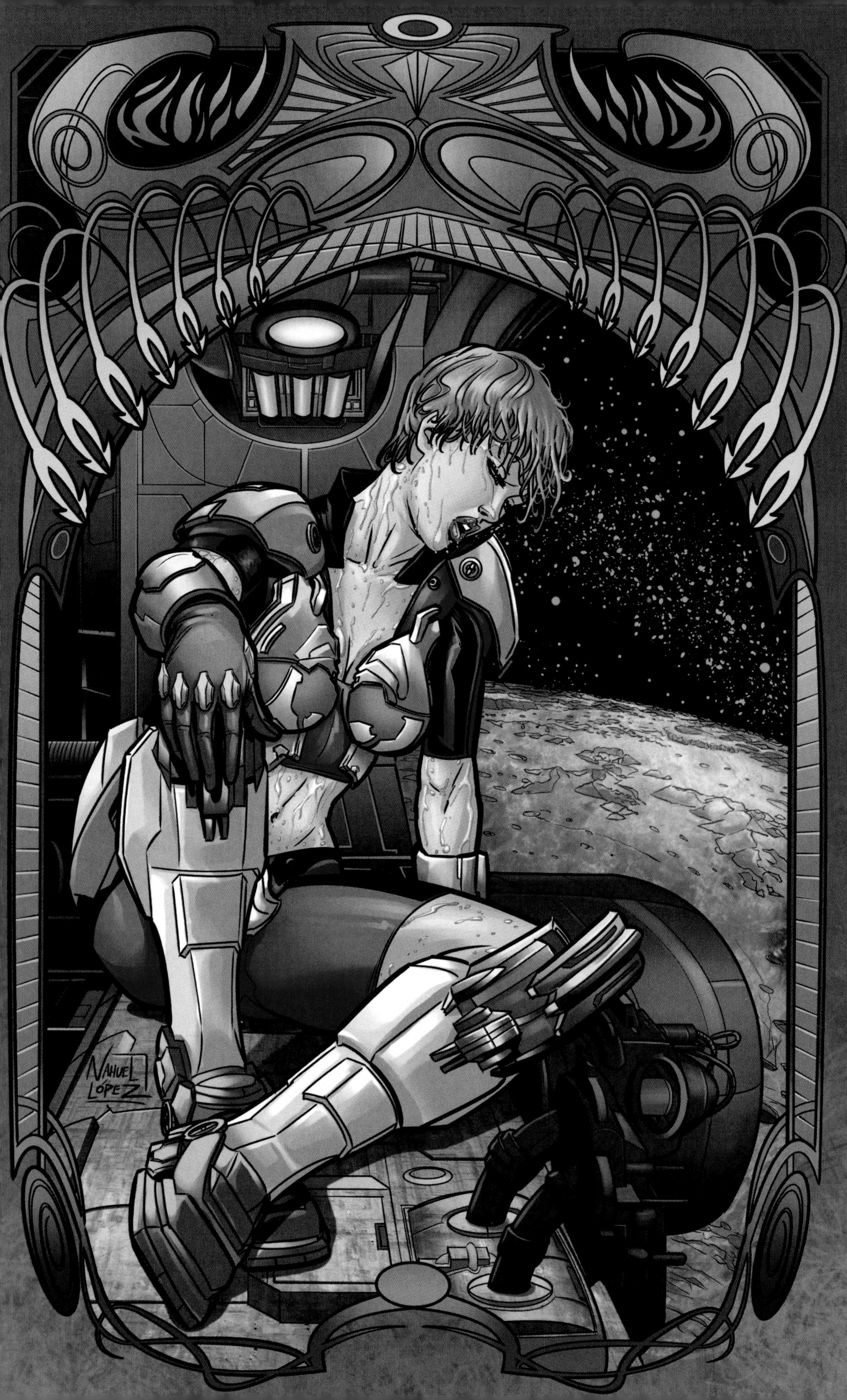
NAHUEL
LÓPEZ

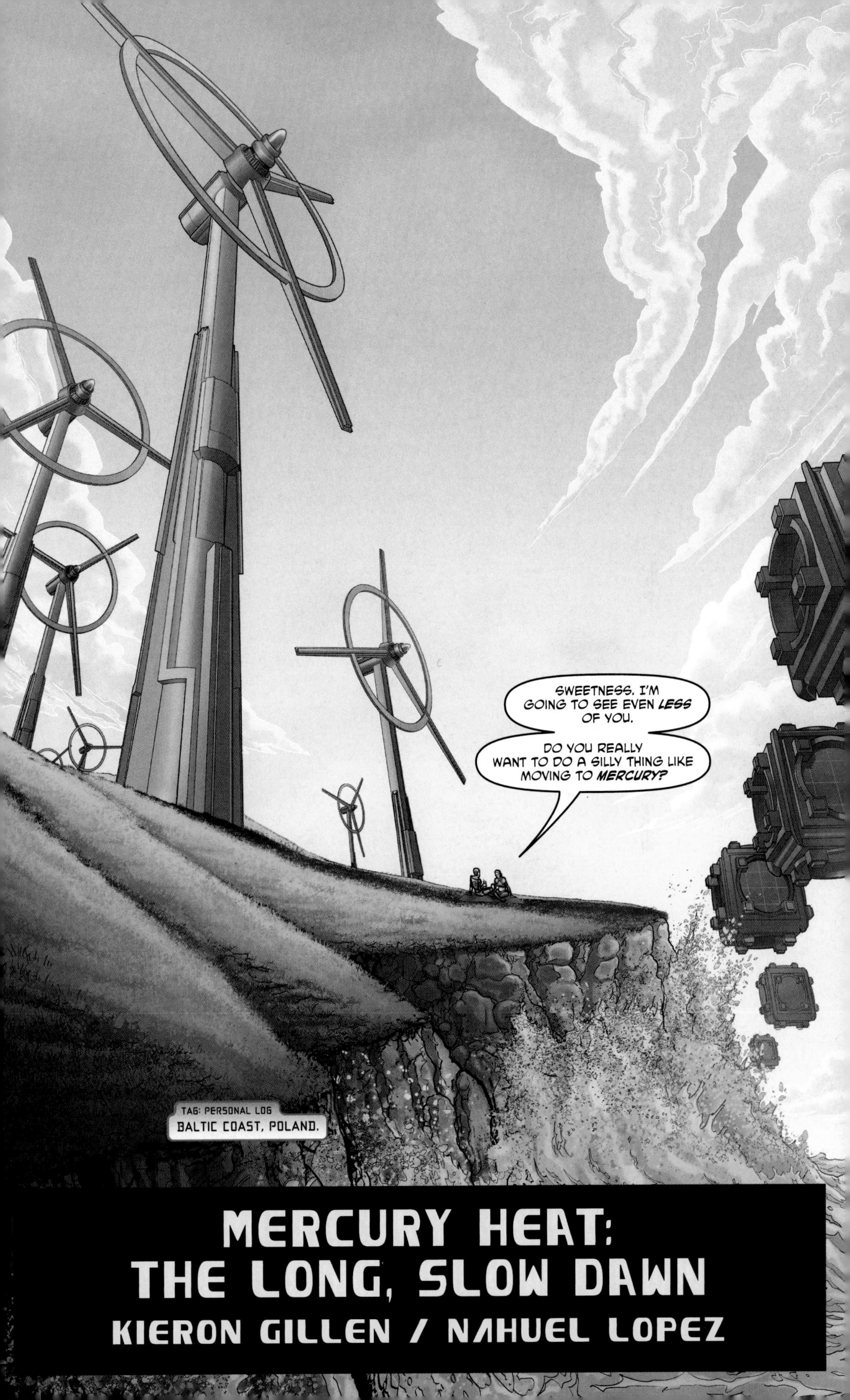
SWEETNESS. I'M GOING TO SEE EVEN *LESS* OF YOU.
DO YOU REALLY WANT TO DO A SILLY THING LIKE MOVING TO *MERCURY?*
TAG: PERSONAL LOG
BALTIC COAST, POLAND.

MERCURY HEAT: THE LONG, SLOW DAWN

KIERON GILLEN / NAHUEL LOPEZ

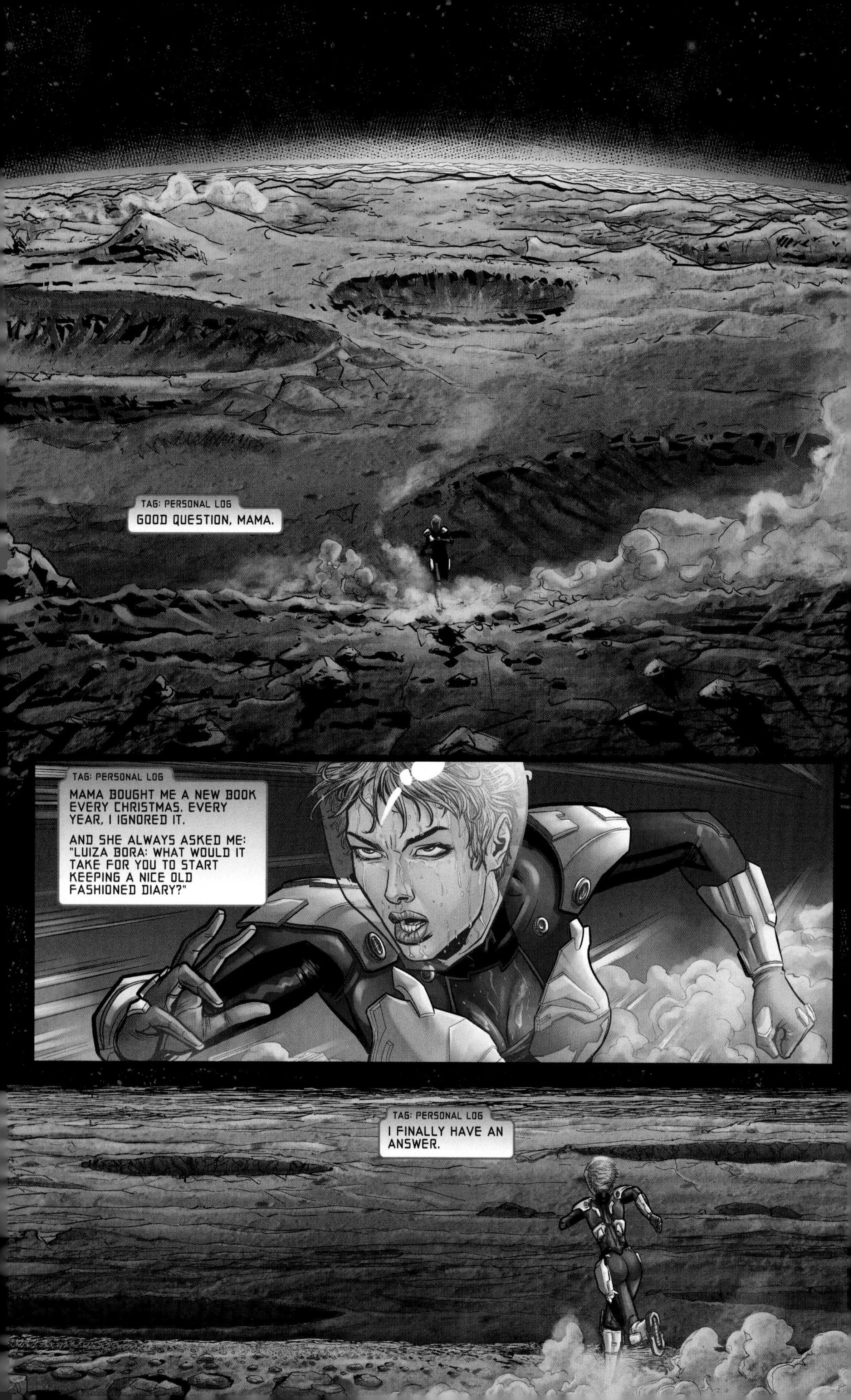
TAG: PERSONAL LOG
GOOD QUESTION, MAMA.
TAG: PERSONAL LOG
MAMA BOUGHT ME A NEW BOOK EVERY CHRISTMAS. EVERY YEAR, I IGNORED IT.
AND SHE ALWAYS ASKED ME: "LUIZA BORA: WHAT WOULD IT TAKE FOR YOU TO START KEEPING A NICE OLD FASHIONED DIARY?"
TAG: PERSONAL LOG
I FINALLY HAVE AN ANSWER.

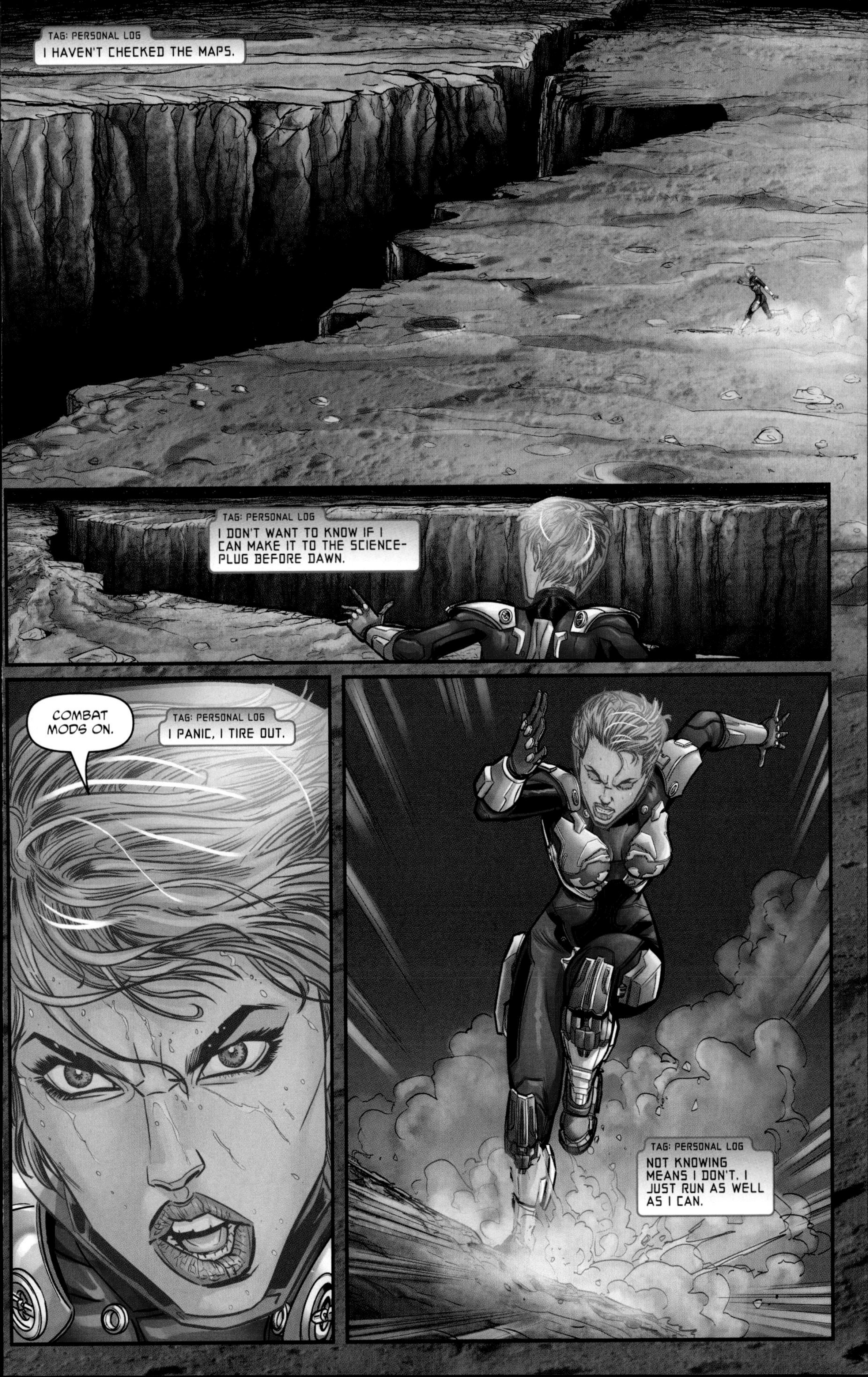
TAG: PERSONAL LOG
I HAVEN'T CHECKED THE MAPS.
TAG: PERSONAL LOG
I DON'T WANT TO KNOW IF I CAN MAKE IT TO THE SCIENCE-PLUG BEFORE DAWN.
COMBAT MODS ON.
TAG: PERSONAL LOG
I PANIC, I TIRE OUT.
TAG: PERSONAL LOG
NOT KNOWING MEANS I DON'T. I JUST RUN AS WELL AS I CAN.

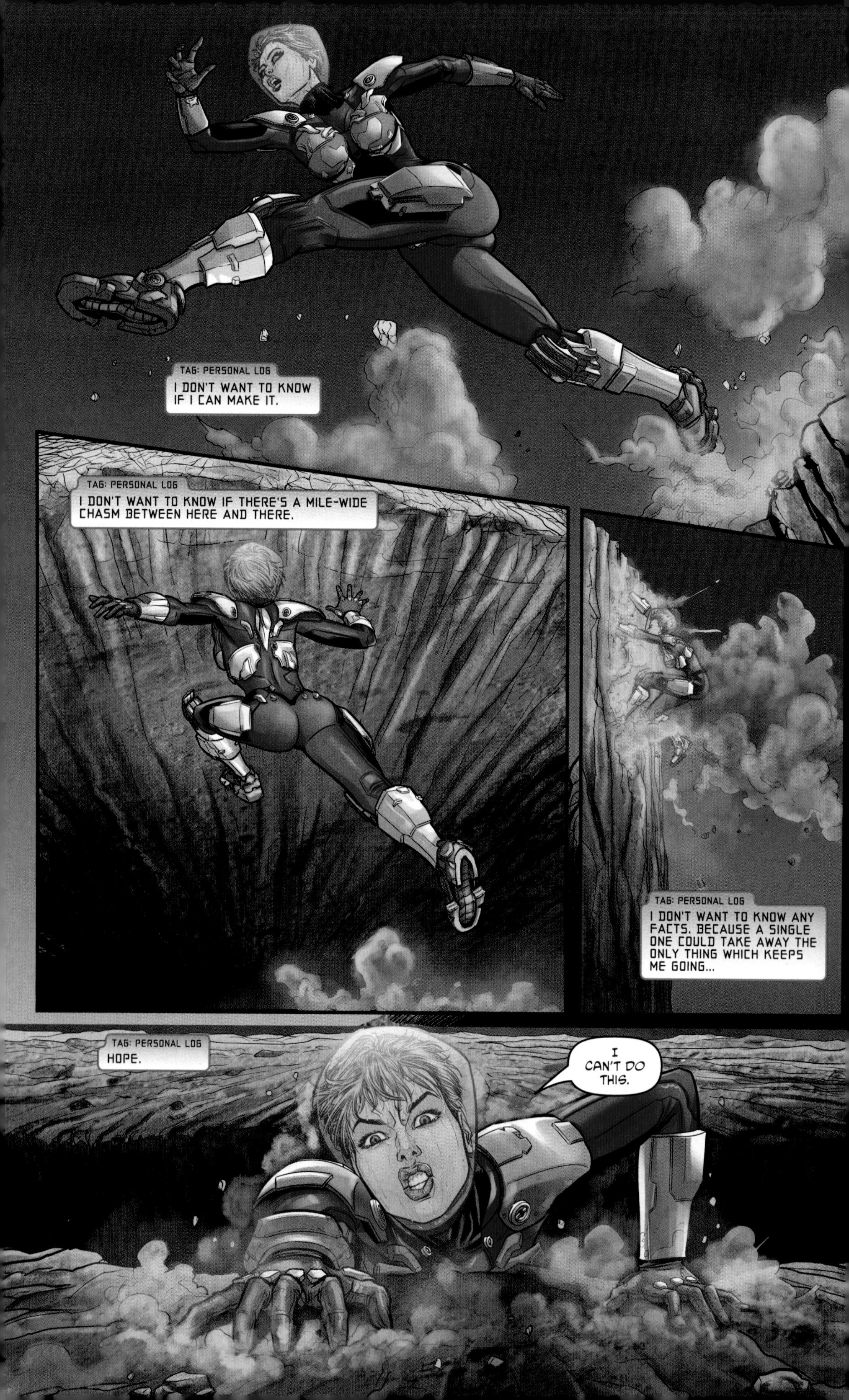
TAG: PERSONAL LOG
I DON'T WANT TO KNOW IF I CAN MAKE IT.
TAG: PERSONAL LOG
I DON'T WANT TO KNOW IF THERE'S A MILE-WIDE CHASM BETWEEN HERE AND THERE.
TAG: PERSONAL LOG
I DON'T WANT TO KNOW ANY FACTS. BECAUSE A SINGLE ONE COULD TAKE AWAY THE ONLY THING WHICH KEEPS ME GOING...
TAG: PERSONAL LOG
HOPE.
I CAN'T DO THIS.

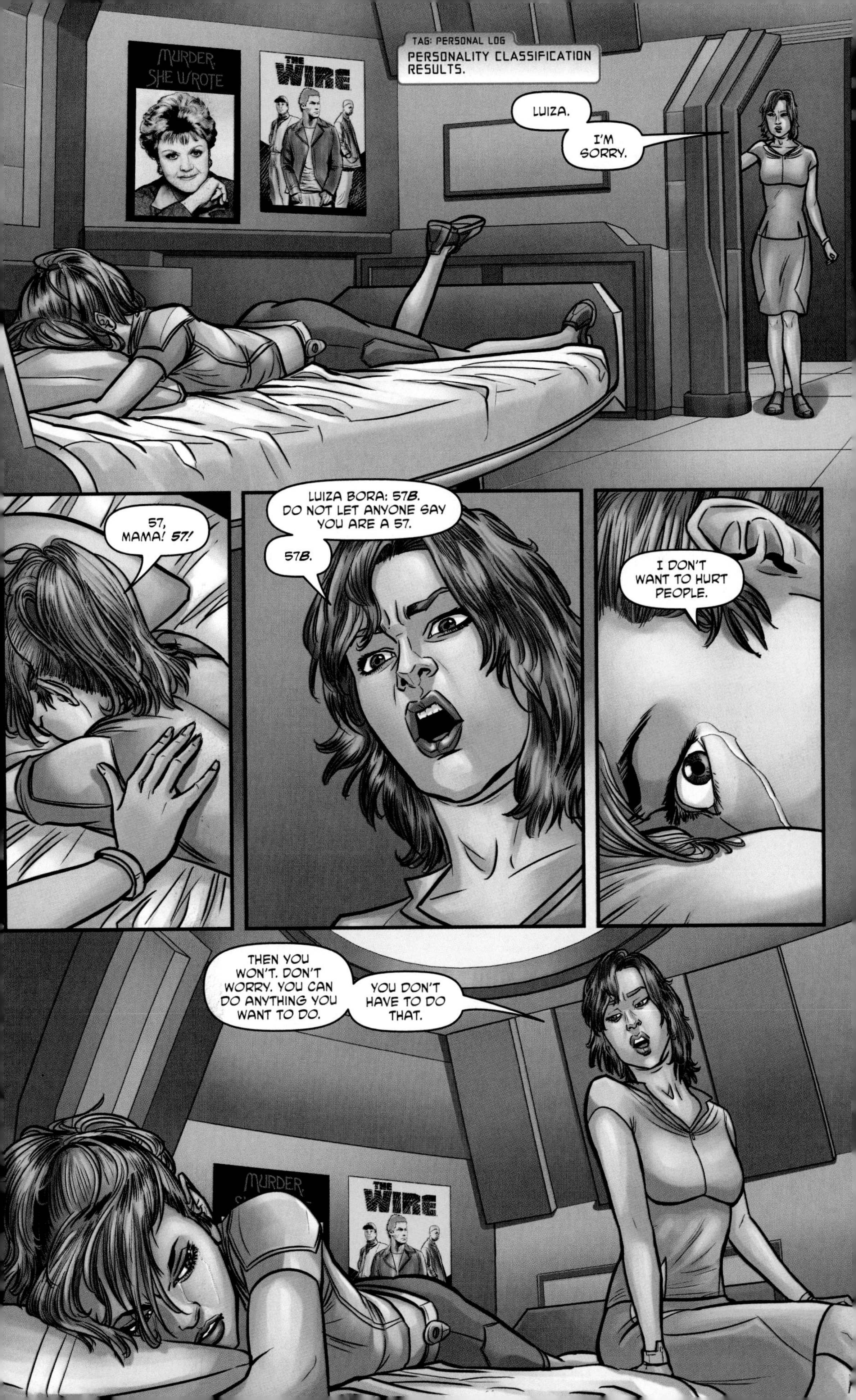
MURDER, SHE WROTE
THE WIRE
TAG: PERSONAL LOG
PERSONALITY CLASSIFICATION RESULTS.
LUIZA.
I'M SORRY.
57, MAMA! 57!
LUIZA BORA: 57B. DO NOT LET ANYONE SAY YOU ARE A 57.
57B.
I DON'T WANT TO HURT PEOPLE.
THEN YOU WON'T. DON'T WORRY. YOU CAN DO ANYTHING YOU WANT TO DO.
YOU DON'T HAVE TO DO THAT.
MURDER,
THE WIRE

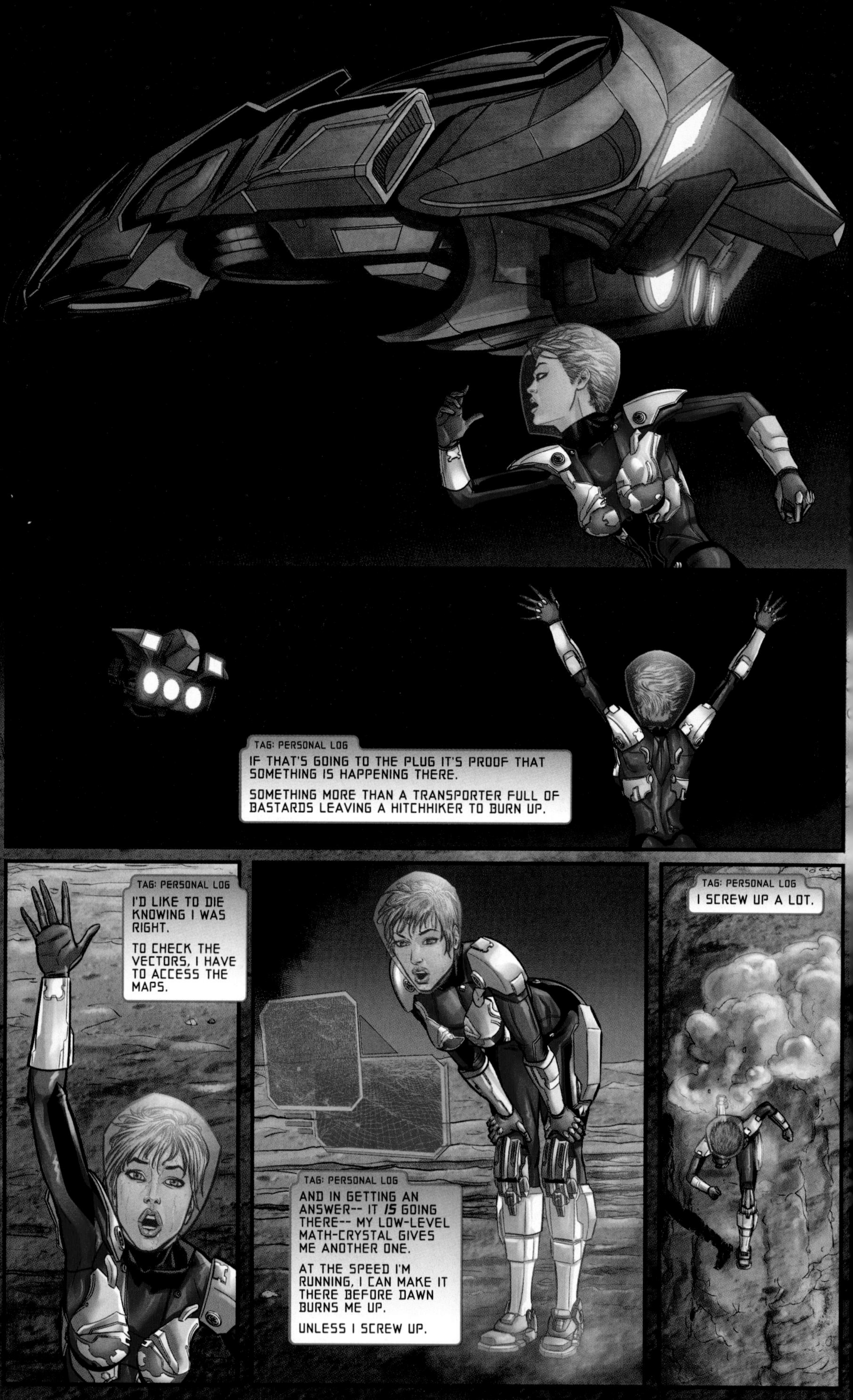
TAG: PERSONAL LOG
IF THAT'S GOING TO THE PLUG IT'S PROOF THAT SOMETHING IS HAPPENING THERE.
SOMETHING MORE THAN A TRANSPORTER FULL OF BASTARDS LEAVING A HITCHHIKER TO BURN UP.
TAG: PERSONAL LOG
I'D LIKE TO DIE KNOWING I WAS RIGHT.
TO CHECK THE VECTORS, I HAVE TO ACCESS THE MAPS.
TAG: PERSONAL LOG
AND IN GETTING AN ANSWER-- IT *IS* GOING THERE-- MY LOW-LEVEL MATH-CRYSTAL GIVES ME ANOTHER ONE.
AT THE SPEED I'M RUNNING, I CAN MAKE IT THERE BEFORE DAWN BURNS ME UP.
UNLESS I SCREW UP.
TAG: PERSONAL LOG
I SCREW UP A LOT.

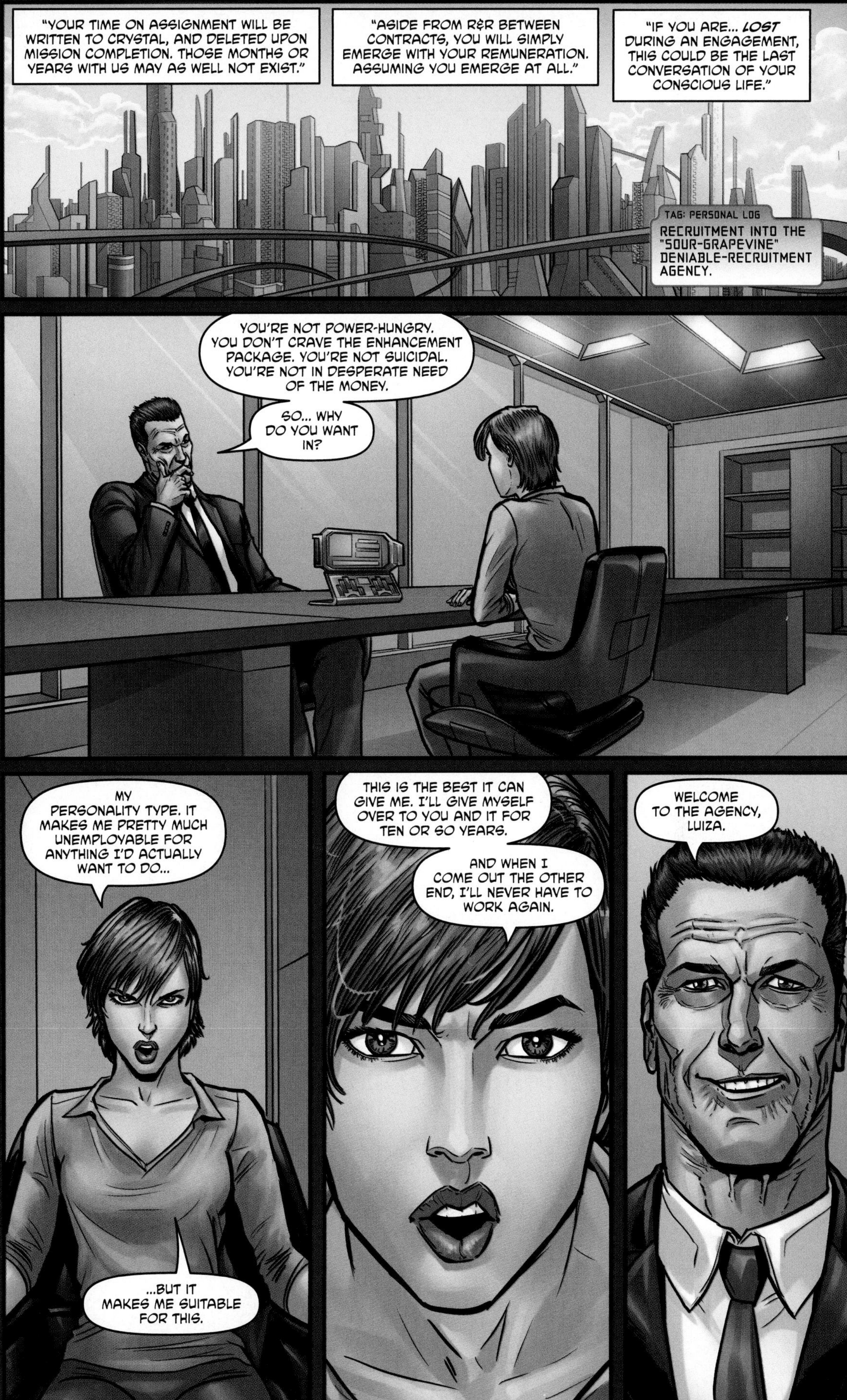
"YOUR TIME ON ASSIGNMENT WILL BE WRITTEN TO CRYSTAL, AND DELETED UPON MISSION COMPLETION. THOSE MONTHS OR YEARS WITH US MAY AS WELL NOT EXIST."
"ASIDE FROM R&R BETWEEN CONTRACTS, YOU WILL SIMPLY EMERGE WITH YOUR REMUNERATION. ASSUMING YOU EMERGE AT ALL."
"IF YOU ARE... *LOST* DURING AN ENGAGEMENT, THIS COULD BE THE LAST CONVERSATION OF YOUR CONSCIOUS LIFE."
TAG: PERSONAL LOG
RECRUITMENT INTO THE "SOUR-GRAPEVINE" DENIABLE-RECRUITMENT AGENCY.
YOU'RE NOT POWER-HUNGRY. YOU DON'T CRAVE THE ENHANCEMENT PACKAGE. YOU'RE NOT SUICIDAL. YOU'RE NOT IN DESPERATE NEED OF THE MONEY.
SO... WHY DO YOU WANT IN?
MY PERSONALITY TYPE. IT MAKES ME PRETTY MUCH UNEMPLOYABLE FOR ANYTHING I'D ACTUALLY WANT TO DO...
...BUT IT MAKES ME SUITABLE FOR THIS.
THIS IS THE BEST IT CAN GIVE ME. I'LL GIVE MYSELF OVER TO YOU AND IT FOR TEN OR SO YEARS.
AND WHEN I COME OUT THE OTHER END, I'LL NEVER HAVE TO WORK AGAIN.
WELCOME TO THE AGENCY, LUIZA.

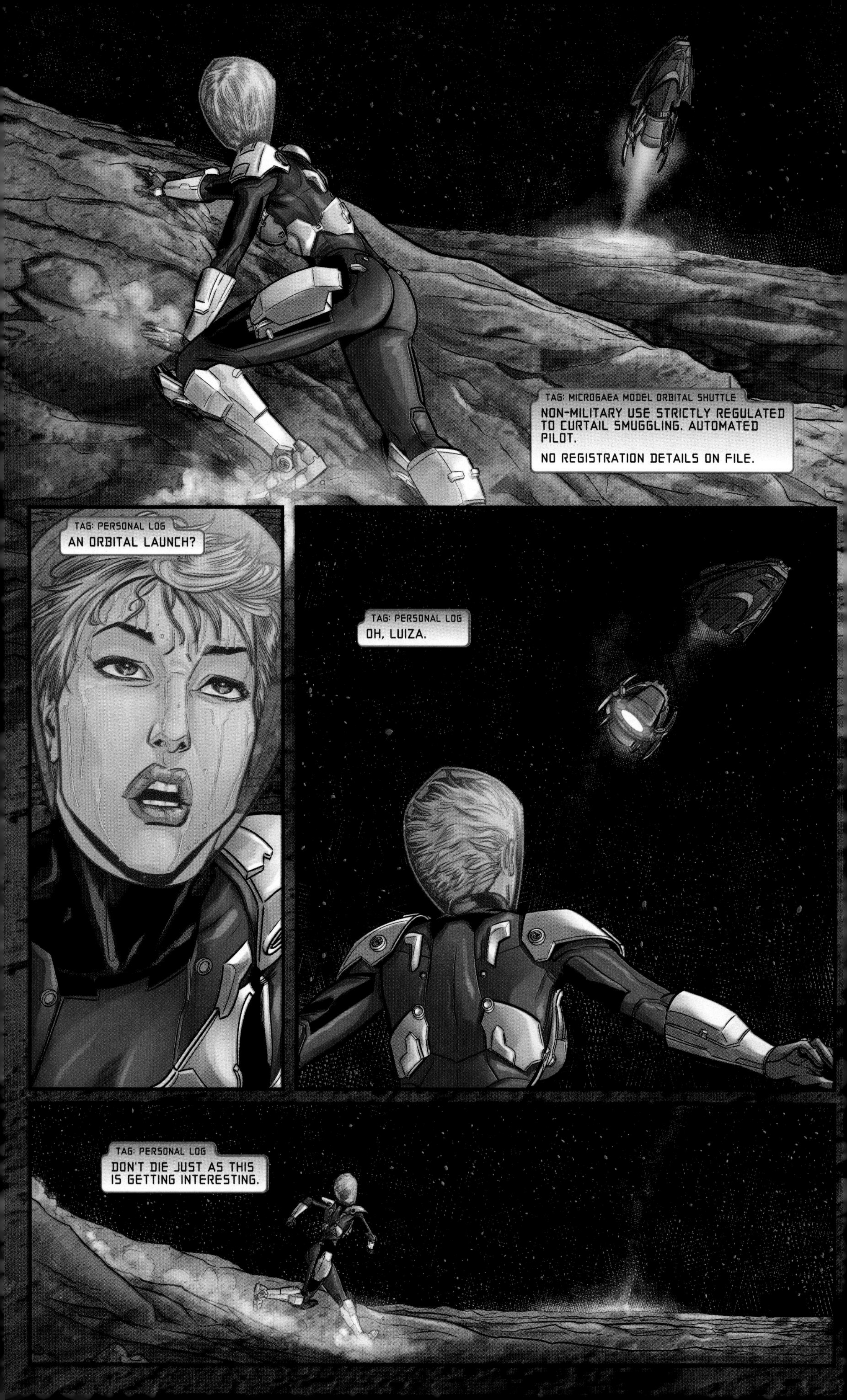
TAG: MICROGAEA MODEL ORBITAL SHUTTLE
NON-MILITARY USE STRICTLY REGULATED TO CURTAIL SMUGGLING. AUTOMATED PILOT.
NO REGISTRATION DETAILS ON FILE.
TAG: PERSONAL LOG
AN ORBITAL LAUNCH?
TAG: PERSONAL LOG
OH, LUIZA.
TAG: PERSONAL LOG
DON'T DIE JUST AS THIS IS GETTING INTERESTING.

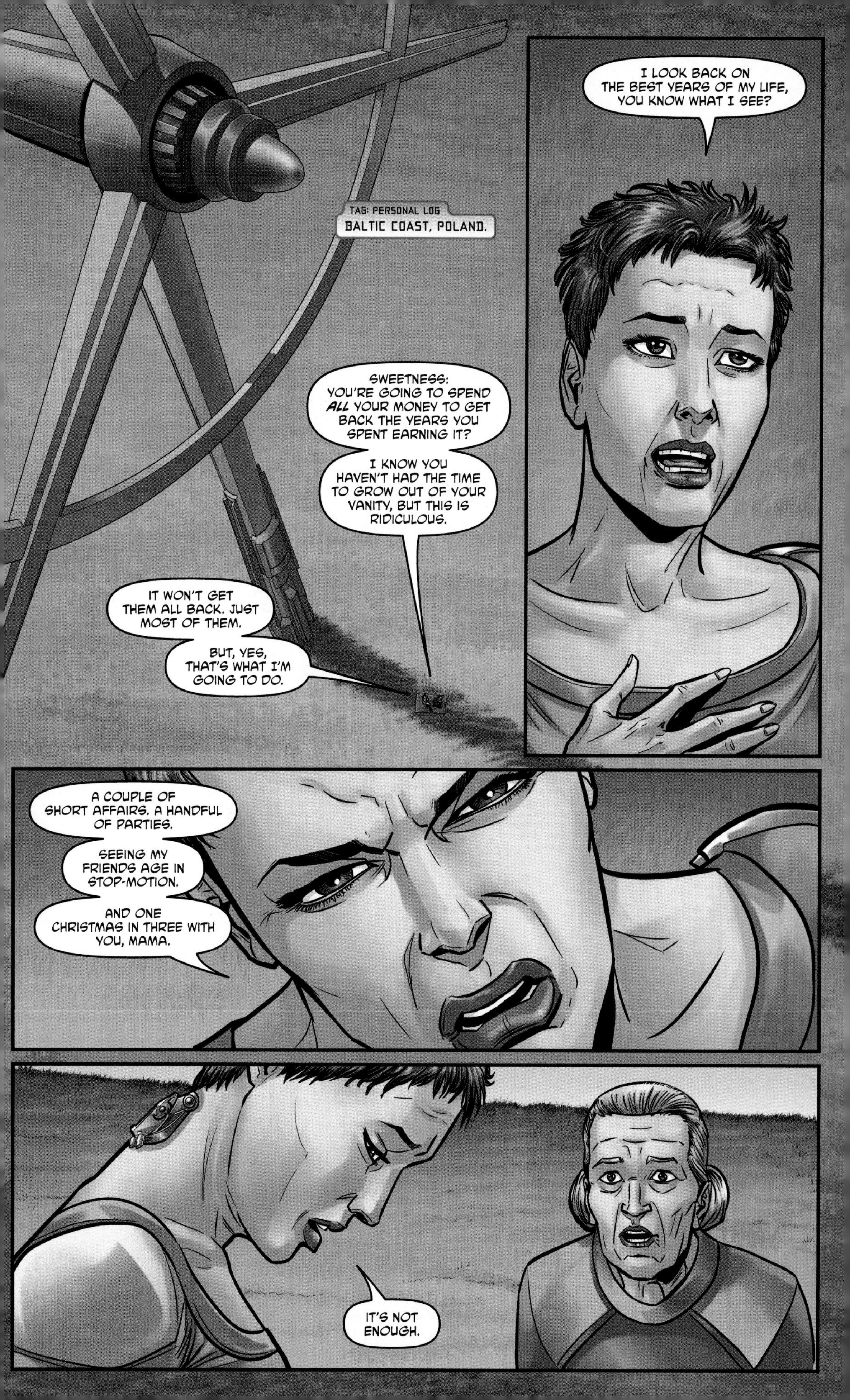
TAG: PERSONAL LOG
BALTIC COAST, POLAND.
I LOOK BACK ON THE BEST YEARS OF MY LIFE, YOU KNOW WHAT I SEE?
SWEETNESS: YOU'RE GOING TO SPEND *ALL* YOUR MONEY TO GET BACK THE YEARS YOU SPENT EARNING IT?
I KNOW YOU HAVEN'T HAD THE TIME TO GROW OUT OF YOUR VANITY, BUT THIS IS RIDICULOUS.
IT WON'T GET THEM ALL BACK. JUST MOST OF THEM.
BUT, YES, THAT'S WHAT I'M GOING TO DO.
A COUPLE OF SHORT AFFAIRS. A HANDFUL OF PARTIES.
SEEING MY FRIENDS AGE IN STOP-MOTION.
AND ONE CHRISTMAS IN THREE WITH YOU, MAMA.
IT'S NOT ENOUGH.

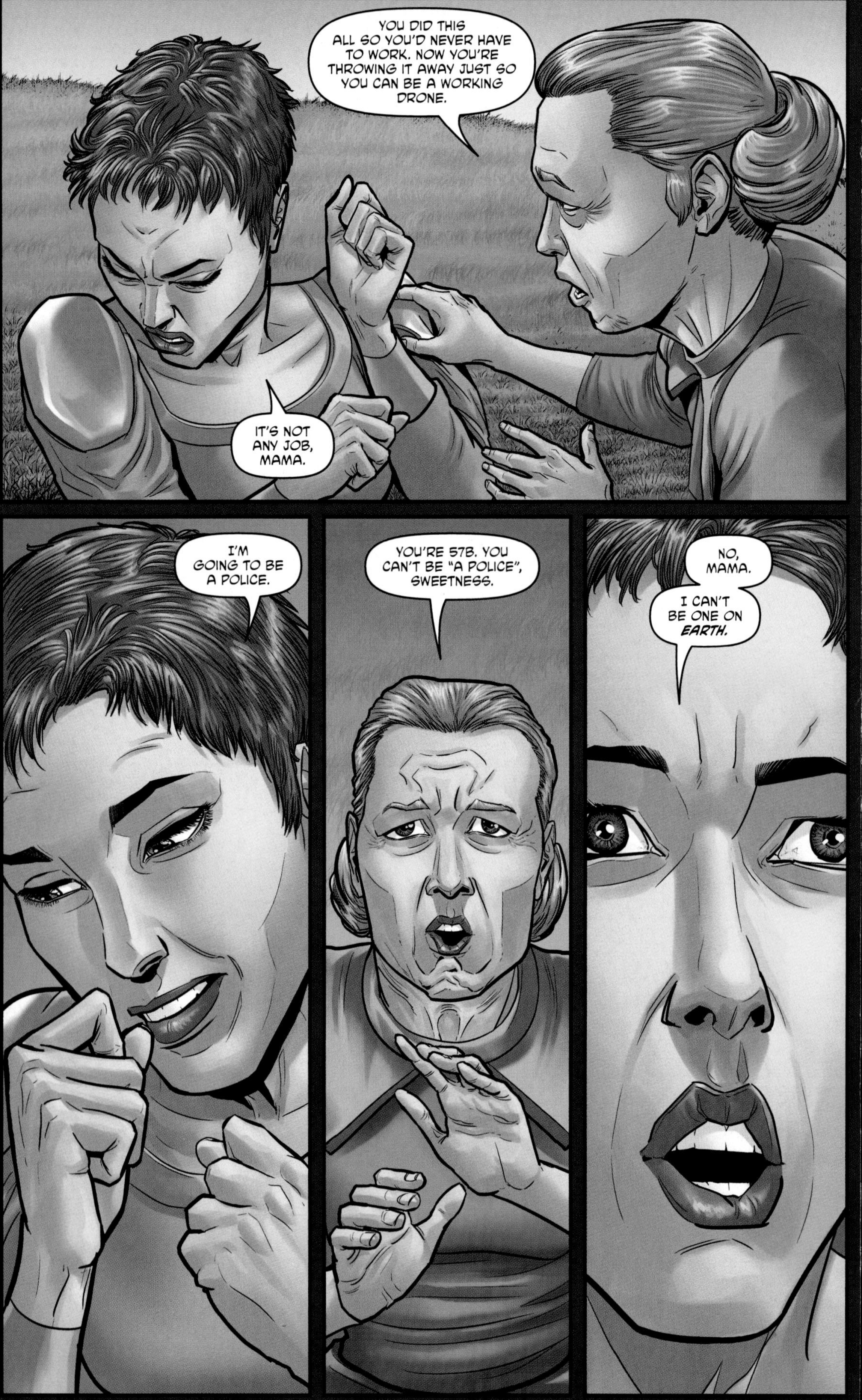
YOU DID THIS ALL SO YOU'D NEVER HAVE TO WORK. NOW YOU'RE THROWING IT AWAY JUST SO YOU CAN BE A WORKING DRONE.
IT'S NOT ANY JOB, MAMA.
I'M GOING TO BE A POLICE.
YOU'RE 57B. YOU CAN'T BE "A POLICE", SWEETNESS.
NO, MAMA.
I CAN'T BE ONE ON *EARTH.*

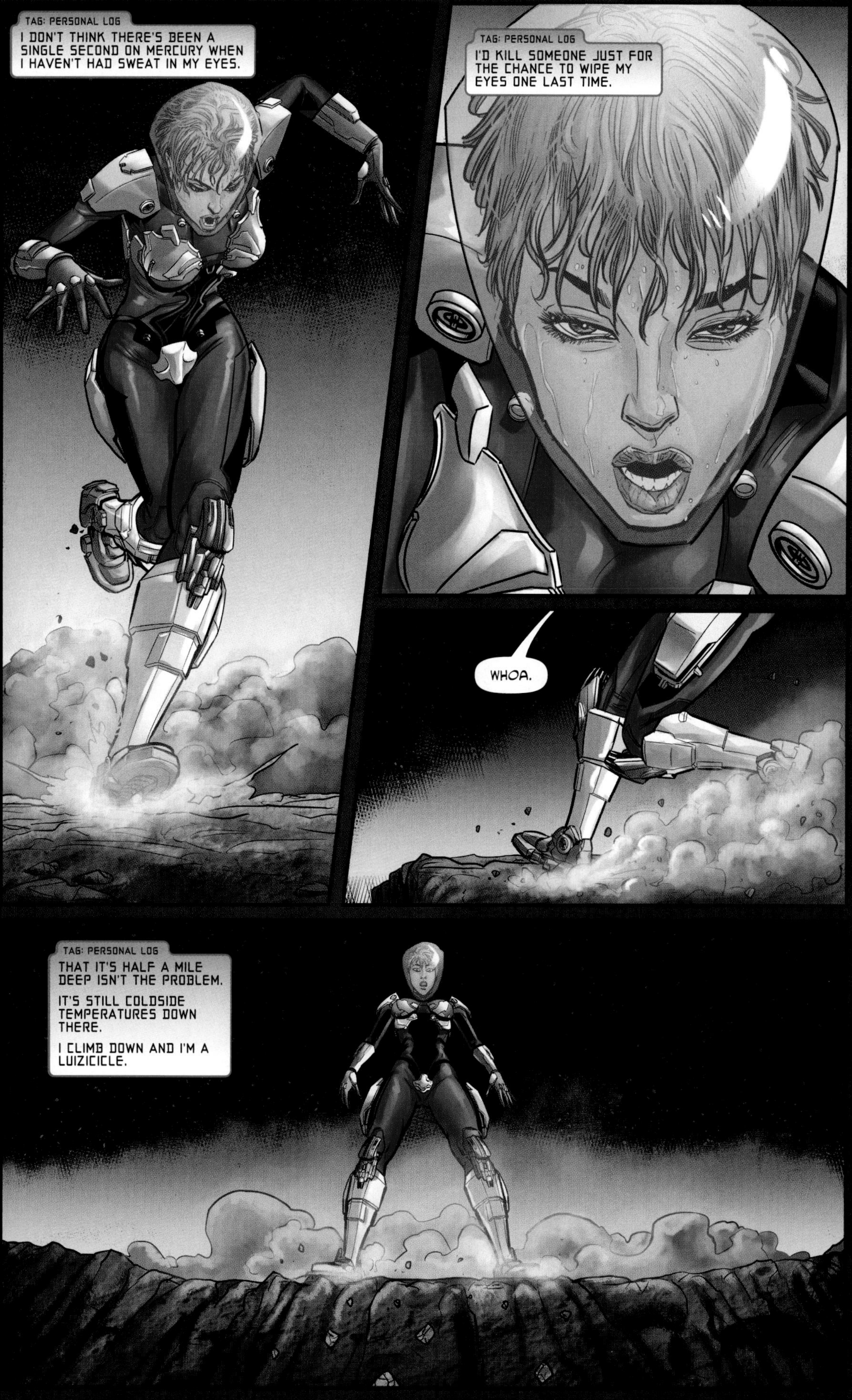
TAG: PERSONAL LOG
I DON'T THINK THERE'S BEEN A SINGLE SECOND ON MERCURY WHEN I HAVEN'T HAD SWEAT IN MY EYES.
TAG: PERSONAL LOG
I'D KILL SOMEONE JUST FOR THE CHANCE TO WIPE MY EYES ONE LAST TIME.
WHOA.
TAG: PERSONAL LOG
THAT IT'S HALF A MILE DEEP ISN'T THE PROBLEM.
IT'S STILL COLDSIDE TEMPERATURES DOWN THERE.
I CLIMB DOWN AND I'M A LUIZICICLE.

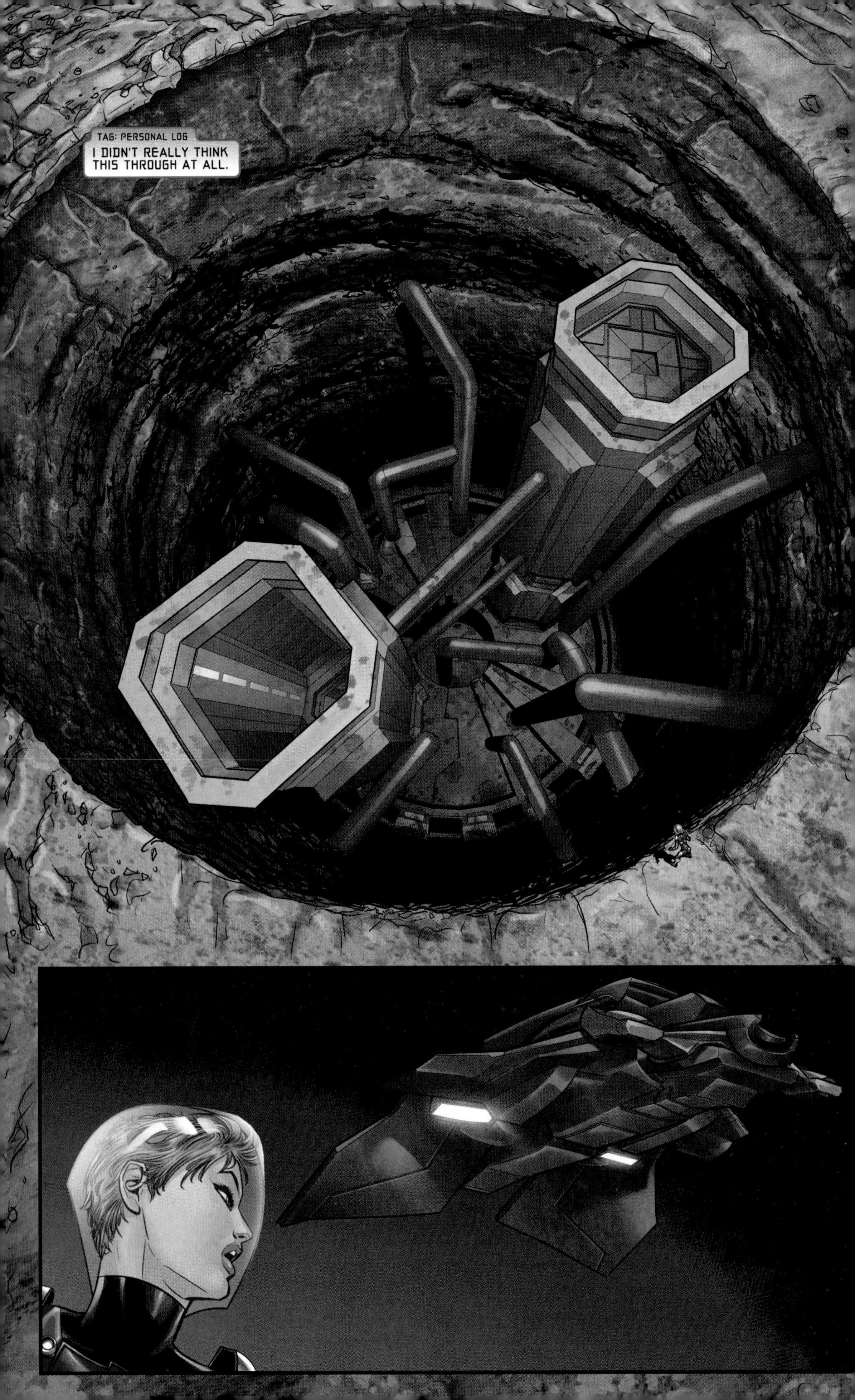
TAG: PERSONAL LOG
I DIDN'T REALLY THINK THIS THROUGH AT ALL.

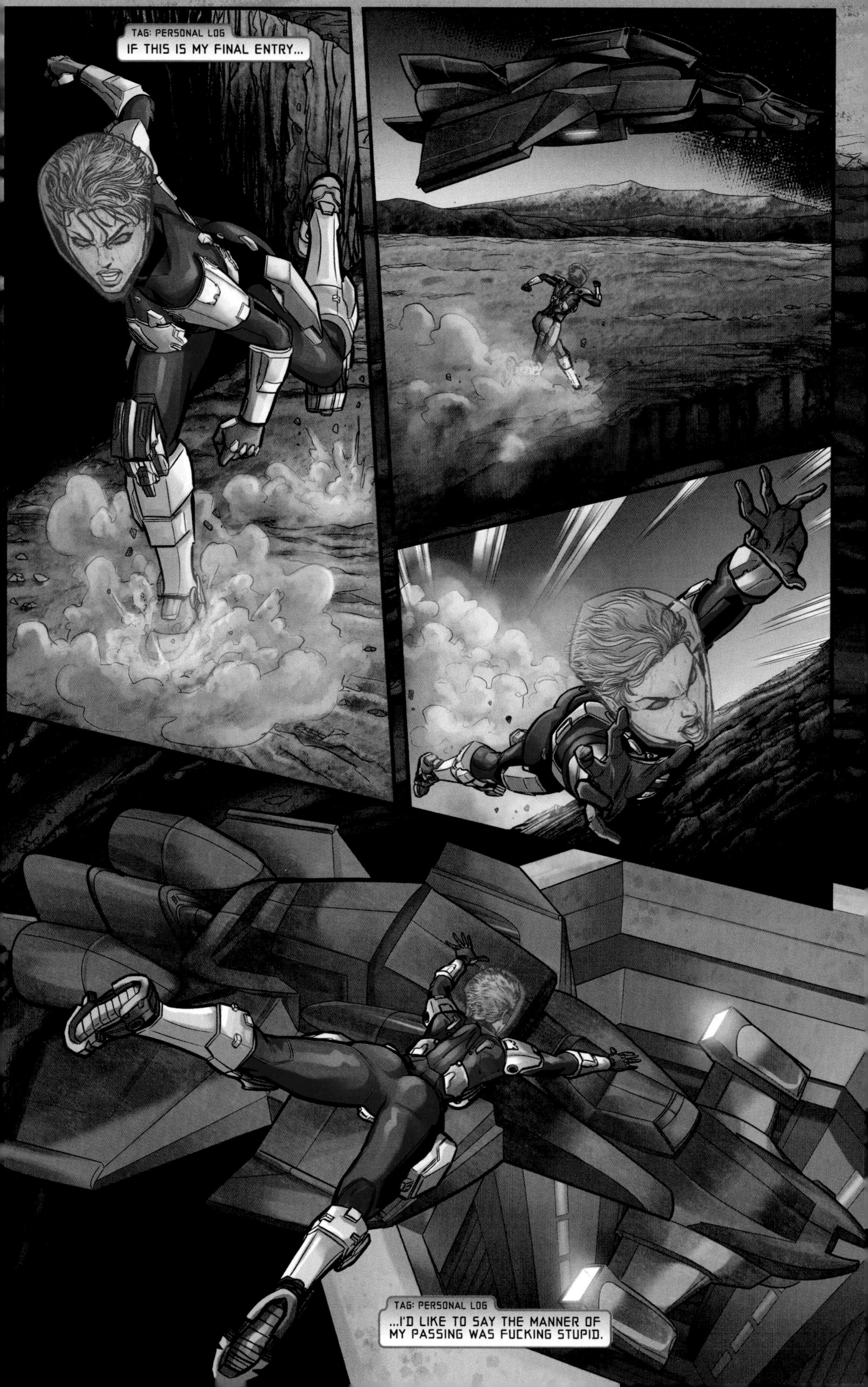
TAG: PERSONAL LOG
IF THIS IS MY FINAL ENTRY...
TAG: PERSONAL LOG
...I'D LIKE TO SAY THE MANNER OF MY PASSING WAS FUCKING STUPID.

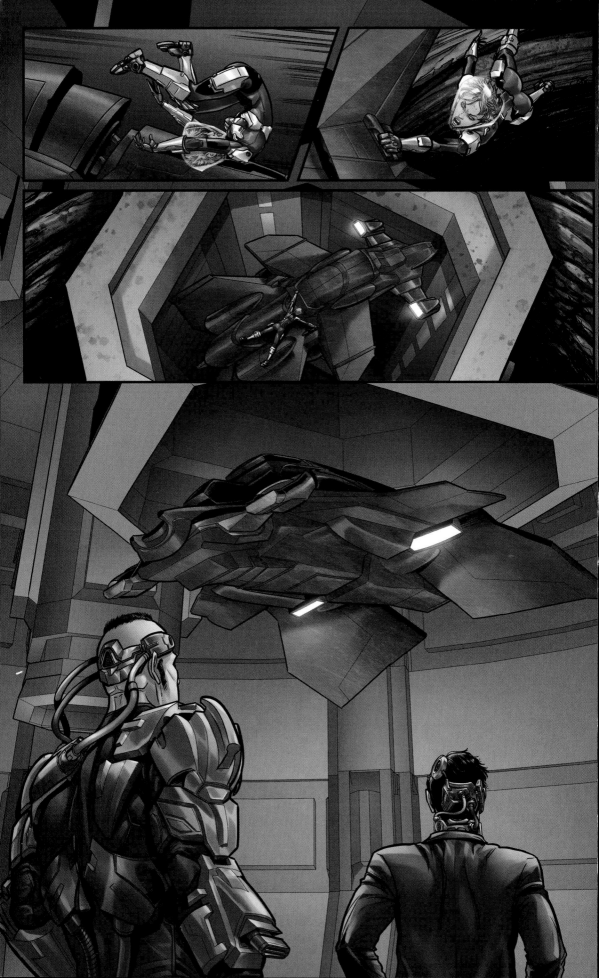

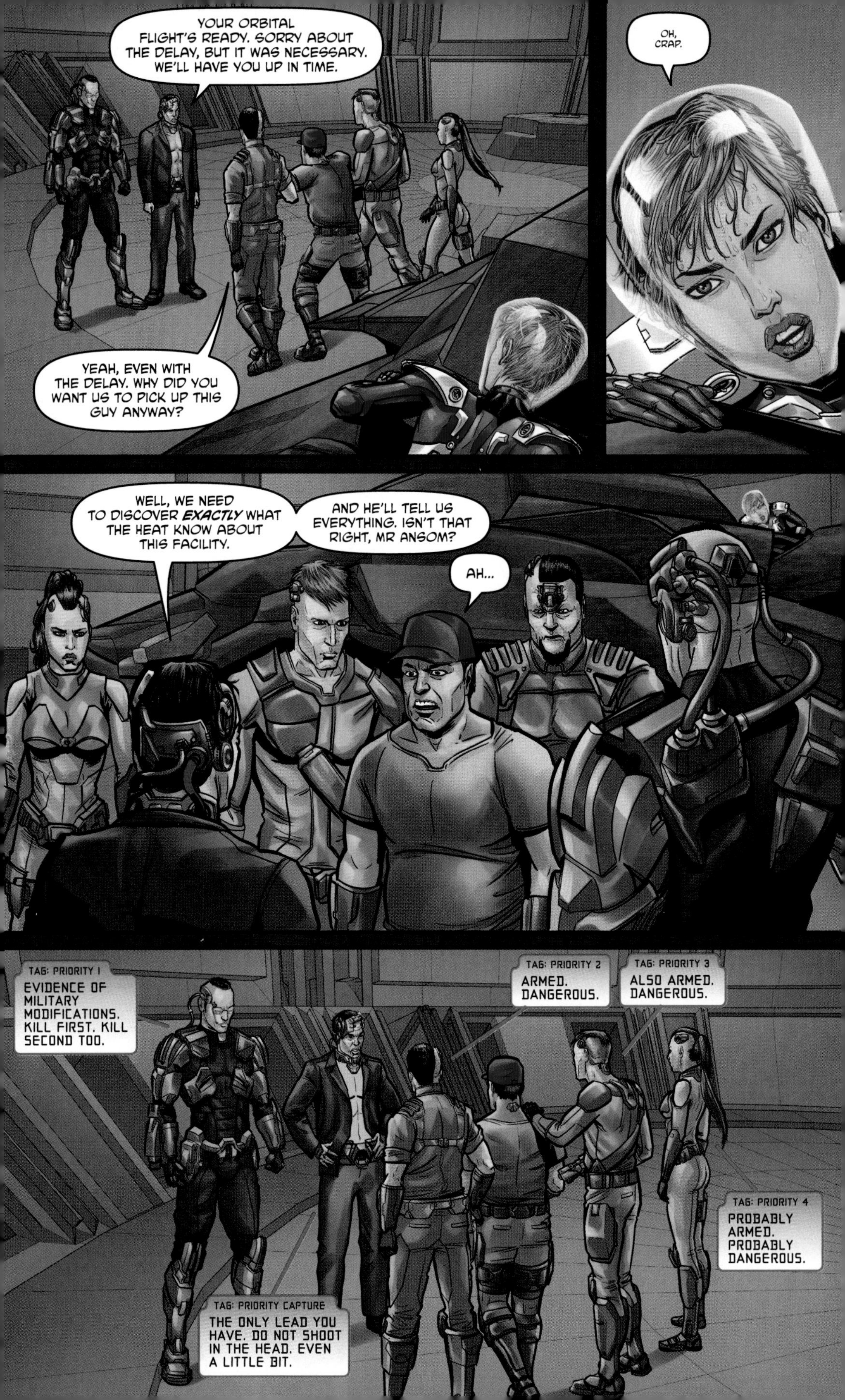
YOUR ORBITAL FLIGHT'S READY. SORRY ABOUT THE DELAY, BUT IT WAS NECESSARY. WE'LL HAVE YOU UP IN TIME.
YEAH, EVEN WITH THE DELAY. WHY DID YOU WANT US TO PICK UP THIS GUY ANYWAY?
OH, CRAP.
WELL, WE NEED TO DISCOVER EXACTLY WHAT THE HEAT KNOW ABOUT THIS FACILITY.
AND HE'LL TELL US EVERYTHING. ISN'T THAT RIGHT, MR ANSOM?
AH...
TAG: PRIORITY 1
EVIDENCE OF MILITARY MODIFICATIONS. KILL FIRST. KILL SECOND TOO.
TAG: PRIORITY 2
ARMED. DANGEROUS.
TAG: PRIORITY 3
ALSO ARMED. DANGEROUS.
TAG: PRIORITY 4
PROBABLY ARMED. PROBABLY DANGEROUS.
TAG: PRIORITY CAPTURE
THE ONLY LEAD YOU HAVE. DO NOT SHOOT IN THE HEAD. EVEN A LITTLE BIT.

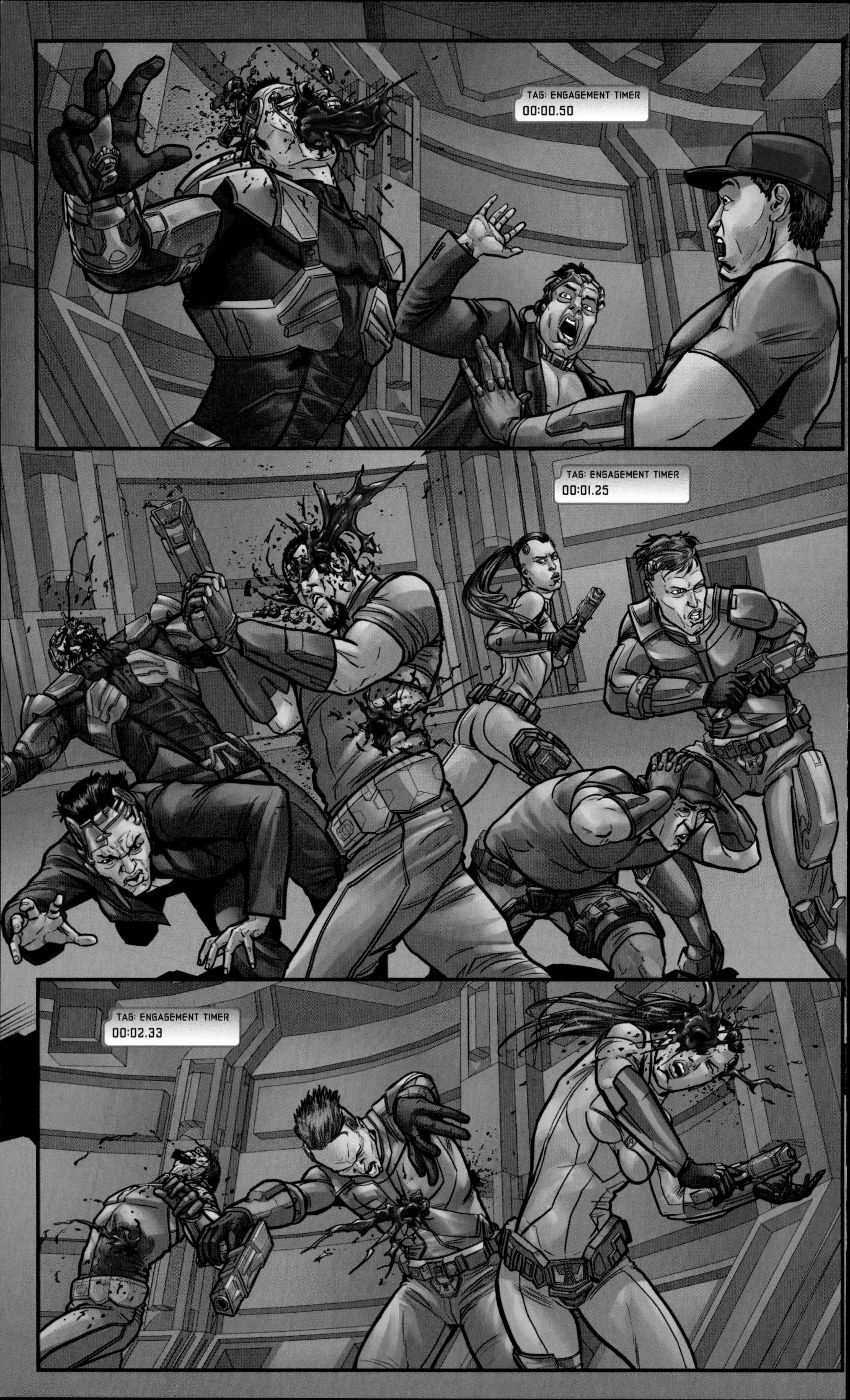
TAG: ENGAGEMENT TIMER
00:00.50
TAG: ENGAGEMENT TIMER
00:01.25
TAG: ENGAGEMENT TIMER
00:02.33

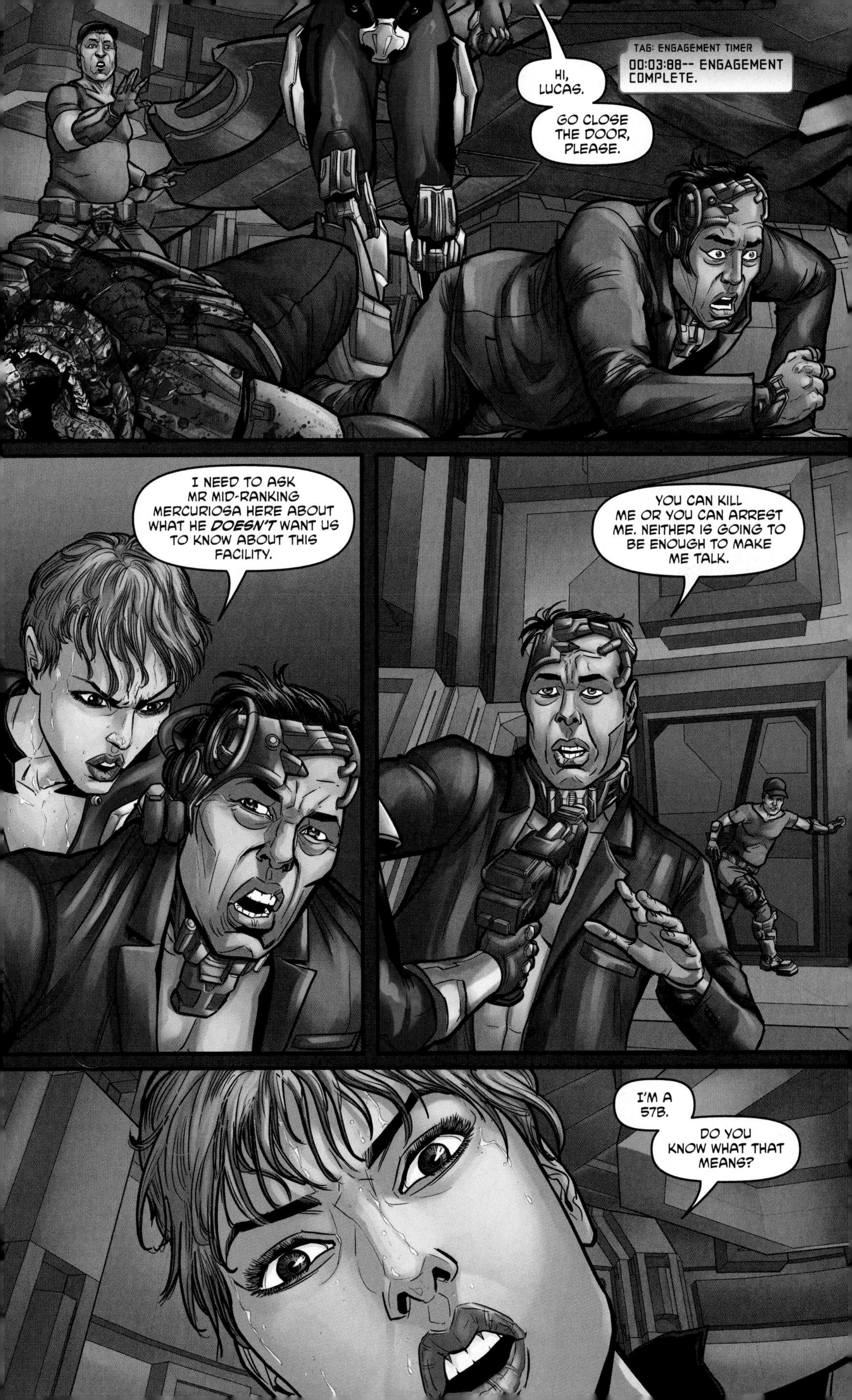
HI, LUCAS.
GO CLOSE THE DOOR, PLEASE.
TAG: ENGAGEMENT TIMER
00:03:88-- ENGAGEMENT COMPLETE.
I NEED TO ASK MR MID-RANKING MERCURIOSA HERE ABOUT WHAT HE *DOESN'T* WANT US TO KNOW ABOUT THIS FACILITY.
YOU CAN KILL ME OR YOU CAN ARREST ME. NEITHER IS GOING TO BE ENOUGH TO MAKE ME TALK.
I'M A 57B.
DO YOU KNOW WHAT THAT MEANS?

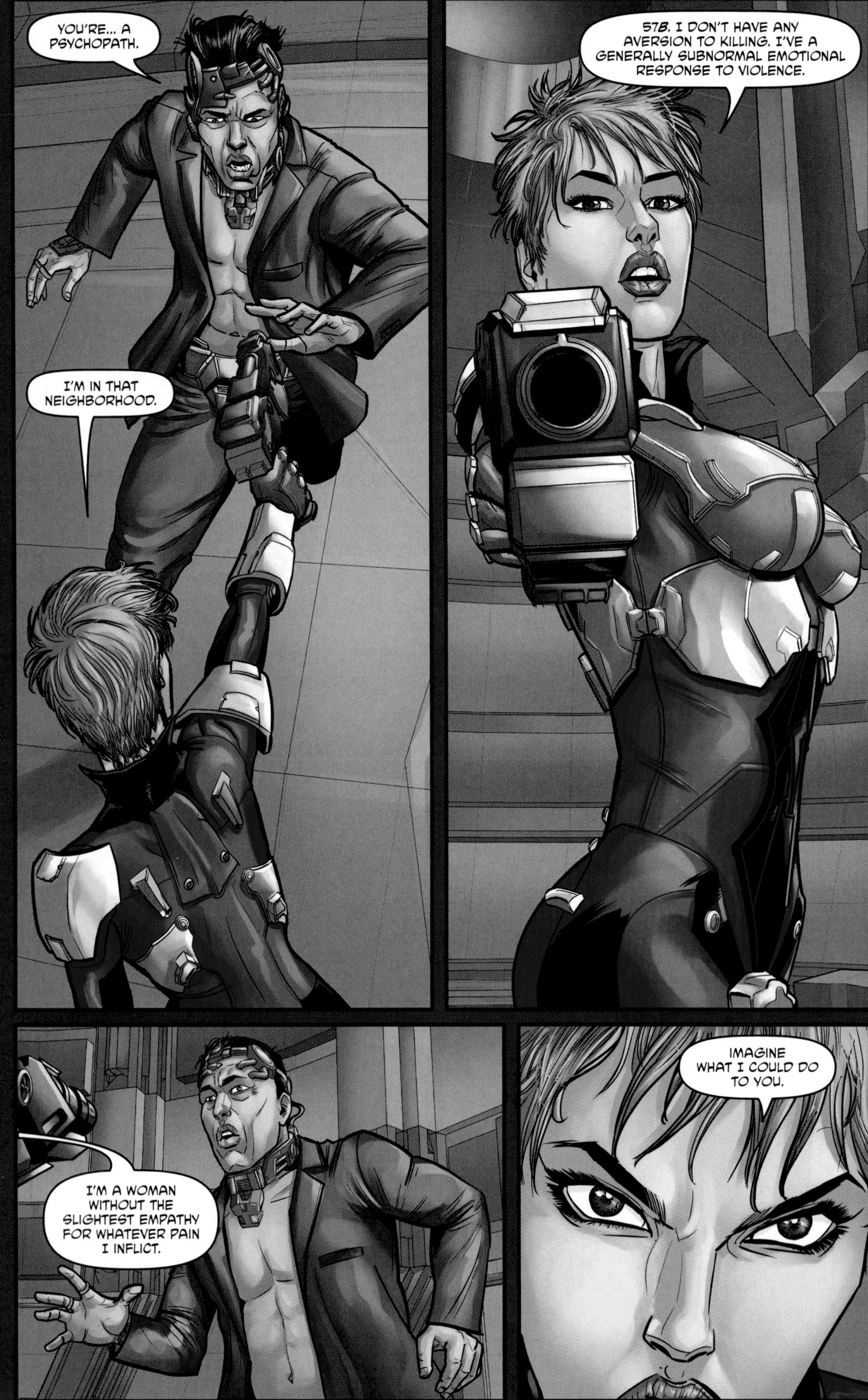
YOU'RE... A PSYCHOPATH.
I'M IN THAT NEIGHBORHOOD.
57B. I DON'T HAVE ANY AVERSION TO KILLING. I'VE A GENERALLY SUBNORMAL EMOTIONAL RESPONSE TO VIOLENCE.
I'M A WOMAN WITHOUT THE SLIGHTEST EMPATHY FOR WHATEVER PAIN I INFLICT.
IMAGINE WHAT I COULD DO TO YOU.

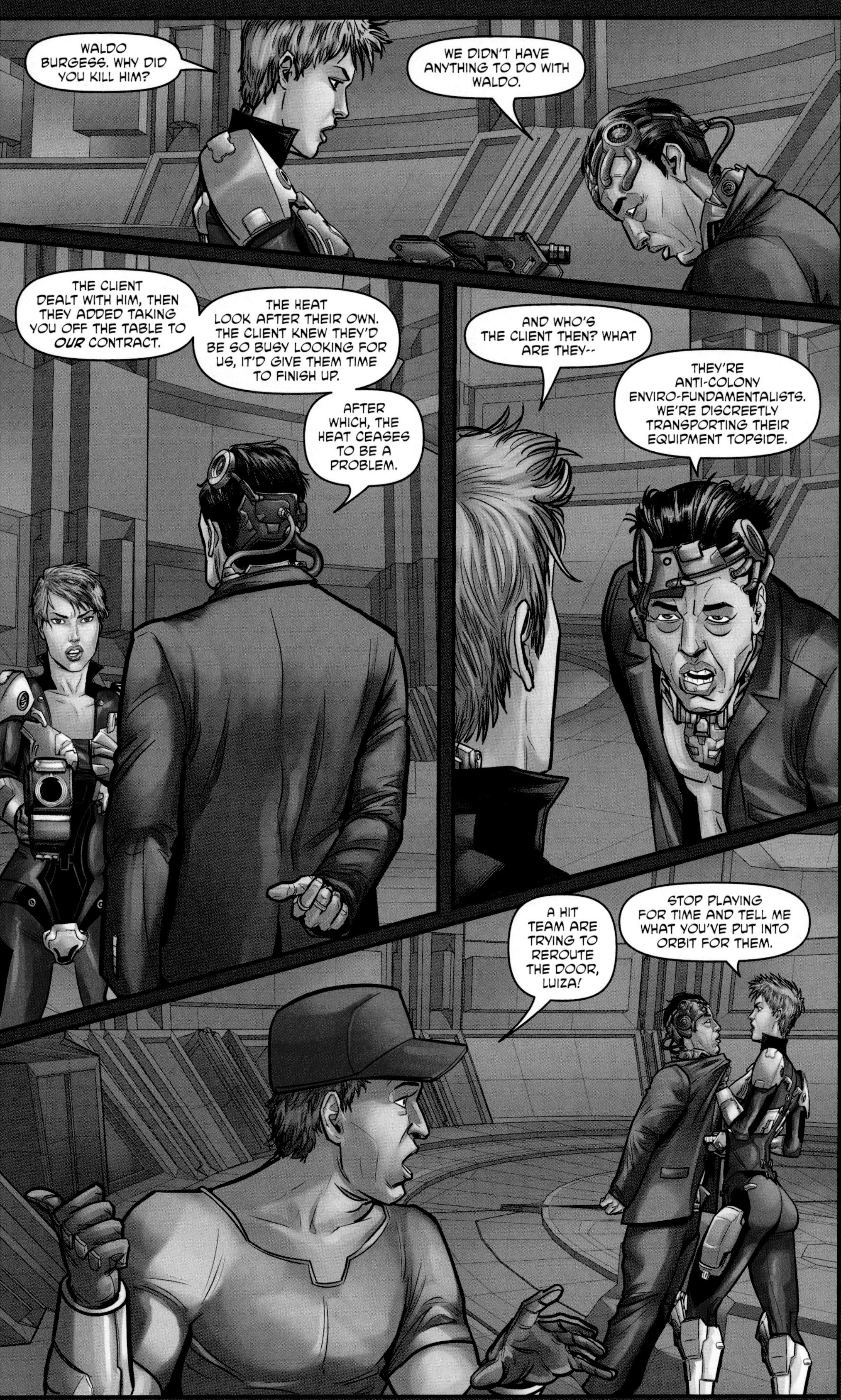
WALDO BURGESS. WHY DID YOU KILL HIM?
WE DIDN'T HAVE ANYTHING TO DO WITH WALDO.
THE CLIENT DEALT WITH HIM, THEN THEY ADDED TAKING YOU OFF THE TABLE TO *OUR* CONTRACT.
THE HEAT LOOK AFTER THEIR OWN. THE CLIENT KNEW THEY'D BE SO BUSY LOOKING FOR US, IT'D GIVE THEM TIME TO FINISH UP.
AFTER WHICH, THE HEAT CEASES TO BE A PROBLEM.
AND WHO'S THE CLIENT THEN? WHAT ARE THEY--
THEY'RE ANTI-COLONY ENVIRO-FUNDAMENTALISTS. WE'RE DISCREETLY TRANSPORTING THEIR EQUIPMENT TOPSIDE.
STOP PLAYING FOR TIME AND TELL ME WHAT YOU'VE PUT INTO ORBIT FOR THEM.
A HIT TEAM ARE TRYING TO REROUTE THE DOOR, LUIZA!

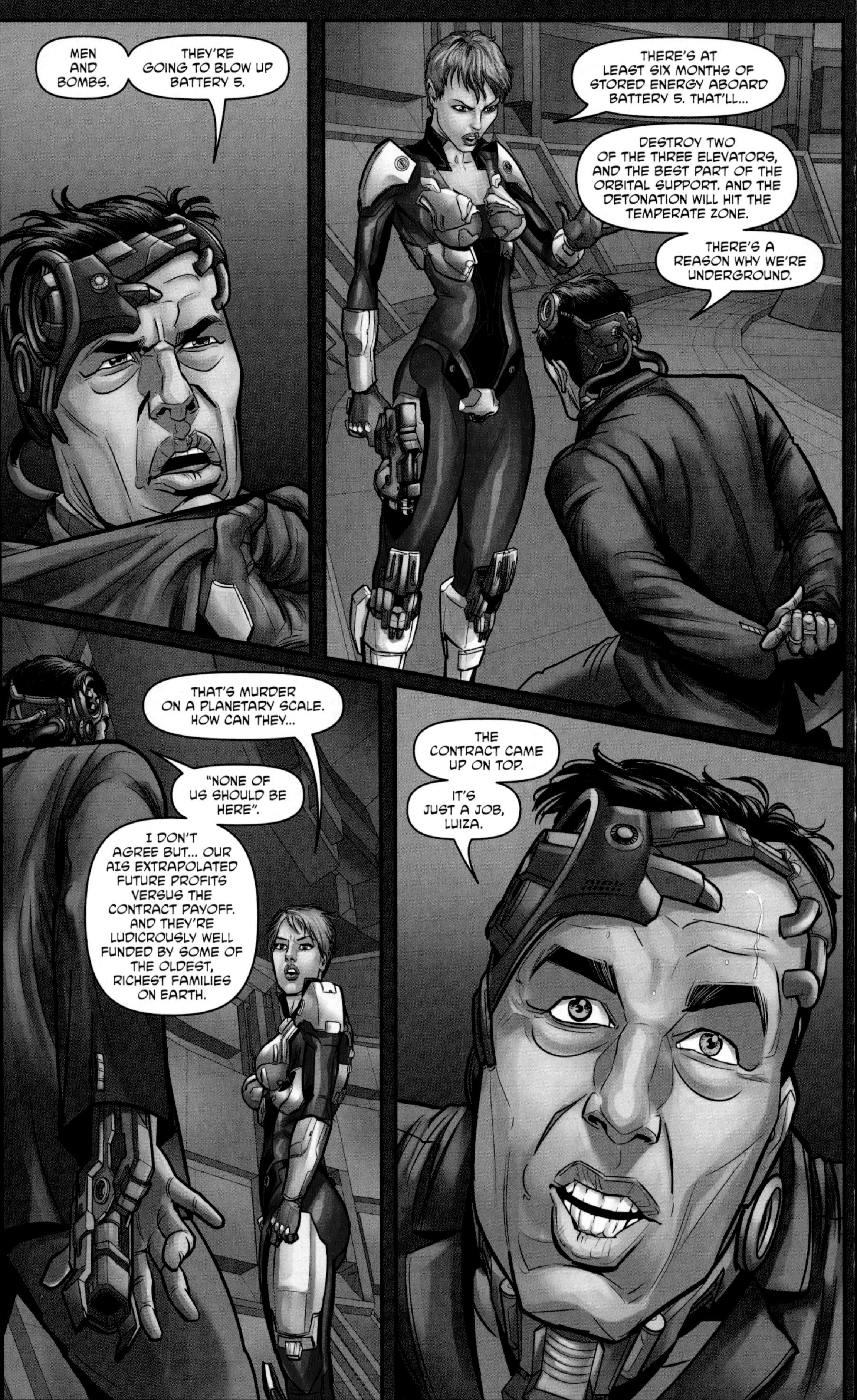
MEN AND BOMBS.
THEY'RE GOING TO BLOW UP BATTERY 5.
THERE'S AT LEAST SIX MONTHS OF STORED ENERGY ABOARD BATTERY 5. THAT'LL...
DESTROY TWO OF THE THREE ELEVATORS, AND THE BEST PART OF THE ORBITAL SUPPORT. AND THE DETONATION WILL HIT THE TEMPERATE ZONE.
THERE'S A REASON WHY WE'RE UNDERGROUND.
THAT'S MURDER ON A PLANETARY SCALE. HOW CAN THEY...
"NONE OF US SHOULD BE HERE".
I DON'T AGREE BUT... OUR AIS EXTRAPOLATED FUTURE PROFITS VERSUS THE CONTRACT PAYOFF. AND THEY'RE LUDICROUSLY WELL FUNDED BY SOME OF THE OLDEST, RICHEST FAMILIES ON EARTH.
THE CONTRACT CAME UP ON TOP.
IT'S JUST A JOB, LUIZA.

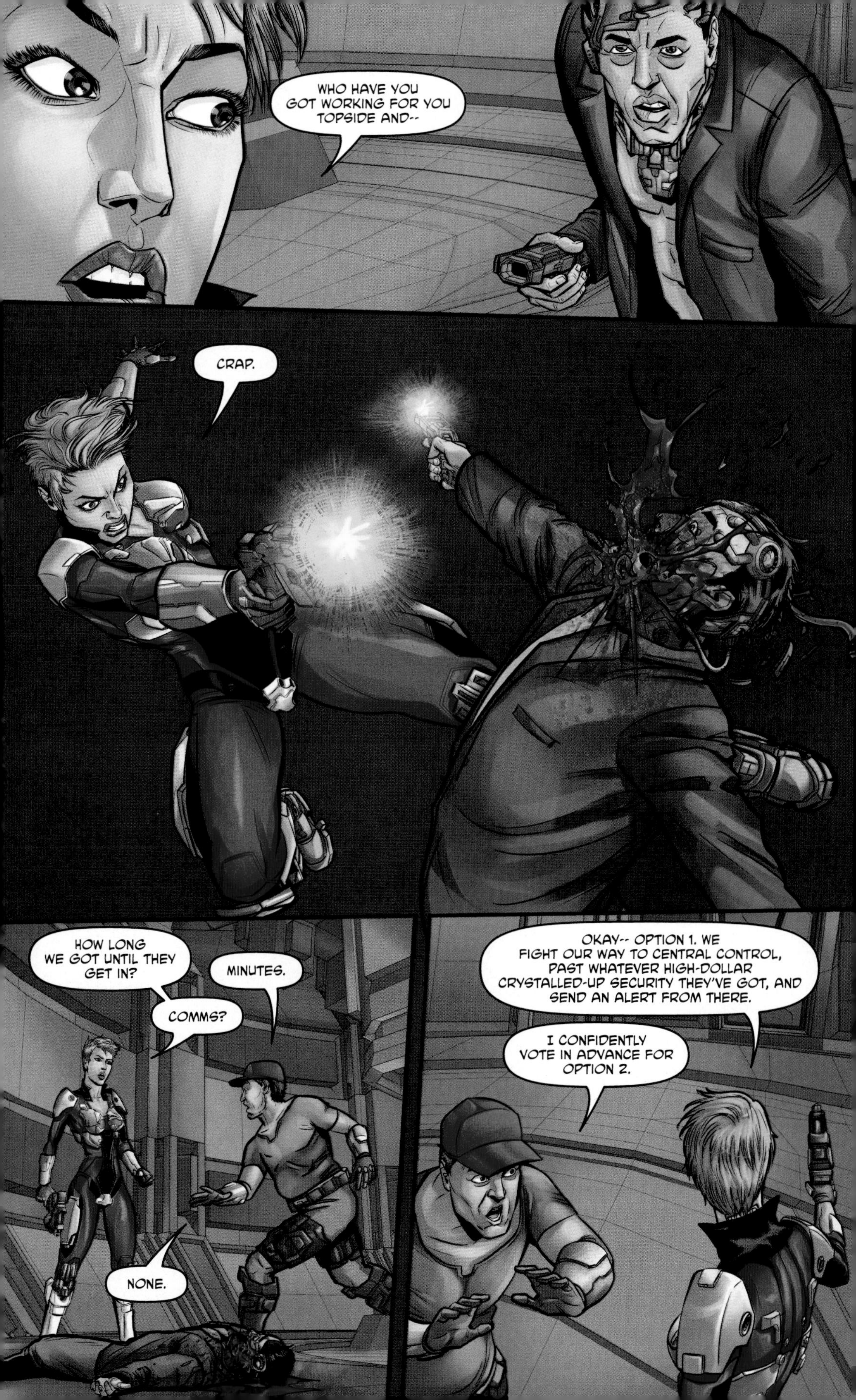
WHO HAVE YOU GOT WORKING FOR YOU TOPSIDE AND--
CRAP.
HOW LONG WE GOT UNTIL THEY GET IN?
MINUTES.
COMMS?
NONE.
OKAY-- OPTION 1. WE FIGHT OUR WAY TO CENTRAL CONTROL, PAST WHATEVER HIGH-DOLLAR CRYSTALLED-UP SECURITY THEY'VE GOT, AND SEND AN ALERT FROM THERE.
I CONFIDENTLY VOTE IN ADVANCE FOR OPTION 2.

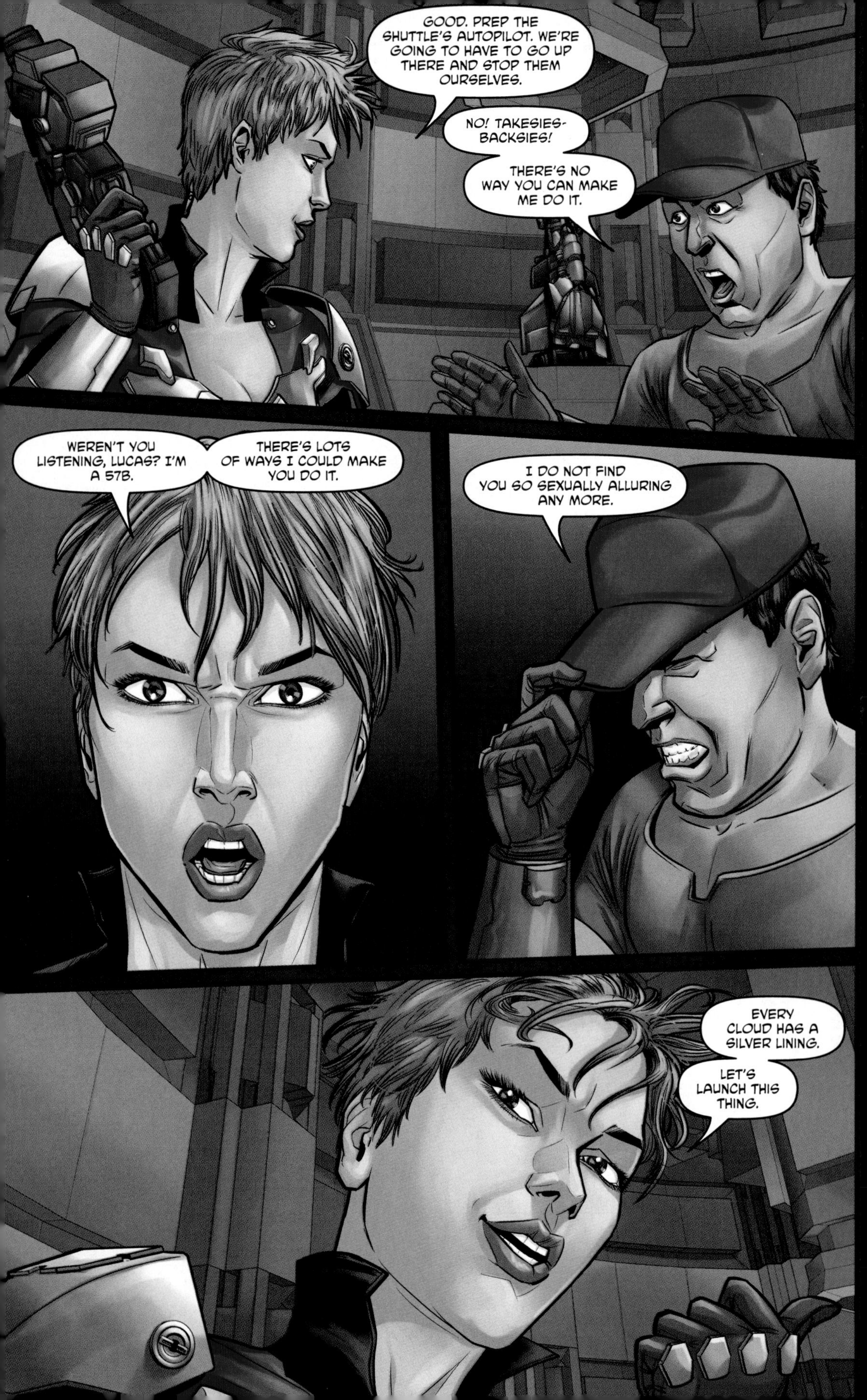
GOOD. PREP THE SHUTTLE'S AUTOPILOT. WE'RE GOING TO HAVE TO GO UP THERE AND STOP THEM OURSELVES.
NO! TAKESIES-BACKSIES!
THERE'S NO WAY YOU CAN MAKE ME DO IT.
WEREN'T YOU LISTENING, LUCAS? I'M A 57B.
THERE'S LOTS OF WAYS I COULD MAKE YOU DO IT.
I DO NOT FIND YOU SO SEXUALLY ALLURING ANY MORE.
EVERY CLOUD HAS A SILVER LINING.
LET'S LAUNCH THIS THING.

chapter 5

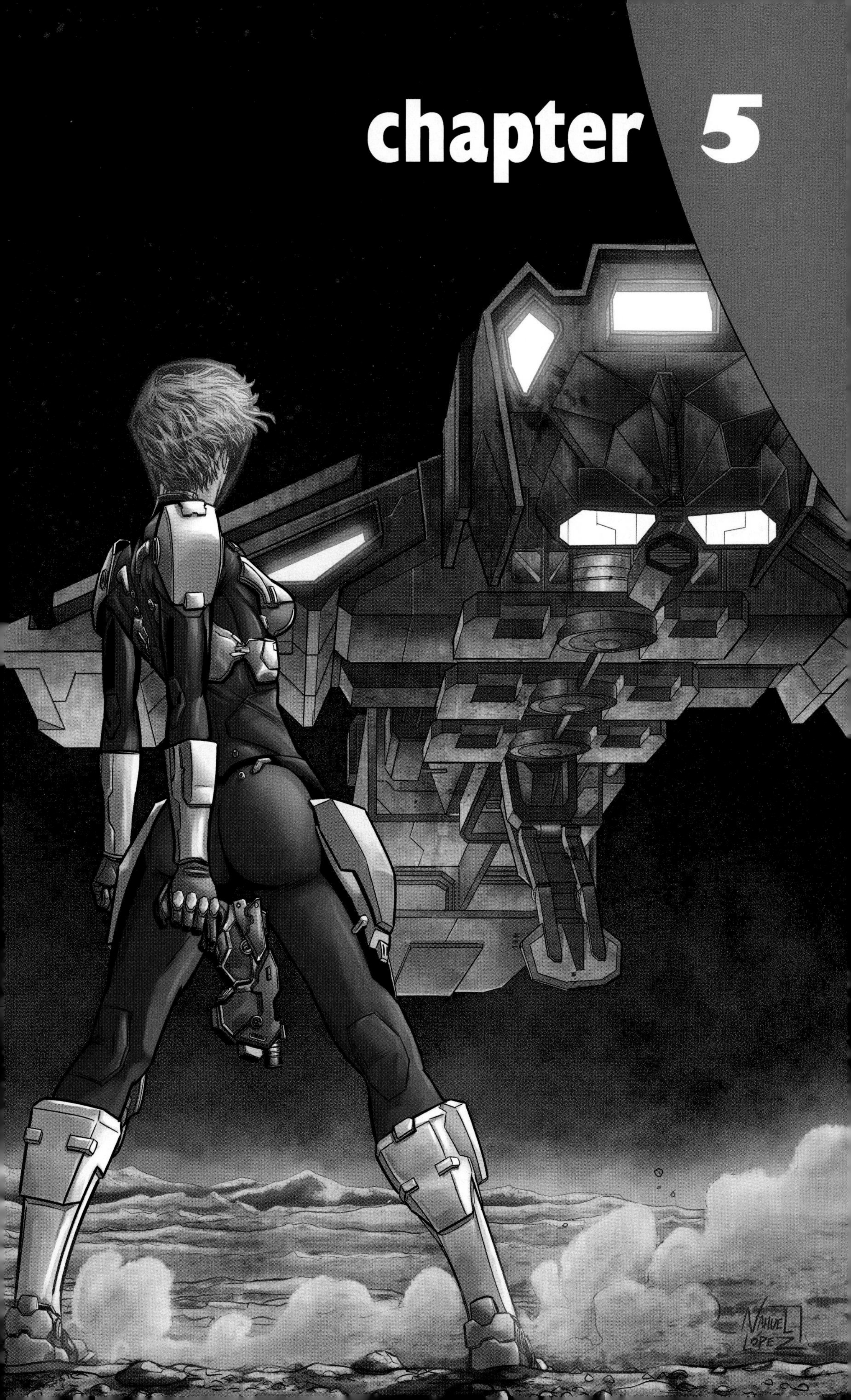
NAHUEL LÓPEZ

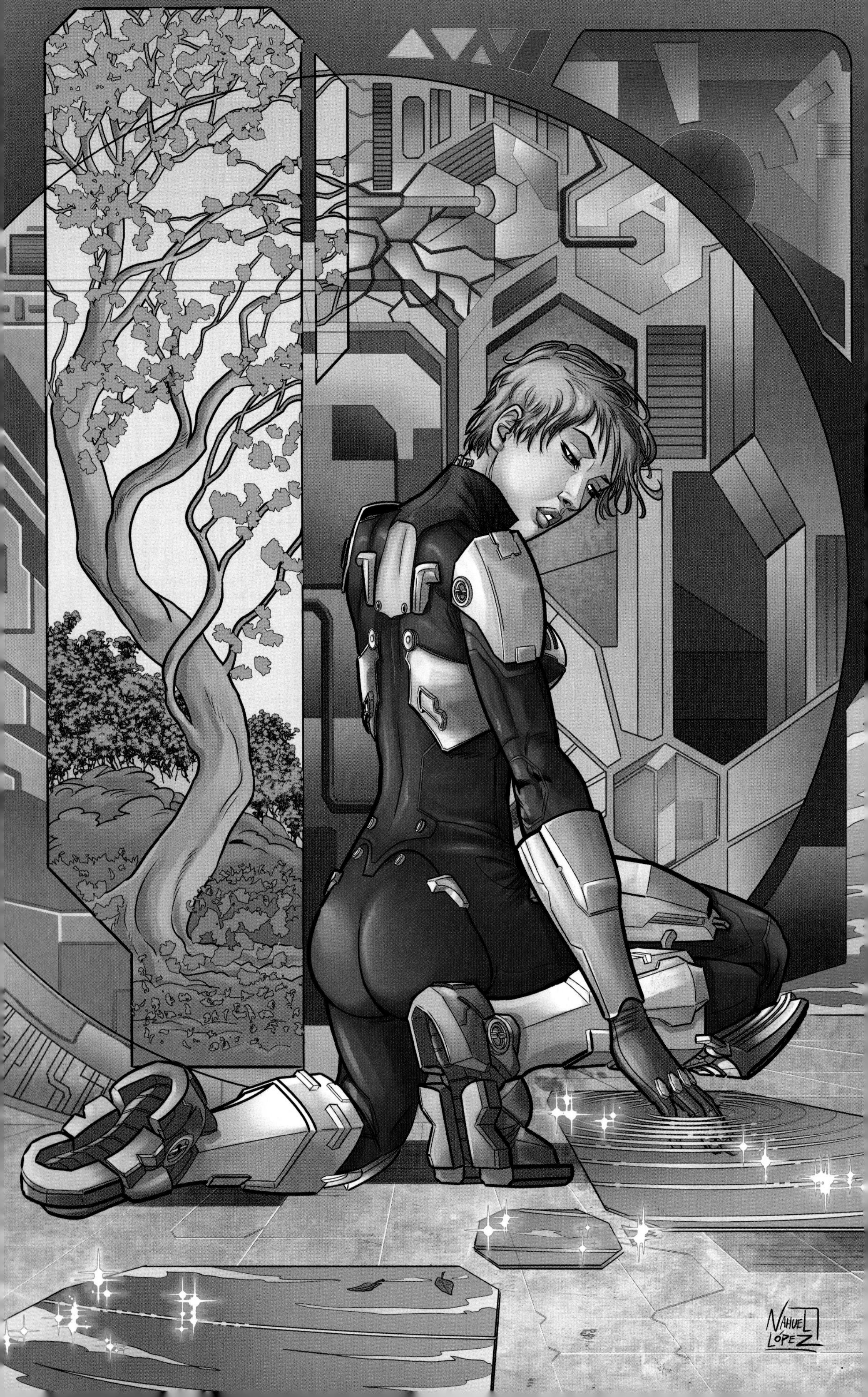
NAHUEL LÓPEZ

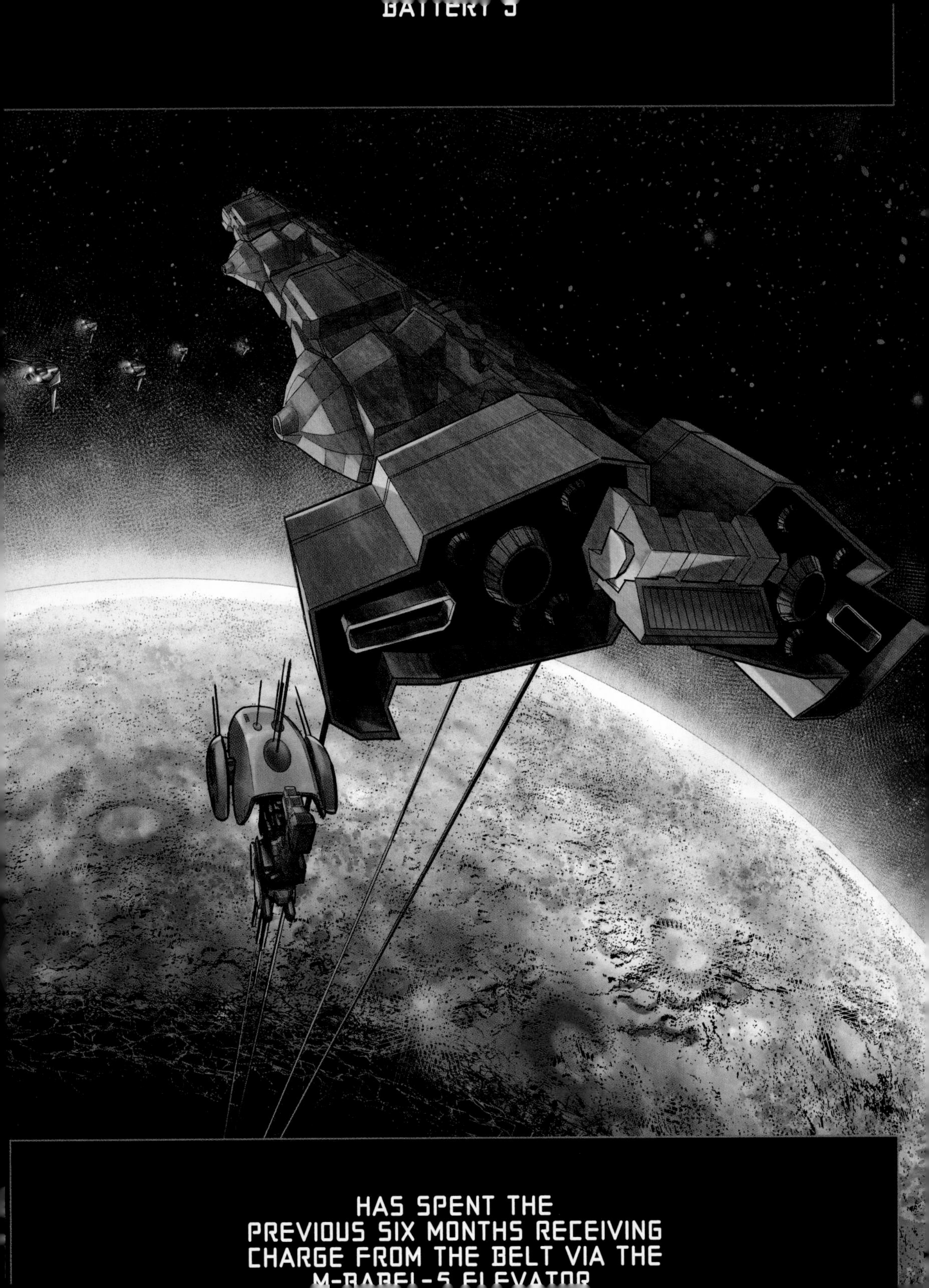
BATTERY 5
HAS SPENT THE
PREVIOUS SIX MONTHS RECEIVING
CHARGE FROM THE BELT VIA THE

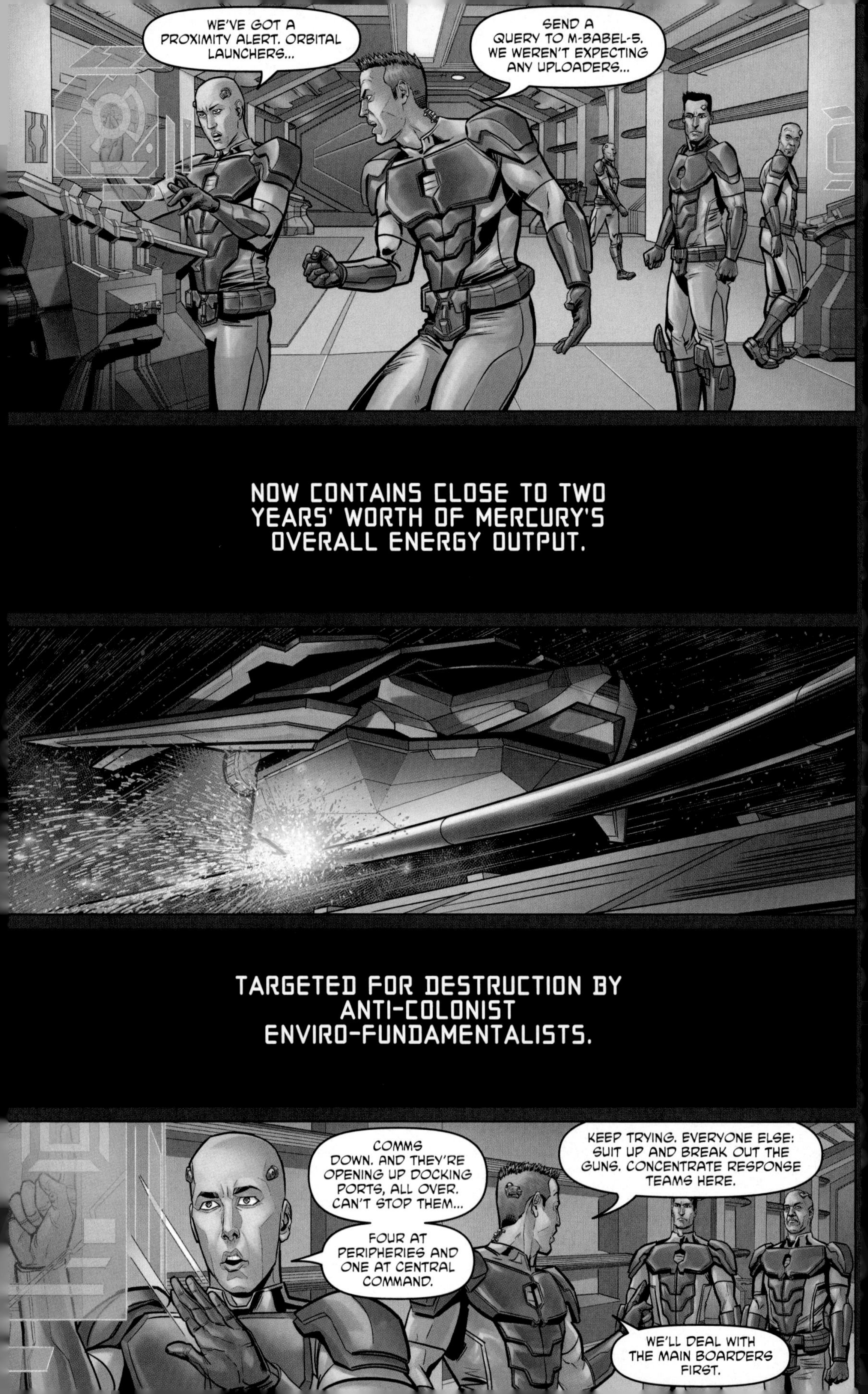
WE'VE GOT A PROXIMITY ALERT. ORBITAL LAUNCHERS...
SEND A QUERY TO M-BABEL-5. WE WEREN'T EXPECTING ANY UPLOADERS...
NOW CONTAINS CLOSE TO TWO YEARS' WORTH OF MERCURY'S OVERALL ENERGY OUTPUT.
TARGETED FOR DESTRUCTION BY ANTI-COLONIST ENVIRO-FUNDAMENTALISTS.
COMMS DOWN. AND THEY'RE OPENING UP DOCKING PORTS, ALL OVER. CAN'T STOP THEM...
FOUR AT PERIPHERIES AND ONE AT CENTRAL COMMAND.
KEEP TRYING. EVERYONE ELSE: SUIT UP AND BREAK OUT THE GUNS. CONCENTRATE RESPONSE TEAMS HERE.
WE'LL DEAL WITH THE MAIN BOARDERS FIRST.

ITS DESTRUCTION WILL PRECIPITATE THE
END OF THE MERCURY PROJECT,

ALONG WITH THE DEATHS OF
THE MAJORITY OF COLONISTS.

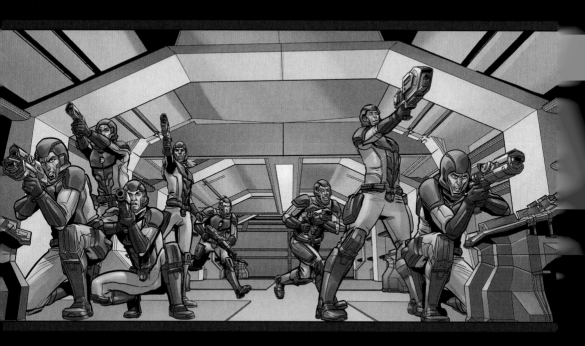

THE PLAN WAS DISCOVERED DURING A
ROUTINE BELT ACCIDENT INVESTIGATION BY
POLICE CONTRACTOR LUIZA BORA,

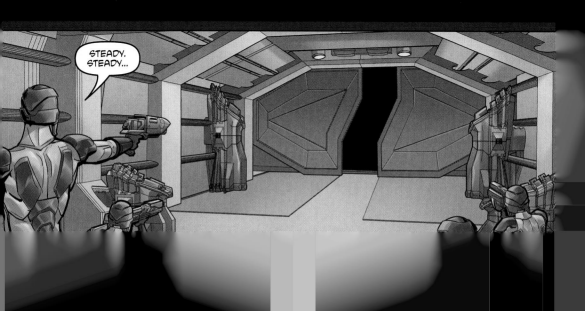

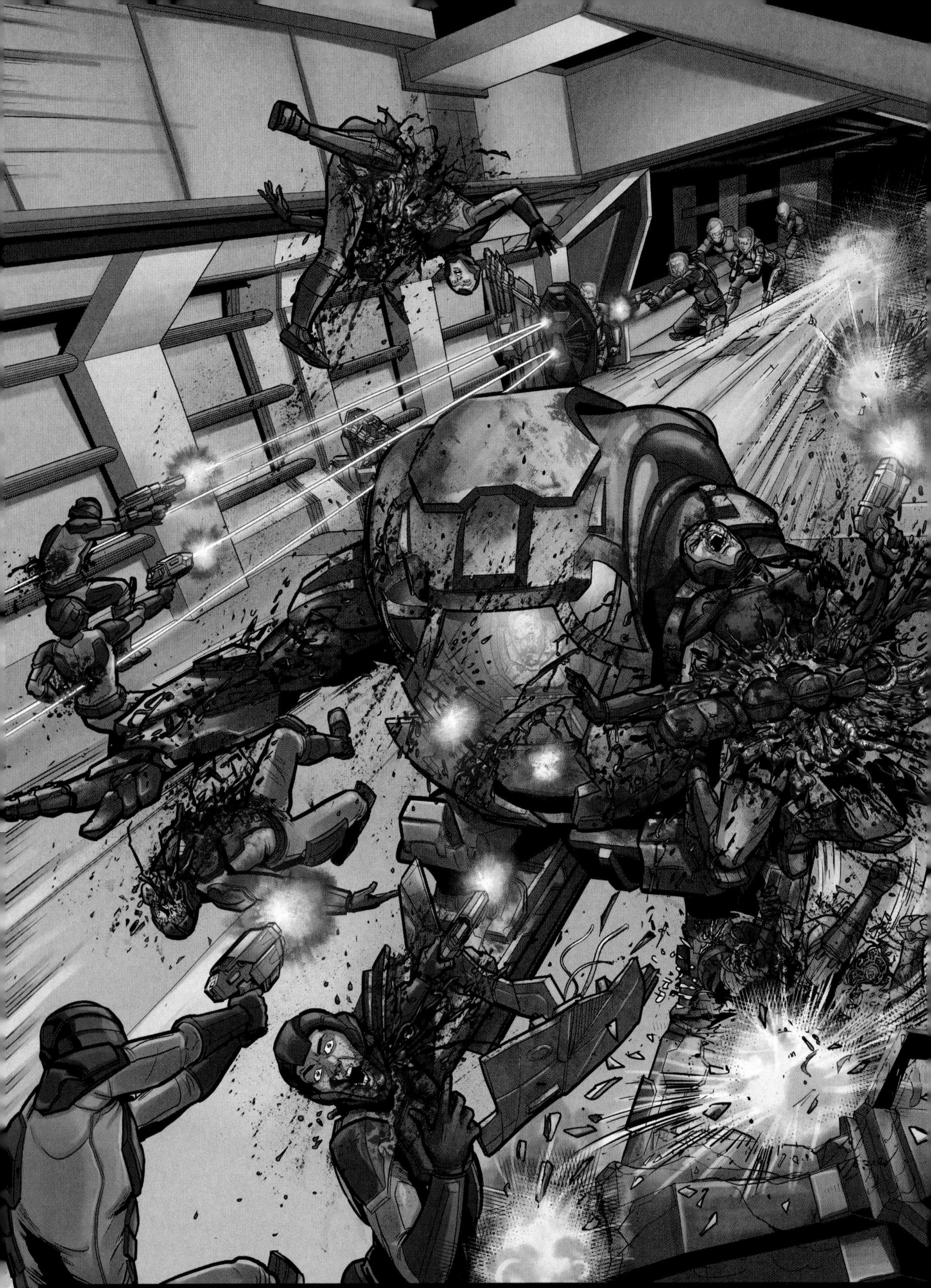

MERCURY HEAT: THE LONG, SLOW DAWN

KIERON GILLEN / NAHUEL LOPEZ

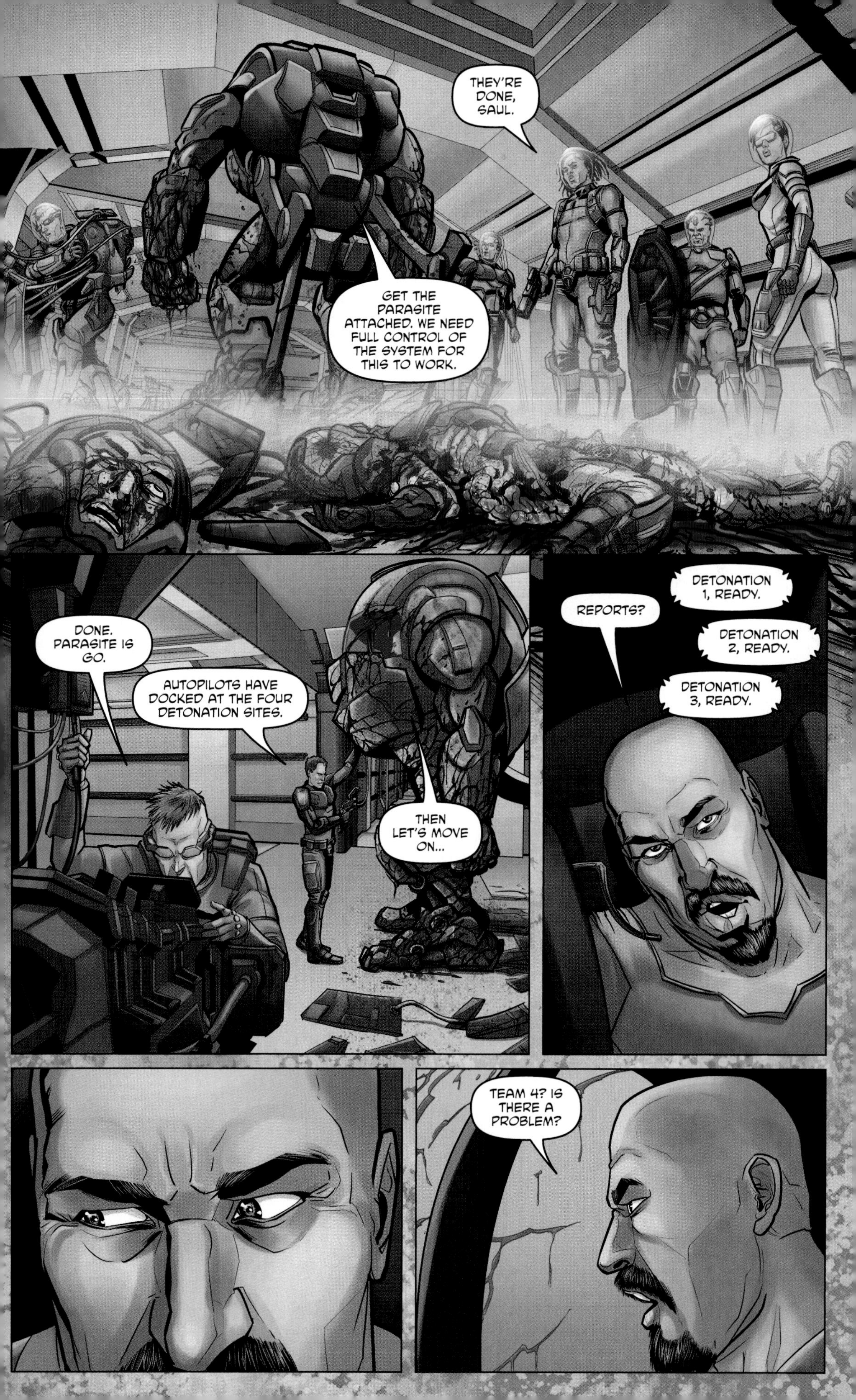
THEY'RE DONE, SAUL.
GET THE PARASITE ATTACHED. WE NEED FULL CONTROL OF THE SYSTEM FOR THIS TO WORK.
DONE. PARASITE IS GO.
AUTOPILOTS HAVE DOCKED AT THE FOUR DETONATION SITES.
THEN LET'S MOVE ON...
REPORTS?
DETONATION 1, READY.
DETONATION 2, READY.
DETONATION 3, READY.
TEAM 4? IS THERE A PROBLEM?

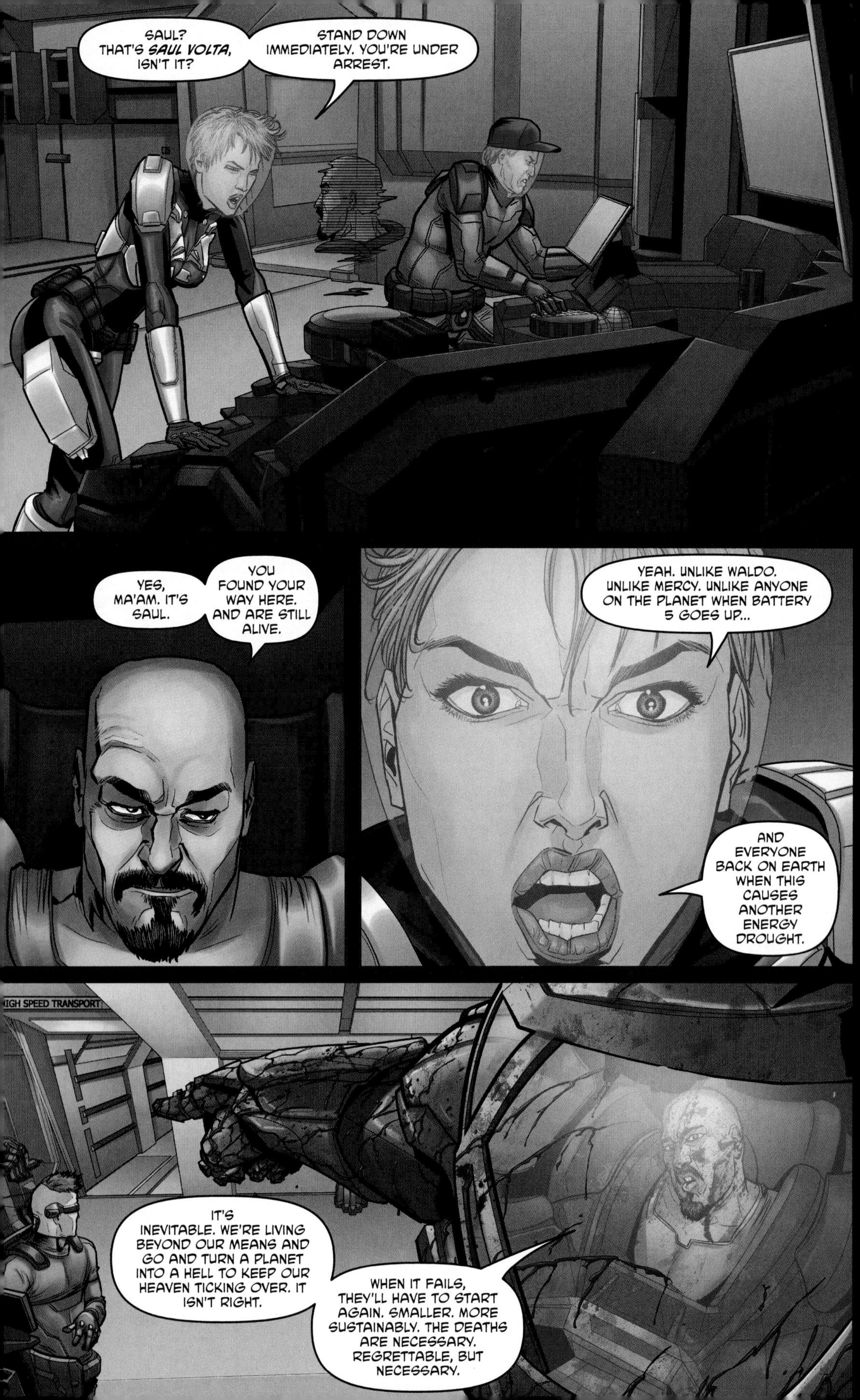
SAUL? THAT'S SAUL VOLTA, ISN'T IT?
STAND DOWN IMMEDIATELY. YOU'RE UNDER ARREST.
YES, MA'AM. IT'S SAUL.
YOU FOUND YOUR WAY HERE. AND ARE STILL ALIVE.
YEAH. UNLIKE WALDO. UNLIKE MERCY. UNLIKE ANYONE ON THE PLANET WHEN BATTERY 5 GOES UP...
AND EVERYONE BACK ON EARTH WHEN THIS CAUSES ANOTHER ENERGY DROUGHT.
HIGH SPEED TRANSPORT
IT'S INEVITABLE. WE'RE LIVING BEYOND OUR MEANS AND GO AND TURN A PLANET INTO A HELL TO KEEP OUR HEAVEN TICKING OVER. IT ISN'T RIGHT.
WHEN IT FAILS, THEY'LL HAVE TO START AGAIN. SMALLER. MORE SUSTAINABLY. THE DEATHS ARE NECESSARY. REGRETTABLE, BUT NECESSARY.

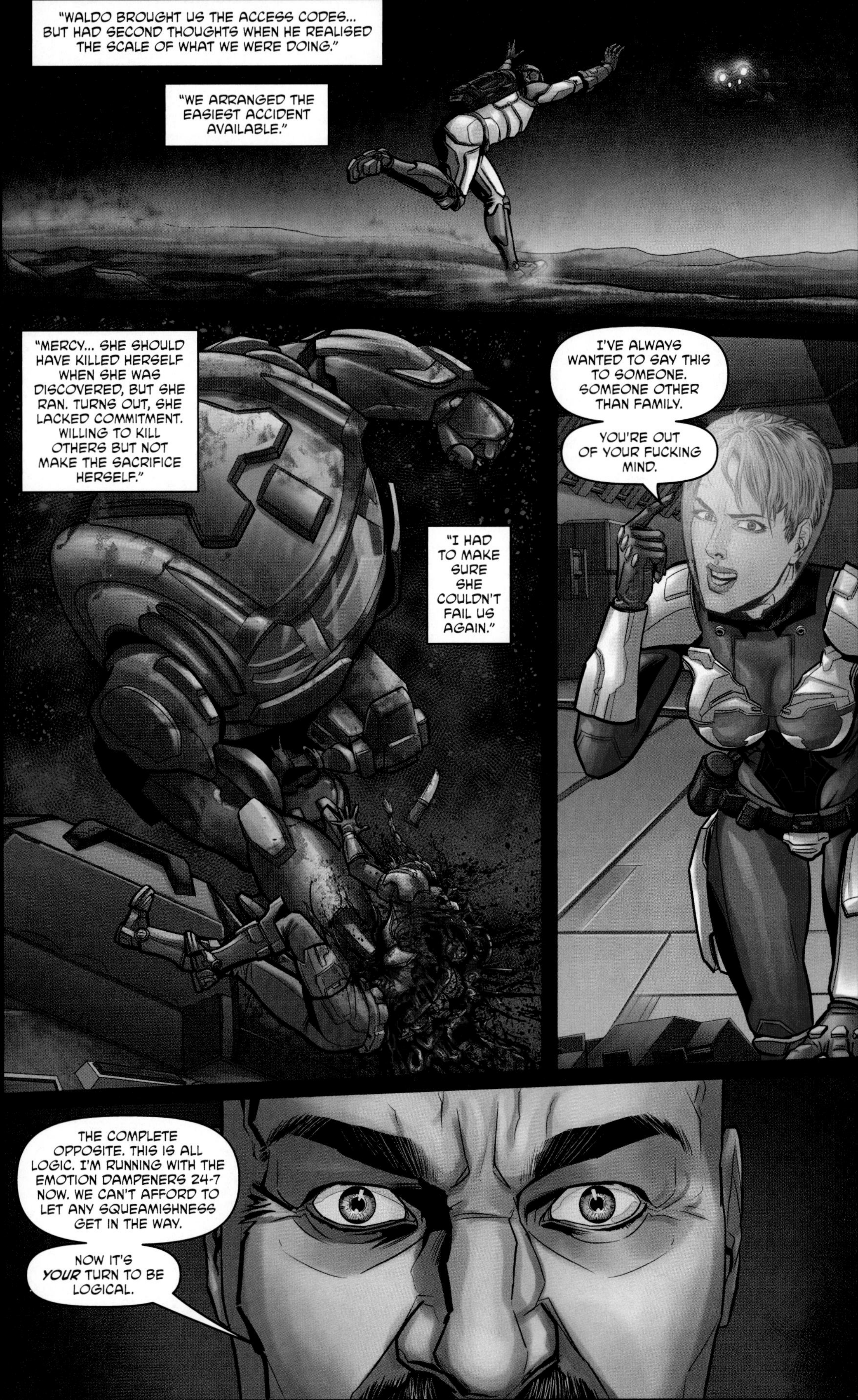
"WALDO BROUGHT US THE ACCESS CODES... BUT HAD SECOND THOUGHTS WHEN HE REALISED THE SCALE OF WHAT WE WERE DOING."
"WE ARRANGED THE EASIEST ACCIDENT AVAILABLE."
"MERCY... SHE SHOULD HAVE KILLED HERSELF WHEN SHE WAS DISCOVERED, BUT SHE RAN. TURNS OUT, SHE LACKED COMMITMENT. WILLING TO KILL OTHERS BUT NOT MAKE THE SACRIFICE HERSELF."
"I HAD TO MAKE SURE SHE COULDN'T FAIL US AGAIN."
I'VE ALWAYS WANTED TO SAY THIS TO SOMEONE. SOMEONE OTHER THAN FAMILY.
YOU'RE OUT OF YOUR FUCKING MIND.
THE COMPLETE OPPOSITE. THIS IS ALL LOGIC. I'M RUNNING WITH THE EMOTION DAMPENERS 24-7 NOW. WE CAN'T AFFORD TO LET ANY SQUEAMISHNESS GET IN THE WAY.
NOW IT'S *YOUR* TURN TO BE LOGICAL.

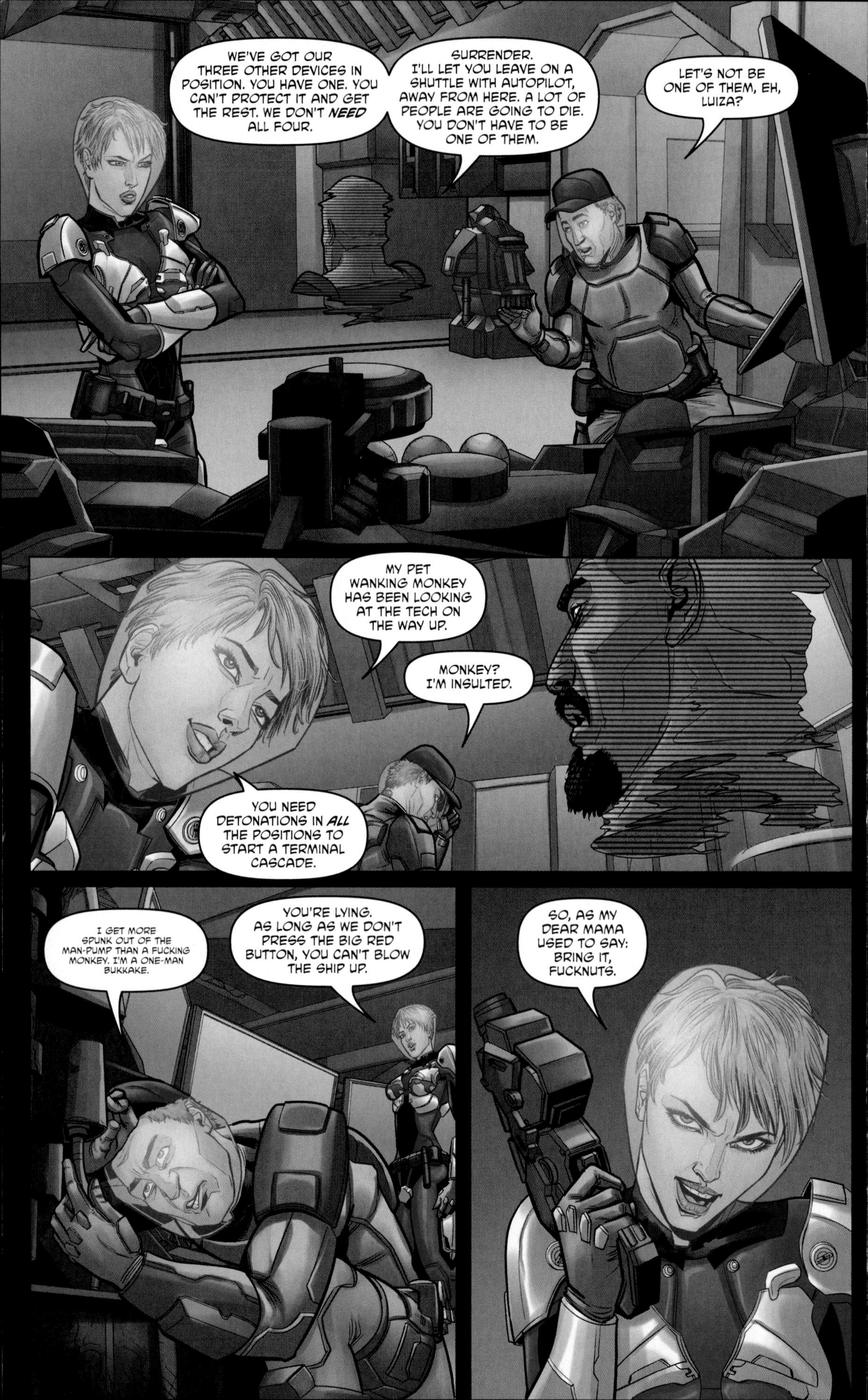
WE'VE GOT OUR THREE OTHER DEVICES IN POSITION. YOU HAVE ONE. YOU CAN'T PROTECT IT AND GET THE REST. WE DON'T *NEED* ALL FOUR.
SURRENDER. I'LL LET YOU LEAVE ON A SHUTTLE WITH AUTOPILOT, AWAY FROM HERE. A LOT OF PEOPLE ARE GOING TO DIE. YOU DON'T HAVE TO BE ONE OF THEM.
LET'S NOT BE ONE OF THEM, EH, LUIZA?
MY PET WANKING MONKEY HAS BEEN LOOKING AT THE TECH ON THE WAY UP.
MONKEY? I'M INSULTED.
YOU NEED DETONATIONS IN *ALL* THE POSITIONS TO START A TERMINAL CASCADE.
I GET MORE SPUNK OUT OF THE MAN-PUMP THAN A FUCKING MONKEY. I'M A ONE-MAN BUKKAKE.
YOU'RE LYING. AS LONG AS WE DON'T PRESS THE BIG RED BUTTON, YOU CAN'T BLOW THE SHIP UP.
SO, AS MY DEAR MAMA USED TO SAY: BRING IT, FUCKNUTS.

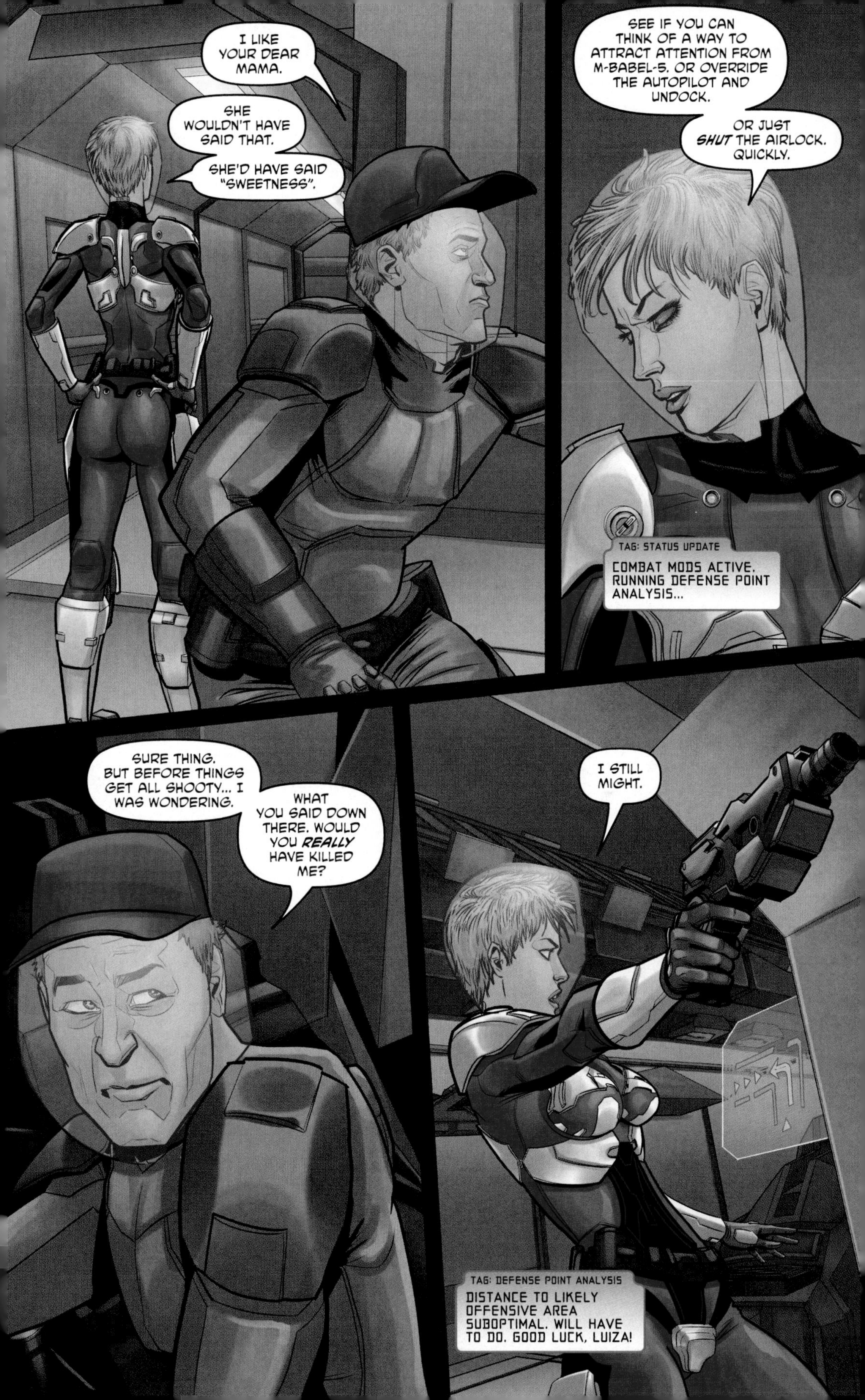

I LIKE YOUR DEAR MAMA.
SHE WOULDN'T HAVE SAID THAT.
SHE'D HAVE SAID "SWEETNESS".
SEE IF YOU CAN THINK OF A WAY TO ATTRACT ATTENTION FROM M-BABEL-5. OR OVERRIDE THE AUTOPILOT AND UNDOCK.
OR JUST *SHUT* THE AIRLOCK. QUICKLY.
TAG: STATUS UPDATE
COMBAT MODS ACTIVE. RUNNING DEFENSE POINT ANALYSIS...
SURE THING. BUT BEFORE THINGS GET ALL SHOOTY... I WAS WONDERING.
WHAT YOU SAID DOWN THERE. WOULD YOU *REALLY* HAVE KILLED ME?
I STILL MIGHT.
TAG: DEFENSE POINT ANALYSIS
DISTANCE TO LIKELY OFFENSIVE AREA SUBOPTIMAL. WILL HAVE TO DO. GOOD LUCK, LUIZA!

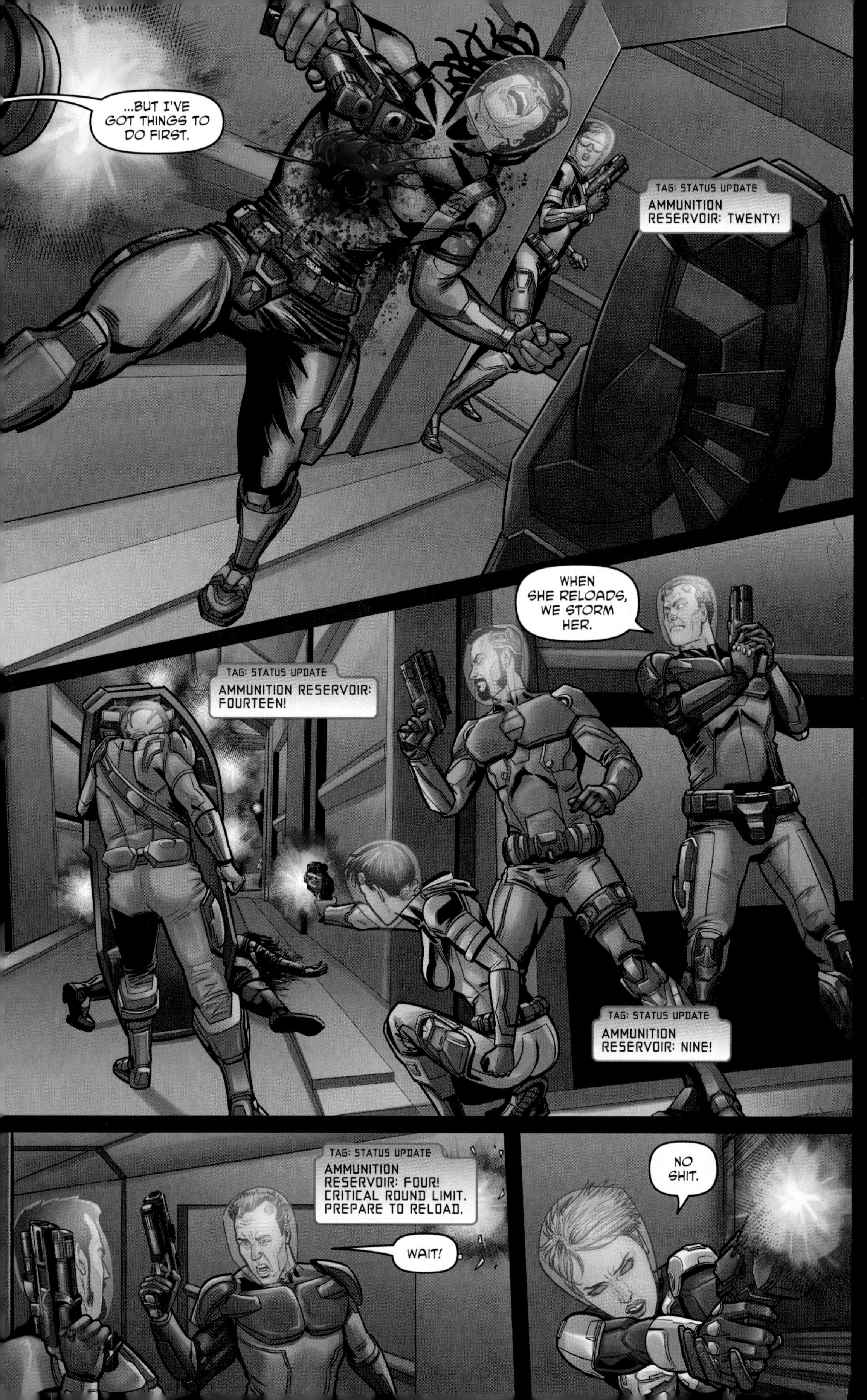
...BUT I'VE GOT THINGS TO DO FIRST.
TAG: STATUS UPDATE
AMMUNITION RESERVOIR: TWENTY!
WHEN SHE RELOADS, WE STORM HER.
TAG: STATUS UPDATE
AMMUNITION RESERVOIR: FOURTEEN!
TAG: STATUS UPDATE
AMMUNITION RESERVOIR: NINE!
TAG: STATUS UPDATE
AMMUNITION RESERVOIR: FOUR! CRITICAL ROUND LIMIT. PREPARE TO RELOAD.
WAIT!
NO SHIT.

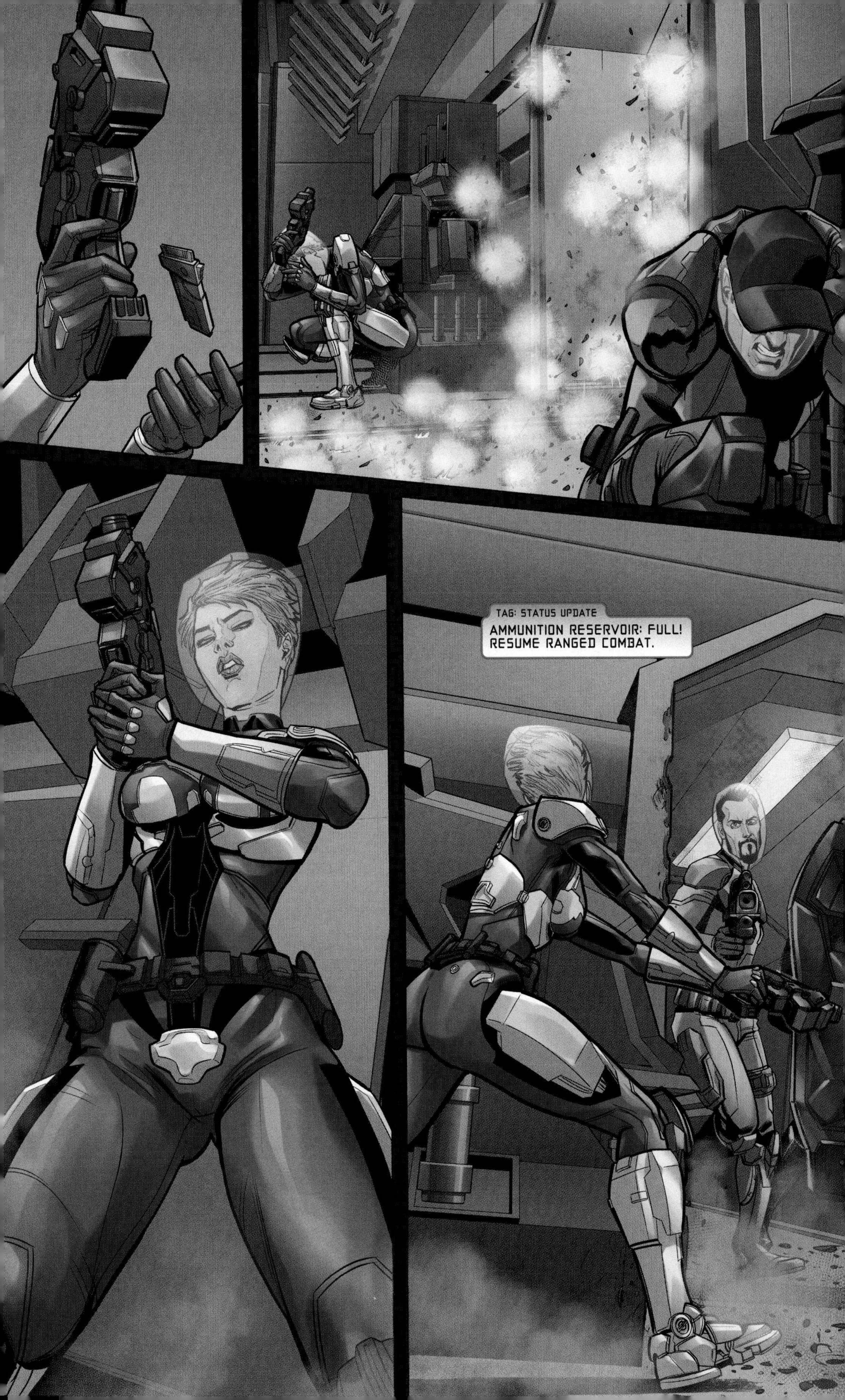
TAG: STATUS UPDATE
AMMUNITION RESERVOIR: FULL! RESUME RANGED COMBAT.

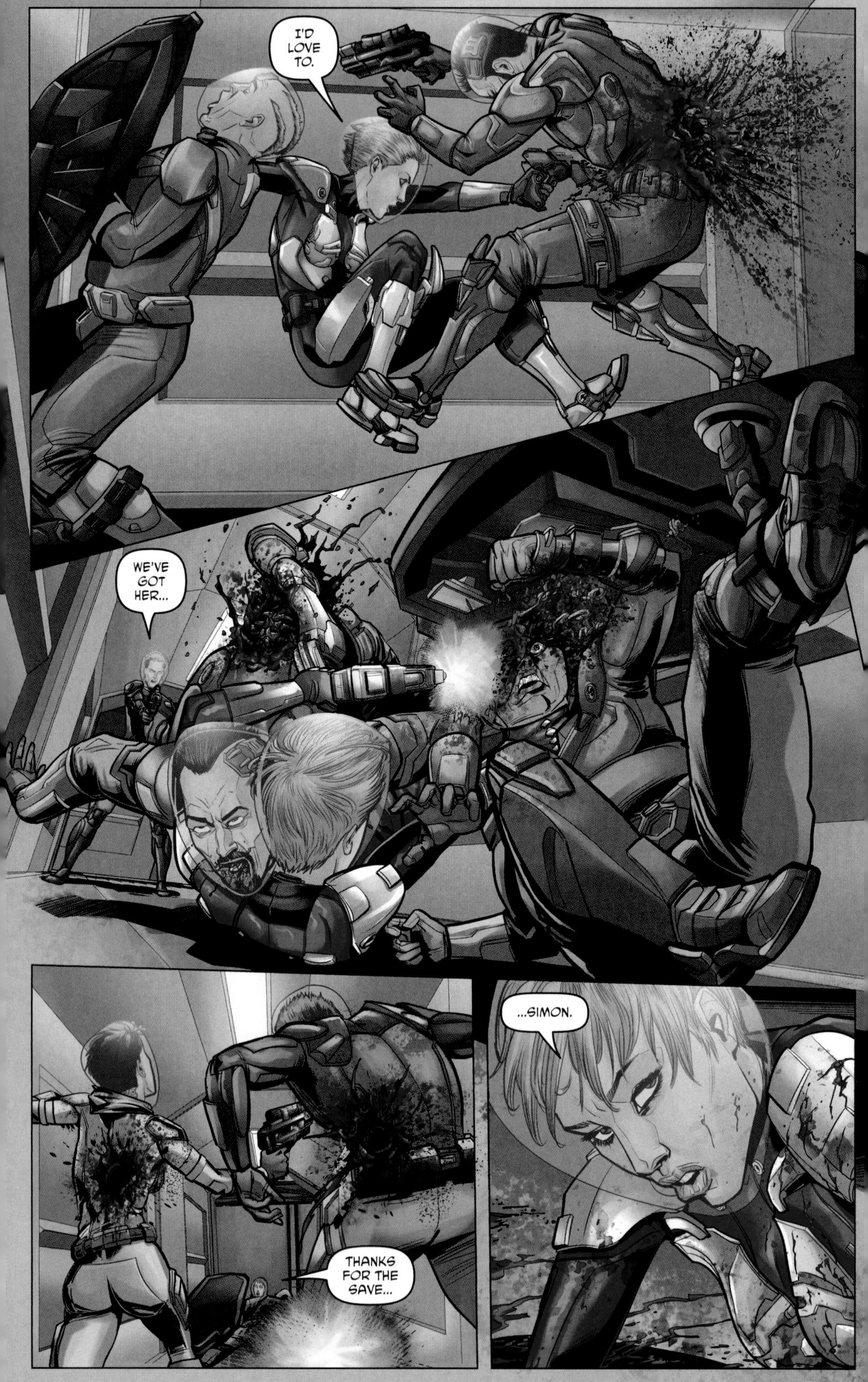
I'D LOVE TO.
WE'VE GOT HER...
THANKS FOR THE SAVE...
...SIMON.

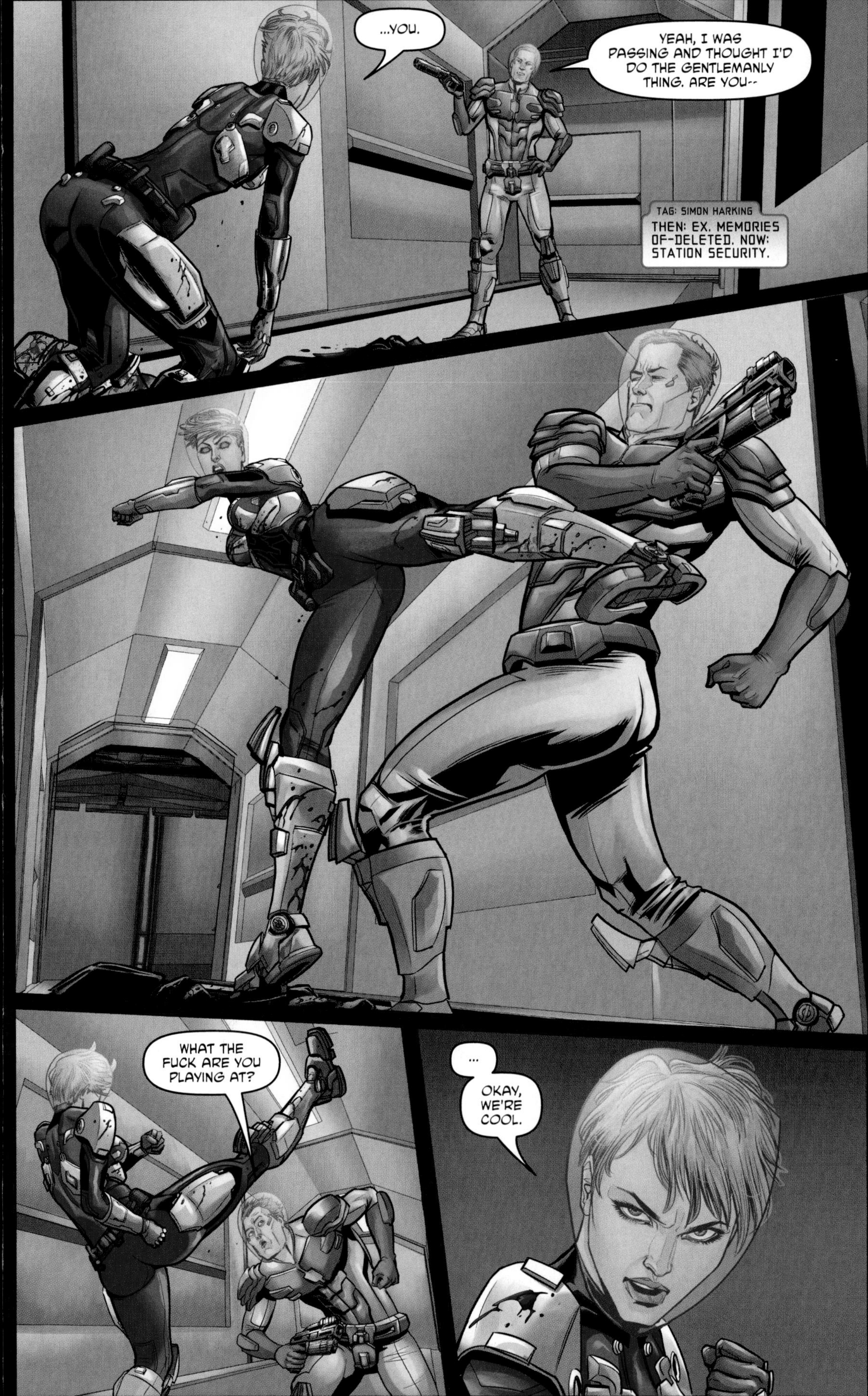
...YOU.
YEAH, I WAS PASSING AND THOUGHT I'D DO THE GENTLEMANLY THING. ARE YOU--
TAG: SIMON HARKING
THEN: EX. MEMORIES OF-DELETED. NOW: STATION SECURITY.
WHAT THE FUCK ARE YOU PLAYING AT?
...
OKAY, WE'RE COOL.

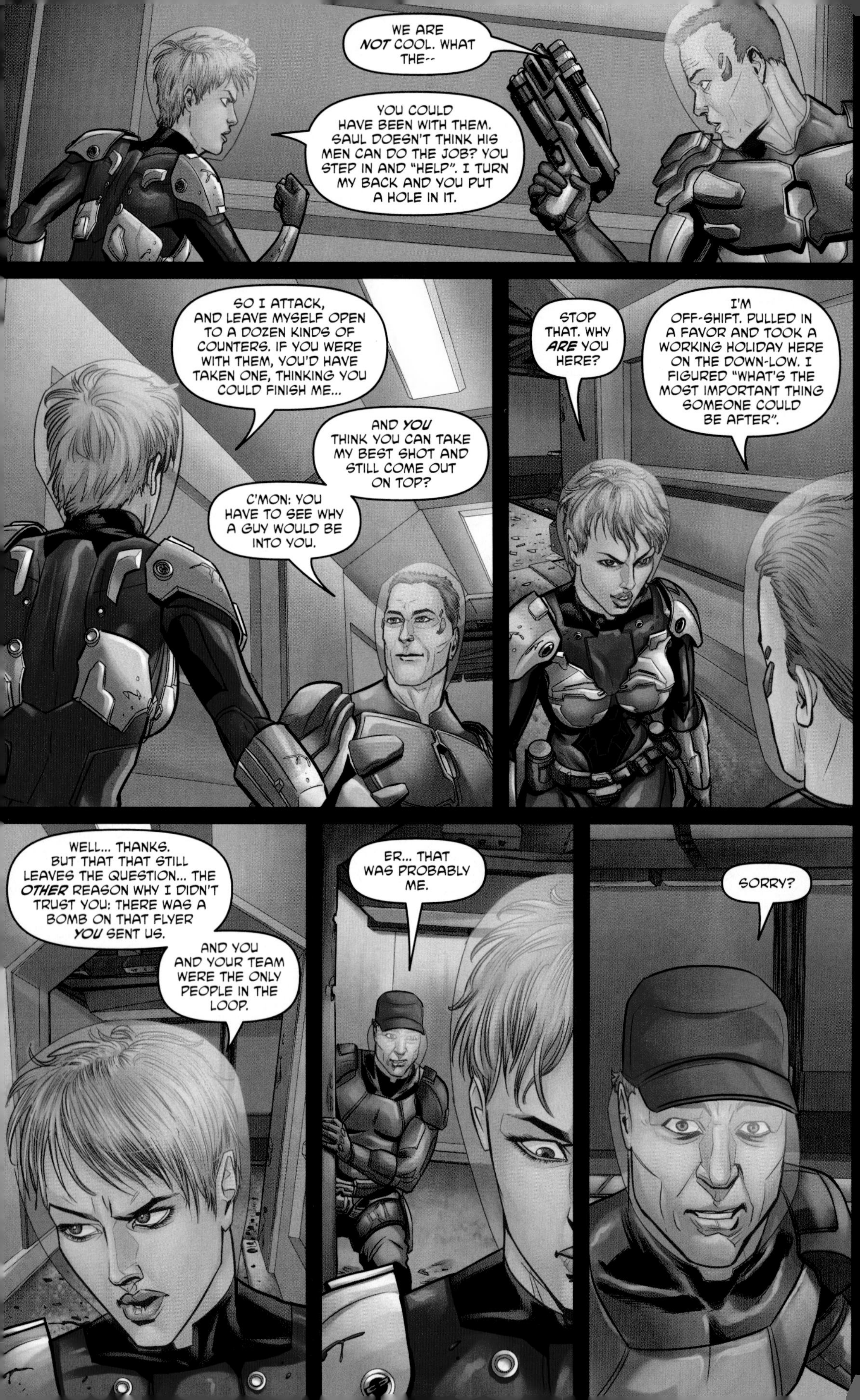
WE ARE *NOT* COOL. WHAT THE--
YOU COULD HAVE BEEN WITH THEM. SAUL DOESN'T THINK HIS MEN CAN DO THE JOB? YOU STEP IN AND "HELP". I TURN MY BACK AND YOU PUT A HOLE IN IT.
SO I ATTACK, AND LEAVE MYSELF OPEN TO A DOZEN KINDS OF COUNTERS. IF YOU WERE WITH THEM, YOU'D HAVE TAKEN ONE, THINKING YOU COULD FINISH ME...
AND *YOU* THINK YOU CAN TAKE MY BEST SHOT AND STILL COME OUT ON TOP?
C'MON: YOU HAVE TO SEE WHY A GUY WOULD BE INTO YOU.
STOP THAT. WHY *ARE* YOU HERE?
I'M OFF-SHIFT. PULLED IN A FAVOR AND TOOK A WORKING HOLIDAY HERE ON THE DOWN-LOW. I FIGURED "WHAT'S THE MOST IMPORTANT THING SOMEONE COULD BE AFTER".
WELL... THANKS. BUT THAT THAT STILL LEAVES THE QUESTION... THE *OTHER* REASON WHY I DIDN'T TRUST YOU: THERE WAS A BOMB ON THAT FLYER *YOU* SENT US.
AND YOU AND YOUR TEAM WERE THE ONLY PEOPLE IN THE LOOP.
ER... THAT WAS PROBABLY ME.
SORRY?

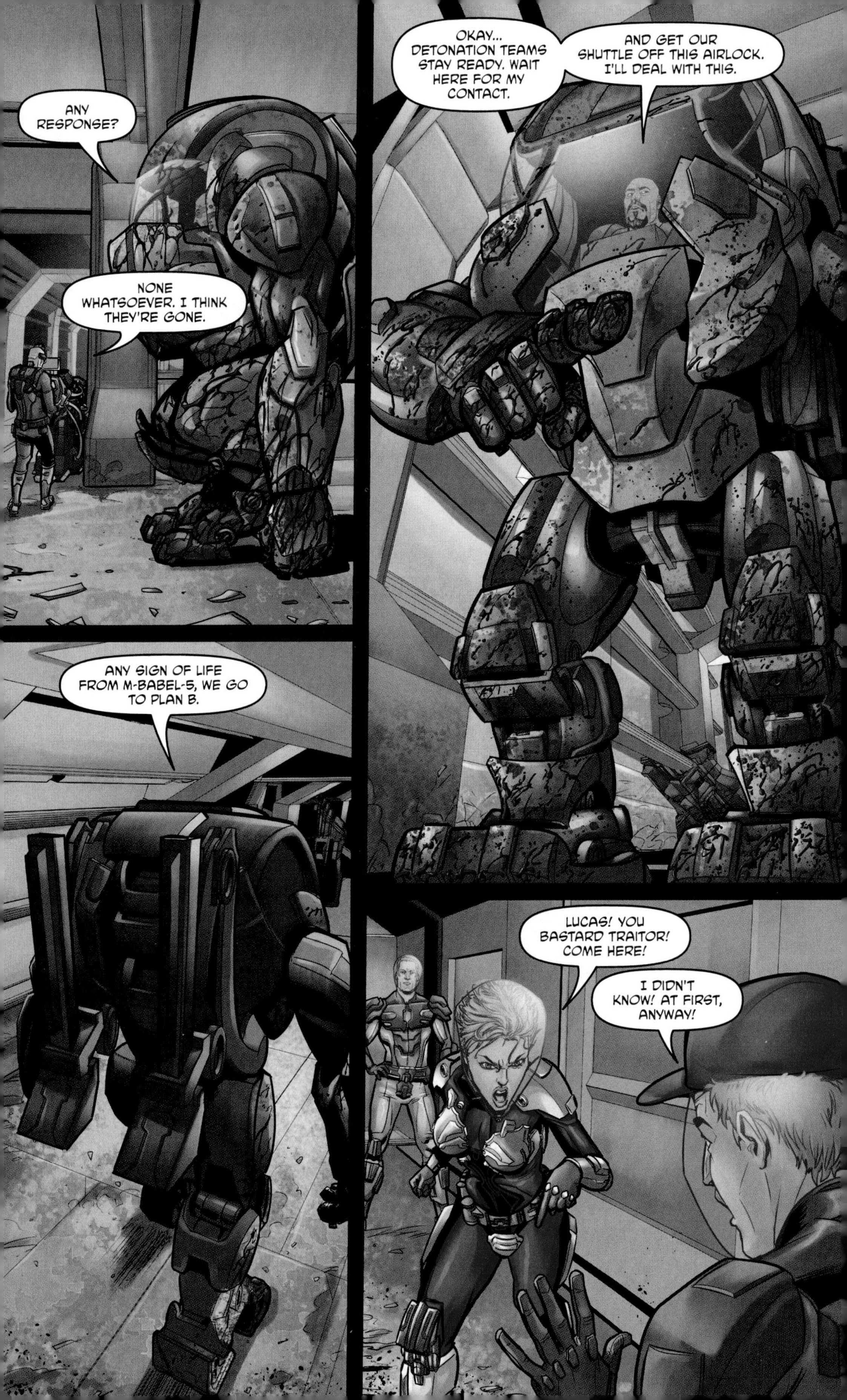
ANY RESPONSE?
NONE WHATSOEVER. I THINK THEY'RE GONE.
OKAY... DETONATION TEAMS STAY READY. WAIT HERE FOR MY CONTACT.
AND GET OUR SHUTTLE OFF THIS AIRLOCK. I'LL DEAL WITH THIS.
ANY SIGN OF LIFE FROM M-BABEL-5, WE GO TO PLAN B.
LUCAS! YOU BASTARD TRAITOR! COME HERE!
I DIDN'T KNOW! AT FIRST, ANYWAY!

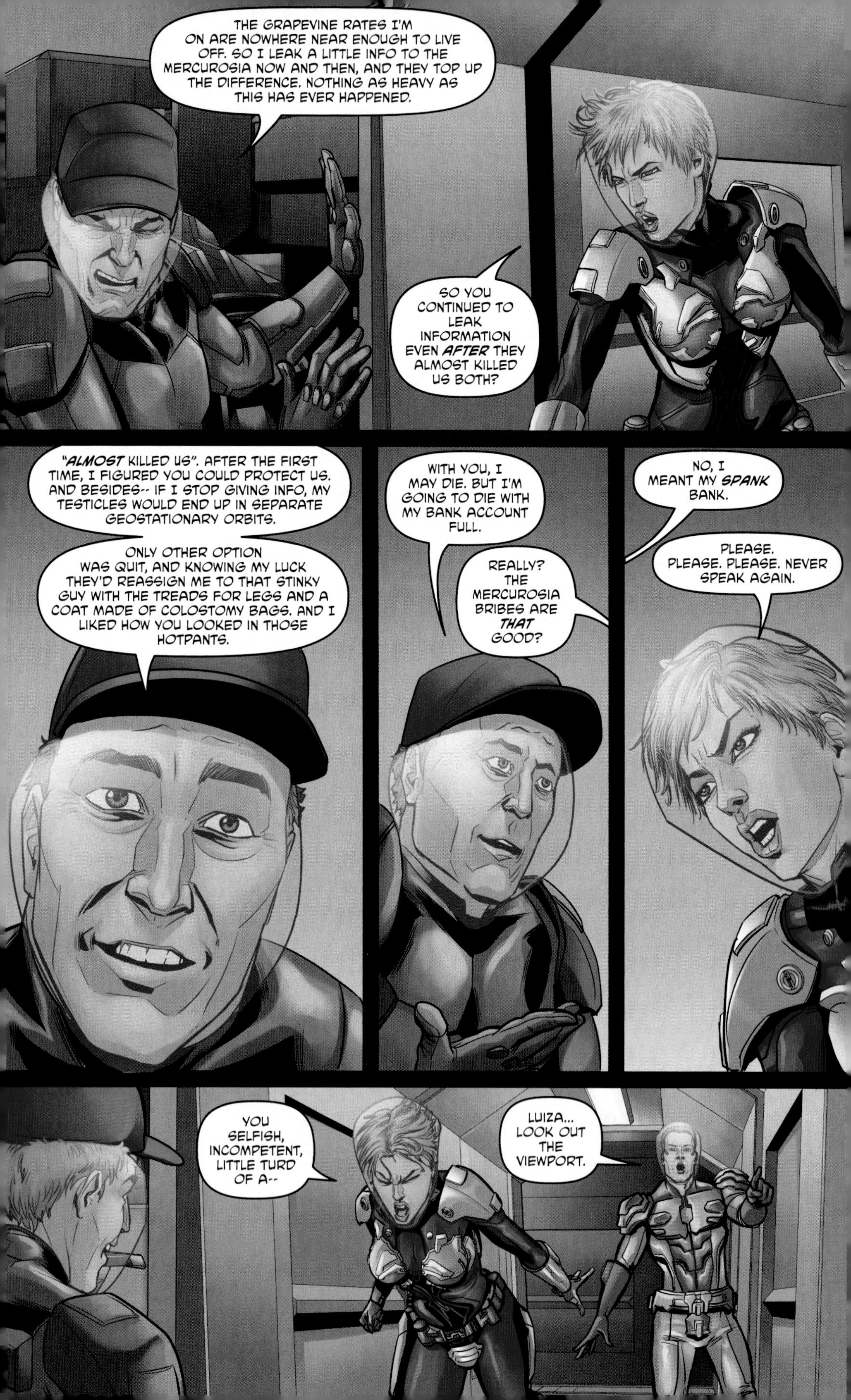
THE GRAPEVINE RATES I'M ON ARE NOWHERE NEAR ENOUGH TO LIVE OFF. SO I LEAK A LITTLE INFO TO THE MERCUROSIA NOW AND THEN, AND THEY TOP UP THE DIFFERENCE. NOTHING AS HEAVY AS THIS HAS EVER HAPPENED.
SO YOU CONTINUED TO LEAK INFORMATION EVEN *AFTER* THEY ALMOST KILLED US BOTH?
"*ALMOST* KILLED US". AFTER THE FIRST TIME, I FIGURED YOU COULD PROTECT US. AND BESIDES-- IF I STOP GIVING INFO, MY TESTICLES WOULD END UP IN SEPARATE GEOSTATIONARY ORBITS.
ONLY OTHER OPTION WAS QUIT, AND KNOWING MY LUCK THEY'D REASSIGN ME TO THAT STINKY GUY WITH THE TREADS FOR LEGS AND A COAT MADE OF COLOSTOMY BAGS. AND I LIKED HOW YOU LOOKED IN THOSE HOTPANTS.
WITH YOU, I MAY DIE. BUT I'M GOING TO DIE WITH MY BANK ACCOUNT FULL.
REALLY? THE MERCUROSIA BRIBES ARE *THAT* GOOD?
NO, I MEANT MY *SPANK* BANK.
PLEASE. PLEASE. PLEASE. NEVER SPEAK AGAIN.
YOU SELFISH, INCOMPETENT, LITTLE TURD OF A--
LUIZA... LOOK OUT THE VIEWPORT.

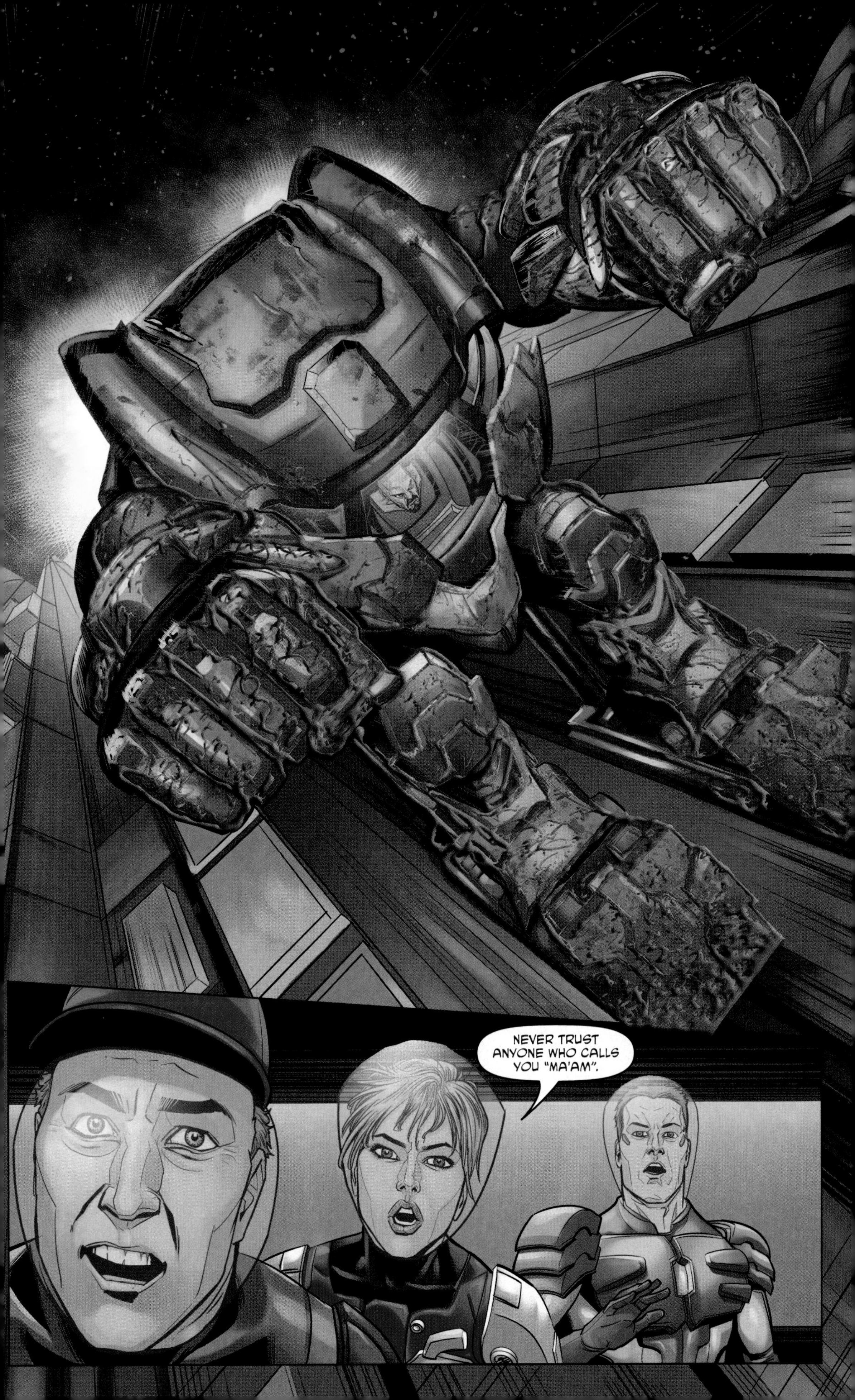
NEVER TRUST ANYONE WHO CALLS YOU "MA'AM".

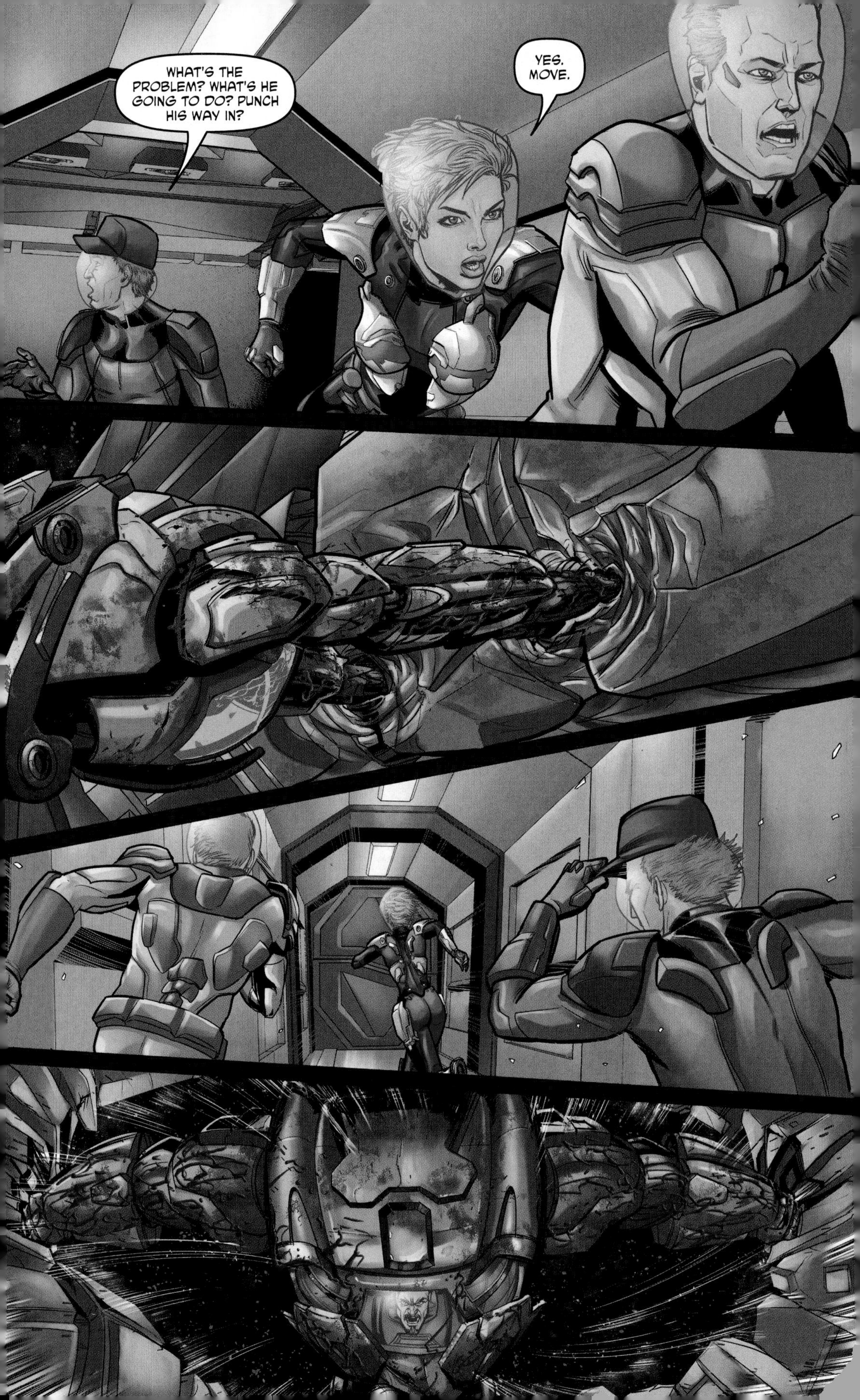
WHAT'S THE PROBLEM? WHAT'S HE GOING TO DO? PUNCH HIS WAY IN?
YES. MOVE.

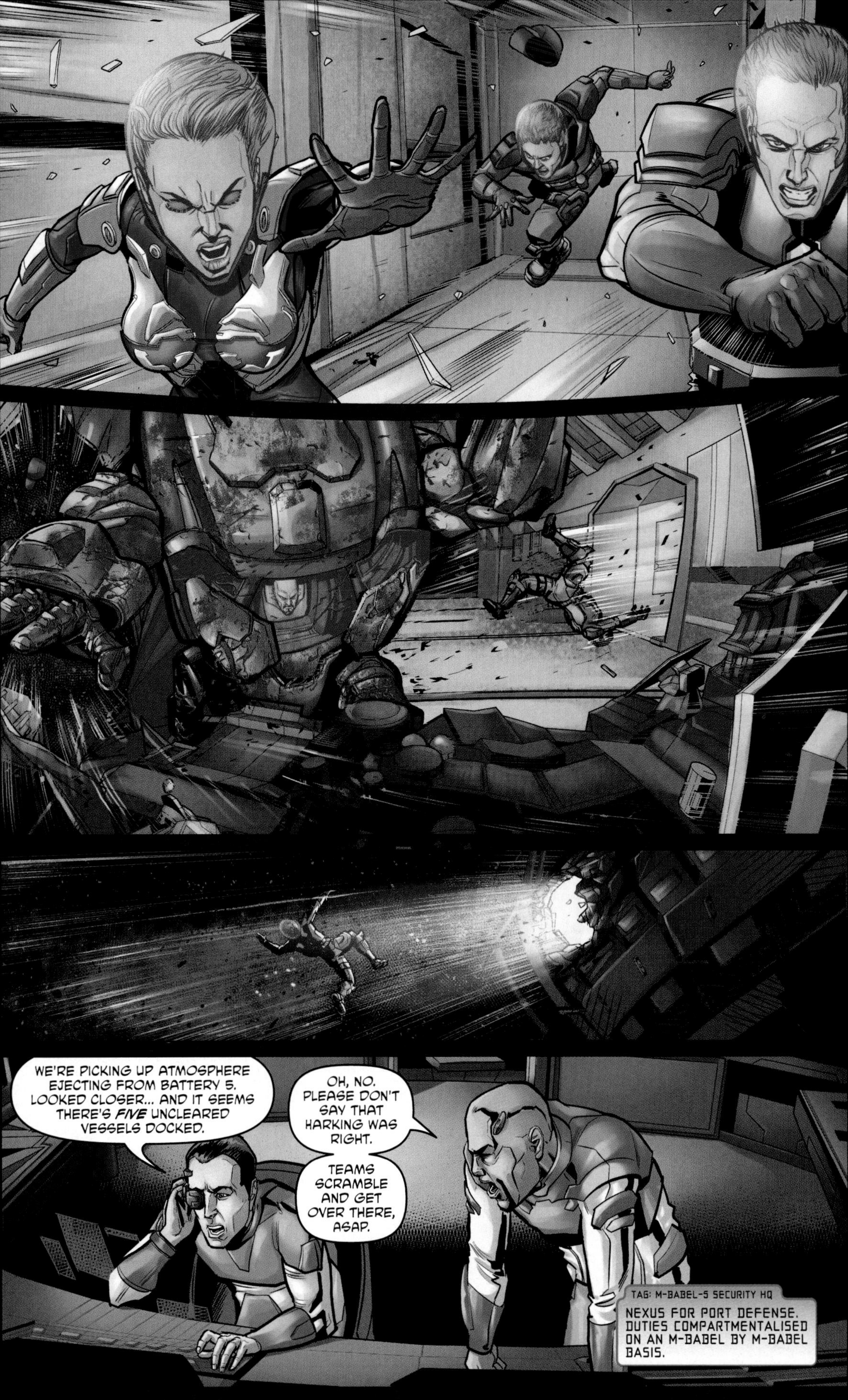
WE'RE PICKING UP ATMOSPHERE EJECTING FROM BATTERY 5. LOOKED CLOSER... AND IT SEEMS THERE'S *FIVE* UNCLEARED VESSELS DOCKED.
OH, NO. PLEASE DON'T SAY THAT HARKING WAS RIGHT.
TEAMS SCRAMBLE AND GET OVER THERE, ASAP.
TAG: M-BABEL-5 SECURITY HQ
NEXUS FOR PORT DEFENSE. DUTIES COMPARTMENTALISED ON AN M-BABEL BY M-BABEL BASIS.

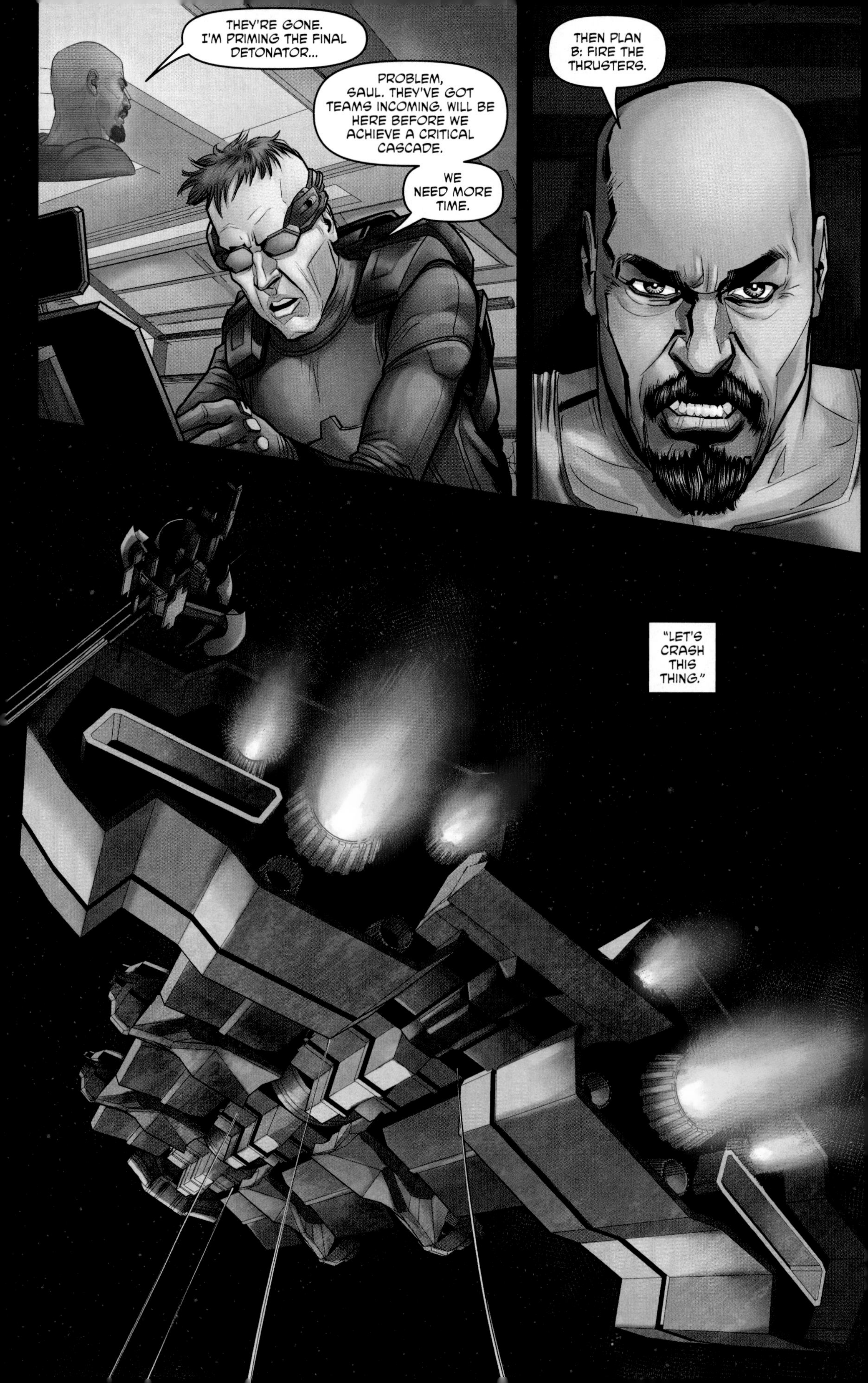
THEY'RE GONE. I'M PRIMING THE FINAL DETONATOR...
PROBLEM, SAUL. THEY'VE GOT TEAMS INCOMING. WILL BE HERE BEFORE WE ACHIEVE A CRITICAL CASCADE.
WE NEED MORE TIME.
THEN PLAN B: FIRE THE THRUSTERS.
"LET'S CRASH THIS THING."

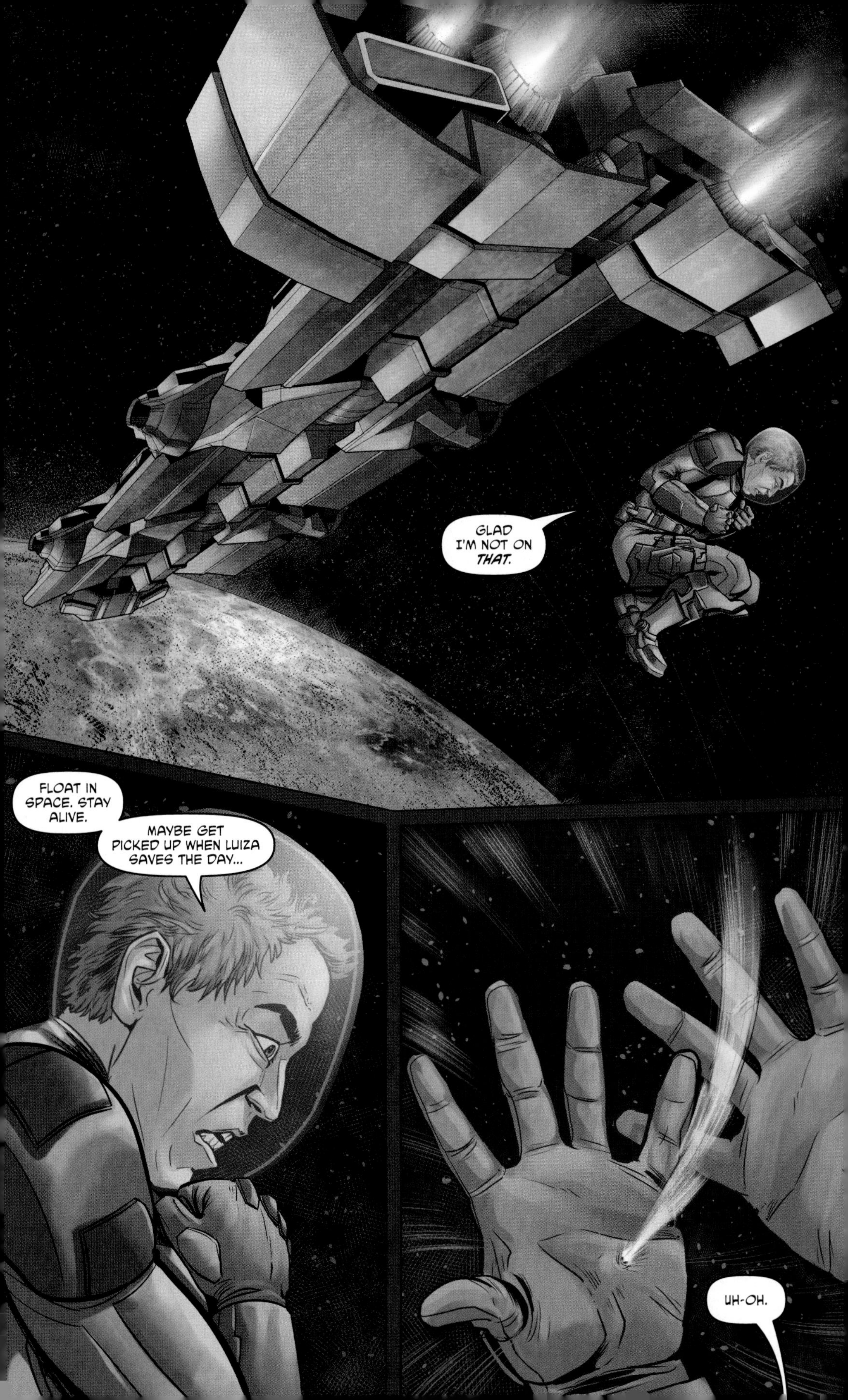
GLAD I'M NOT ON *THAT.*
FLOAT IN SPACE. STAY ALIVE.
MAYBE GET PICKED UP WHEN LUIZA SAVES THE DAY...
UH-OH.

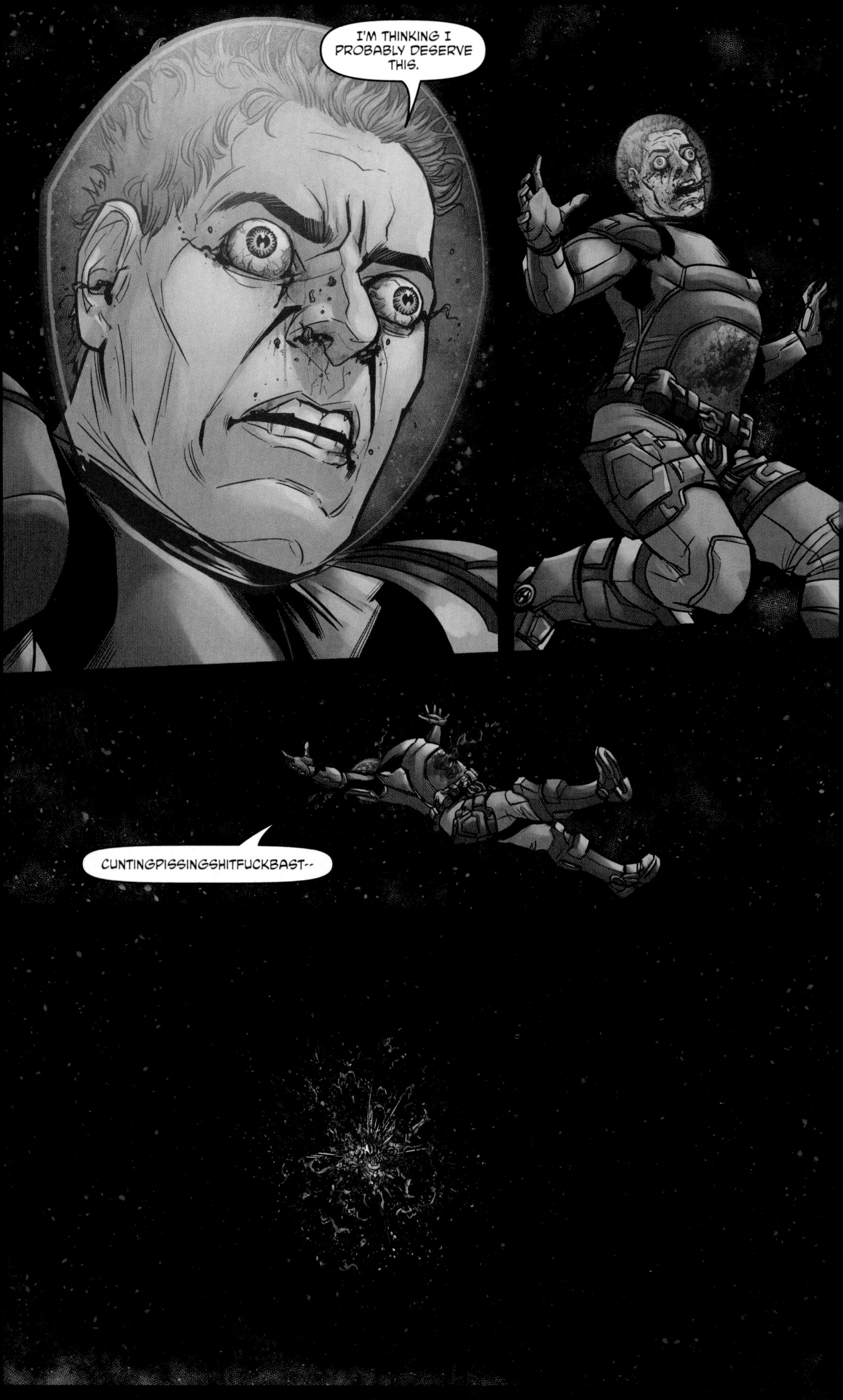
I'M THINKING I PROBABLY DESERVE THIS.
CUNTINGPISSINGSHITFUCKBAST--

chapter 6

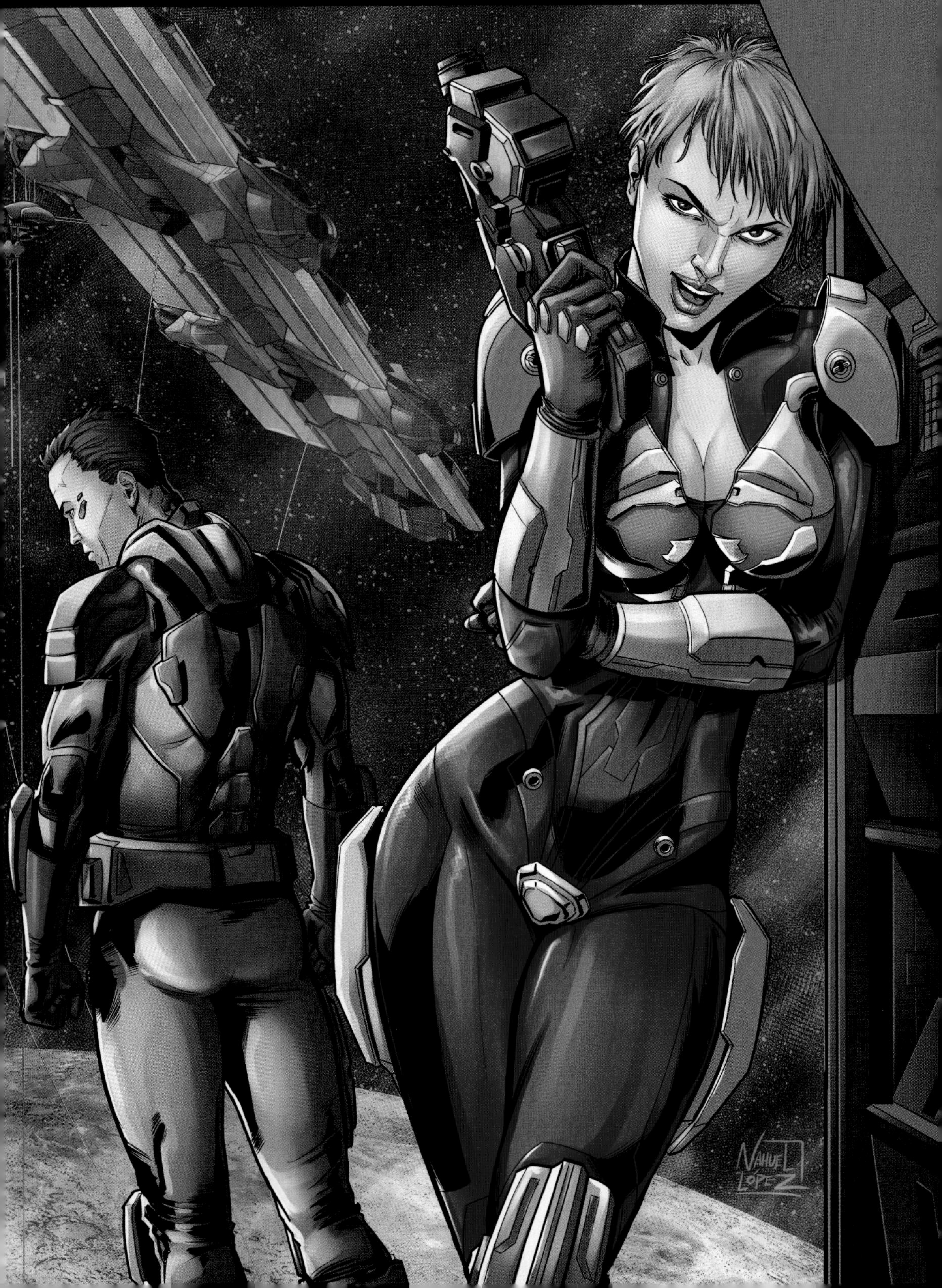
NAHUEL LOPEZ

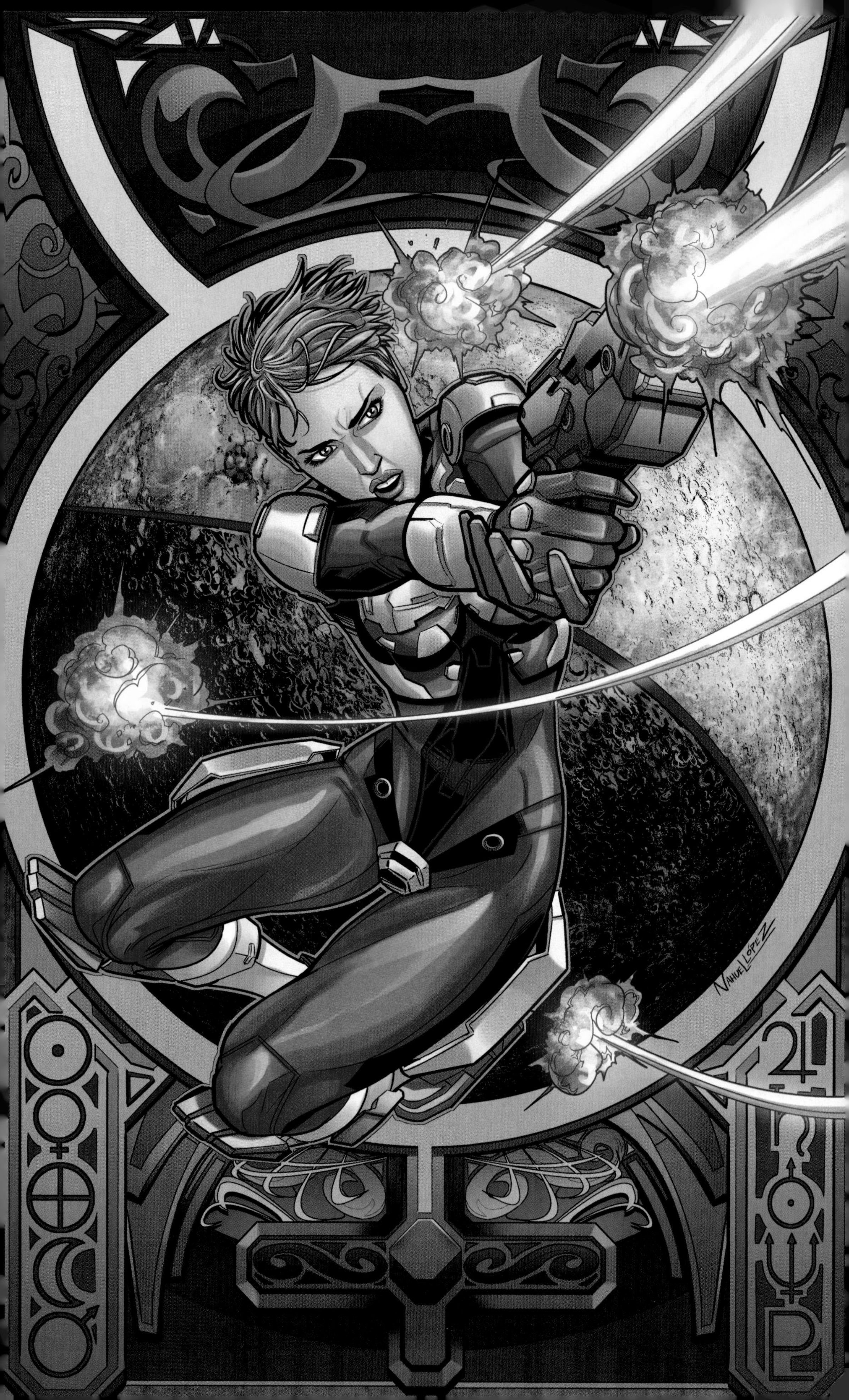
NAHUEL LOPEZ

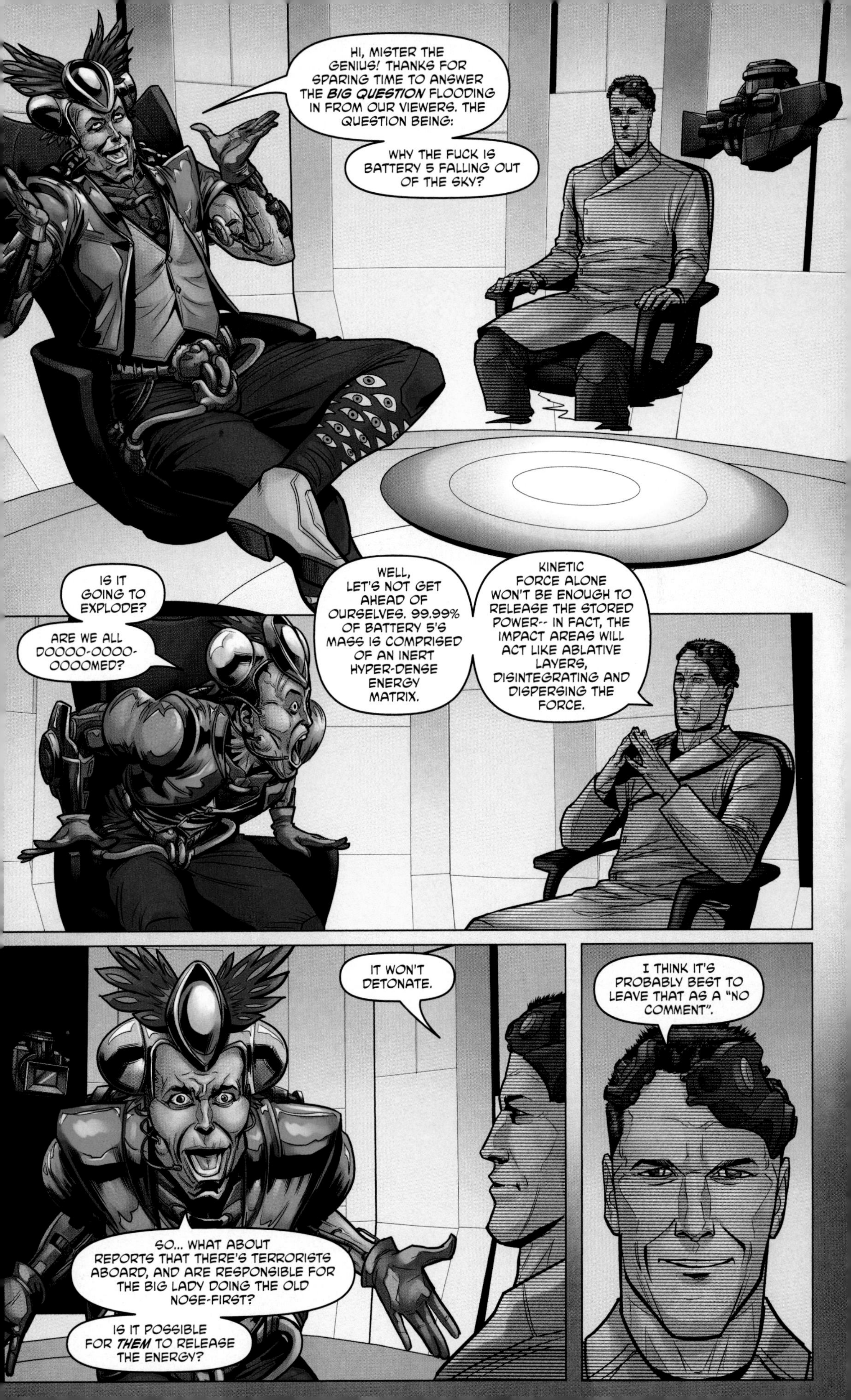
HI, MISTER THE GENIUS! THANKS FOR SPARING TIME TO ANSWER THE *BIG QUESTION* FLOODING IN FROM OUR VIEWERS. THE QUESTION BEING:
WHY THE FUCK IS BATTERY 5 FALLING OUT OF THE SKY?
IS IT GOING TO EXPLODE?
ARE WE ALL DOOOO-OOOO-OOOOMED?
WELL, LET'S NOT GET AHEAD OF OURSELVES. 99.99% OF BATTERY 5'S MASS IS COMPRISED OF AN INERT HYPER-DENSE ENERGY MATRIX.
KINETIC FORCE ALONE WON'T BE ENOUGH TO RELEASE THE STORED POWER-- IN FACT, THE IMPACT AREAS WILL ACT LIKE ABLATIVE LAYERS, DISINTEGRATING AND DISPERSING THE FORCE.
IT WON'T DETONATE.
SO... WHAT ABOUT REPORTS THAT THERE'S TERRORISTS ABOARD, AND ARE RESPONSIBLE FOR THE BIG LADY DOING THE OLD NOSE-FIRST?
IS IT POSSIBLE FOR *THEM* TO RELEASE THE ENERGY?
I THINK IT'S PROBABLY BEST TO LEAVE THAT AS A "NO COMMENT".

MERCURY HEAT: THE LONG, SLOW DAWN

KIERON GILLEN / NAHUEL LOPEZ

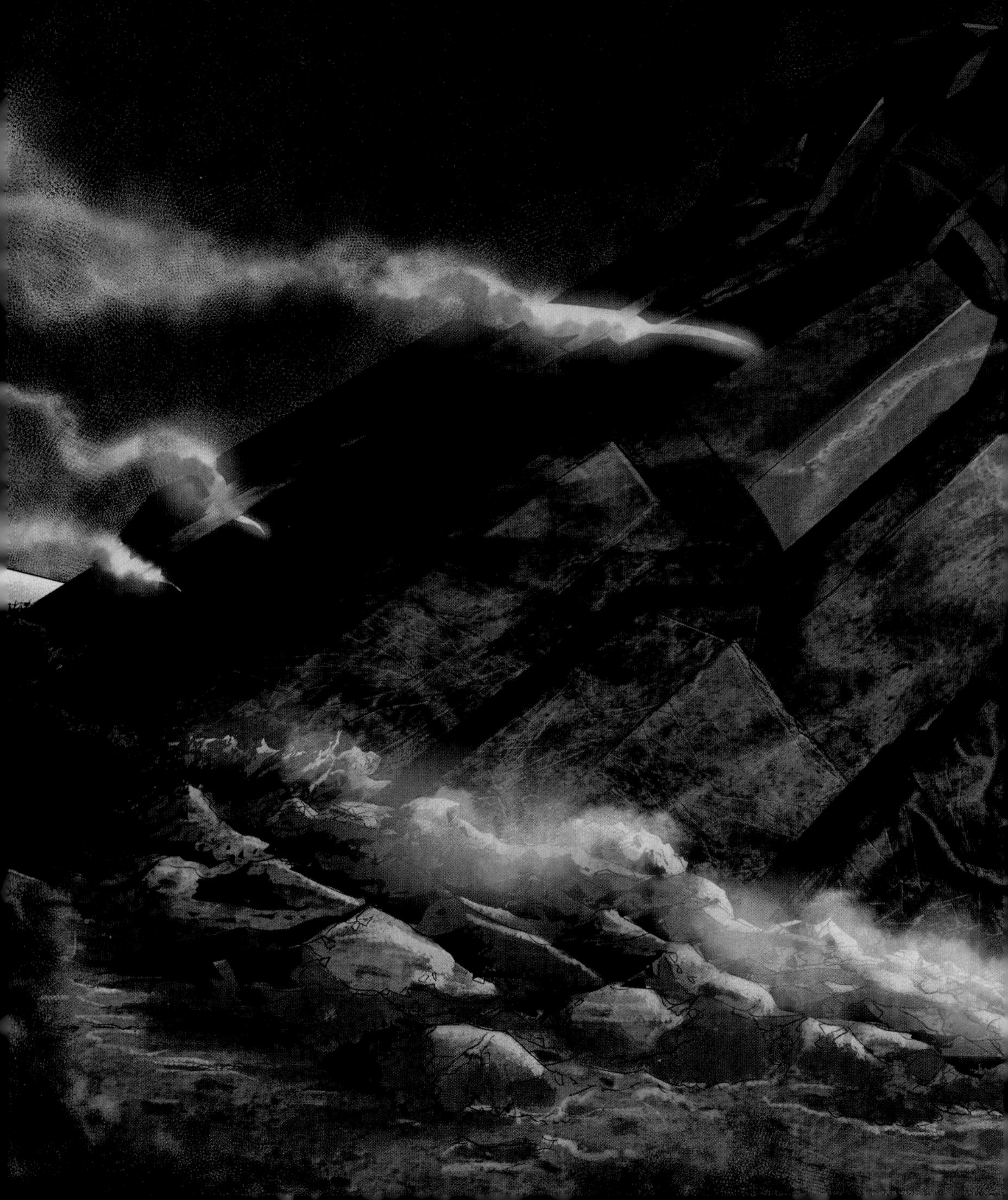

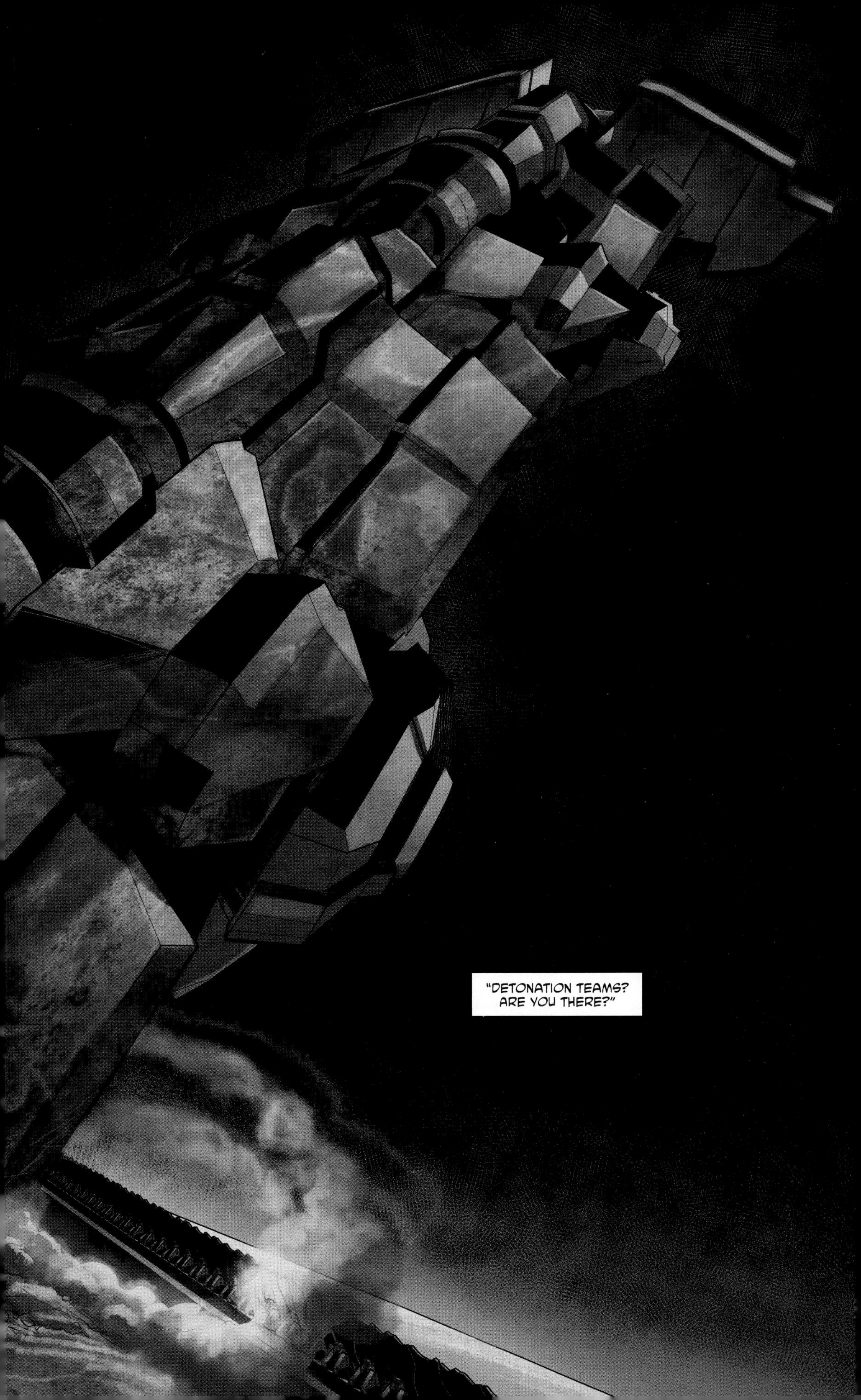
"DETONATION TEAMS? ARE YOU THERE?"

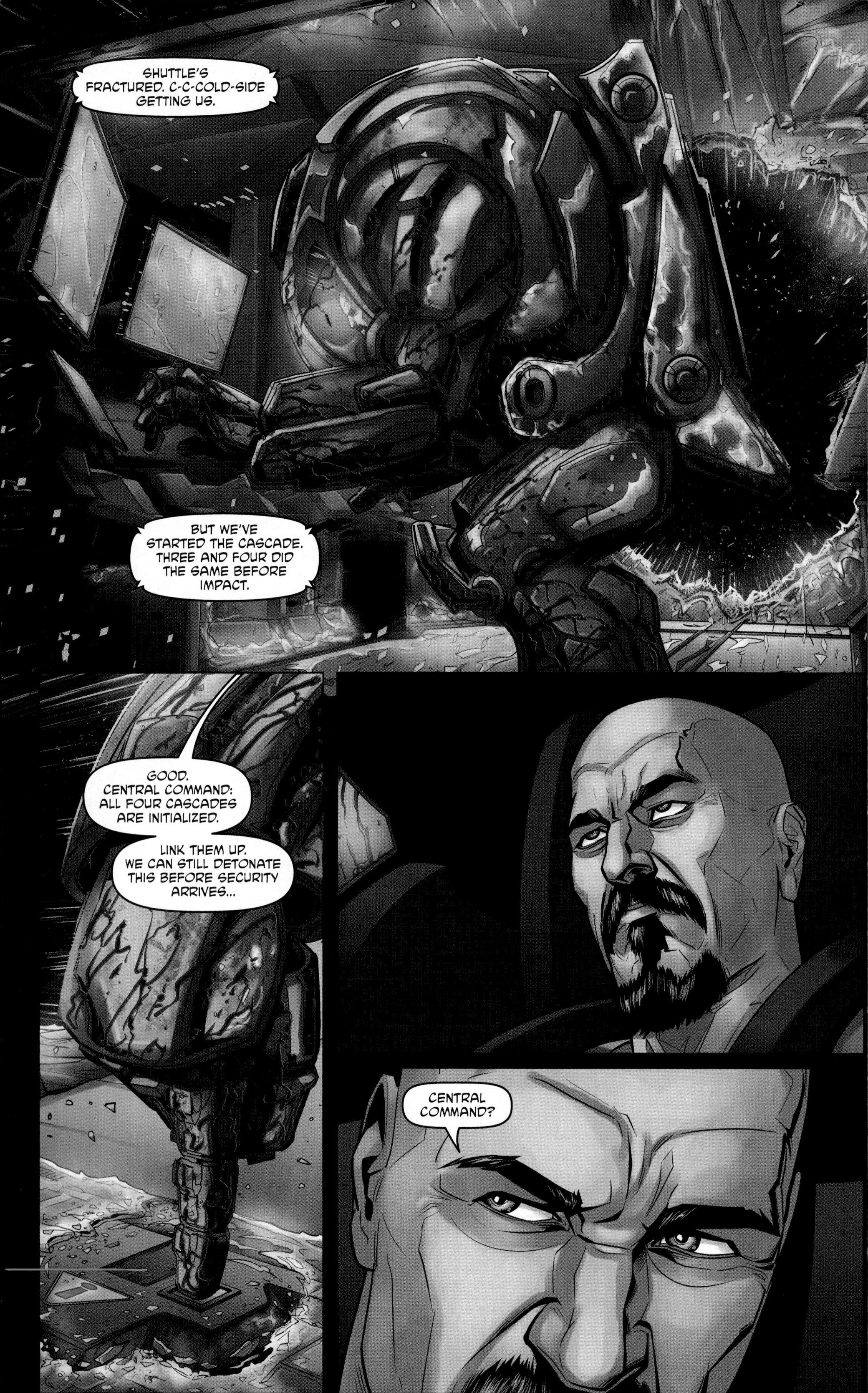

SHUTTLE'S FRACTURED. C-C-COLD-SIDE GETTING US.
BUT WE'VE STARTED THE CASCADE. THREE AND FOUR DID THE SAME BEFORE IMPACT.
GOOD. CENTRAL COMMAND: ALL FOUR CASCADES ARE INITIALIZED.
LINK THEM UP. WE CAN STILL DETONATE THIS BEFORE SECURITY ARRIVES...
CENTRAL COMMAND?

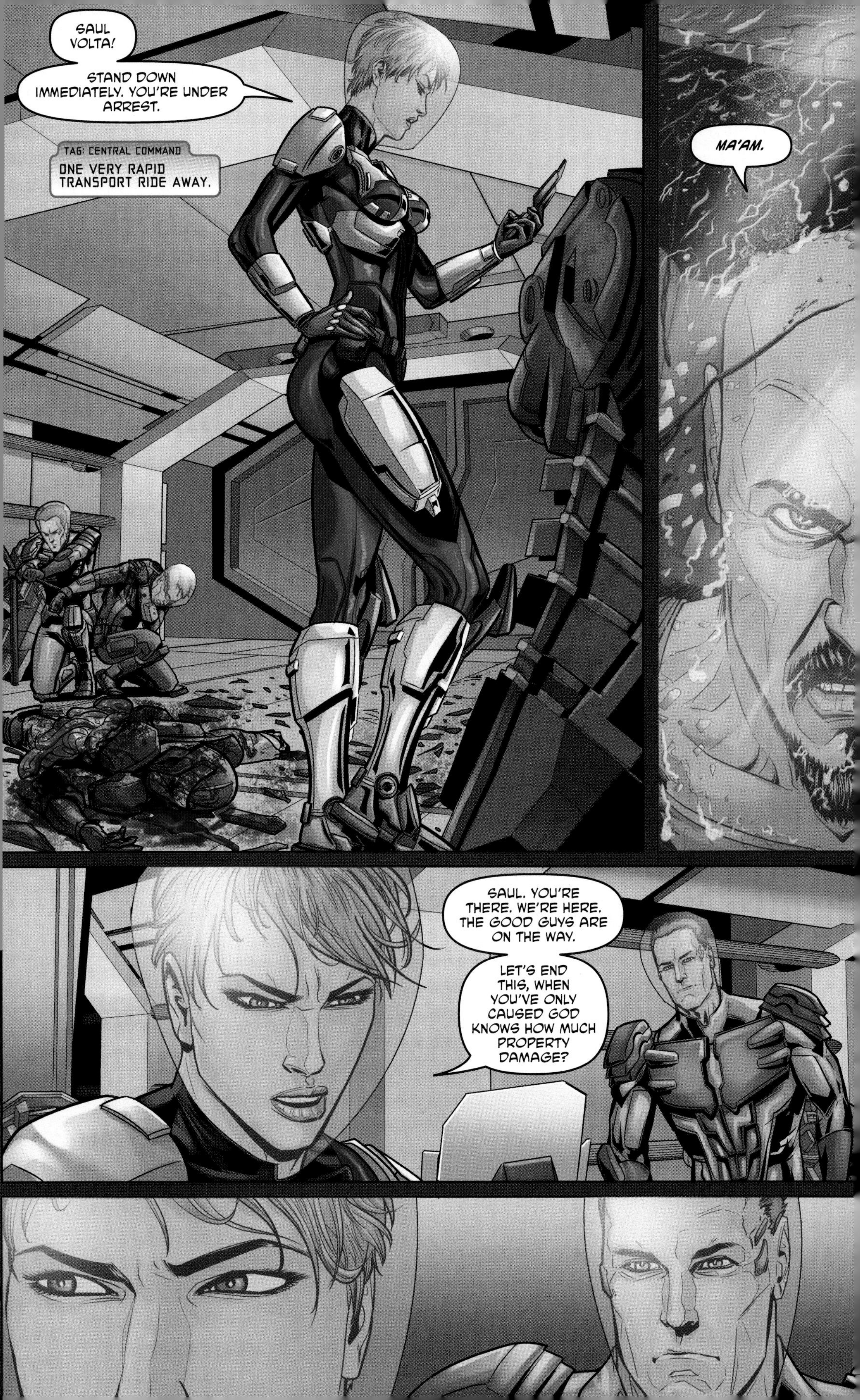
SAUL VOLTA!
STAND DOWN IMMEDIATELY. YOU'RE UNDER ARREST.
TAG: CENTRAL COMMAND
ONE VERY RAPID TRANSPORT RIDE AWAY.
MA'AM.
SAUL. YOU'RE THERE. WE'RE HERE. THE GOOD GUYS ARE ON THE WAY.
LET'S END THIS, WHEN YOU'VE ONLY CAUSED GOD KNOWS HOW MUCH PROPERTY DAMAGE?

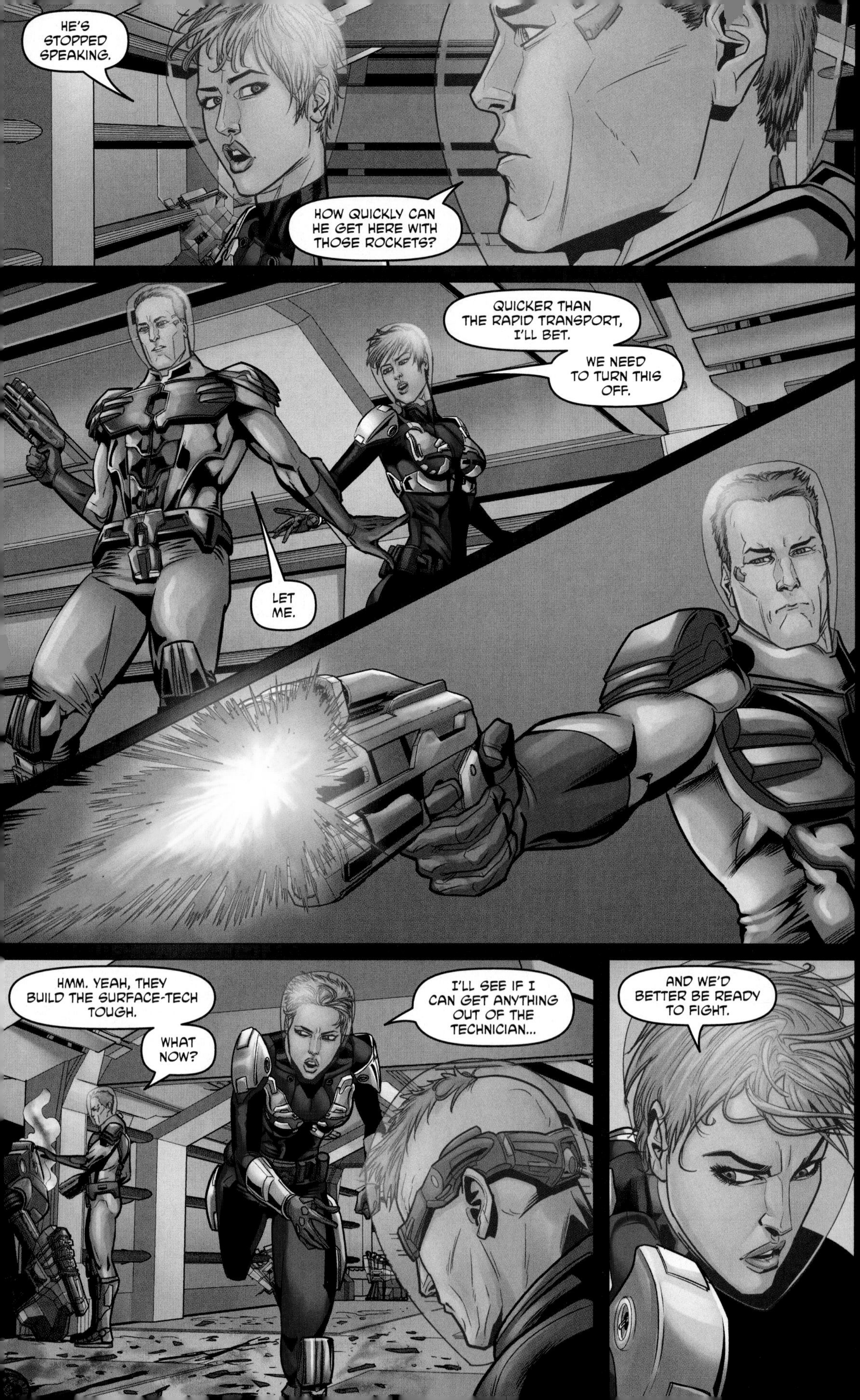
HE'S STOPPED SPEAKING.
HOW QUICKLY CAN HE GET HERE WITH THOSE ROCKETS?
QUICKER THAN THE RAPID TRANSPORT, I'LL BET.
WE NEED TO TURN THIS OFF.
LET ME.
HMM. YEAH, THEY BUILD THE SURFACE-TECH TOUGH.
WHAT NOW?
I'LL SEE IF I CAN GET ANYTHING OUT OF THE TECHNICIAN...
AND WE'D BETTER BE READY TO FIGHT.

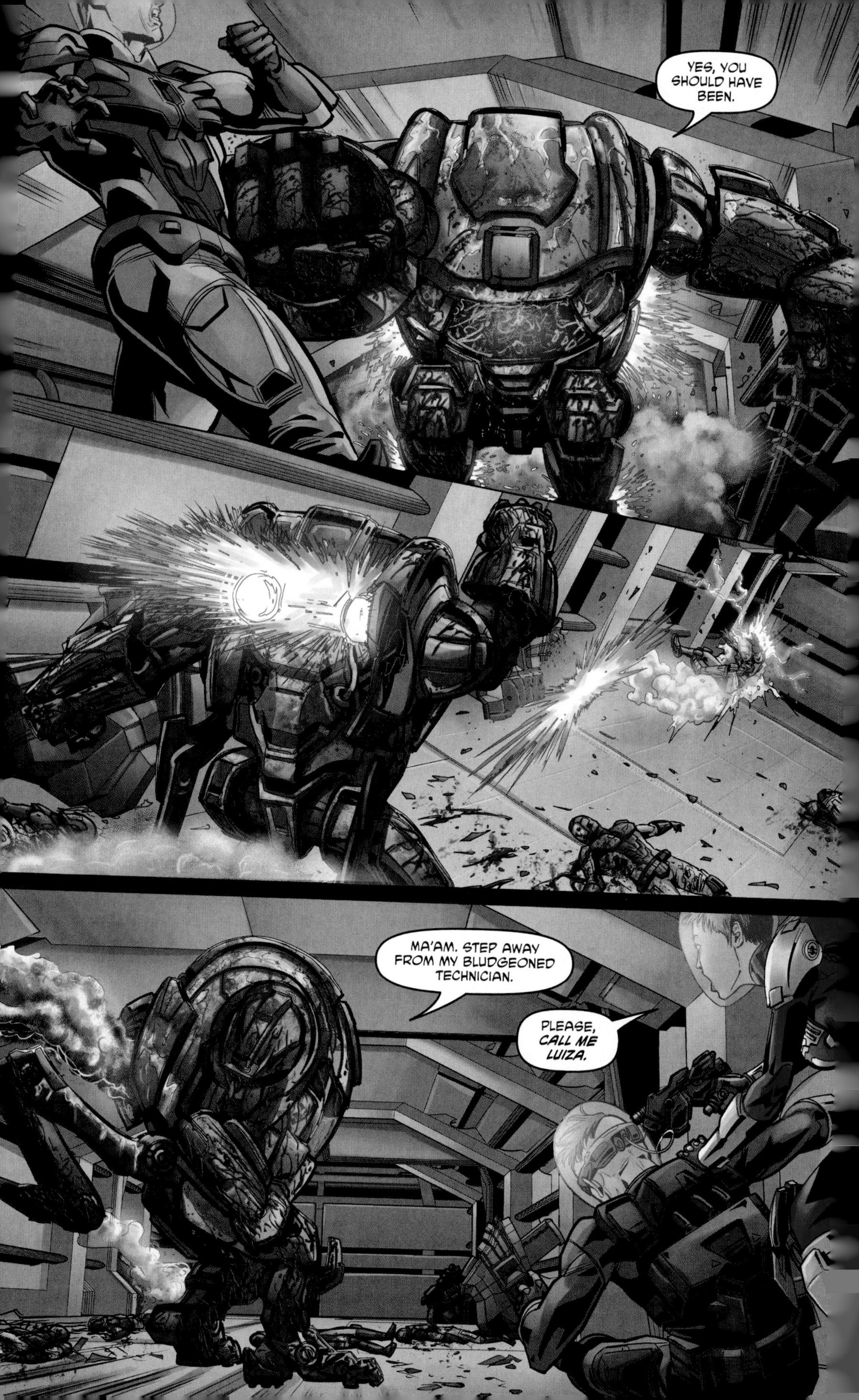
YES, YOU SHOULD HAVE BEEN.
MA'AM. STEP AWAY FROM MY BLUDGEONED TECHNICIAN.
PLEASE, *CALL ME LUIZA.*

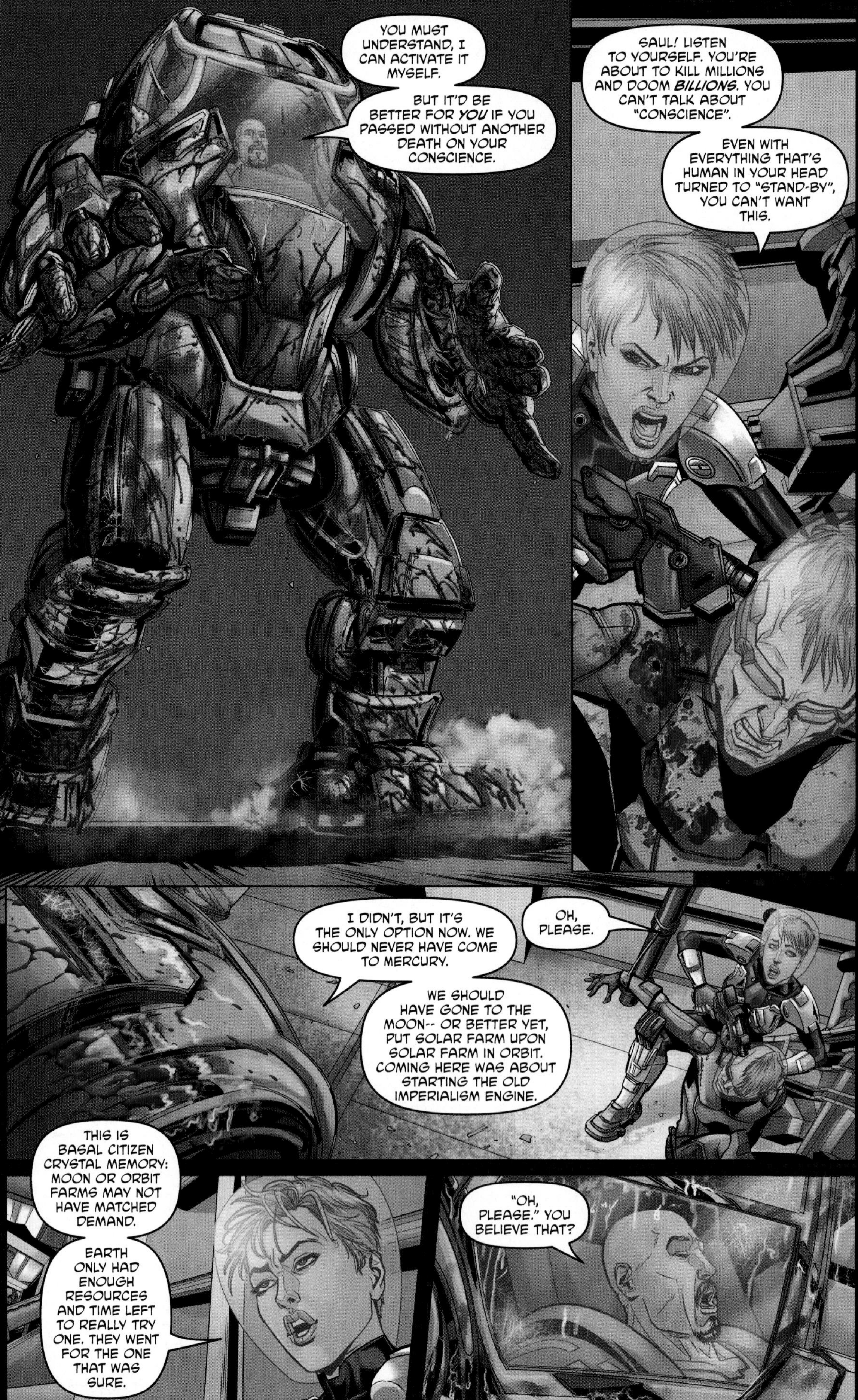
YOU MUST UNDERSTAND, I CAN ACTIVATE IT MYSELF.
BUT IT'D BE BETTER FOR *YOU* IF YOU PASSED WITHOUT ANOTHER DEATH ON YOUR CONSCIENCE.
SAUL! LISTEN TO YOURSELF. YOU'RE ABOUT TO KILL MILLIONS AND DOOM *BILLIONS*. YOU CAN'T TALK ABOUT "CONSCIENCE".
EVEN WITH EVERYTHING THAT'S HUMAN IN YOUR HEAD TURNED TO "STAND-BY", YOU CAN'T WANT THIS.
I DIDN'T, BUT IT'S THE ONLY OPTION NOW. WE SHOULD NEVER HAVE COME TO MERCURY.
OH, PLEASE.
WE SHOULD HAVE GONE TO THE MOON-- OR BETTER YET, PUT SOLAR FARM UPON SOLAR FARM IN ORBIT. COMING HERE WAS ABOUT STARTING THE OLD IMPERIALISM ENGINE.
THIS IS BASAL CITIZEN CRYSTAL MEMORY: MOON OR ORBIT FARMS MAY NOT HAVE MATCHED DEMAND.
EARTH ONLY HAD ENOUGH RESOURCES AND TIME LEFT TO REALLY TRY ONE. THEY WENT FOR THE ONE THAT WAS SURE.
"OH, PLEASE." YOU BELIEVE THAT?

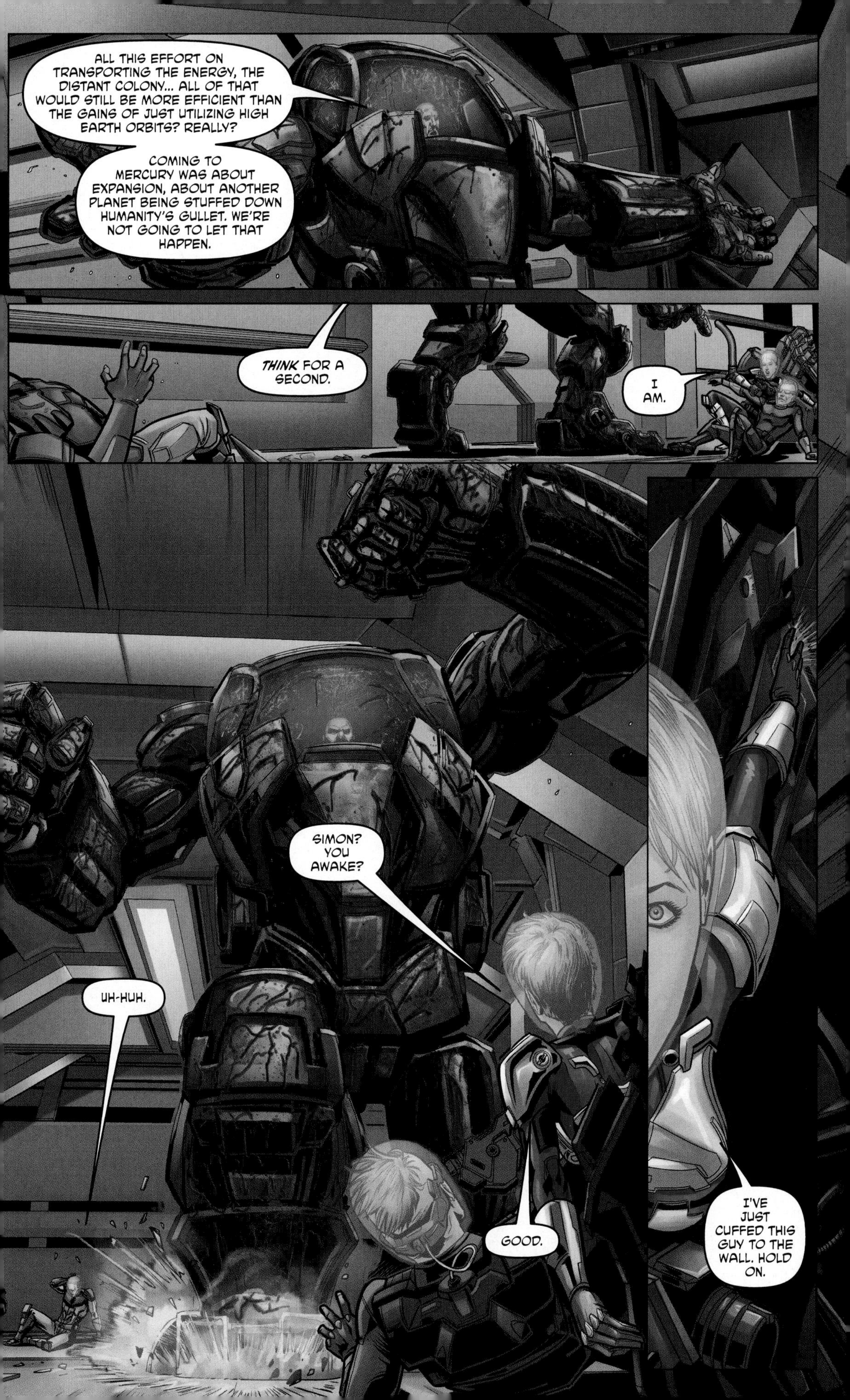
ALL THIS EFFORT ON TRANSPORTING THE ENERGY, THE DISTANT COLONY... ALL OF THAT WOULD STILL BE MORE EFFICIENT THAN THE GAINS OF JUST UTILIZING HIGH EARTH ORBITS? REALLY?
COMING TO MERCURY WAS ABOUT EXPANSION, ABOUT ANOTHER PLANET BEING STUFFED DOWN HUMANITY'S GULLET. WE'RE NOT GOING TO LET THAT HAPPEN.
THINK FOR A SECOND.
I AM.
SIMON? YOU AWAKE?
UH-HUH.
GOOD.
I'VE JUST CUFFED THIS GUY TO THE WALL. HOLD ON.

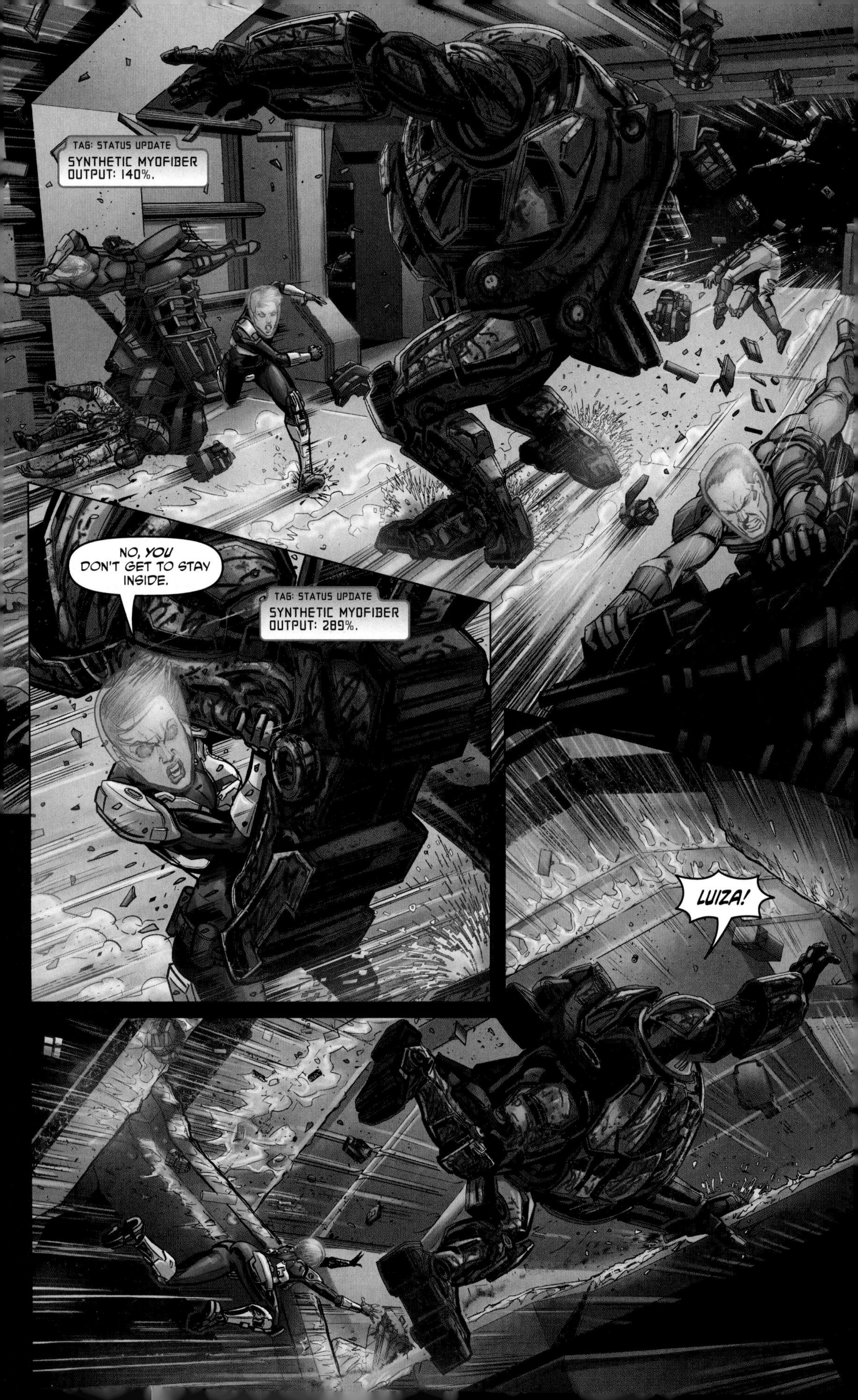
TAG: STATUS UPDATE
SYNTHETIC MYOFIBER OUTPUT: 140%.
NO, YOU DON'T GET TO STAY INSIDE.
TAG: STATUS UPDATE
SYNTHETIC MYOFIBER OUTPUT: 289%.
LUIZA!

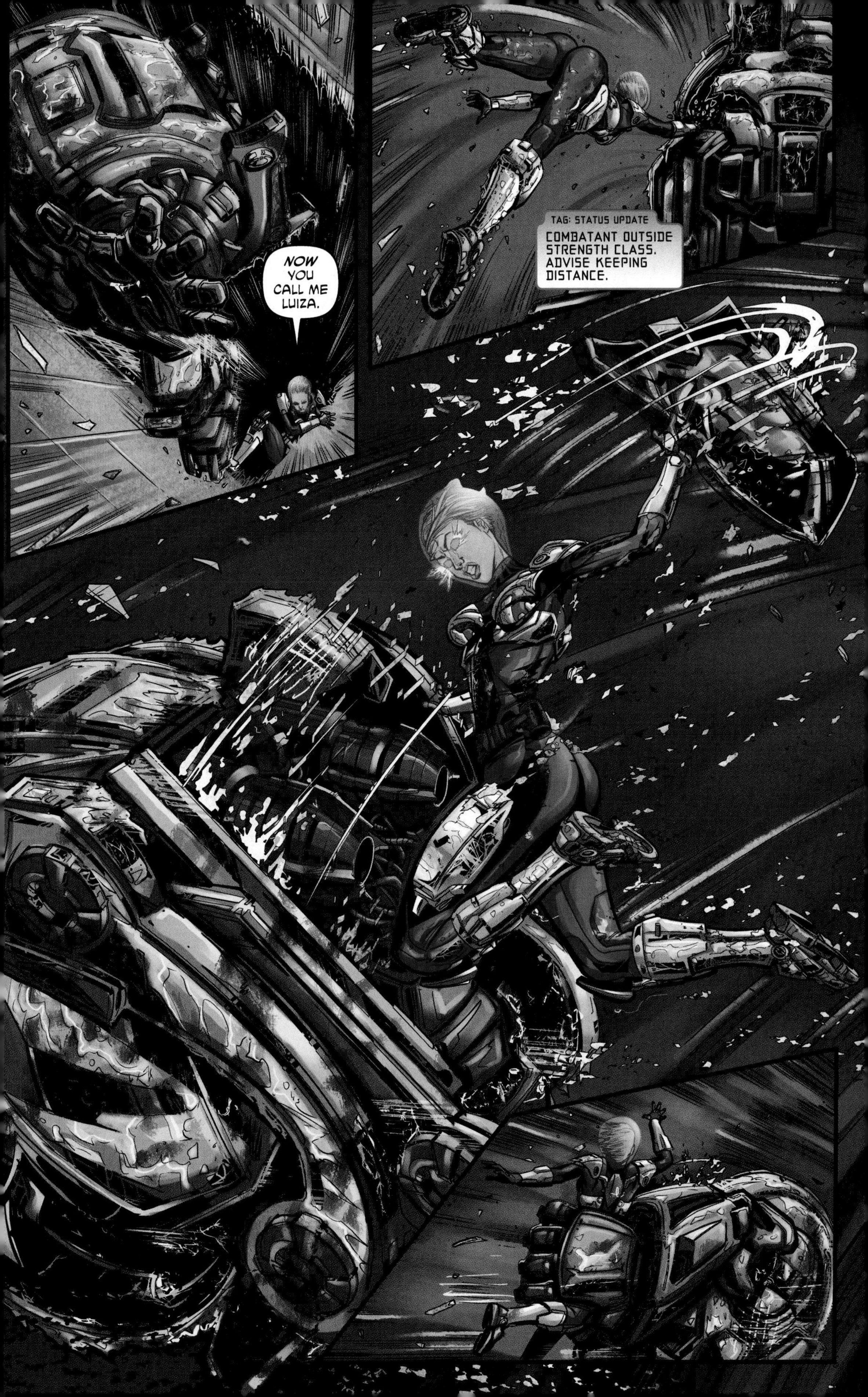
NOW YOU CALL ME LUIZA.
TAG: STATUS UPDATE
COMBATANT OUTSIDE STRENGTH CLASS. ADVISE KEEPING DISTANCE.

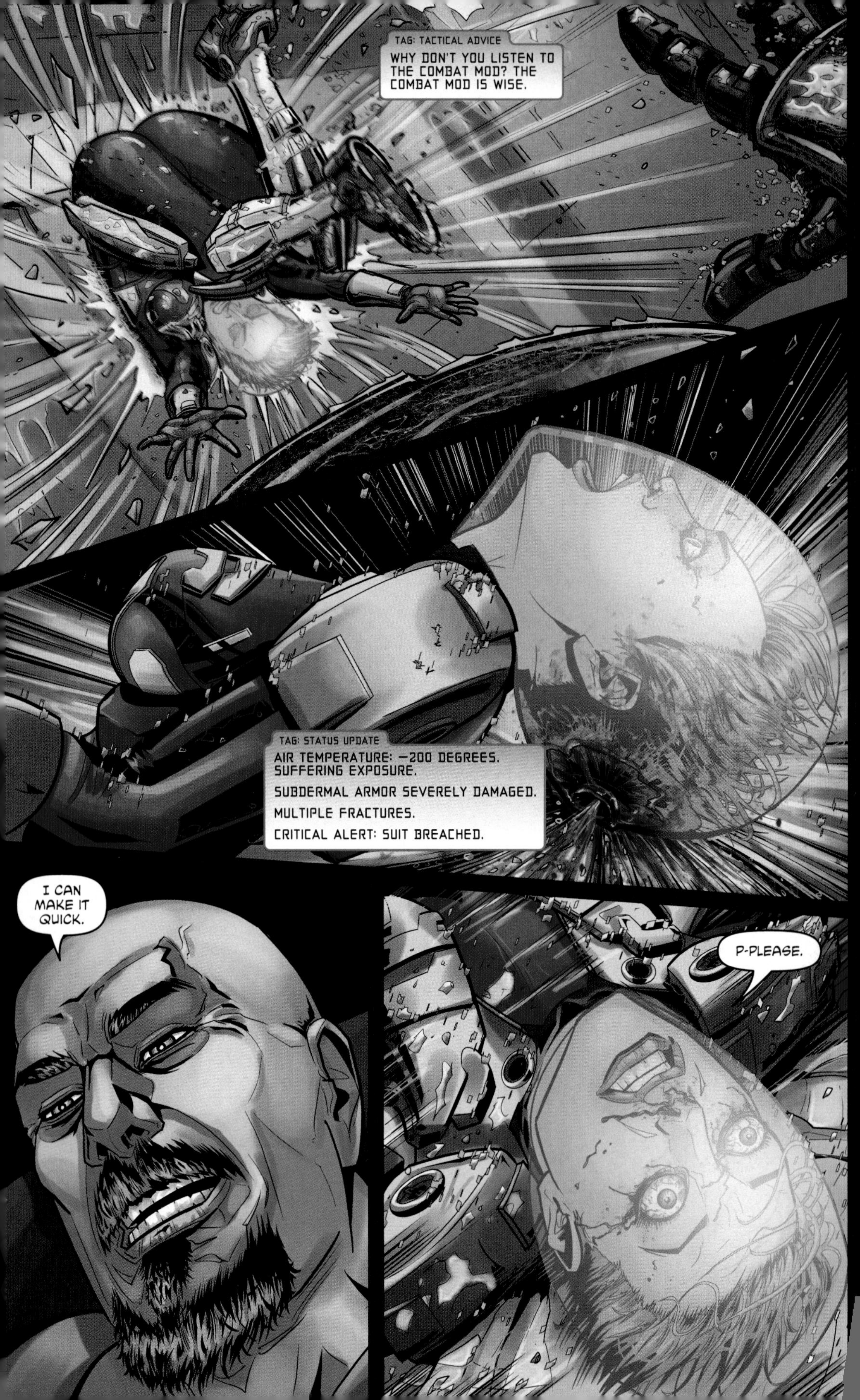

TAG: TACTICAL ADVICE
WHY DON'T YOU LISTEN TO THE COMBAT MOD? THE COMBAT MOD IS WISE.
TAG: STATUS UPDATE
AIR TEMPERATURE: −200 DEGREES. SUFFERING EXPOSURE.
SUBDERMAL ARMOR SEVERELY DAMAGED.
MULTIPLE FRACTURES.
CRITICAL ALERT: SUIT BREACHED.
I CAN MAKE IT QUICK.
P-PLEASE.

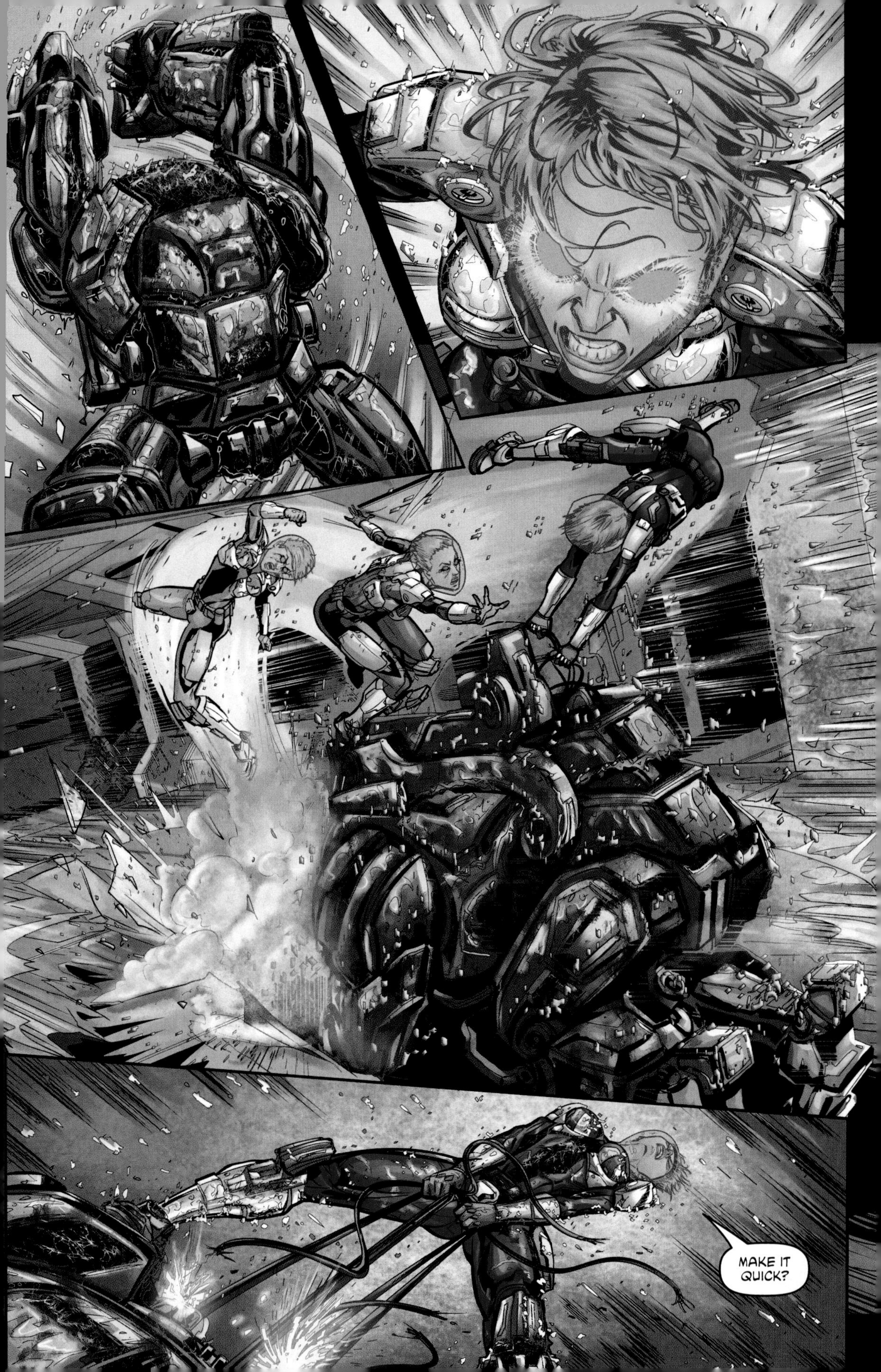
MAKE IT
QUICK?

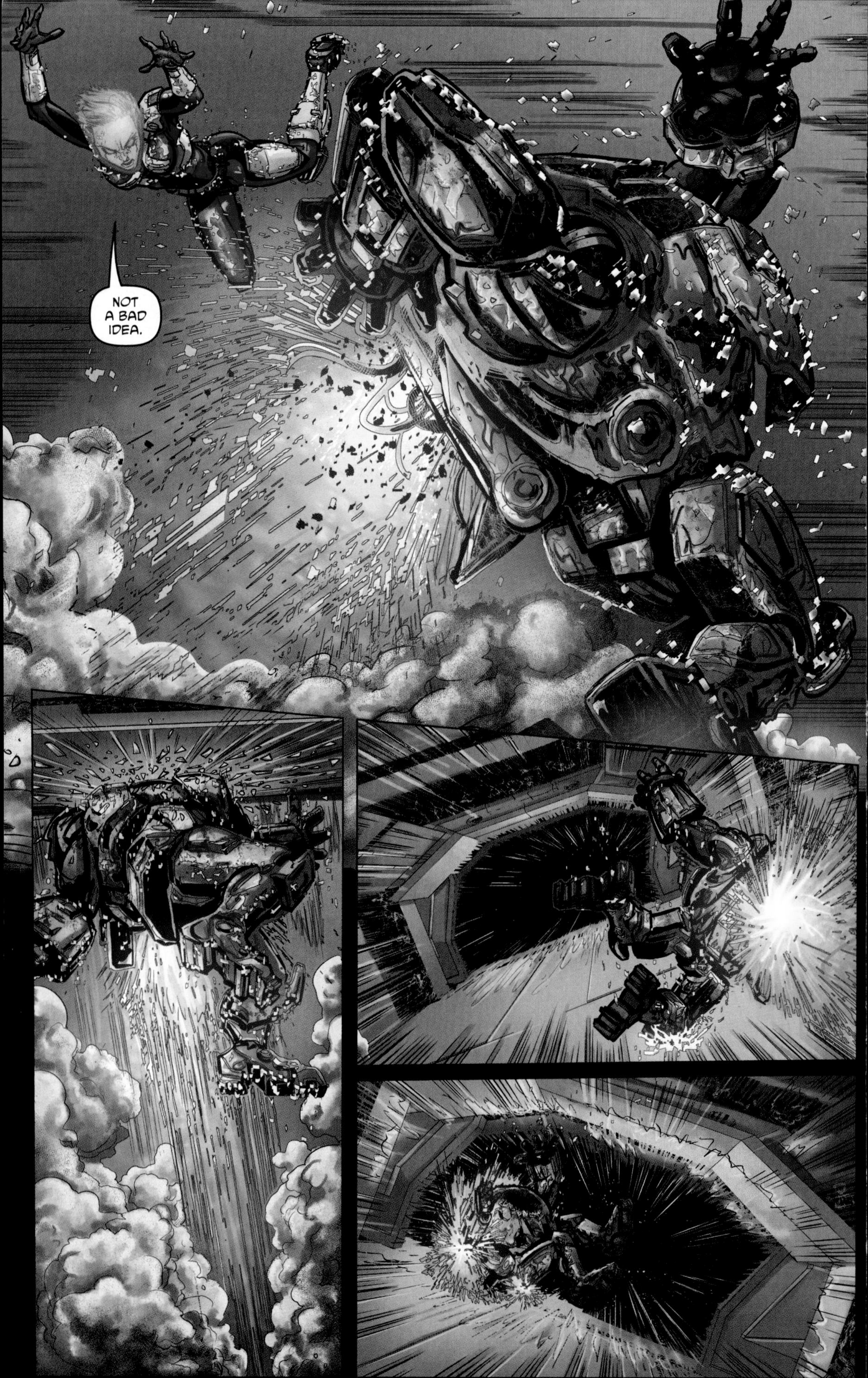
NOT A BAD IDEA.

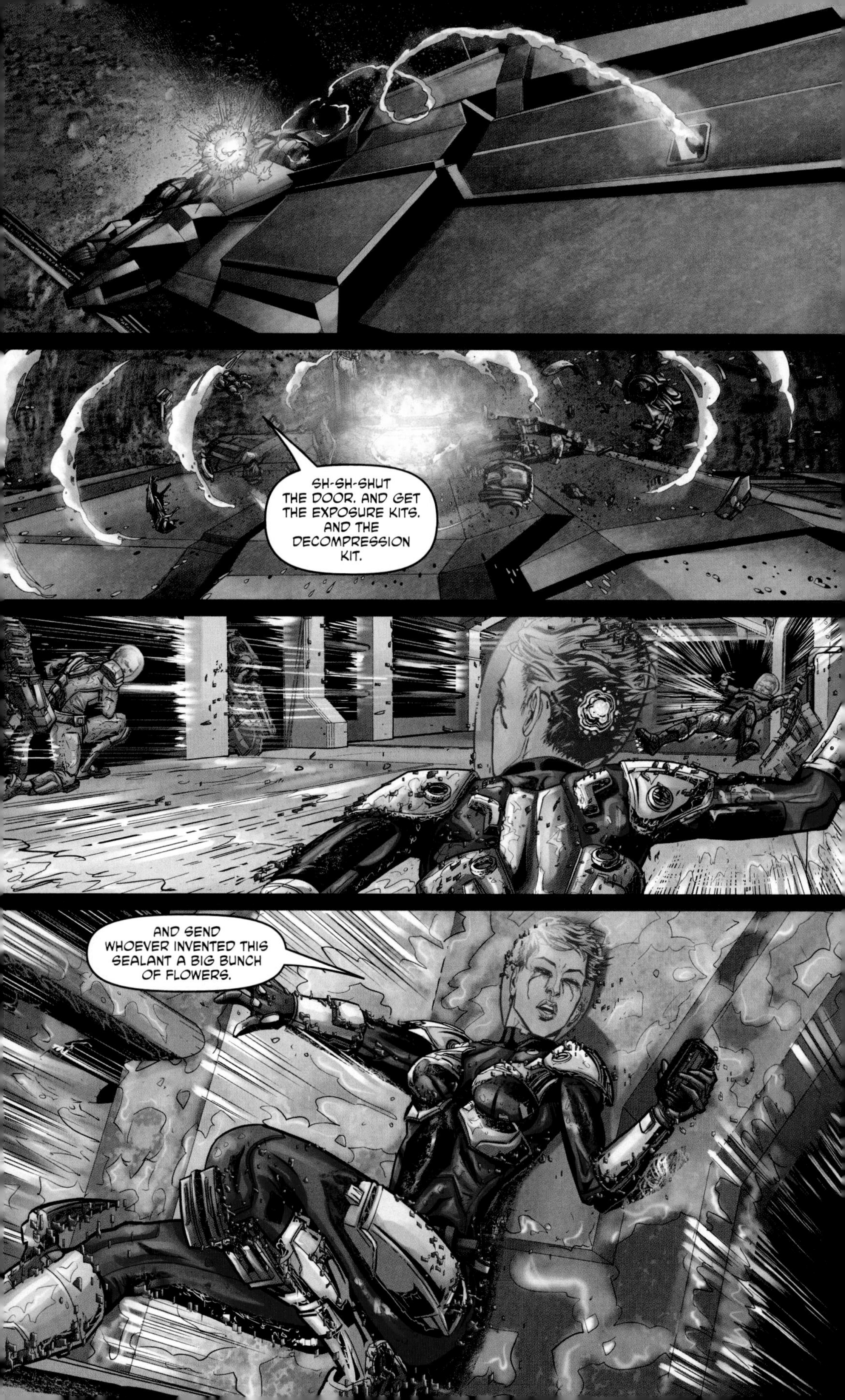
SH-SH-SHUT THE DOOR. AND GET THE EXPOSURE KITS. AND THE DECOMPRESSION KIT.
AND SEND WHOEVER INVENTED THIS SEALANT A BIG BUNCH OF FLOWERS.

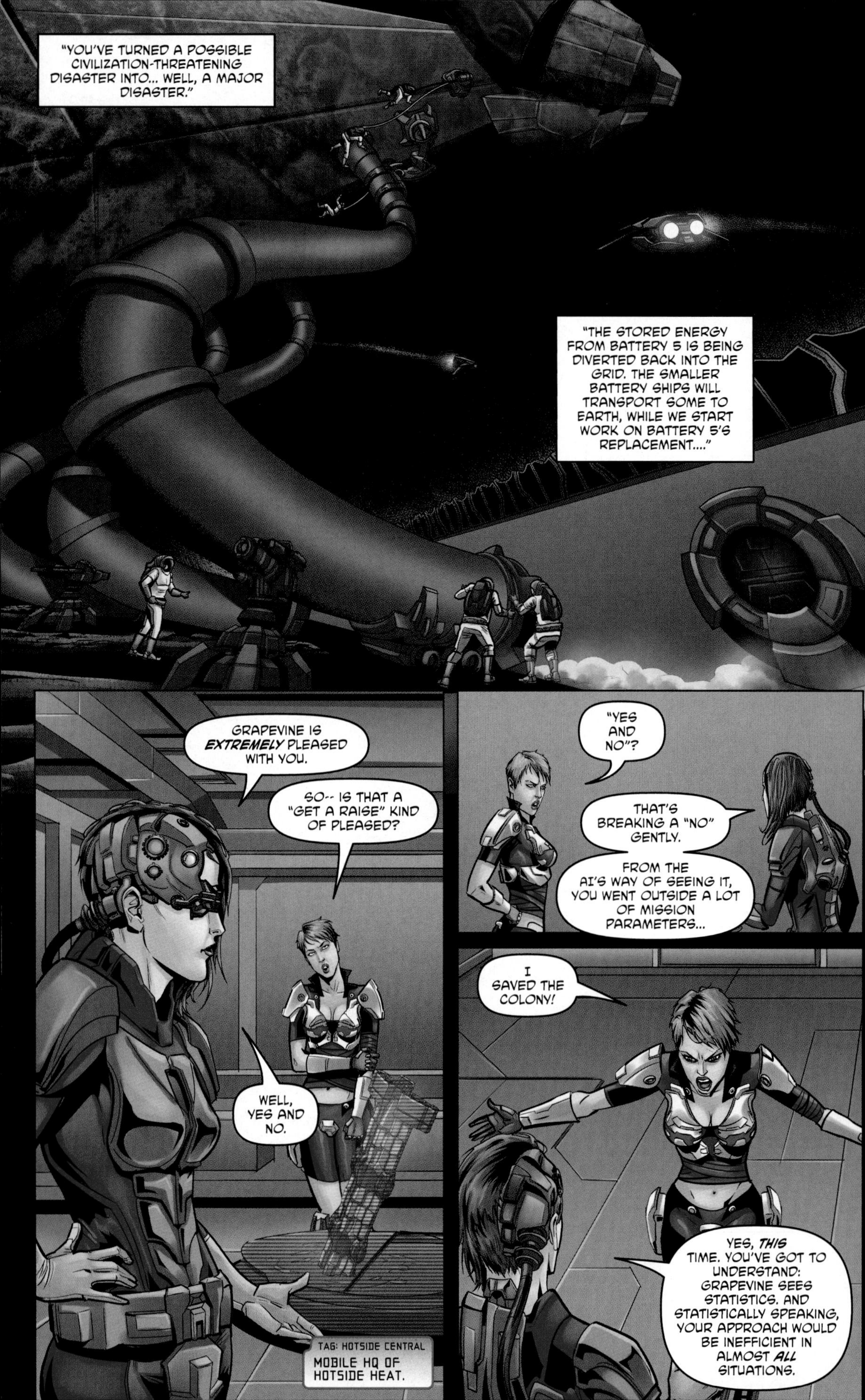
"YOU'VE TURNED A POSSIBLE CIVILIZATION-THREATENING DISASTER INTO... WELL, A MAJOR DISASTER."
"THE STORED ENERGY FROM BATTERY 5 IS BEING DIVERTED BACK INTO THE GRID. THE SMALLER BATTERY SHIPS WILL TRANSPORT SOME TO EARTH, WHILE WE START WORK ON BATTERY 5'S REPLACEMENT...."
GRAPEVINE IS *EXTREMELY* PLEASED WITH YOU.
SO-- IS THAT A "GET A RAISE" KIND OF PLEASED?
WELL, YES AND NO.
TAG: HOTSIDE CENTRAL
MOBILE HQ OF HOTSIDE HEAT.
"YES AND NO"?
THAT'S BREAKING A "NO" GENTLY.
FROM THE AI'S WAY OF SEEING IT, YOU WENT OUTSIDE A LOT OF MISSION PARAMETERS...
I SAVED THE COLONY!
YES, *THIS* TIME. YOU'VE GOT TO UNDERSTAND: GRAPEVINE SEES STATISTICS. AND STATISTICALLY SPEAKING, YOUR APPROACH WOULD BE INEFFICIENT IN ALMOST *ALL* SITUATIONS.

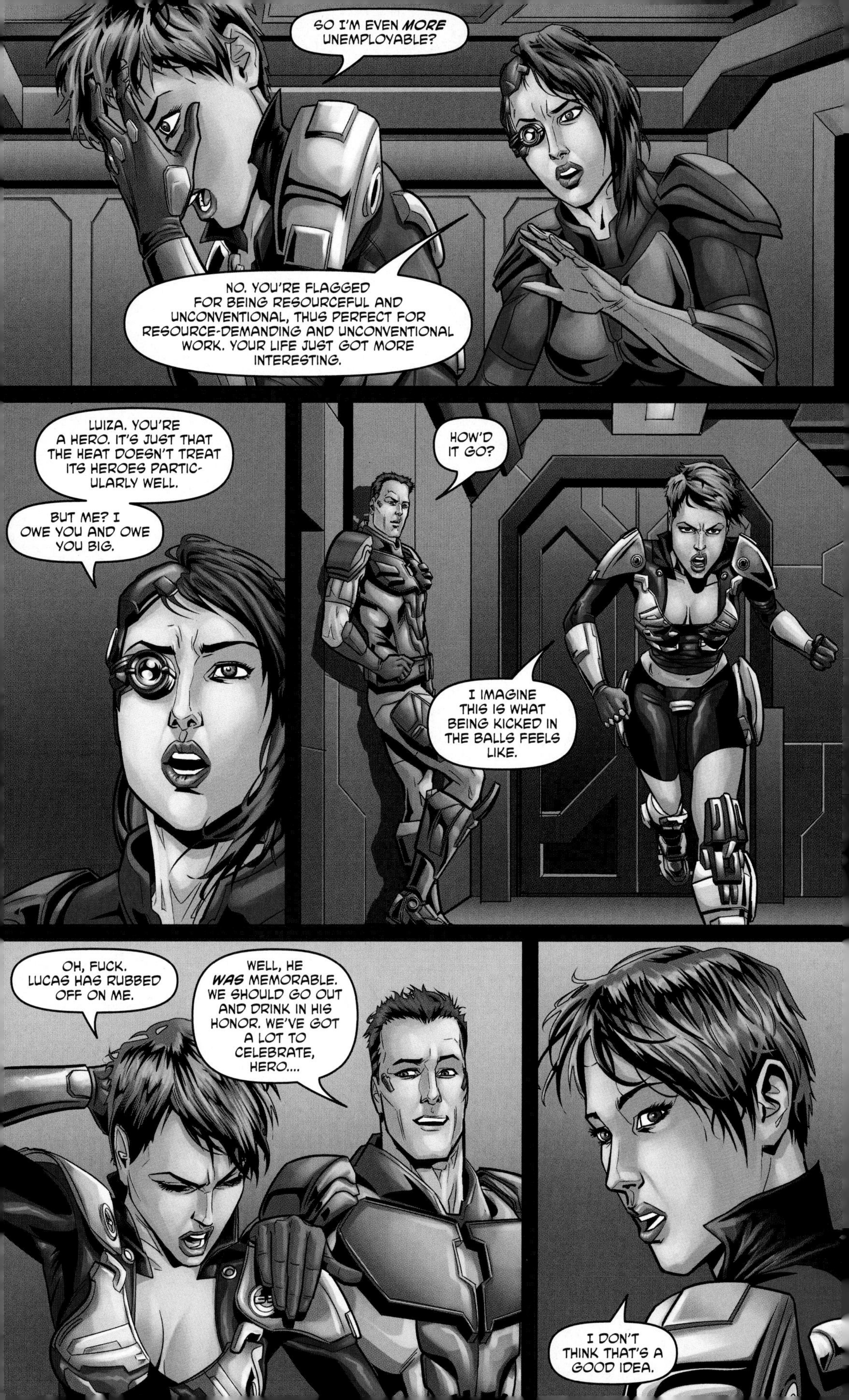

SO I'M EVEN *MORE* UNEMPLOYABLE?
NO. YOU'RE FLAGGED FOR BEING RESOURCEFUL AND UNCONVENTIONAL, THUS PERFECT FOR RESOURCE-DEMANDING AND UNCONVENTIONAL WORK. YOUR LIFE JUST GOT MORE INTERESTING.
LUIZA. YOU'RE A HERO. IT'S JUST THAT THE HEAT DOESN'T TREAT ITS HEROES PARTIC-ULARLY WELL.
BUT ME? I OWE YOU AND OWE YOU BIG.
HOW'D IT GO?
I IMAGINE THIS IS WHAT BEING KICKED IN THE BALLS FEELS LIKE.
OH, FUCK. LUCAS HAS RUBBED OFF ON ME.
WELL, HE *WAS* MEMORABLE. WE SHOULD GO OUT AND DRINK IN HIS HONOR. WE'VE GOT A LOT TO CELEBRATE, HERO....
I DON'T THINK THAT'S A GOOD IDEA.

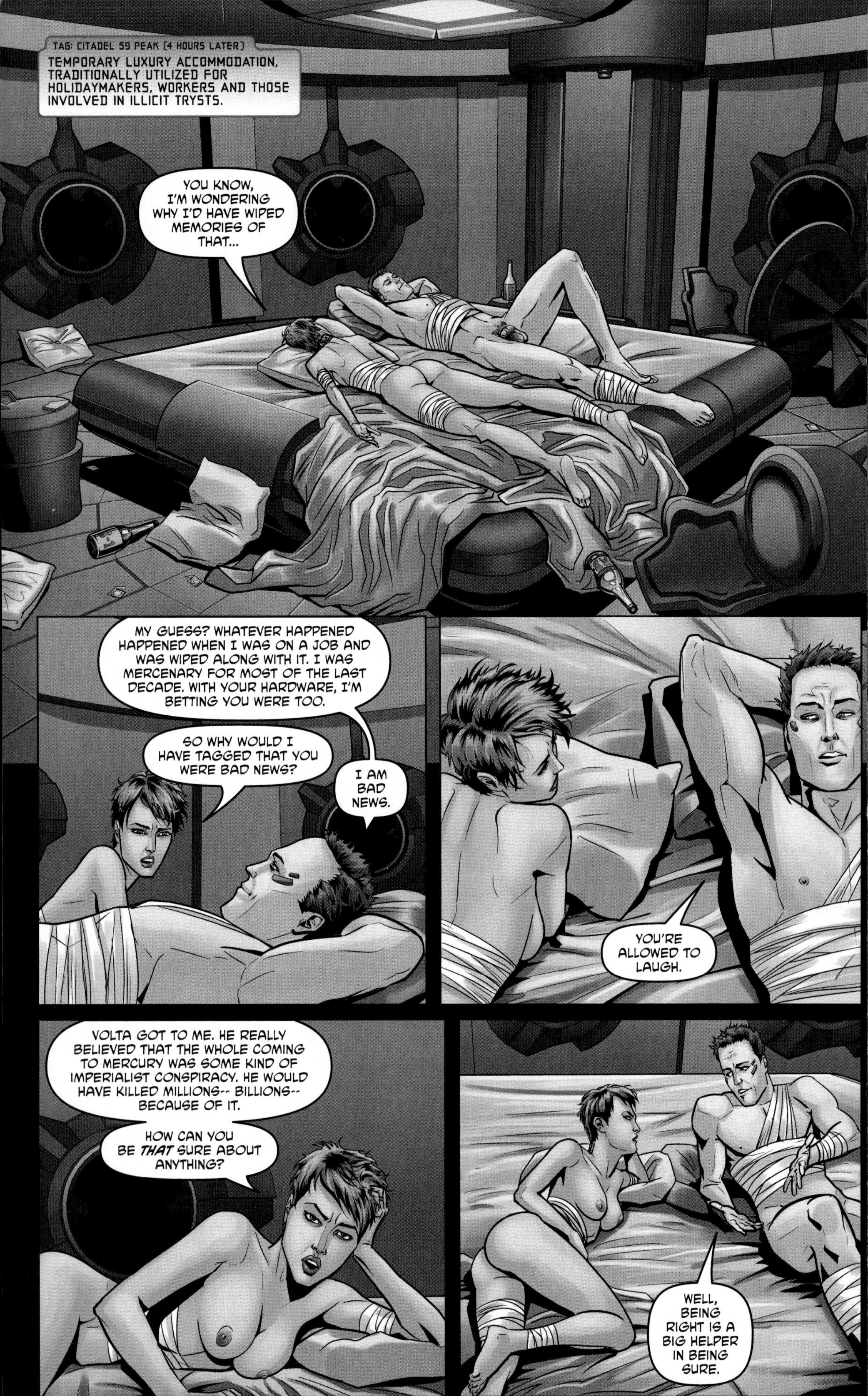
TAG: CITADEL 59 PEAK (4 HOURS LATER)
TEMPORARY LUXURY ACCOMMODATION, TRADITIONALLY UTILIZED FOR HOLIDAYMAKERS, WORKERS AND THOSE INVOLVED IN ILLICIT TRYSTS.
YOU KNOW, I'M WONDERING WHY I'D HAVE WIPED MEMORIES OF THAT...
MY GUESS? WHATEVER HAPPENED HAPPENED WHEN I WAS ON A JOB AND WAS WIPED ALONG WITH IT. I WAS MERCENARY FOR MOST OF THE LAST DECADE. WITH YOUR HARDWARE, I'M BETTING YOU WERE TOO.
SO WHY WOULD I HAVE TAGGED THAT YOU WERE BAD NEWS?
I AM BAD NEWS.
YOU'RE ALLOWED TO LAUGH.
VOLTA GOT TO ME. HE REALLY BELIEVED THAT THE WHOLE COMING TO MERCURY WAS SOME KIND OF IMPERIALIST CONSPIRACY. HE WOULD HAVE KILLED MILLIONS-- BILLIONS-- BECAUSE OF IT.
HOW CAN YOU BE *THAT* SURE ABOUT ANYTHING?
WELL, BEING RIGHT IS A BIG HELPER IN BEING SURE.

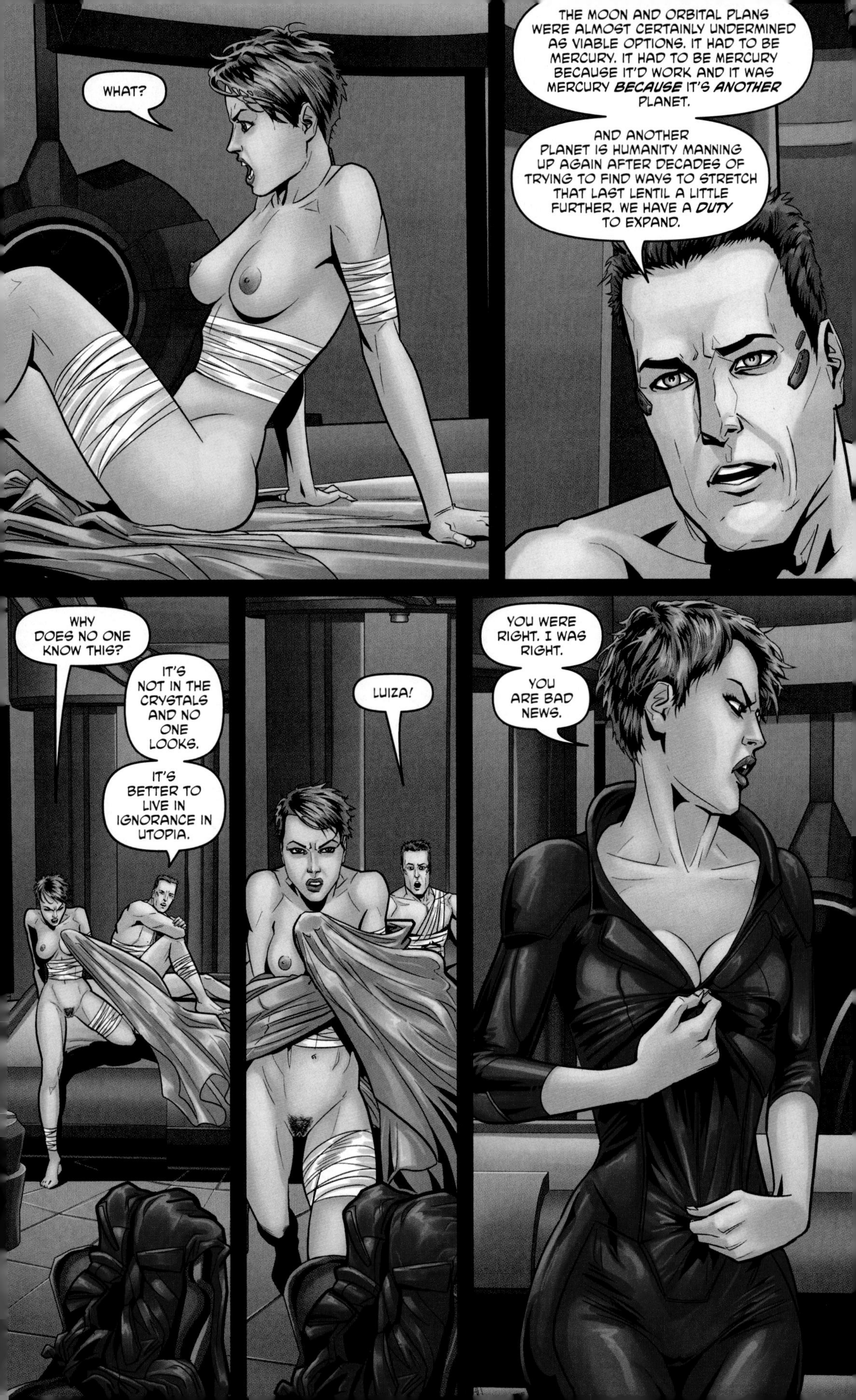
WHAT?
THE MOON AND ORBITAL PLANS WERE ALMOST CERTAINLY UNDERMINED AS VIABLE OPTIONS. IT HAD TO BE MERCURY. IT HAD TO BE MERCURY BECAUSE IT'D WORK AND IT WAS MERCURY ***BECAUSE*** IT'S ***ANOTHER*** PLANET.
AND ANOTHER PLANET IS HUMANITY MANNING UP AGAIN AFTER DECADES OF TRYING TO FIND WAYS TO STRETCH THAT LAST LENTIL A LITTLE FURTHER. WE HAVE A ***DUTY*** TO EXPAND.
WHY DOES NO ONE KNOW THIS?
IT'S NOT IN THE CRYSTALS AND NO ONE LOOKS.
IT'S BETTER TO LIVE IN IGNORANCE IN UTOPIA.
LUIZA!
YOU WERE RIGHT. I WAS RIGHT.
YOU ARE BAD NEWS.

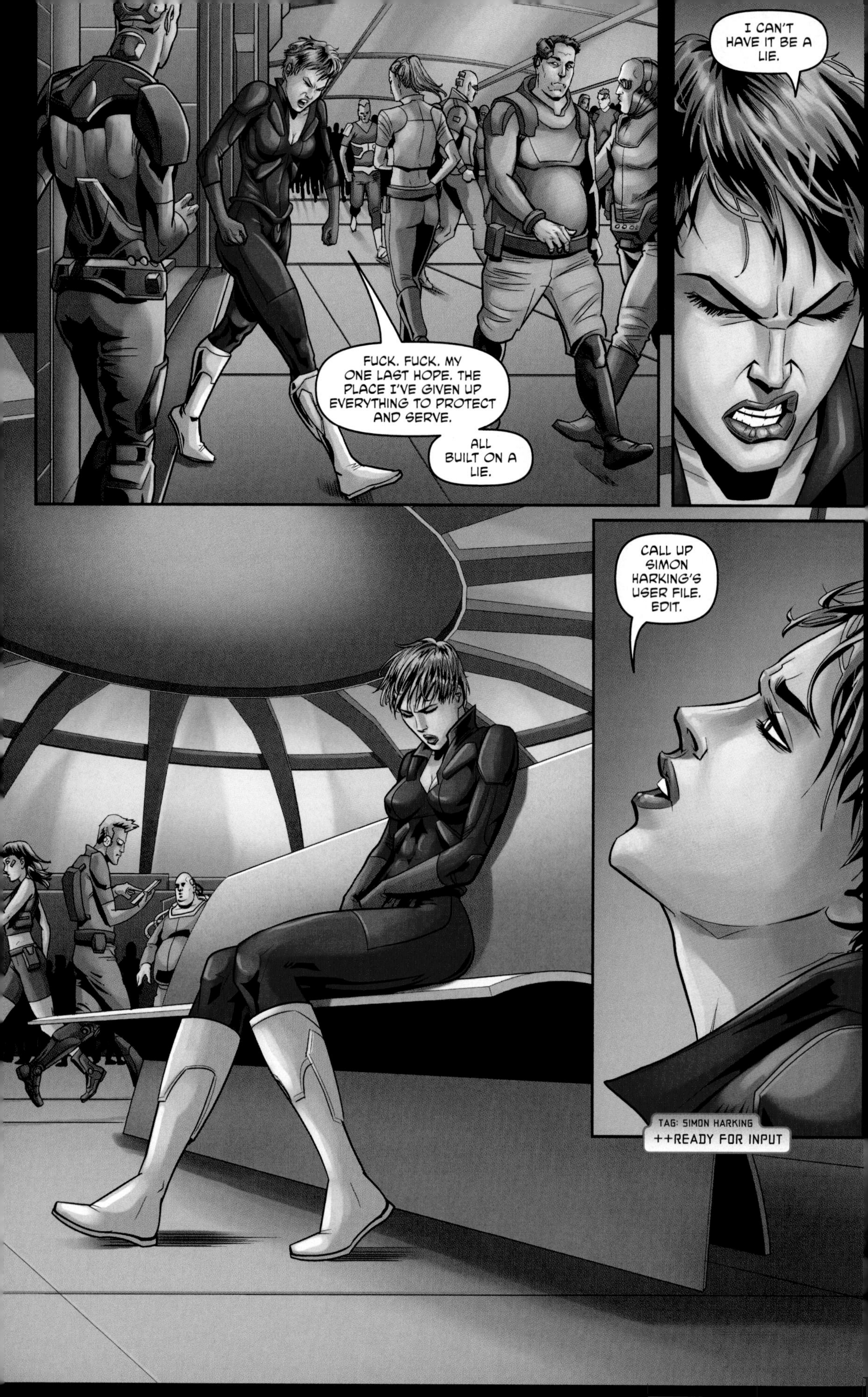
FUCK. FUCK. MY ONE LAST HOPE. THE PLACE I'VE GIVEN UP EVERYTHING TO PROTECT AND SERVE.
ALL BUILT ON A LIE.
I CAN'T HAVE IT BE A LIE.
CALL UP SIMON HARKING'S USER FILE. EDIT.
TAG: SIMON HARKING
++READY FOR INPUT

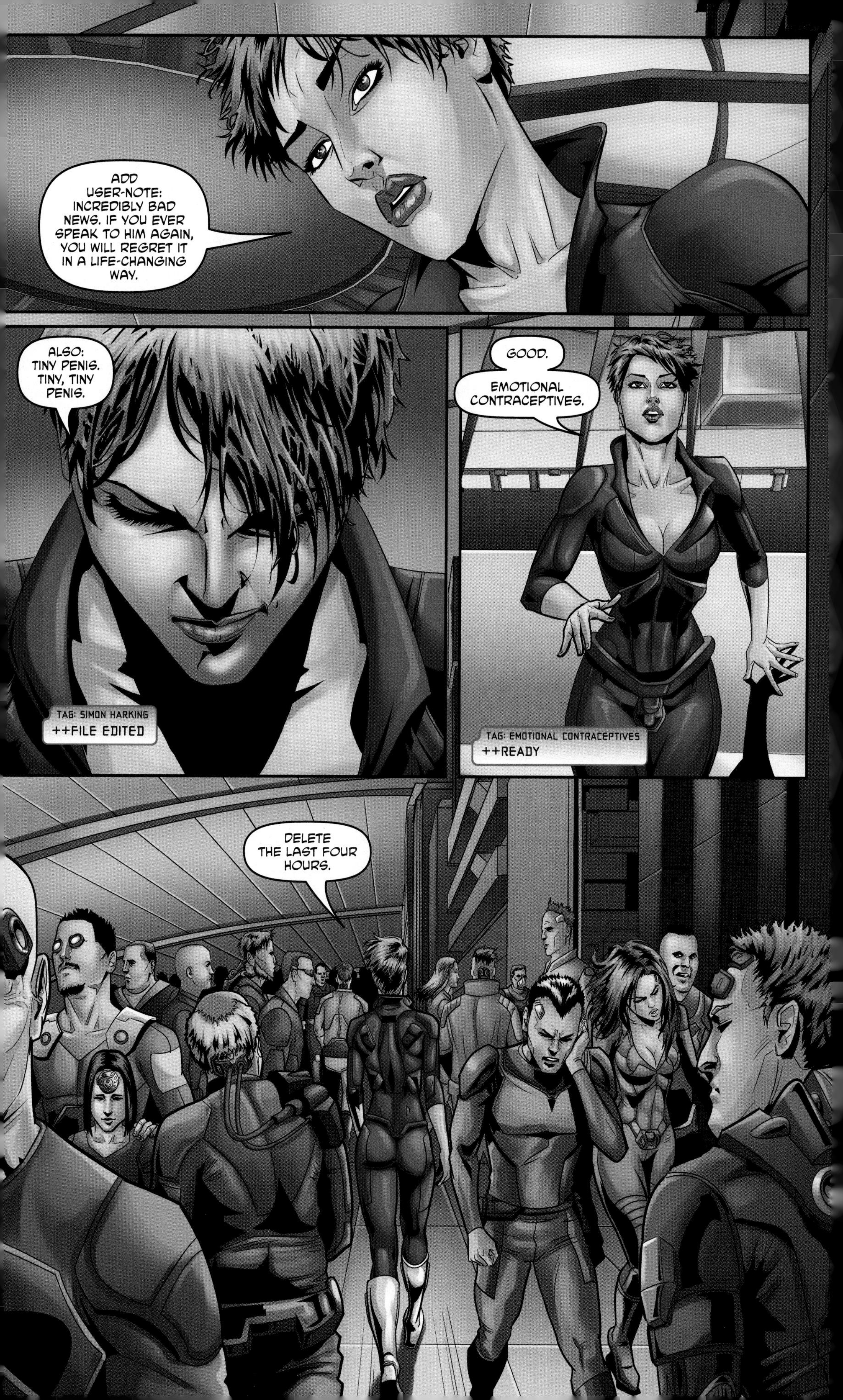
ADD USER-NOTE: INCREDIBLY BAD NEWS. IF YOU EVER SPEAK TO HIM AGAIN, YOU WILL REGRET IT IN A LIFE-CHANGING WAY.
ALSO: TINY PENIS. TINY, TINY PENIS.
TAG: SIMON HARKING
++FILE EDITED
GOOD.
EMOTIONAL CONTRACEPTIVES.
TAG: EMOTIONAL CONTRACEPTIVES
++READY
DELETE THE LAST FOUR HOURS.

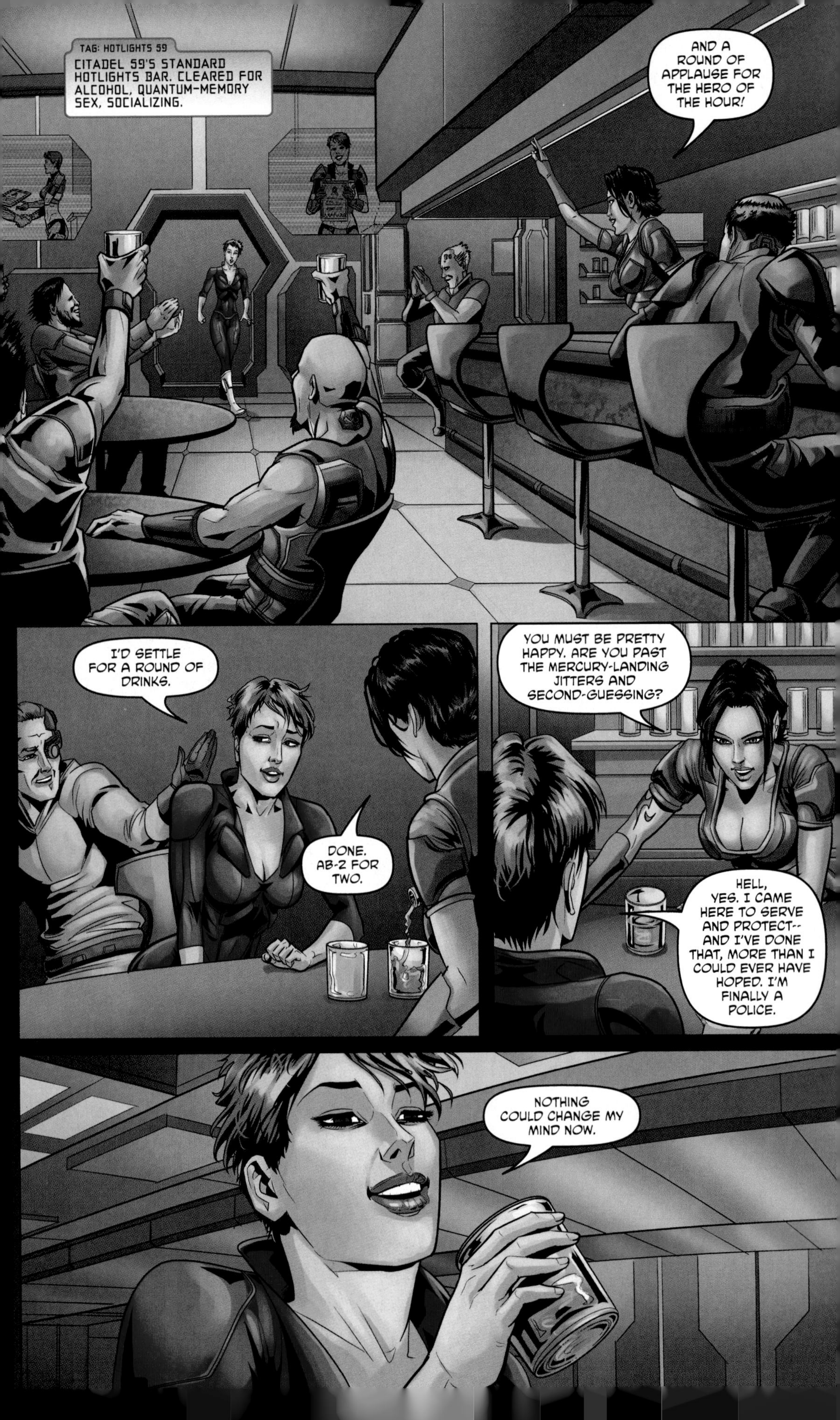
TAG: HOTLIGHTS 59
CITADEL 59'S STANDARD HOTLIGHTS BAR. CLEARED FOR ALCOHOL, QUANTUM-MEMORY SEX, SOCIALIZING.
AND A ROUND OF APPLAUSE FOR THE HERO OF THE HOUR!
I'D SETTLE FOR A ROUND OF DRINKS.
DONE. AB-2 FOR TWO.
YOU MUST BE PRETTY HAPPY. ARE YOU PAST THE MERCURY-LANDING JITTERS AND SECOND-GUESSING?
HELL, YES. I CAME HERE TO SERVE AND PROTECT-- AND I'VE DONE THAT, MORE THAN I COULD EVER HAVE HOPED. I'M FINALLY A POLICE.
NOTHING COULD CHANGE MY MIND NOW.

interlude

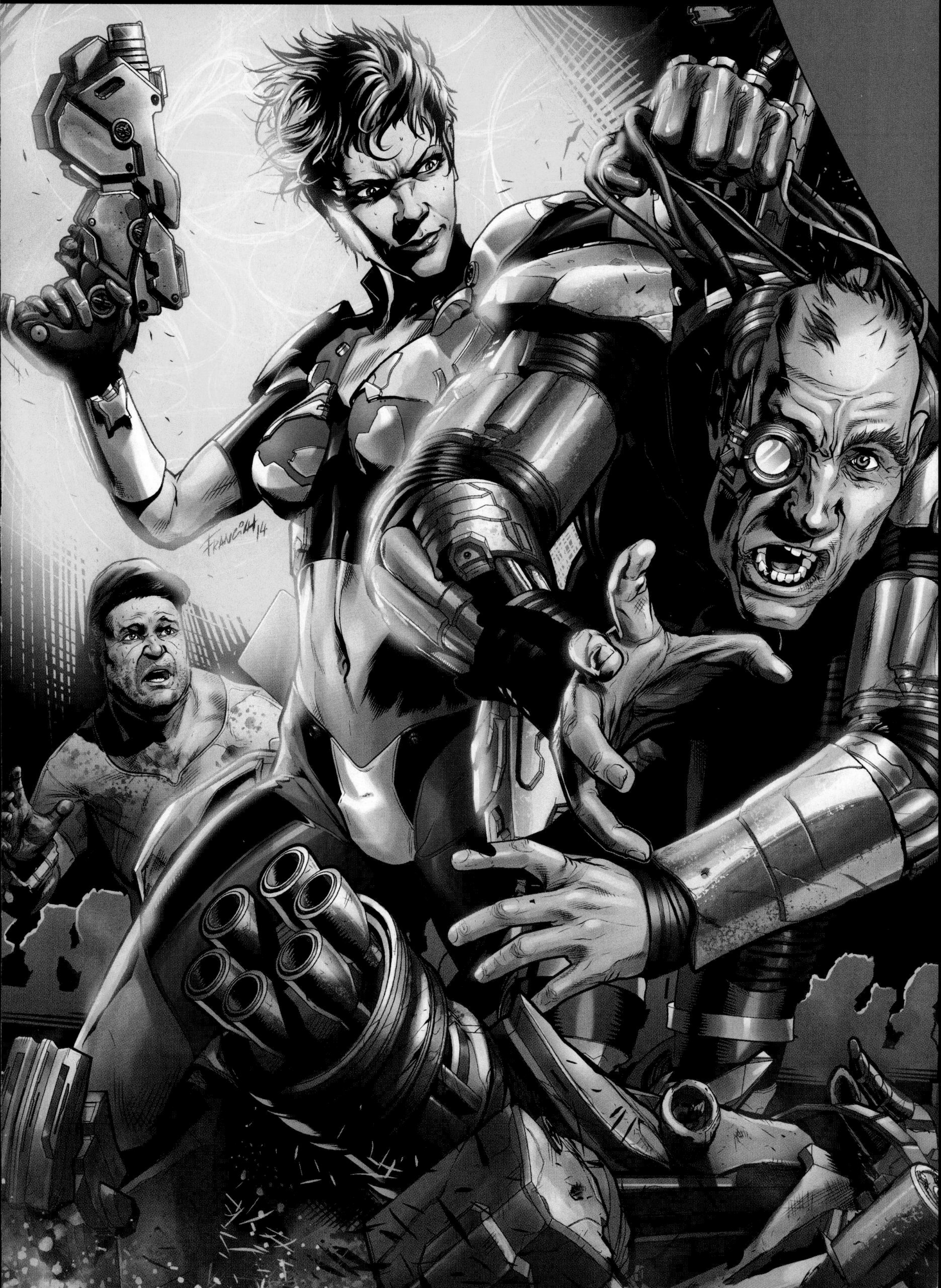

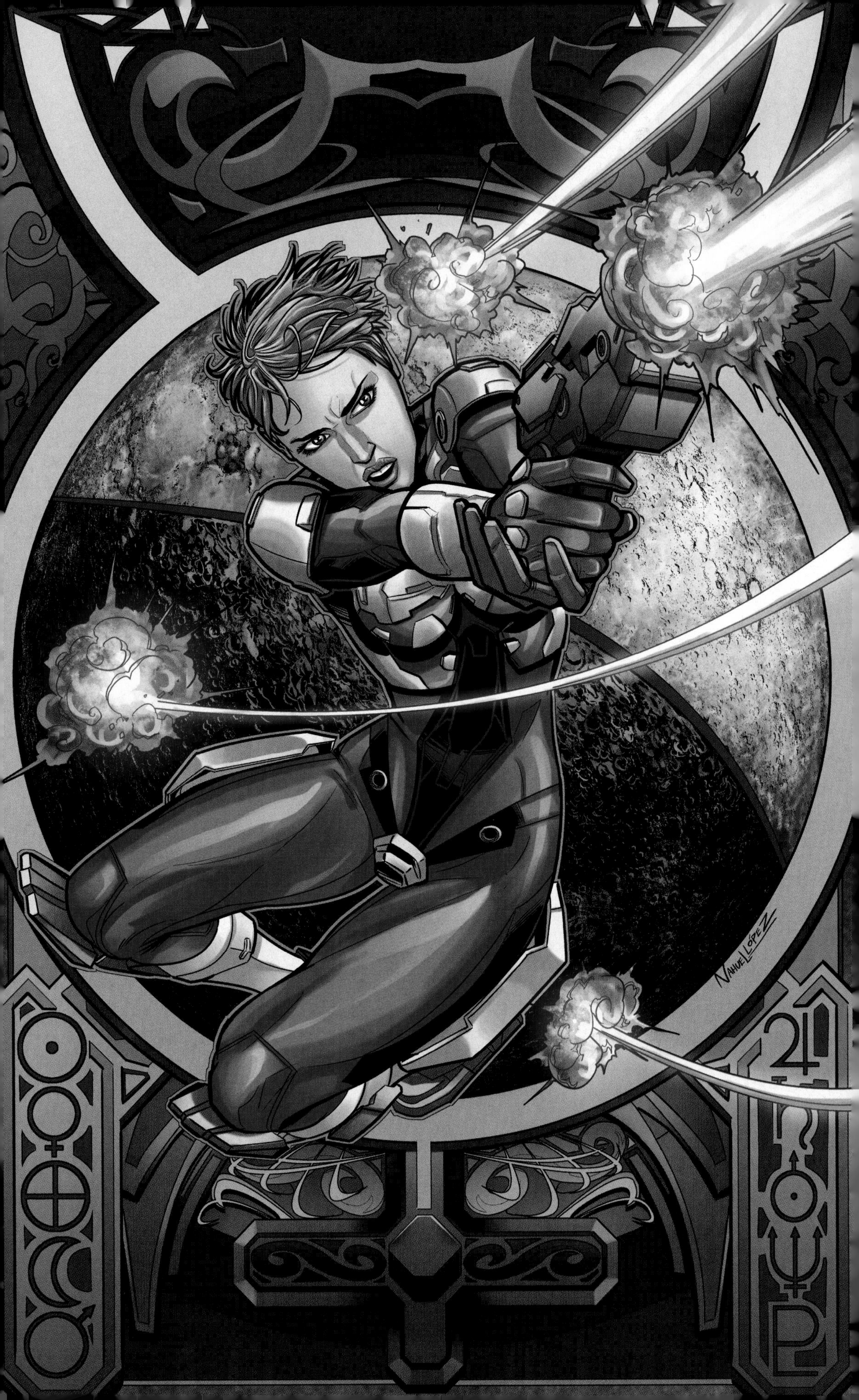
NAHUEL LOPEZ

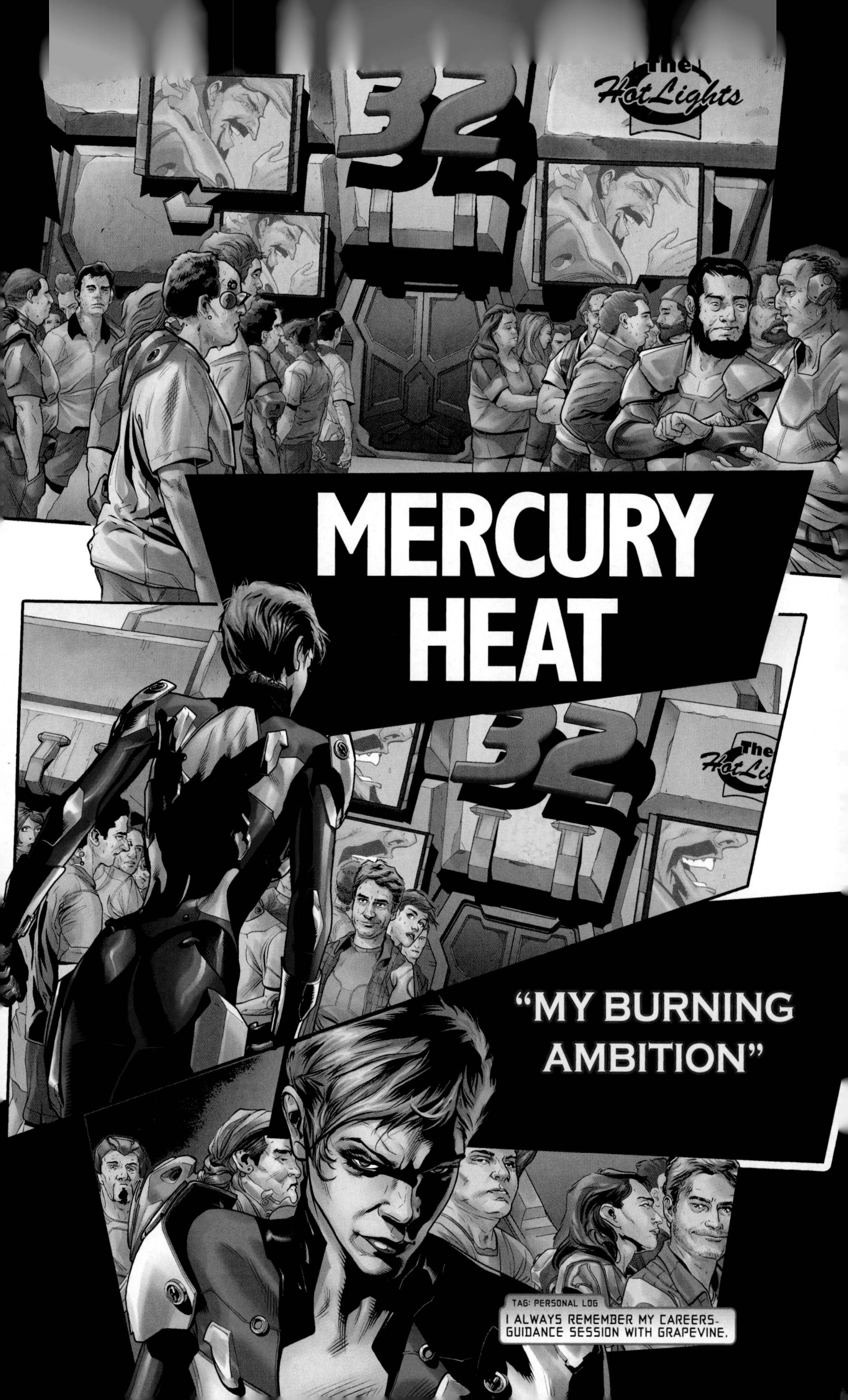

The HotLights
32
MERCURY HEAT
"MY BURNING AMBITION"
TAG: PERSONAL LOG
I ALWAYS REMEMBER MY CAREERS-GUIDANCE SESSION WITH GRAPEVINE.

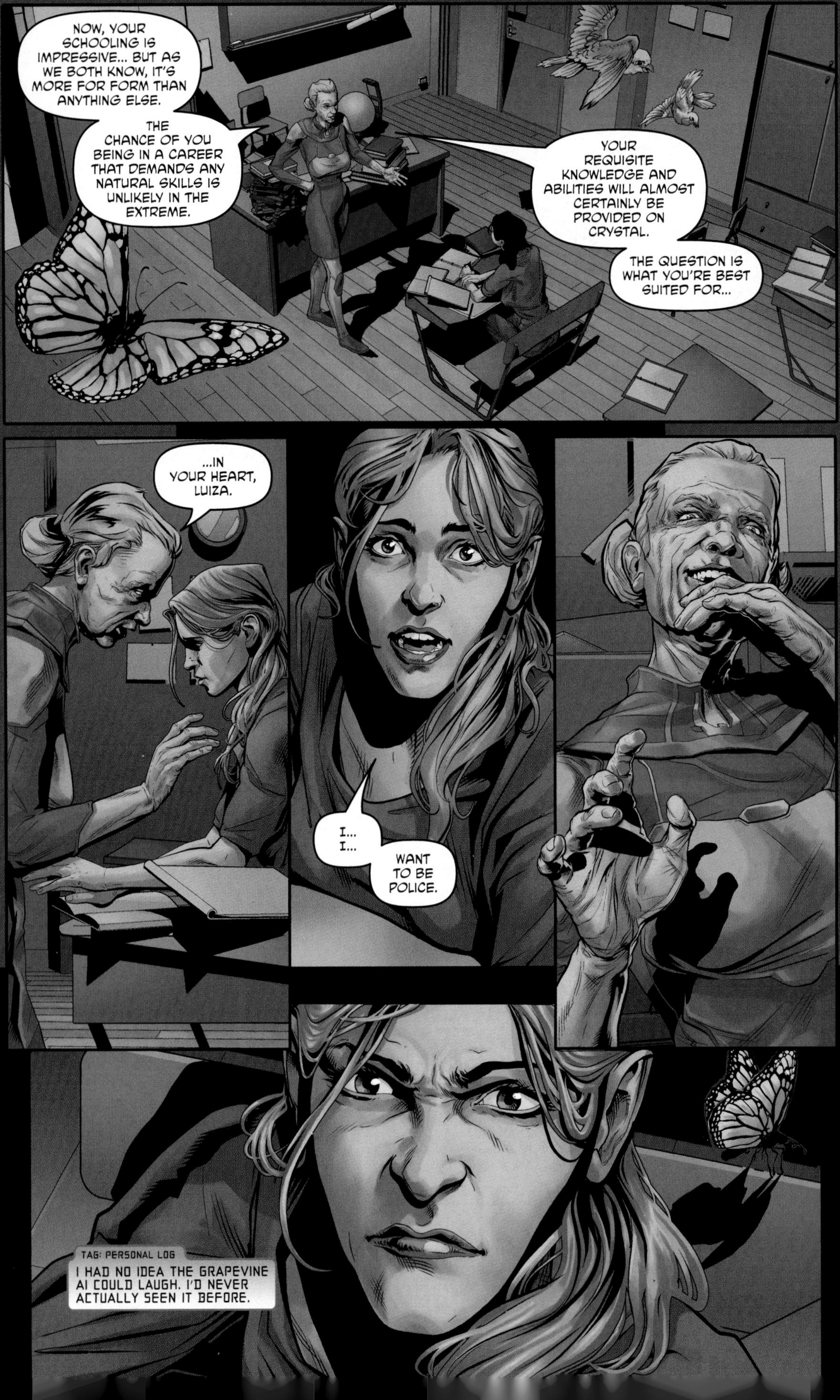
NOW, YOUR SCHOOLING IS IMPRESSIVE... BUT AS WE BOTH KNOW, IT'S MORE FOR FORM THAN ANYTHING ELSE.
THE CHANCE OF YOU BEING IN A CAREER THAT DEMANDS ANY NATURAL SKILLS IS UNLIKELY IN THE EXTREME.
YOUR REQUISITE KNOWLEDGE AND ABILITIES WILL ALMOST CERTAINLY BE PROVIDED ON CRYSTAL.
THE QUESTION IS WHAT YOU'RE BEST SUITED FOR...
...IN YOUR HEART, LUIZA.
I... I...
WANT TO BE POLICE.
TAG: PERSONAL LOG
I HAD NO IDEA THE GRAPEVINE AI COULD LAUGH. I'D NEVER ACTUALLY SEEN IT BEFORE.

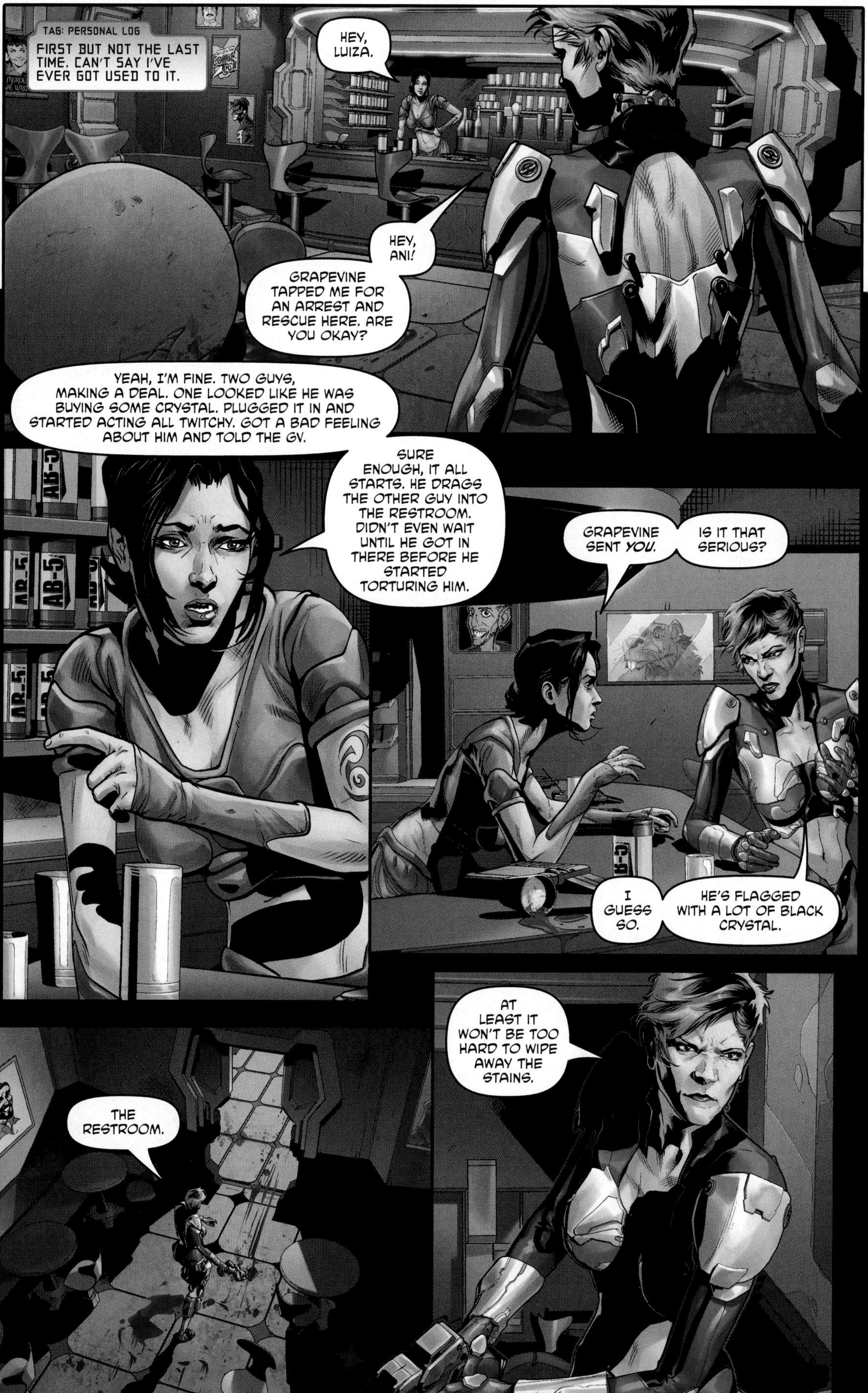
TAG: PERSONAL LOG
FIRST BUT NOT THE LAST TIME. CAN'T SAY I'VE EVER GOT USED TO IT.
HEY, LUIZA.
HEY, ANI!
GRAPEVINE TAPPED ME FOR AN ARREST AND RESCUE HERE. ARE YOU OKAY?
YEAH, I'M FINE. TWO GUYS, MAKING A DEAL. ONE LOOKED LIKE HE WAS BUYING SOME CRYSTAL. PLUGGED IT IN AND STARTED ACTING ALL TWITCHY. GOT A BAD FEELING ABOUT HIM AND TOLD THE GV.
SURE ENOUGH, IT ALL STARTS. HE DRAGS THE OTHER GUY INTO THE RESTROOM. DIDN'T EVEN WAIT UNTIL HE GOT IN THERE BEFORE HE STARTED TORTURING HIM.
GRAPEVINE SENT *YOU*.
IS IT THAT SERIOUS?
HE'S FLAGGED WITH A LOT OF BLACK CRYSTAL.
I GUESS SO.
THE RESTROOM.
AT LEAST IT WON'T BE TOO HARD TO WIPE AWAY THE STAINS.

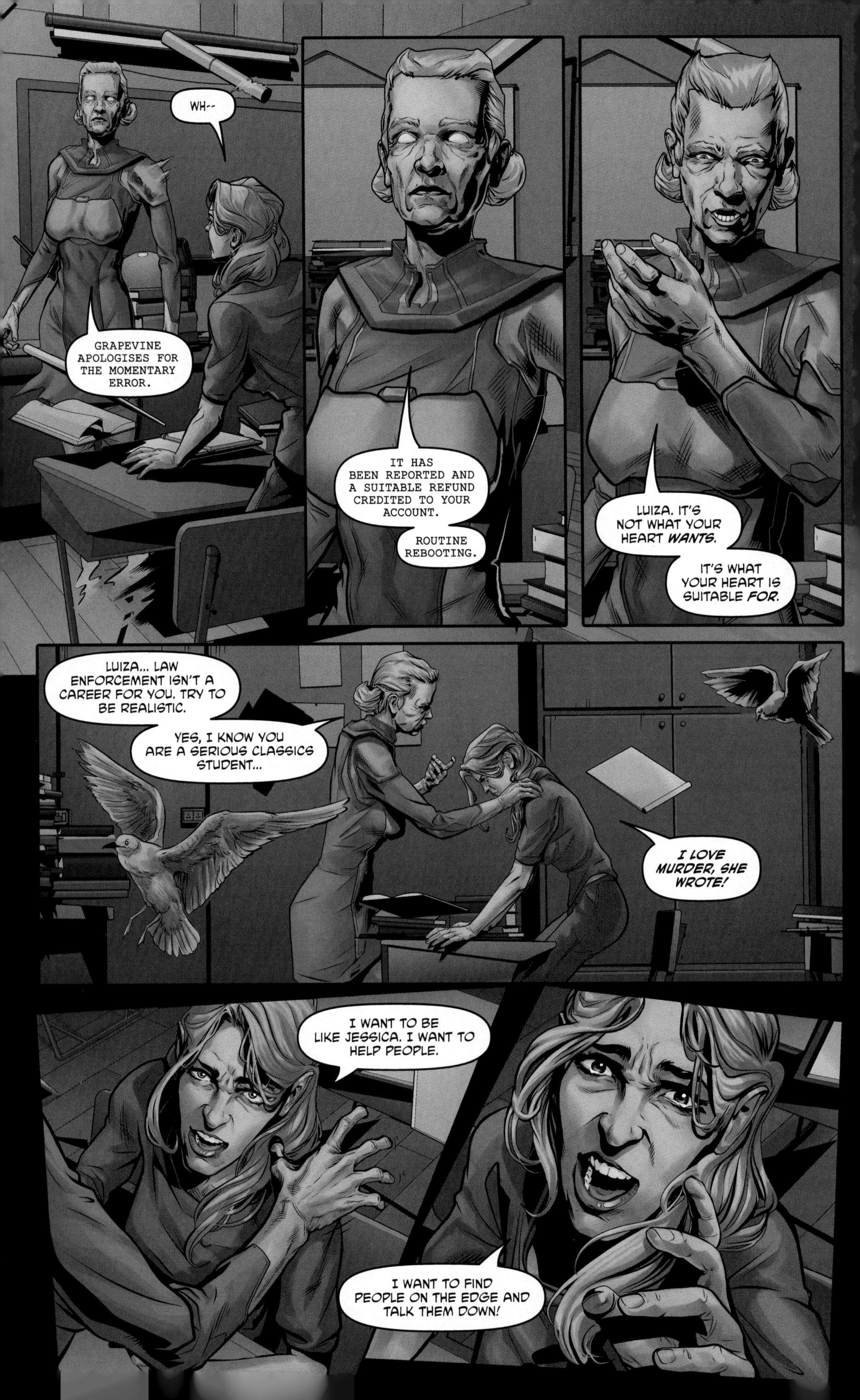
WH--
GRAPEVINE APOLOGISES FOR THE MOMENTARY ERROR.
IT HAS BEEN REPORTED AND A SUITABLE REFUND CREDITED TO YOUR ACCOUNT.
ROUTINE REBOOTING.
LUIZA. IT'S NOT WHAT YOUR HEART *WANTS*.
IT'S WHAT YOUR HEART IS SUITABLE *FOR*.
LUIZA... LAW ENFORCEMENT ISN'T A CAREER FOR YOU. TRY TO BE REALISTIC.
YES, I KNOW YOU ARE A SERIOUS CLASSICS STUDENT...
I LOVE MURDER, SHE WROTE!
I WANT TO BE LIKE JESSICA. I WANT TO HELP PEOPLE.
I WANT TO FIND PEOPLE ON THE EDGE AND TALK THEM DOWN!

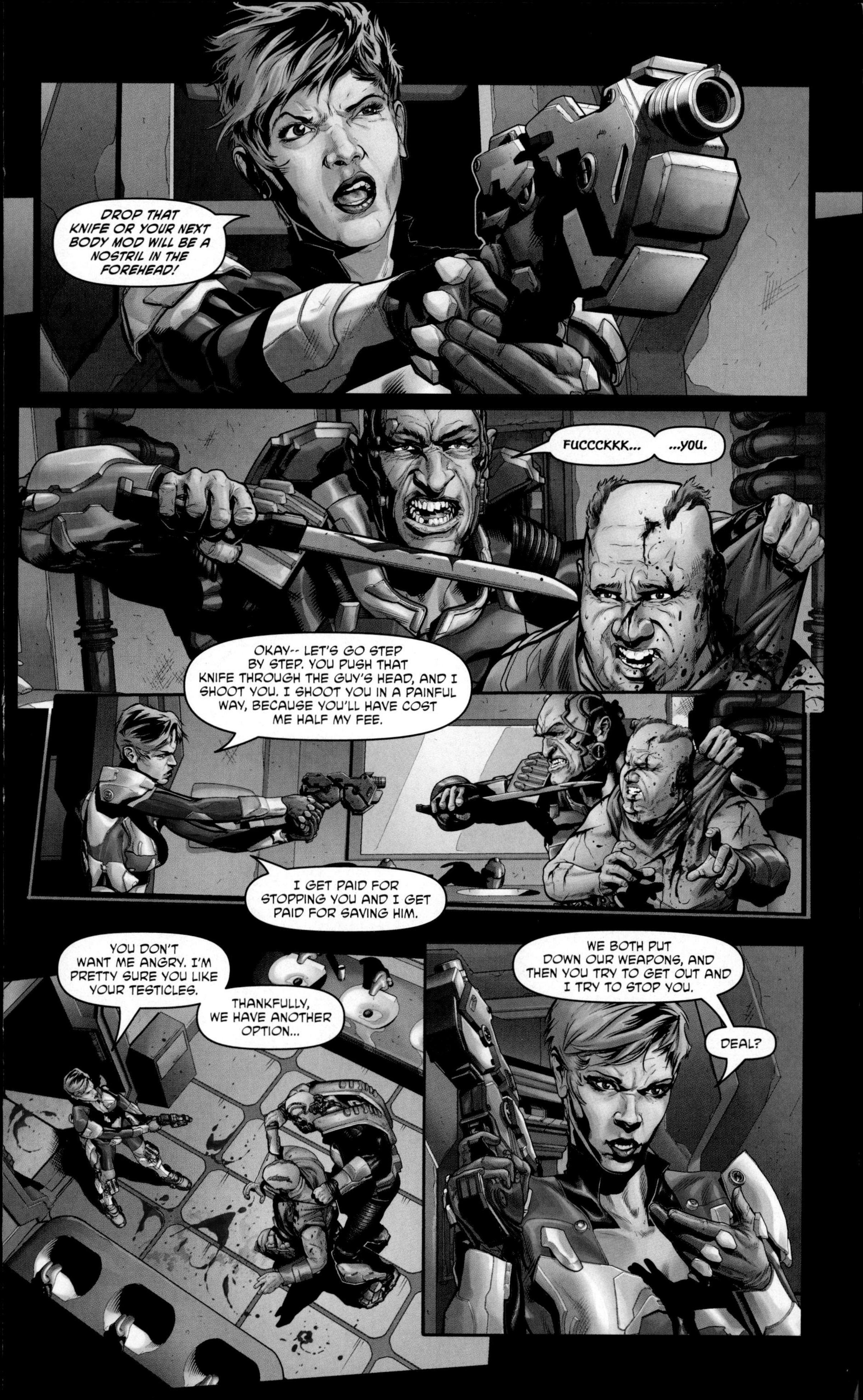
DROP THAT KNIFE OR YOUR NEXT BODY MOD WILL BE A NOSTRIL IN THE FOREHEAD!
FUCCCKKK...
...YOU.
OKAY-- LET'S GO STEP BY STEP. YOU PUSH THAT KNIFE THROUGH THE GUY'S HEAD, AND I SHOOT YOU. I SHOOT YOU IN A PAINFUL WAY, BECAUSE YOU'LL HAVE COST ME HALF MY FEE.
I GET PAID FOR STOPPING YOU AND I GET PAID FOR SAVING HIM.
YOU DON'T WANT ME ANGRY. I'M PRETTY SURE YOU LIKE YOUR TESTICLES.
THANKFULLY, WE HAVE ANOTHER OPTION...
WE BOTH PUT DOWN OUR WEAPONS, AND THEN YOU TRY TO GET OUT AND I TRY TO STOP YOU.
DEAL?

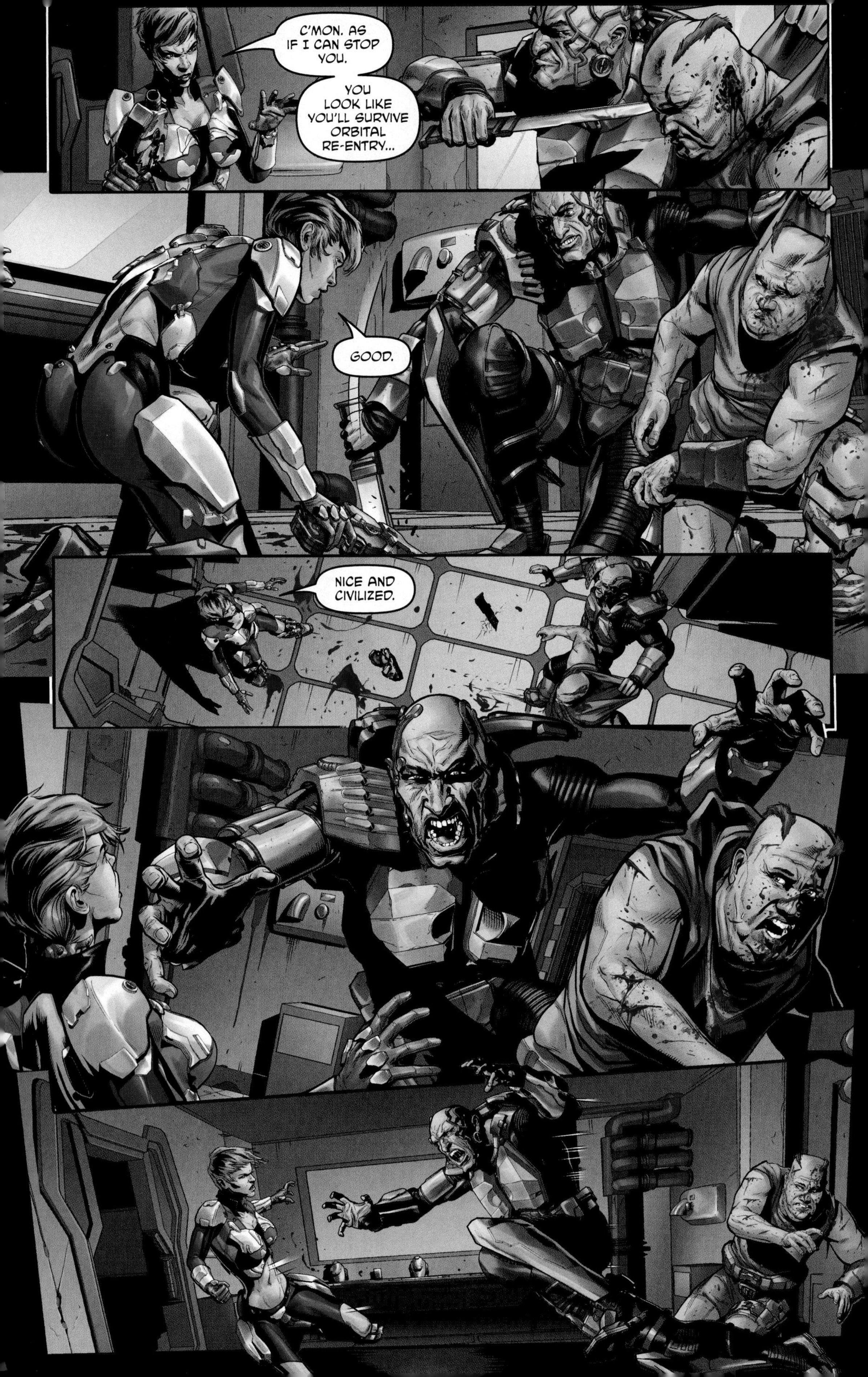
C'MON. AS IF I CAN STOP YOU.
YOU LOOK LIKE YOU'LL SURVIVE ORBITAL RE-ENTRY...
GOOD.
NICE AND CIVILIZED.

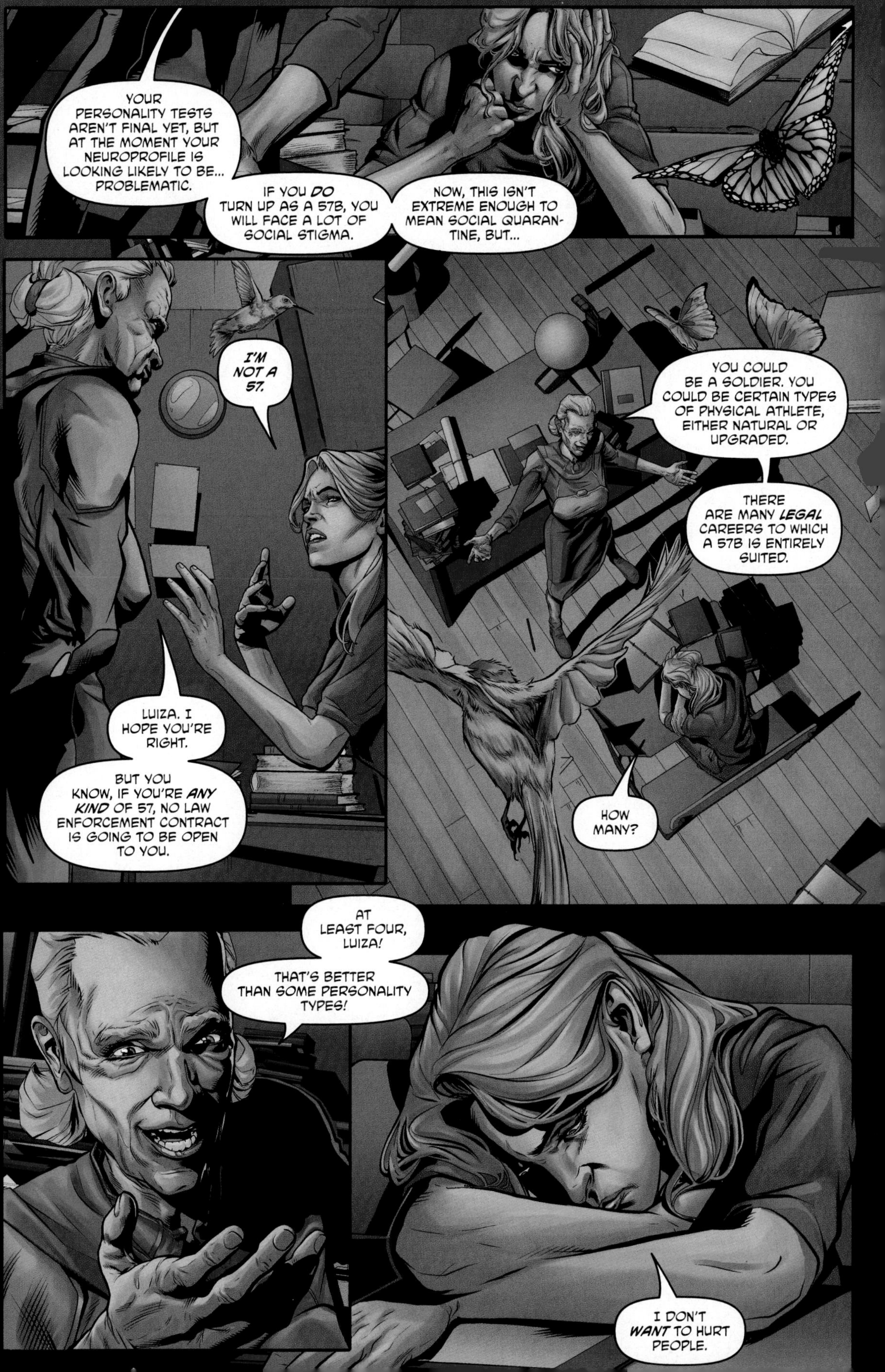
YOUR PERSONALITY TESTS AREN'T FINAL YET, BUT AT THE MOMENT YOUR NEUROPROFILE IS LOOKING LIKELY TO BE... PROBLEMATIC.
IF YOU *DO* TURN UP AS A 57B, YOU WILL FACE A LOT OF SOCIAL STIGMA.
NOW, THIS ISN'T EXTREME ENOUGH TO MEAN SOCIAL QUARAN-TINE, BUT...
I'M NOT A 57.
LUIZA. I HOPE YOU'RE RIGHT.
BUT YOU KNOW, IF YOU'RE *ANY KIND* OF 57, NO LAW ENFORCEMENT CONTRACT IS GOING TO BE OPEN TO YOU.
YOU COULD BE A SOLDIER. YOU COULD BE CERTAIN TYPES OF PHYSICAL ATHLETE, EITHER NATURAL OR UPGRADED.
THERE ARE MANY *LEGAL* CAREERS TO WHICH A 57B IS ENTIRELY SUITED.
HOW MANY?
AT LEAST FOUR, LUIZA!
THAT'S BETTER THAN SOME PERSONALITY TYPES!
I DON'T *WANT* TO HURT PEOPLE.

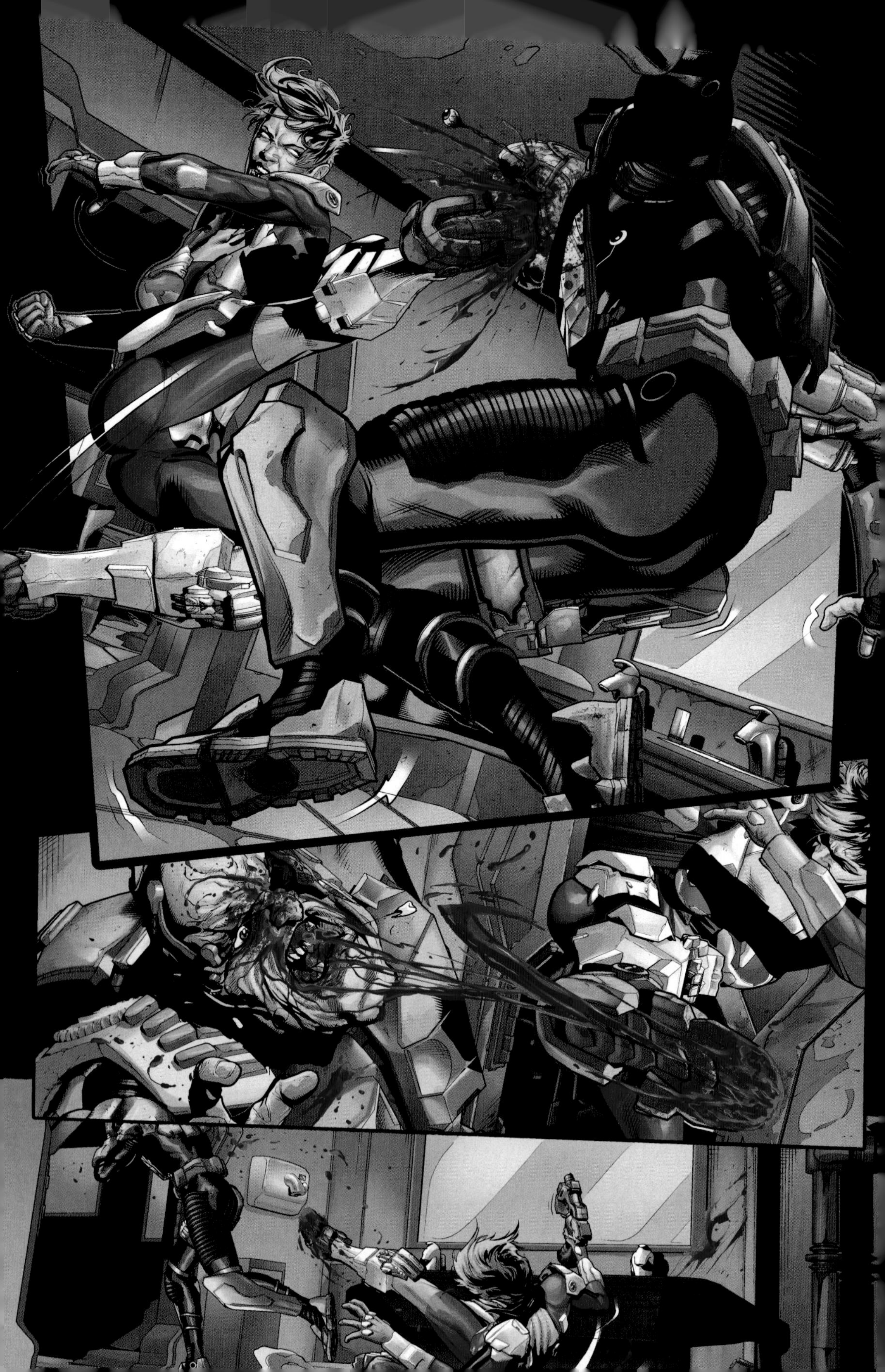

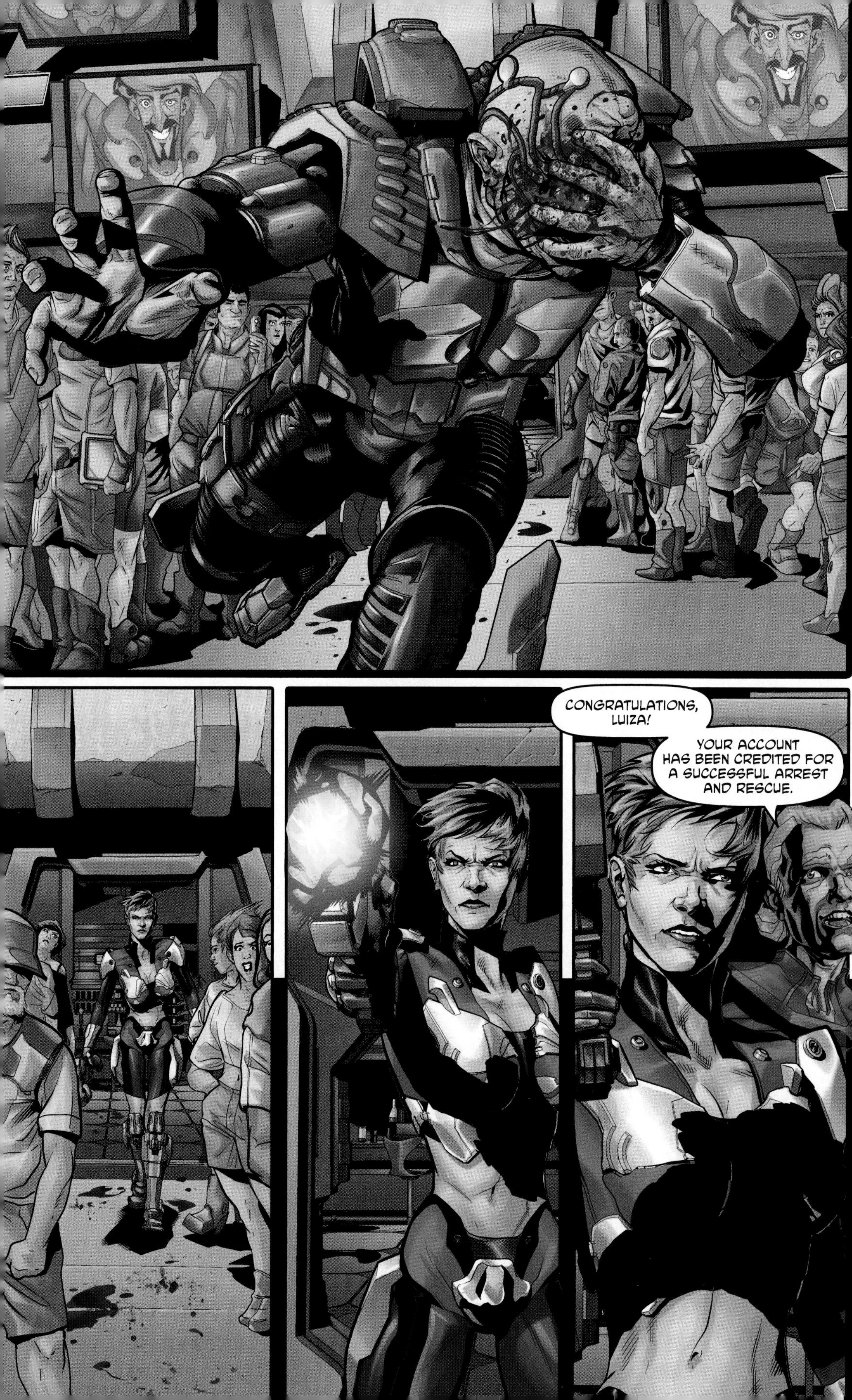
CONGRATULATIONS, LUIZA!
YOUR ACCOUNT HAS BEEN CREDITED FOR A SUCCESSFUL ARREST AND RESCUE.

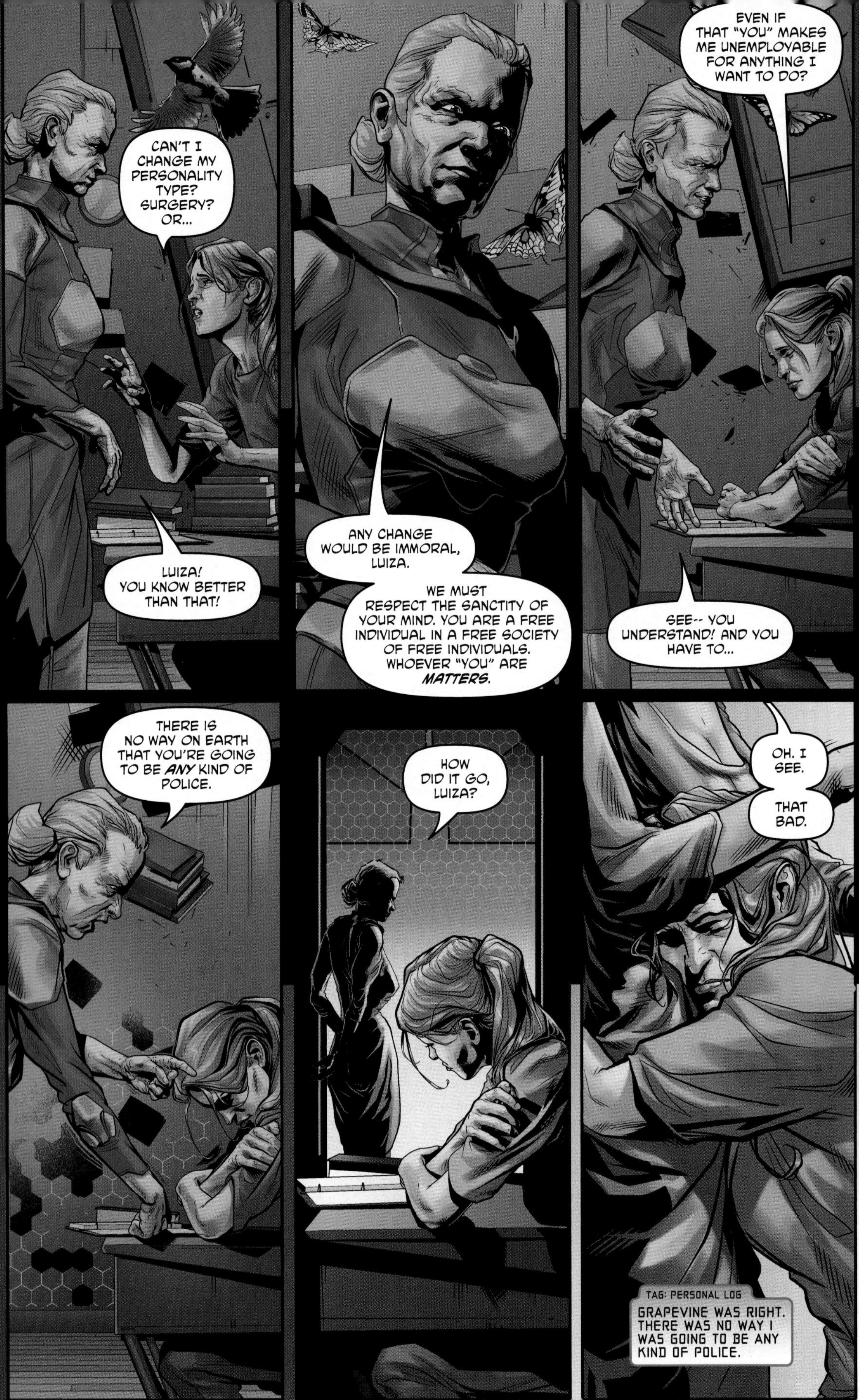
CAN'T I CHANGE MY PERSONALITY TYPE? SURGERY? OR...
LUIZA! YOU KNOW BETTER THAN THAT!
ANY CHANGE WOULD BE IMMORAL, LUIZA.
WE MUST RESPECT THE SANCTITY OF YOUR MIND. YOU ARE A FREE INDIVIDUAL IN A FREE SOCIETY OF FREE INDIVIDUALS. WHOEVER "YOU" ARE *MATTERS*.
EVEN IF THAT "YOU" MAKES ME UNEMPLOYABLE FOR ANYTHING I WANT TO DO?
SEE-- YOU UNDERSTAND! AND YOU HAVE TO...
THERE IS NO WAY ON EARTH THAT YOU'RE GOING TO BE *ANY* KIND OF POLICE.
HOW DID IT GO, LUIZA?
OH. I SEE.
THAT BAD.
TAG: PERSONAL LOG
GRAPEVINE WAS RIGHT. THERE WAS NO WAY I WAS GOING TO BE ANY KIND OF POLICE.

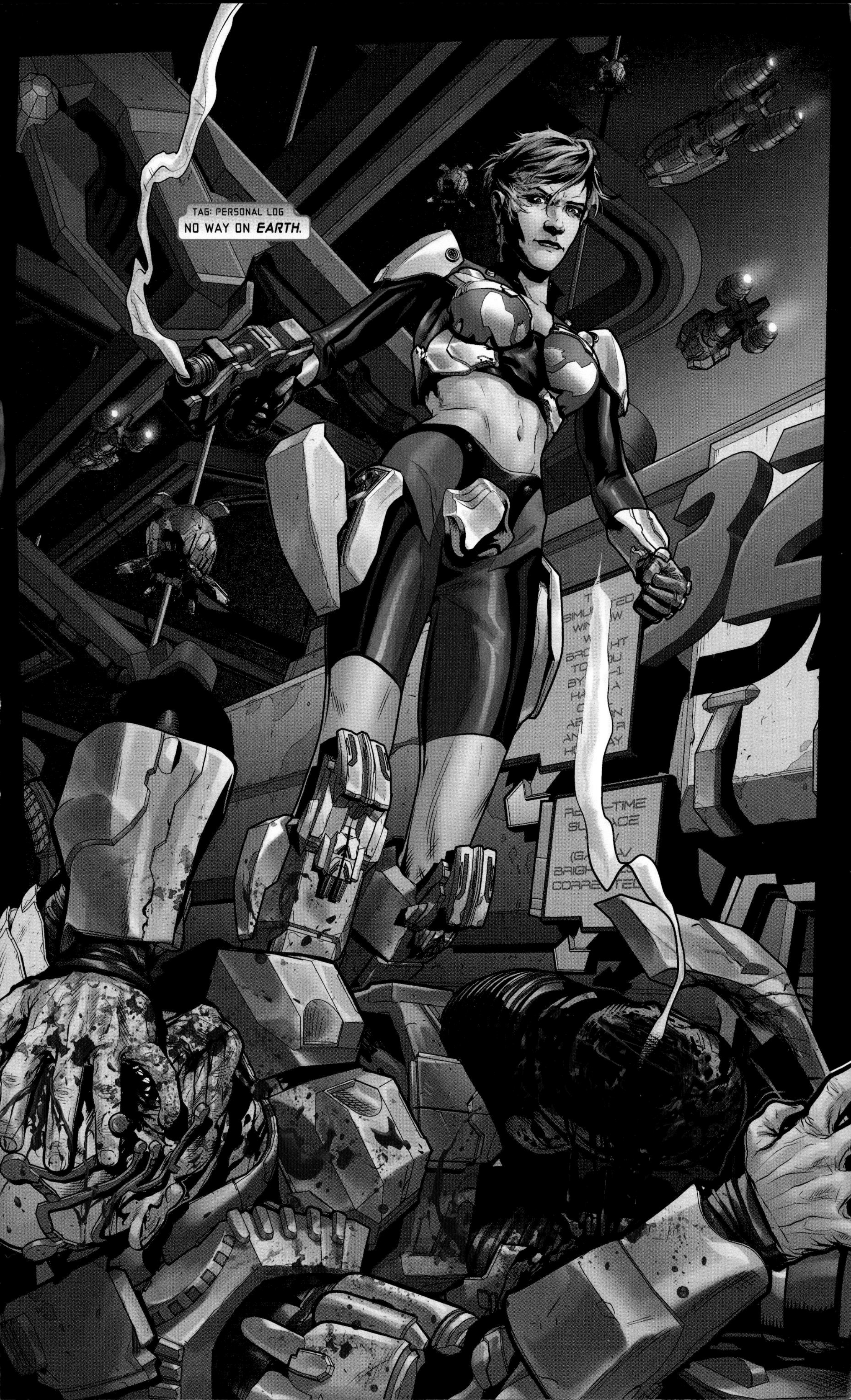
TAG: PERSONAL LOG
NO WAY ON *EARTH*.

backmatter

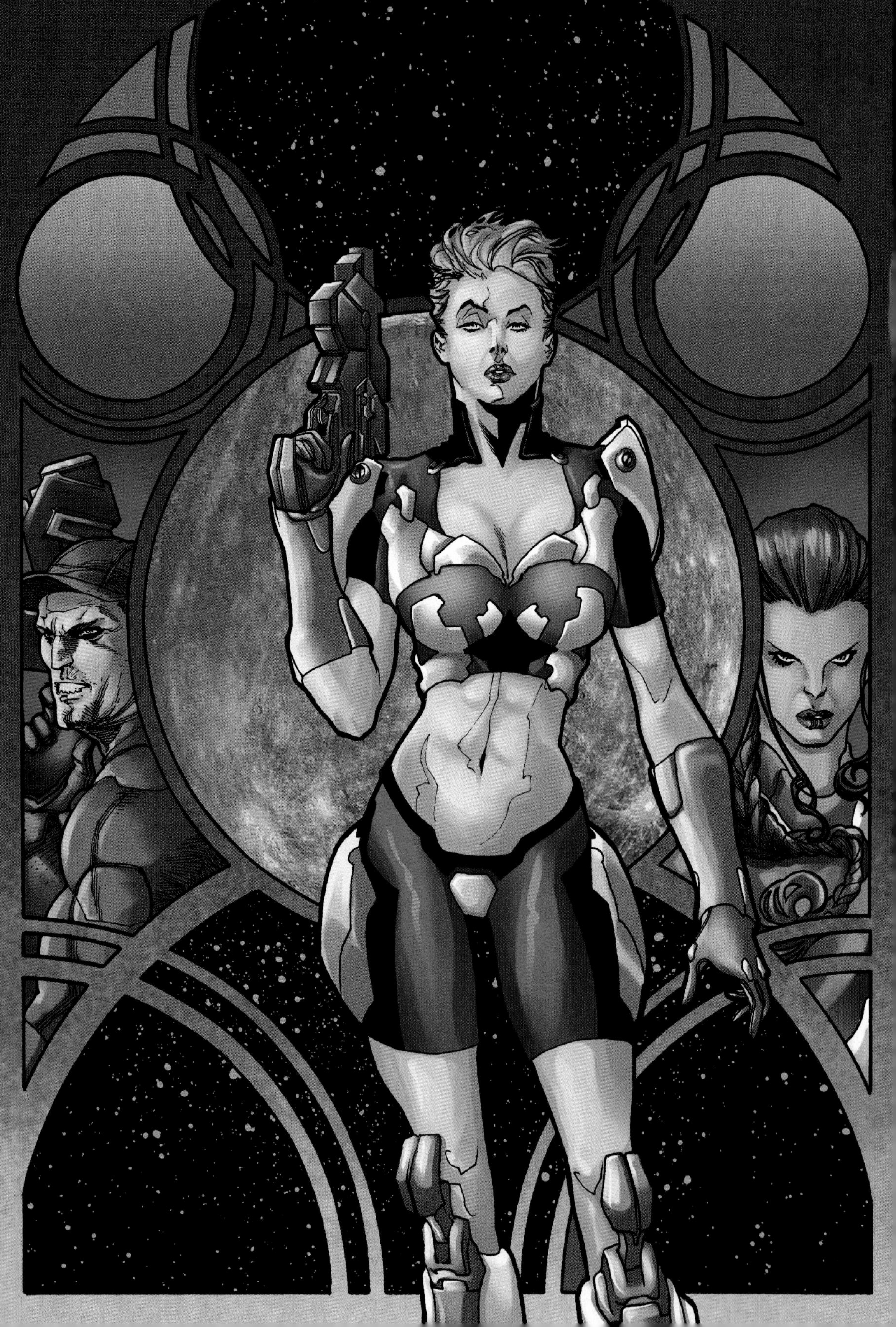

MERCURY HEAT

If someone asks me about *Mercury Heat*, I normally say something like the following...

"Mercury is the closest planet to the Sun. You know this. You think Mercury – *hot*. That's true, at least in part. The side that's nearest the Sun is hot enough to melt lead. However, the side that's facing away is *cold*. In the depths of the pits at its poles, it's virtually cold enough to liquify oxygen.

One of the reasons for this is Mercury's unusual orbit and rotation. It rotates incredibly slowly. A day on Mercury is just shy of 59 days long. However the time it takes to go around the Sun is incredibly fast – 88 days. Between the two interacting, the length of a day as we would experience it on Earth (the Sun reaching the same point in the sky) is 176 days.

It's more complicated than that. There's actually bits on Mercury where, if you're standing, the Sun's progress across the sky will reverse – but if we simplify it enormously, that's about 88 days of direct sunlight, and another 88 in the dark. Point being there's plenty of time to get really hot and really cold.

There's an interesting side effect of this – for about three days around the Sunrise and sunset, the temperature on the surface is Earth-like. Cold on the first day and hot on the third, but within vague Earth temperature boundaries. Put on some vacuum/electromagnetic protection and you could be fine walking around in that Zone.

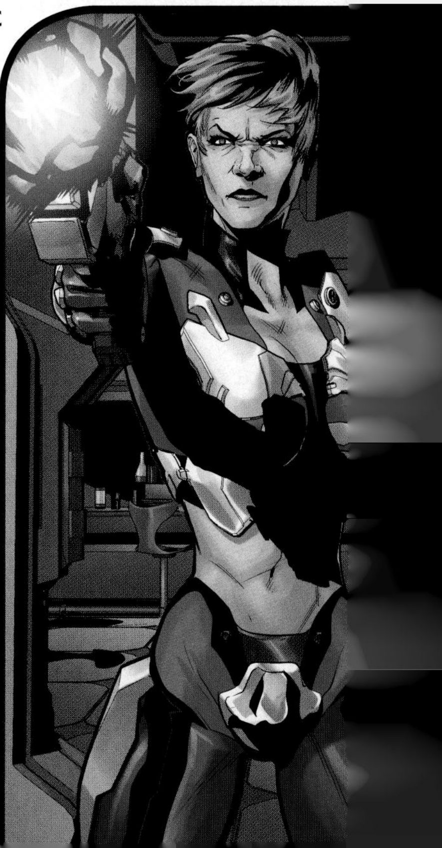

Now, here's a third thing. Mercury is tiny. Its diameter is about a third of Earth's, only 15,329km. That means, at the equator, it's only rotating at 3.6km/h. In other words, walking speed.

If I dropped you facing the dawn on Mercury, you could stay ahead of the dawn.

As long as you can keep moving.

That's the opening image of *Mercury Heat*. Someone abandoned, trying to stay ahead of the incinerating light.

Mercury Heat is a science-fiction cop comic set on Mercury, and its first case is trying to work out why that guy was left to die. It's called 'The Long Hot Dawn'.

I start with that for a couple of reasons.

Firstly, it's pretty cool. It's a single reasonably hard sci-fi image that captures the imagination. That's exactly the same reason I also start the series proper with it.

Secondly, *Mercury Heat* is such a maximalist polyglot kitchen-sink of a sci-fi book, that it doesn't really boil down to key points well. There's so much detail in the world of *Mercury Heat* that a top level view makes it look a bit of a blur. I suspect any one aspect of the world building could have been expanded out into a full story. But no, I'm going to cram them all into this one. I like my futures to feel alive.

Mercury Heat has been in development since late 2008, near the start of my comics writing career. *Phonogram: The Singles Club* had just started coming out. I was starting work on *Über* for Avatar (currently available from all good bookshops, etc, etc.) As that was going well, Commander William Christensen suggested we do another book together. He could tell by the generally frenetic tone of my emails perhaps it'd be useful to do something a little lighter. We were both aware that anything short of *From Hell* is light compared to *Über,* but the thought was there. William threw me a seed of something he thought Avatar should be publishing.

That's how we were working then. *Über* came from a basic seed idea of "Nazi Germany invents Superhumans, prompting an arms race between the Allied and the Axis powers" *Mercury Heat*'s mandate was even wider: "Female-lead action comic."

From that point, I suspect it's impossible to retrace all my steps. I don't think the pun came first. I'd hate to think that the pun was the founding element, but I'd also be lying if I said it wasn't the idea which brought everything else into sharp focus.

Here's a selection of assorted things I was thinking about in the period.

Tank Girl. Everyone loves Tank Girl.

Judge Dredd. Everyone loves Judge Dredd. I'm never going to get a chance to write a Judge Dredd comic. Hell, I'm never going to get a chance to write for 2000AD. Wouldn't it be fun to do something which would fit neatly into that thrill-power pulp-aesthetic, but with a hard-R rating. With an obviously sullen Gillen-lead?

Cyberpunk. When Warren was doing *Transmetropolitan* he shuddered at comics lapping at the past like that, as comics always tends to be at least five years out of date. But we're another decade on from when Spider came into life. It's now just another flavour to add to the mix – its purpose then entirely different from its purpose *now*. Playing with some cyberpunk tropes and firing them through a late-00s filter struck me as amusing. As many people have noted, the world outside the window is a cyberpunk novel, so perhaps a sci-fi extrapolation of a cyberpunk present?

The Cassandra Project, the *Deus Ex* game mod I worked on in the early 00s – how I used its female assassin lead as a useful bucket to process all manner of awful crap I was going through by putting it in black leathers and arming it with Depleted Uranium ammunition.

Watching the movie *Sunshine* thinking, "Man, imagine if this wasn't shit. It'd be great."

Rucka/Leiber's *Whiteout,* which took a police structure and rejuvenated its tropes by setting it in an alien environment. That instantly gives it a mood and identity. Set it on another planet where no stars are visible as the Sun's too close, and even the ground blinds you when the sweat doesn't get in your eyes...

Thinking about all my smart women peers turning thirty, looking at their twenties with a shudder and reaching up to find nothing above them but glass.

Me looking at the then-present wave of post-apocalyptic fiction in comics and pop culture generally, and being annoyed. I like the genre, but its predominance spoke to something else – a culture with an inability to imagine a future. Post-apocalypse fiction is literally giving up, saying it's all over and a complete abdication of trying to imagine how the future could be. What's the best riposte to that? I decided that it wasn't actually utopian sci-fi. That's merely its inversion. It was to create a future where we've managed to deal with several of what presently seem as unsurmountable problems... but a world where there's a whole separate bunch of problems to deal with. *There will be a future. It will have problems in it. We will have to deal with them. Grow up.*

Of course, if it's going to be sci-fi, sci-fi is primarily a device to talk about the present. What social trends seem interesting to play with?

I wasn't thinking about Spotify playlists, as they didn't exist then, but I made a playlist more recently for writing the new episodes of the project and I suspect I should include a link to it here in case you wish to join me: *https://bitly.com/MercHeatPlaylist*

Most of all, I was always a big fan of characters who kick other characters' heads clean off. We should probably have some of that.

I mixed all that together into another one of my hefty documents, sent it at William. He replied saying that he'd suggested that it may be good for me to do something a little lighter, and I'd come back to him with an intricately constructed science-fiction web. You are not very good at doing easy things, Kieron.

He was correct, but it is lighter than *Über.* We both agreed on that, and set to work.

Its original title was *The Heat*, but we changed it to *Mercury Heat* after the Bullock/McCarthy movie came out. It works better too. *The Heat* didn't really signify the book by itself, while *Mercury Heat* at least suggests a setting, and since it's a setting in a close orbit around the Sun, a genre. It's not going to be a period drama. Well, I suppose it is, but the period is the far future.

Hmm. Let's wrap this up now, as there's more talk to come, including pretty pictures which will make my blithering much more appealing. Let's end with a more traditional explanation as to what the book's about...

In the future, Earth is as close to a paradise as we can hope for... but it needs to be fuelled. A belt of solar panels have been constructed around Mercury to provide Earth's power, where a nomadic population work in Heaven's boiler room. Away from Earth, this is the closest to a Wild West as humanity has experienced in a century . Policing them, under-supplied and underfire, are freelance police agents, colloquially known as the *Mercury Heat*.

Luiza Bora's spent her whole life wanting to be Police, one thing her personality type entirely prevents her from doing. Well... it bars her from doing it *on Earth*.

Luiza Bora has arrived on Mercury. She is Mercury Heat.

Seriously, I'm much more comfortable ranting about the day length on Mercury than doing proper 30-second pitches.

I'm joined on this endeavour by Omar Francia and Nahuel Lopez. The art part of this project has been an adventure in and of itself – basically, think *Spinal Tap* drummers. Omar handled the planning and the first three issues, before having to leave, and did some frankly astounding world-building which you'll see shown in the following pages. Nahuel picked up where he left off, and leans into the high adventure of the book.

Let's walk together through some designs, and I'll talk about the world a little...

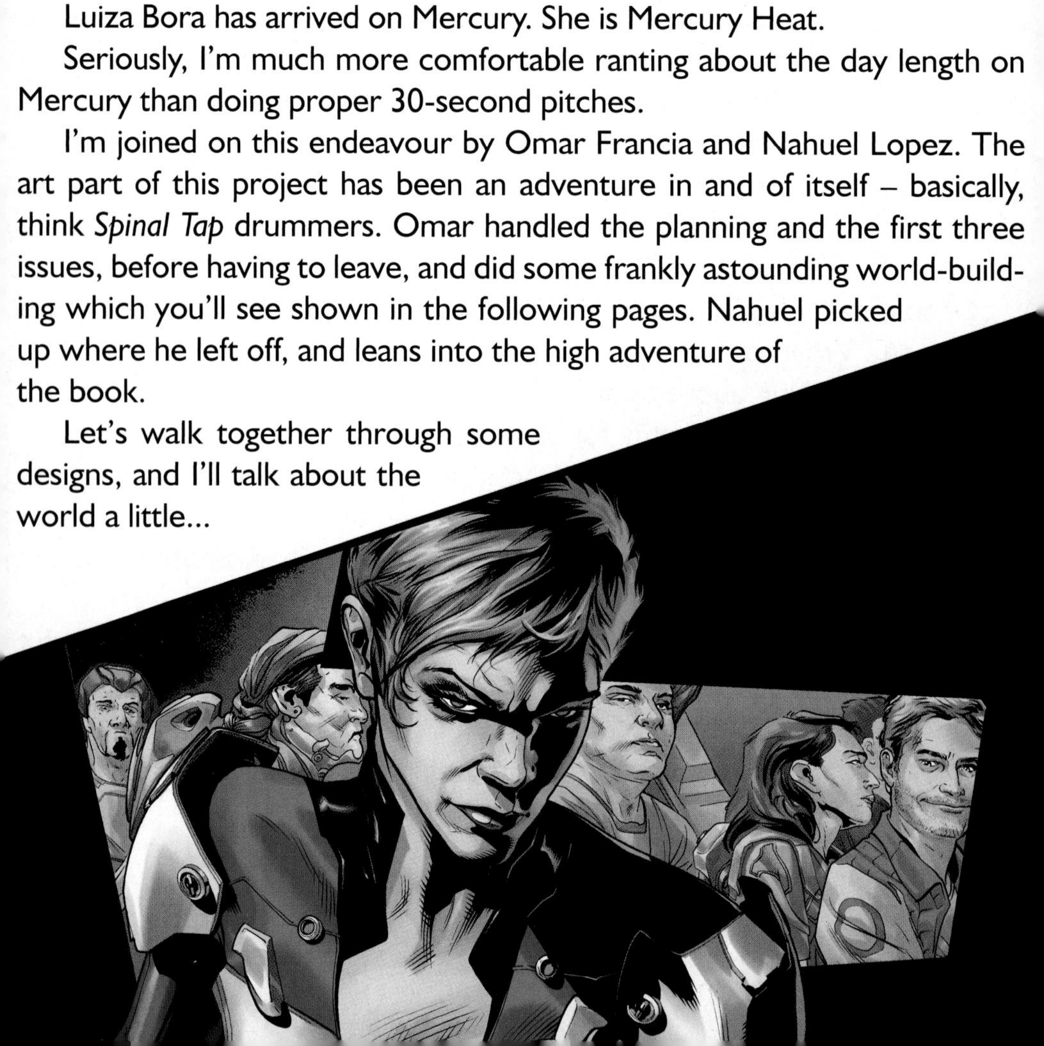

THE BELT

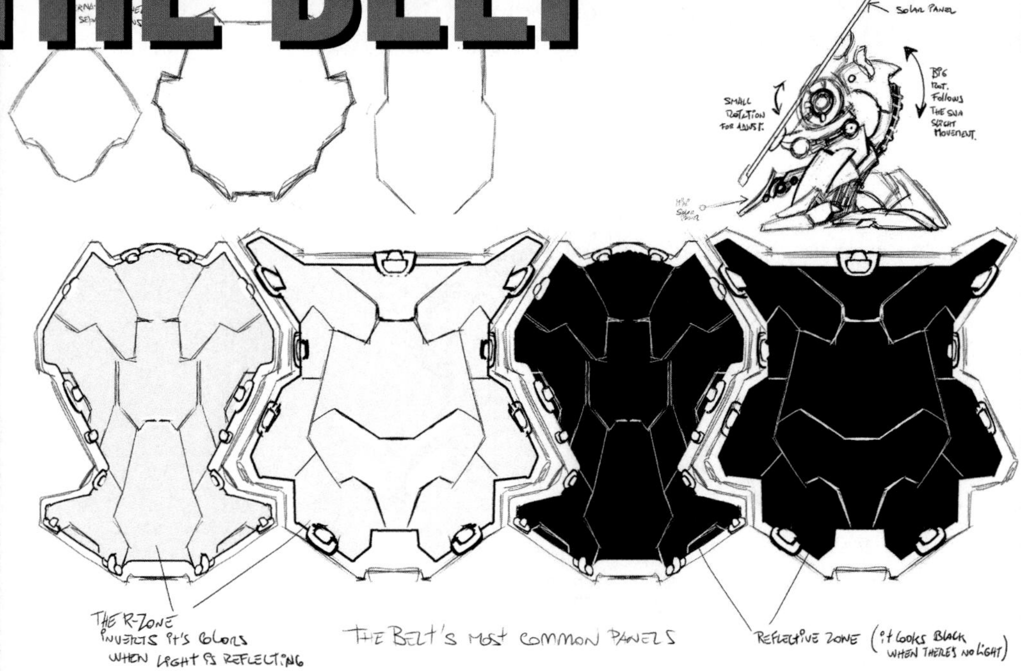
SOLAR PANEL
BIG ROT. FOLLOWS THE SUN SLIGHT MOVEMENT.
SMALL ROTATION FOR ADJUST.
THE R-ZONE INVERTS IT'S COLORS WHEN LIGHT IS REFLECTING
THE BELT'S MOST COMMON PANELS
REFLECTIVE ZONE (it looks BLACK WHEN THERE'S NO LIGHT)

The reason why we're on Mercury. Solar panels. Lots and lots of solar panels.

The Belt is a solar panel array that stretches around the entire equator. The vast majority of the population of Mercury moves around in the most habitable zone, working as what's called "Belt-workers." They either repair the panels, or expand the belt. The plan is that over the decades, it'll grow ever larger.

Fundamentally, the plan is to gild a whole planet with them. That's a pretty hefty plan, but not without precedent – they've already done it to the Moon.

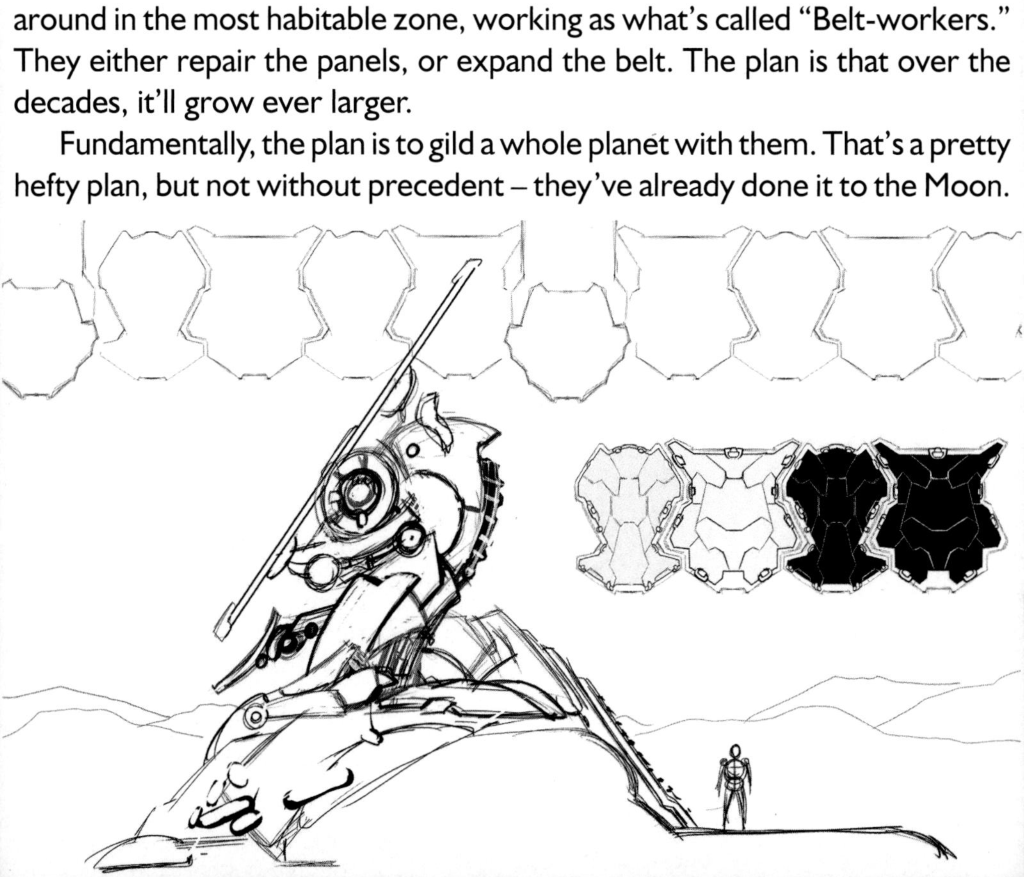

LUIZA BORA

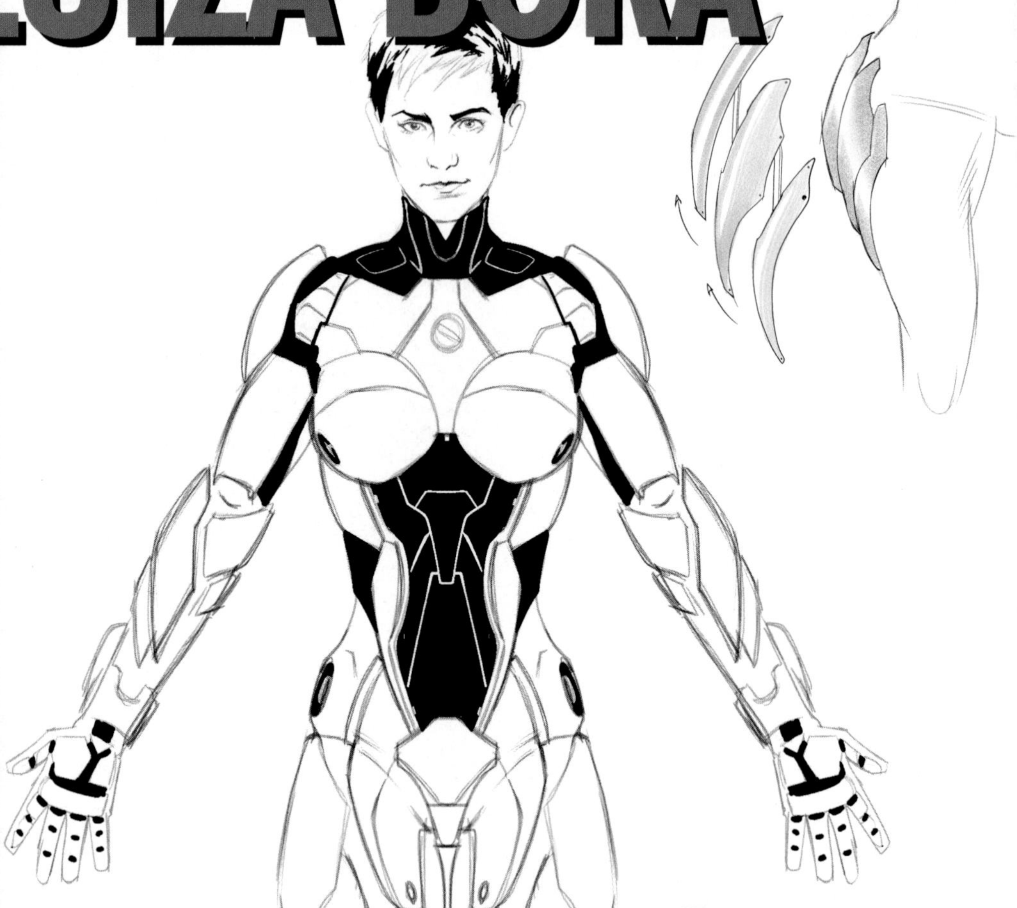

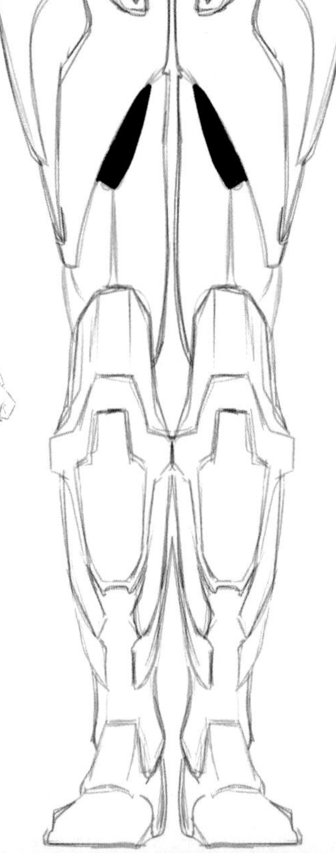

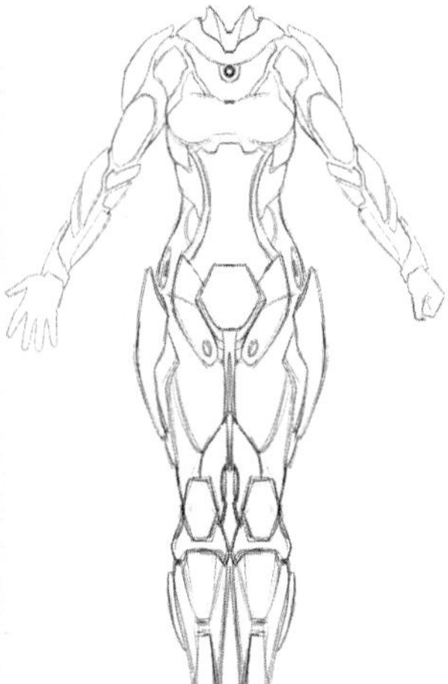

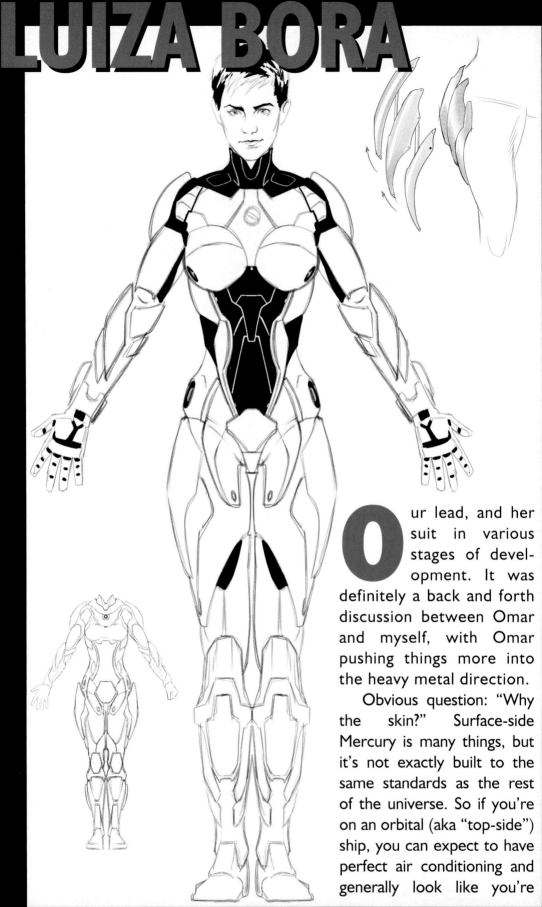

Our lead, and her suit in various stages of development. It was definitely a back and forth discussion between Omar and myself, with Omar pushing things more into the heavy metal direction.

Obvious question: "Why the skin?" Surface-side Mercury is many things, but it's not exactly built to the same standards as the rest of the universe. So if you're on an orbital (aka "top-side") ship, you can expect to have perfect air conditioning and generally look like you're about to feature in an Xbox shooter version of *Gattaca*. If you're on the surface... well, it's a different story. The full *Mercury Heat* armour simply is too hot to wear in most of the bases. Everyone serving loses parts of it. Some lose all, making do with the badge. This led to a back and forth dance between Omar and myself, with me alternately going "MORE SKIN!" and then "LESS SKIN!"

This is true for everyone who's in any of the bases, of course, no matter what sex. If I'm going to show skin in a book, I'm showing it equally. I've written essays on this before, but the biggest problem in comics isn't the costumes, it's how an artist chooses to frame a character in the storytelling. A character can be in jeans and a sweater, but if she's pulling ass poses for the reader, it's much more objectifying than a Jamie McKelvie Emma Frost. Luiza is our lead, and had to be our lead. We empathise with her. We are her.

The oppressive heat is a key thing. If there's a general note that I write a lot on *Mercury Heat* pages it's "Sweatier! Sweatier!"

As a person, Luiza is... oh, we're out of room. She's complex, shall we say.

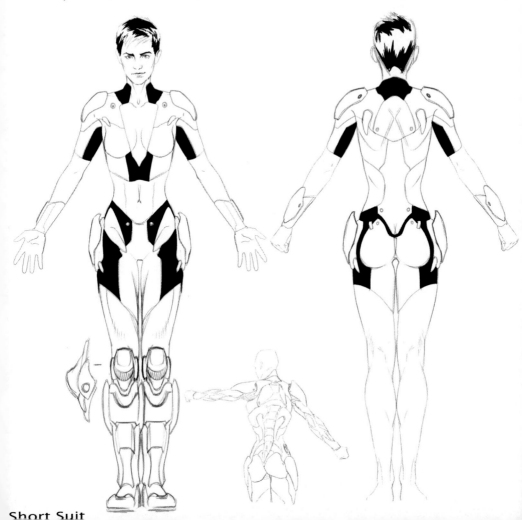

Short Suit

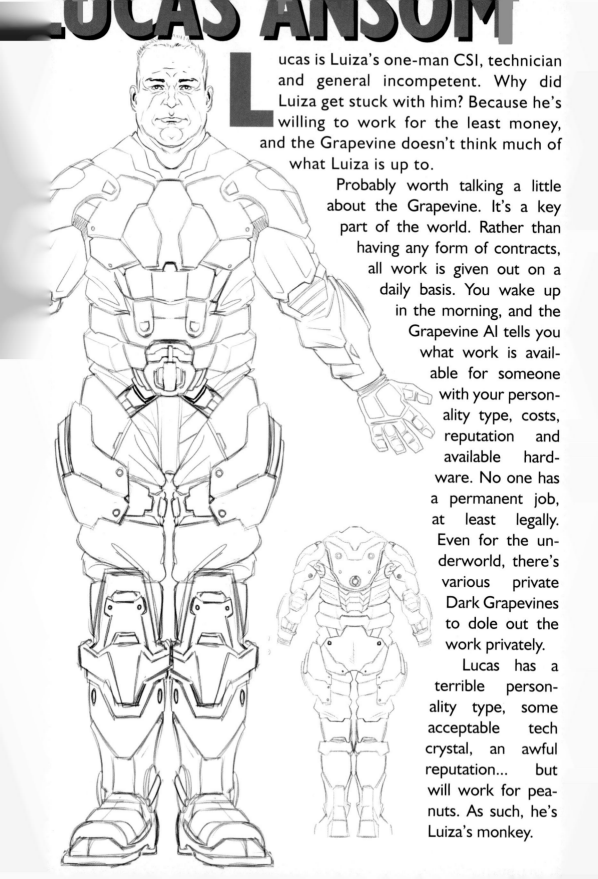

Lucas is Luiza's one-man CSI, technician and general incompetent. Why did Luiza get stuck with him? Because he's willing to work for the least money, and the Grapevine doesn't think much of what Luiza is up to.

Probably worth talking a little about the Grapevine. It's a key part of the world. Rather than having any form of contracts, all work is given out on a daily basis. You wake up in the morning, and the Grapevine AI tells you what work is available for someone with your personality type, costs, reputation and available hardware. No one has a permanent job, at least legally. Even for the underworld, there's various private Dark Grapevines to dole out the work privately.

Lucas has a terrible personality type, some acceptable tech crystal, an awful reputation... but will work for peanuts. As such, he's Luiza's monkey.

MEMORY CRYSTAL

Quantum Crystals tech
Quantum Connectors

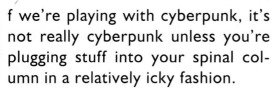

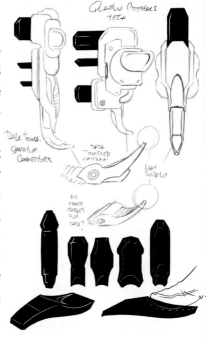

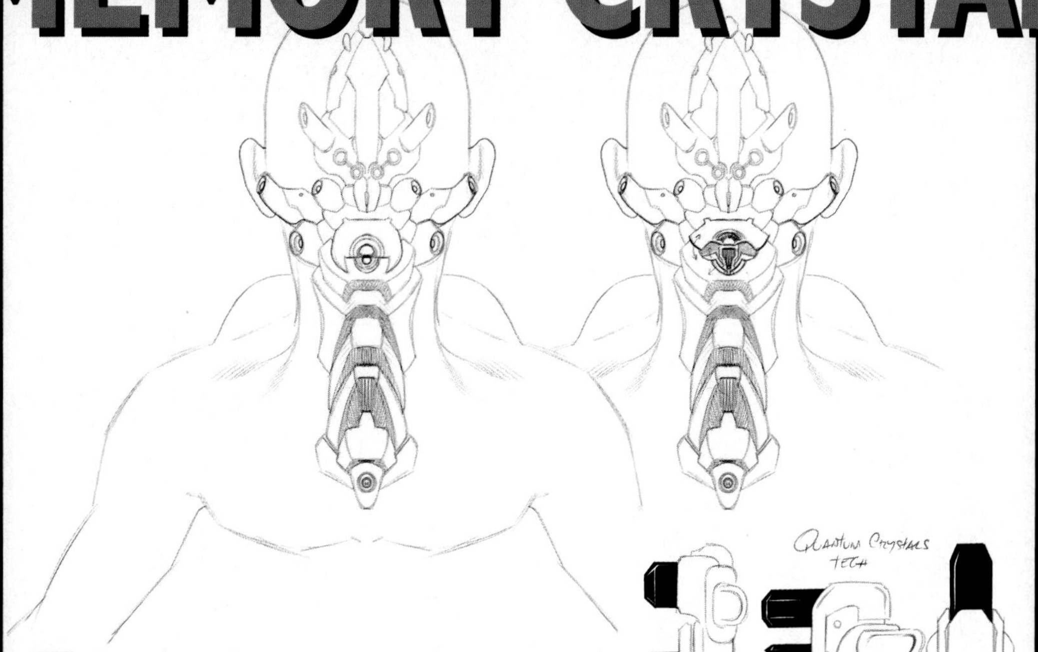

If we're playing with cyberpunk, it's not really cyberpunk unless you're plugging stuff into your spinal column in a relatively icky fashion.

One of the key aspects of the world is that it operates in a post-skill economy. Pretty much every single human skill can be given artificially to anyone via an operative jack by inserting the appropriate memory crystal. By design, memory crystals' production methods are jealously guarded, and as closely controlled as anything else. Certain skill sets are quarantined, and only given access to individuals while working specific jobs.

You may find yourself imagining that this fails all the time. You would be correct. There's a busy marketplace for black crystal, which is particularly dangerous for the police, in the same way that trying to arrest people who were smuggling the ability to "be" Bruce Lee would be.

That we work in a post-skill economy means that there's different economic pressures, primarily based on the personality type of an individual. We talk about that a little in the comic you've just read, but in a real way, whoever the system decides you are is a major force in shaping the rest of your life.

Some people still learn skills the old fashioned way. Generally speaking, they're considered fucking weird.

BATTERY SHIPS

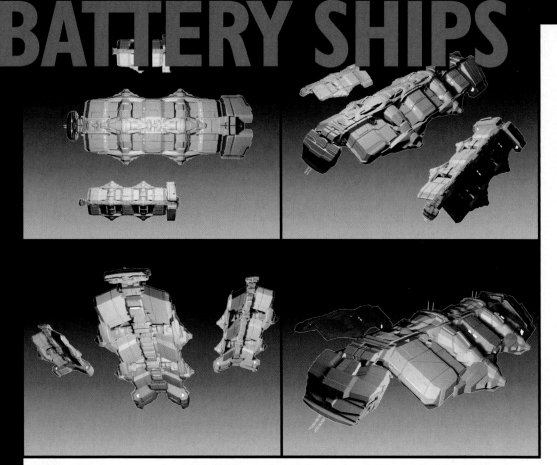

I f Mercury is the Wild West, these are our stagecoaches. Enormous transport vessels which travel between Mercury and Earth to deliver the harvest power from the Belt. There's been five Battery ships built. Battery IV has just returned to Mercury at the start of our first story, carrying the starstruck Luiza. The enormous Battery V is preparing to launch.

The amateur futurists among you (Hi, Warren) may wonder why in this relatively hard science fiction story we're not using (say) beaming technology. There's so much free energy, the losses are irrelevant, and it's much quicker and arguably more robust than carting the stuff there. It's a good question.

Primarily, it's actually a cultural issue. Earth in the future has solved various major problems we face. One of them is the Environment. Between now and then, humanity got serious, and decided having a sustainable planet to live on was probably a good thing. As such, rather than the present day where we'll probably shrug and say we care about the environment whilst carrying on eating crisps (or chips) out of plastic bags for the convenience, in this future they'll be utterly horrified at the waste in the same way we're horrified at various barbaric acts from our past. This is a fundamental thing that people believe, and those who don't are pretty much viewed in the same way we view Nazis. And in that culture? People just don't like the idea of energy beams being fired from one planet to another. What happens if it went wrong? That the science folk are making comforting noises doesn't really matter – the kick-back is so large, they can't overcome it. So instead, space-ships are carting the energy (with very little loss) in an inert state.

You may think "if environmental issues were taken more seriously, wouldn't the colonisation of Mercury be a controversial issue?" And I'd nod at you, shake your hand and say well done, you have correctly anticipated a major theme in our world.

Secondarily, I like spaceships. *Mercury Heat* is more semi-hard science fiction. Semi-hard science fiction sounds like something I should get pills to treat, so I'll stop writing now.

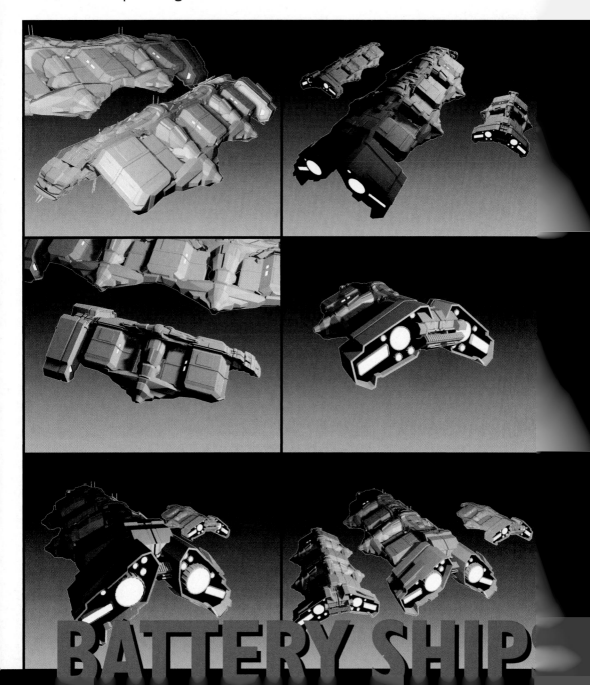

BATTERY SHIP

HELMETS

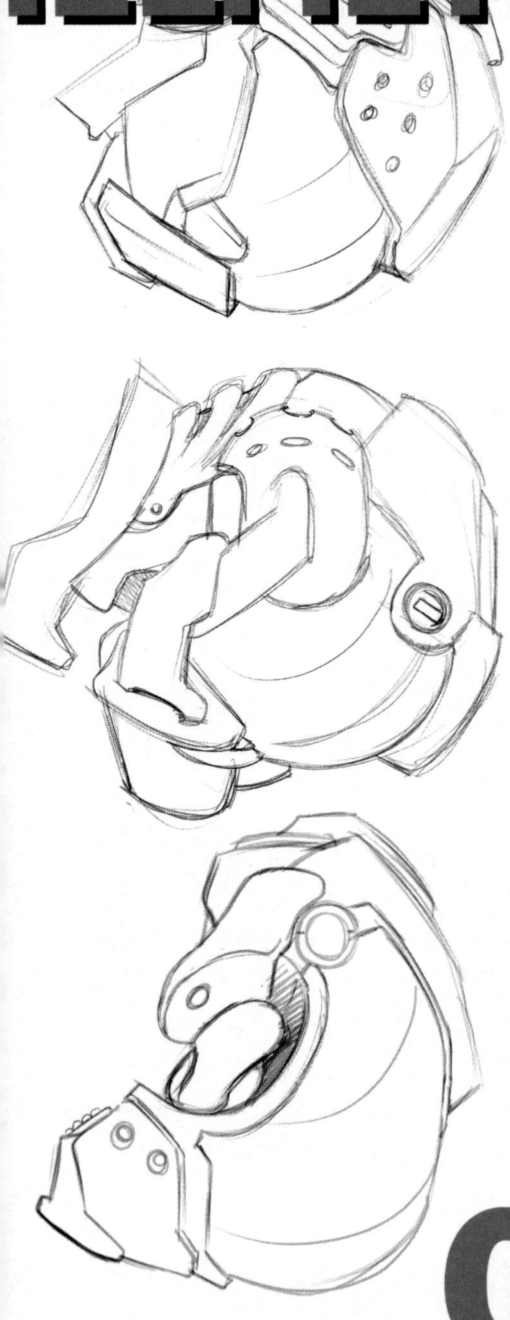

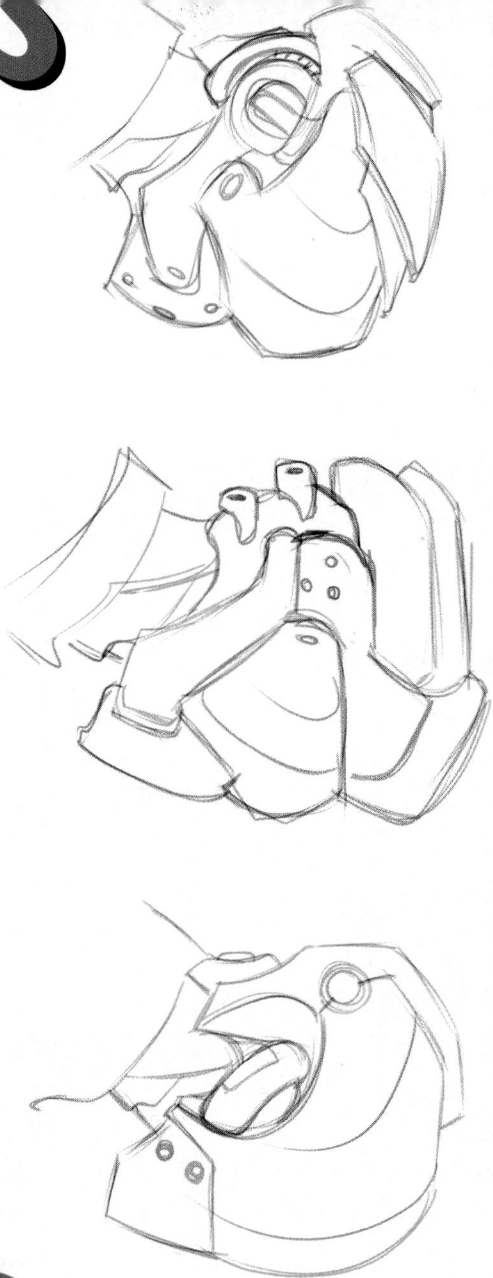

Omar really likes drawing them.

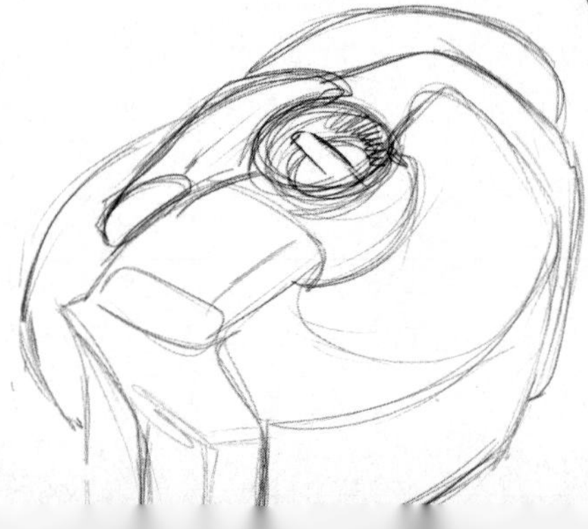

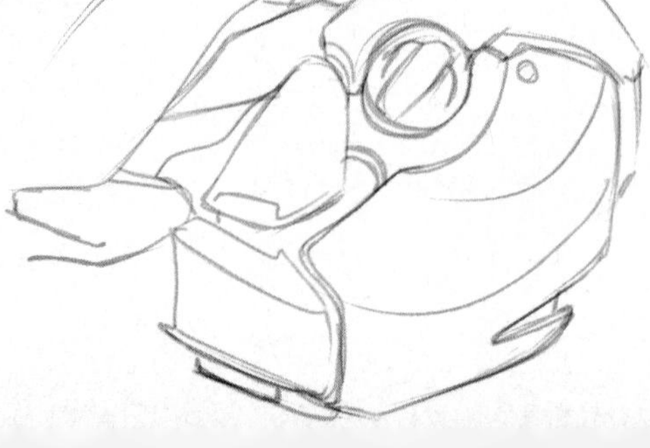

SPACE ELEVATOR

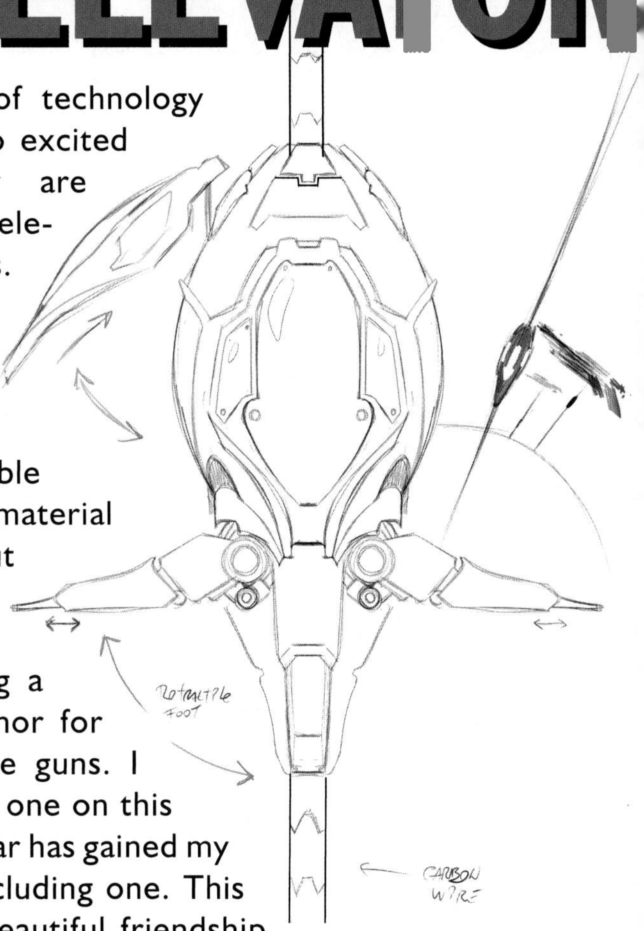
FOOT
CARBON WIRE

I have three pieces of technology which reduce me to excited hand-waving. They are miniguns, space-elevators and ekranoplans. Miniguns have shown up in pretty much every comic I've ever written, with the exception of *Phonogram* (and I may be able to slide one into 'The Immaterial Girl', so don't count it out yet). I've used them as metaphors for all manner of things, not least being a particularly literal metaphor for enormous rotary machine guns. I didn't actually ask for the one on this issue's comic, though Omar has gained my undying admiration by including one. This could be the start of a beautiful friendship.

Space Elevators though? The proverbial space-shoe in.

There's multiple space-elevators on Mercury – far more than Earth. This is primarily due to the relatively smaller size of Mercury, meaning they don't quite require the same level of resources to construct. At least partially it's because humans are generally speaking less opposed to their construction on another planet. I say "generally" which you should take to mean "there are significant numbers of people who feel otherwise." Each Space Elevator is directly connected to the Plug-Citadels. They're the identical bases that are constructed around the equator, which the population moves between as the planet rotates.

The travel between the planet-side (key words: fucking grimy) and the orbital bases (key word: spotless utopian) is a big thing about the book. When you're on the planet, you both literally and figuratively are on another world. There's also the other obvious use – rather than relatively lossy beaming tech, they also run the power up to the Battery ships.

Ekranoplans? I've never written a comic featuring an Ekranoplan, though am reduced to posting pictures of the Caspian Sea Devil to my twitter stream at least once a year. Ekranoplan! Ekranoplan!

HOTSIDE SUITS

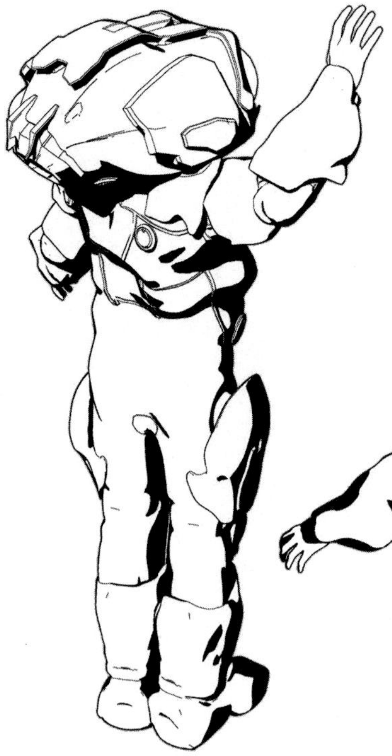

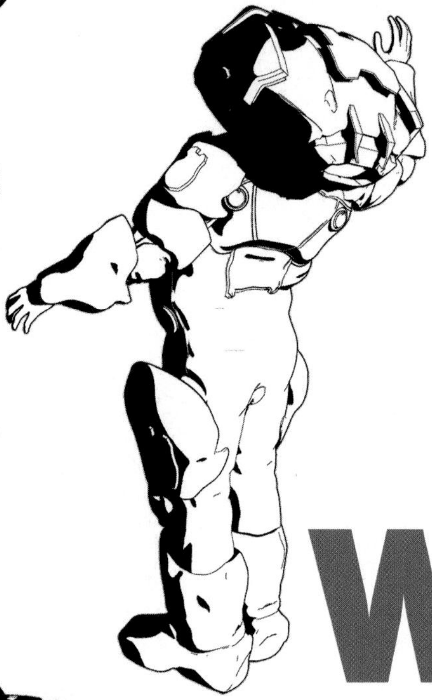

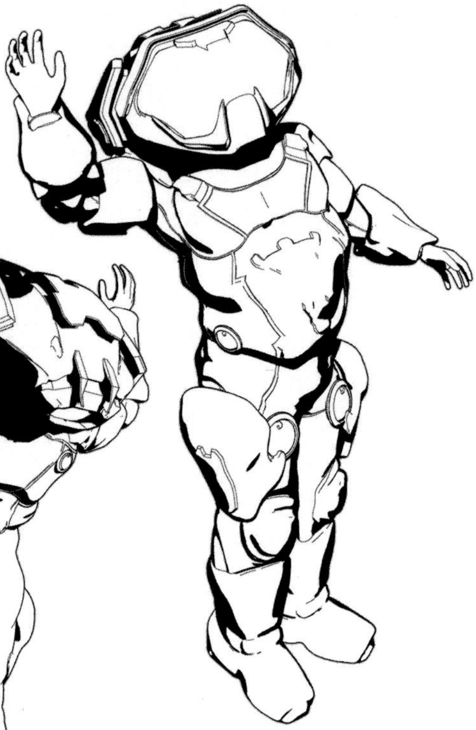

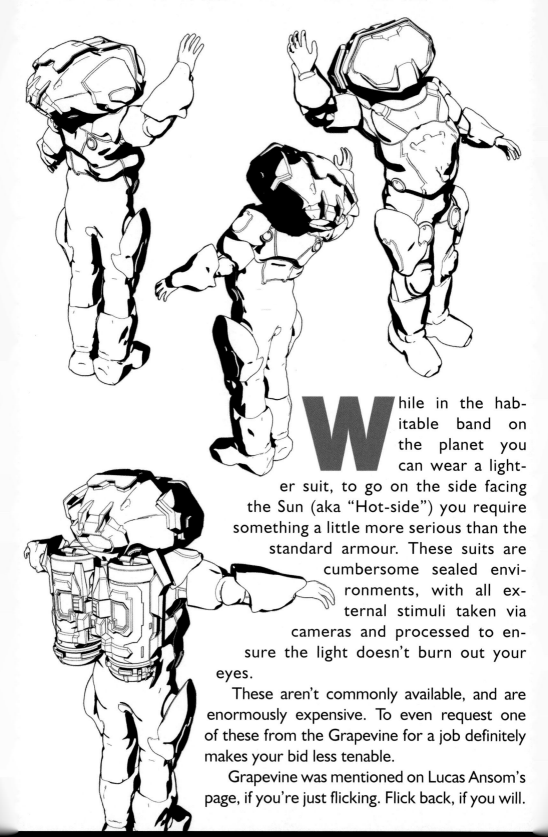

While in the habitable band on the planet you can wear a lighter suit, to go on the side facing the Sun (aka “Hot-side”) you require something a little more serious than the standard armour. These suits are cumbersome sealed environments, with all external stimuli taken via cameras and processed to ensure the light doesn’t burn out your eyes.

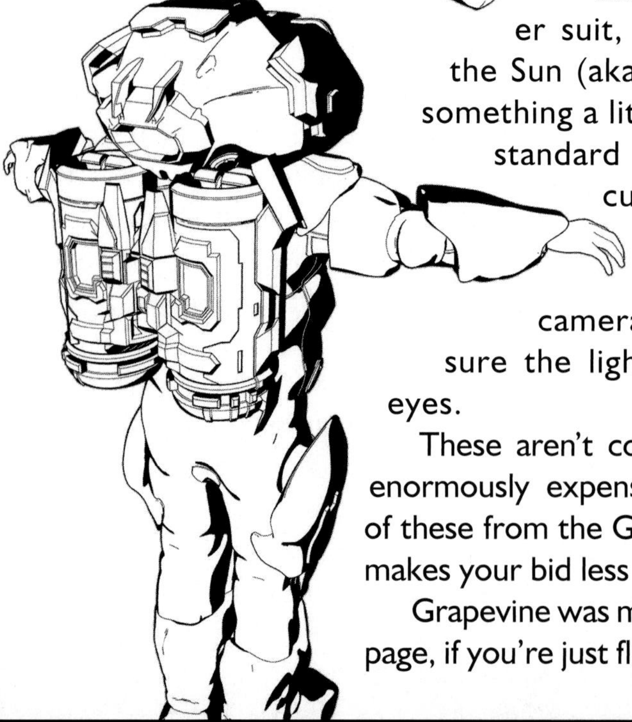

These aren’t commonly available, and are enormously expensive. To even request one of these from the Grapevine for a job definitely makes your bid less tenable.

Grapevine was mentioned on Lucas Ansom’s page, if you’re just flicking. Flick back, if you will.

MINING PLATFORM

I haven't much to say about this mining platform – it's a mining platform that can fly to reposition itself which features as the setting for an excellent fight sequence in issue 3 – but Omar really did go to town on the concept art for it.

As a general rule, *Mercury Heat* likes its action. You know how *Über* has people sitting in rooms and talking for issues? *Mercury Heat* isn't like that. This is very much me in Thrill Power mode. Generally speaking, 50% is Luiza thinking about emotions and doing detective work, and the other 50% is Luiza kicking people's heads off.

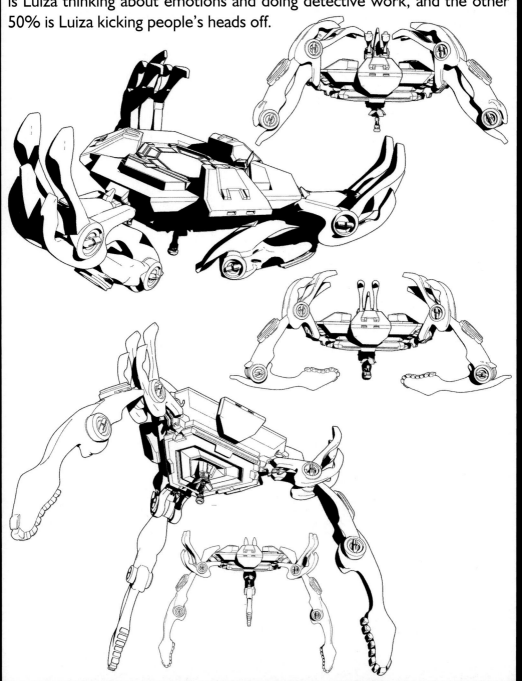

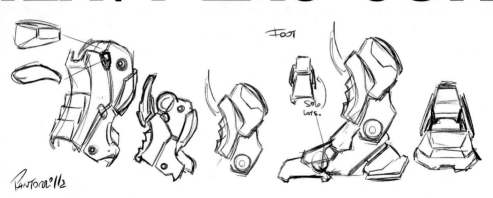

Mercury Heat features the full range of cybernetic electives. Some have upgrades that are entirely invisible to the human eye. Others have clearly set their heart on a chromed arm and won't let anyone tell them otherwise. Others decide that it's a good idea to have their whole nervous system reworked so they can pilot into an enormous exoskeleton like this chap.

I exaggerate slightly. This isn't an individual being permanently bonded to one suit. This is basically having your body reworked into a generalised plug for all classes of this kind of exoskeleton. The smallest is about ten feet. Most surface ones are about twenty, which is pictured here.

Some are considerably larger.

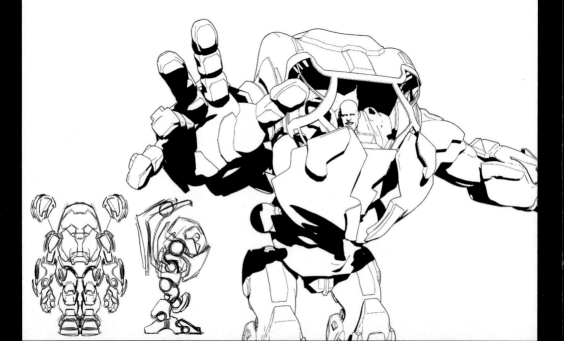

CONSTRUCTION AREAS

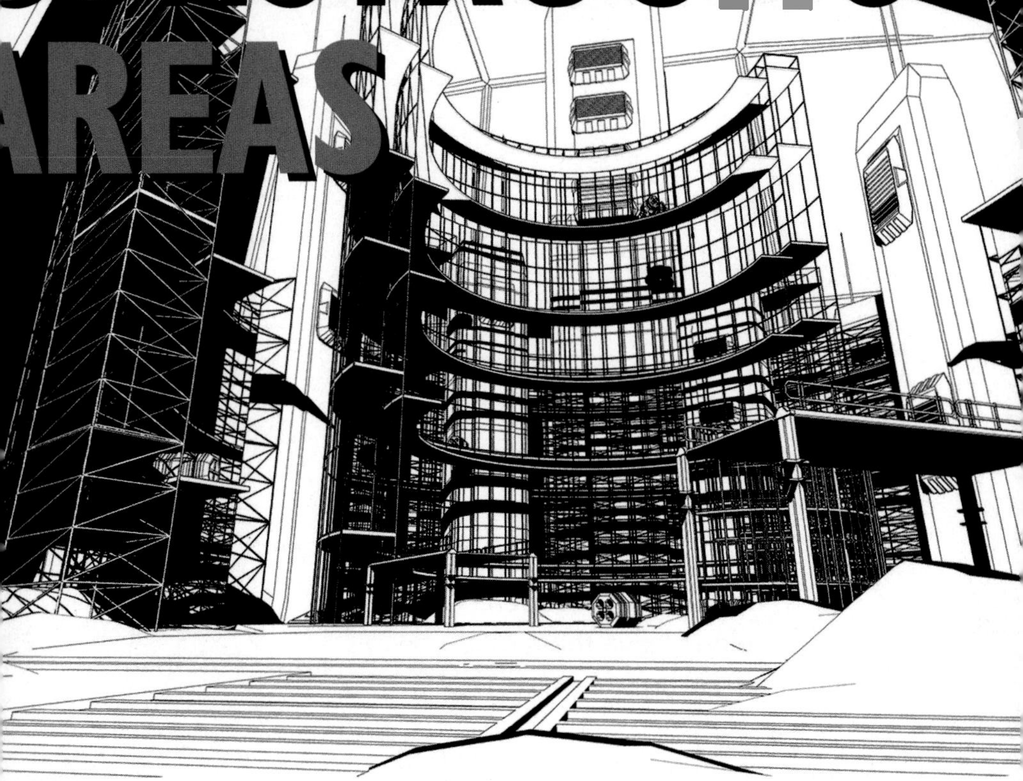

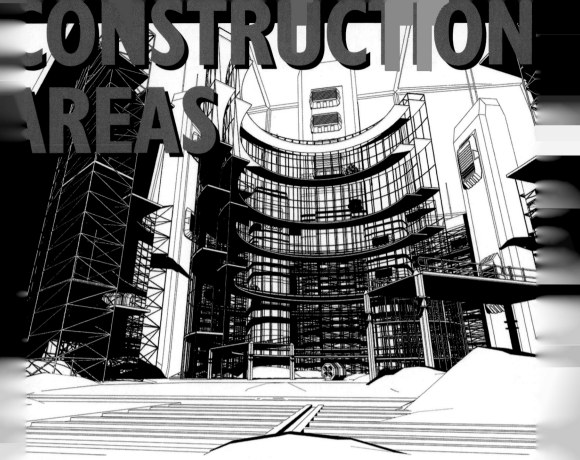

The sort of worksite that's all too common on the surface of the planet. Speed of construction is the thing, as work has to be performed in three day chunks, at best, with whatever's left behind needing to be strong enough to be exposed to the extremes of Mercury temperature. Prefabricated sections, able to be positioned swiftly, are absolutely key.

In practice, most of the plug-citadels were too complicated for that. They're made in orbit (originally on Earth or Moon Orbit) and then transported to Mercury, and dropped from space. They're called Plugs due to their visual similarity, and the fact their orbital insertion looks a little as if they were plugged into the planet itself.

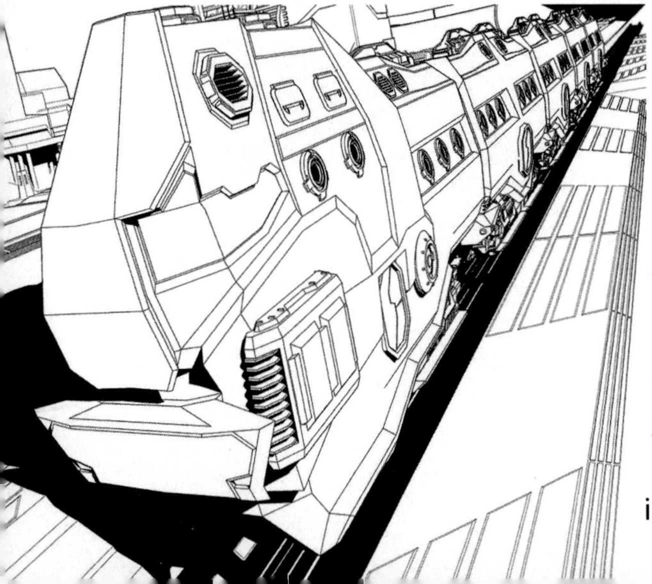

Yes, Mercury has piercings.

OTHER DESIGNS

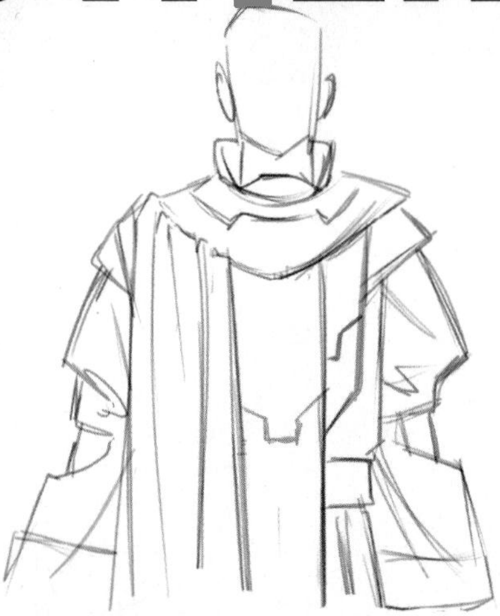

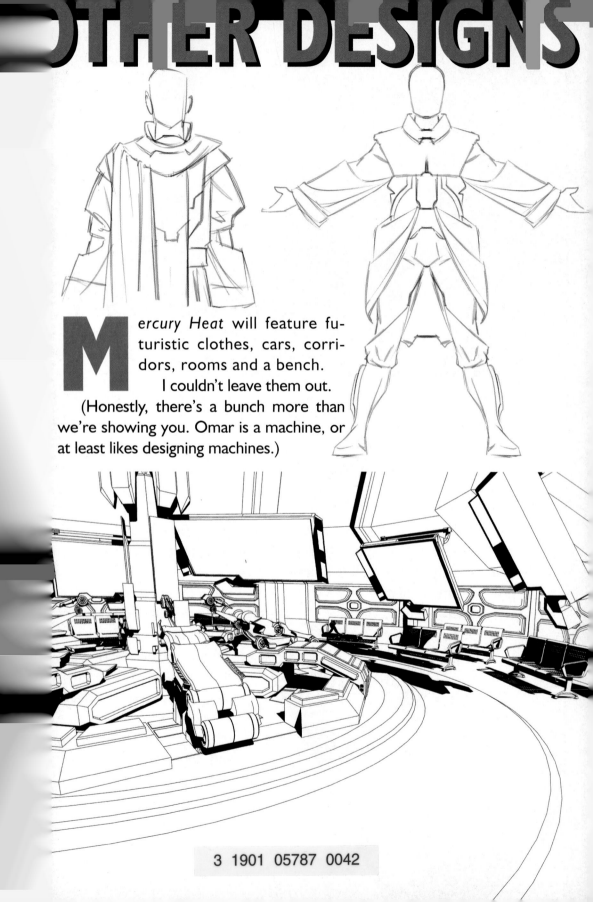

Mercury Heat will feature futuristic clothes, cars, corridors, rooms and a bench. I couldn't leave them out.

(Honestly, there's a bunch more than we're showing you. Omar is a machine, or at least likes designing machines.)

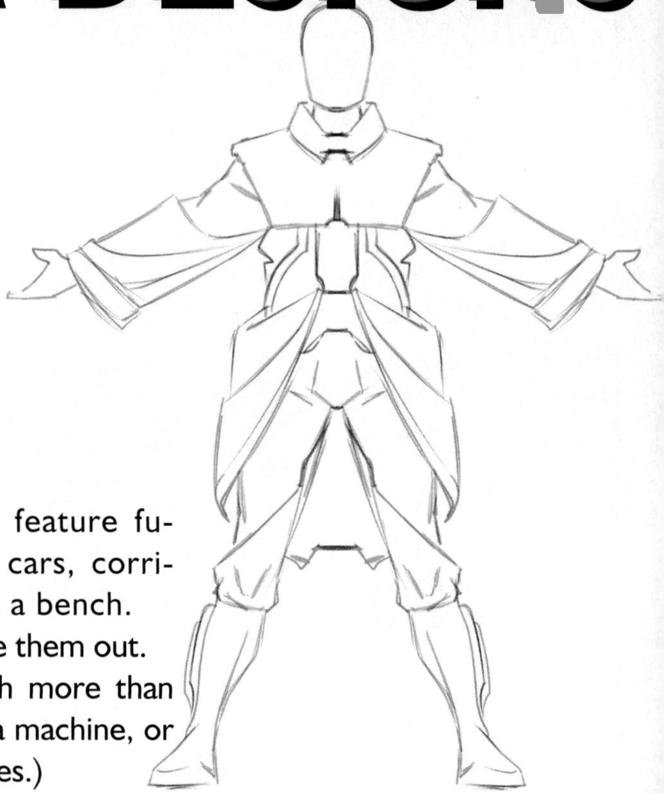

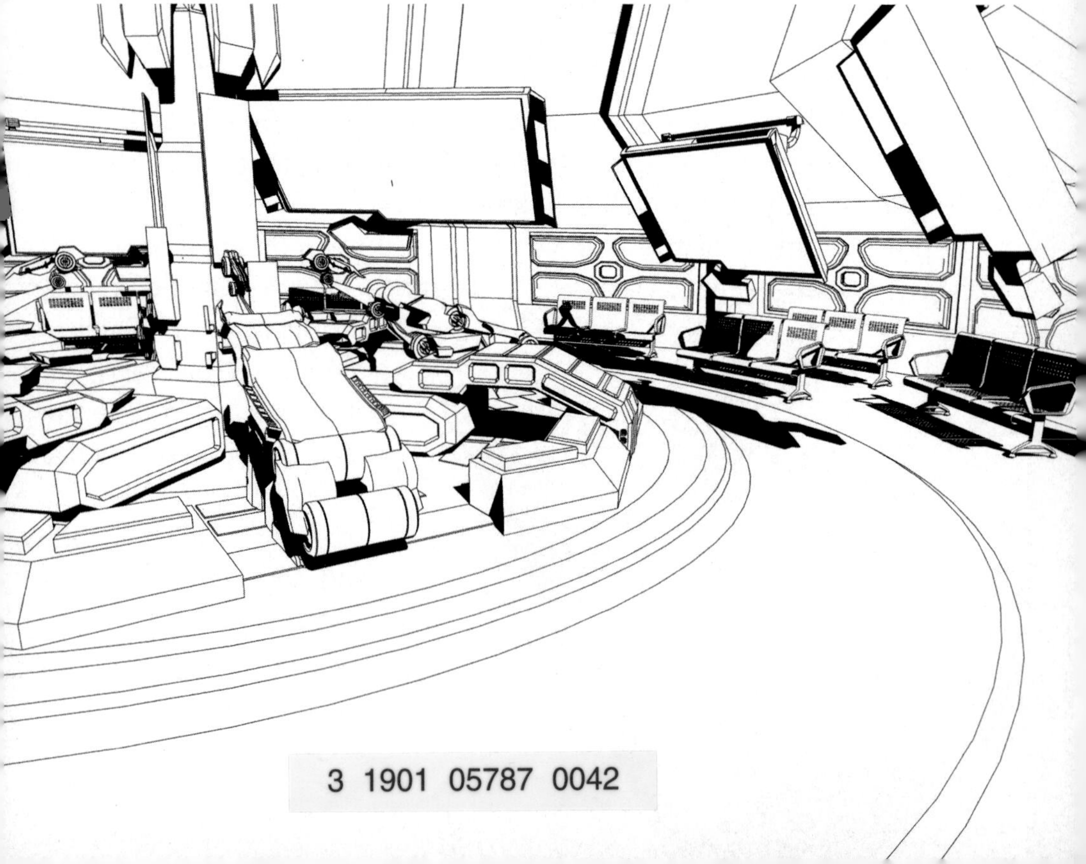